W9-BCK-634

ZIMBABWE

WANA

MOZAMBIQUE

VENDA

LEBOWA

Olifants R.

Potchef...

Kimberley

Bloemfon...

Orange

...burg

...AN

GOOD HOPE

FRANSKEI

Umtata

Port St. Johns

CISKEI

Great Kei

Alice

King William's Town

East London

Grahamstown

N2

Humansdorp

Port Elizabeth

Jeffreys Bay

Cape St. Francis

Great Fish R.

INDIAN OCEAN

South Africa

| 0 | 50 | 100 | 150 | 200 | 250 | 300 Kilometers |

| 0 | 50 | 100 | 150 | 200 Miles |

CROSSING the LINE

William Finnegan

CROSSING the LINE

A YEAR IN THE
LAND OF APARTHEID

1817

HARPER & ROW, PUBLISHERS, New York

Cambridge, Philadelphia, San Francisco, Washington
London, Mexico City, São Paulo, Singapore, Sydney

FIRST EDITION

Designed by Ruth Bornschlegel

Copyeditor: Mary Jane Alexander

Maps by George Colbert

Library of Congress Cataloging-in-Publication Data
Finnegan, William.
   Crossing the line.

   Includes index.
   1. Finnegan, William. 2. High school teachers—
South Africa—Biography. 3. High school teachers—
United States—Biography. 4. Grassy Park High (Cape
Town, South Africa)—Case studies. 5. Discrimination in
education—South Africa—Case studies. I. Title.
LG414.C374F56 1986   373.11′0092′4   85-45633
ISBN 0-06-015568-X

86 87 88 89 90 HC 10 9 8 7 6 5 4 3 2 1

For Caroline

CONTENTS

NOTE TO THE READER

Although this book is a factual account, the names, and in some cases the appearances, of the people described in it (apart from public figures) have been changed. This precaution is made necessary by the present reign of state terror in South Africa, which also makes it impossible to thank individually here the many South Africans to whom I owe a debt of gratitude. Fortunately, they know who they are. Their patience, kindness, humor, and courage were the inspiration for this book. I am especially indebted to my students at Grassy Park High, who never seemed to tire of teaching me about their country.

With friends and family in the United States, I can be more specific. Kevin Finnegan, Caroline Rule, Gay Seidman, Cherryl Walker, Jane Foress-Betty, and Nicholas Wellington read *Crossing the Line* in manuscript and made many valuable suggestions. I would also like to thank Terry Karten and Aaron Asher at Harper & Row, my agent Jean Naggar, and Jo-Anne Rosen. My deepest thanks, finally, to the people whose love and faith made writing this book possible: Bryan Di Salvatore, Caroline Rule, and my parents, Pat and Bill Finnegan.

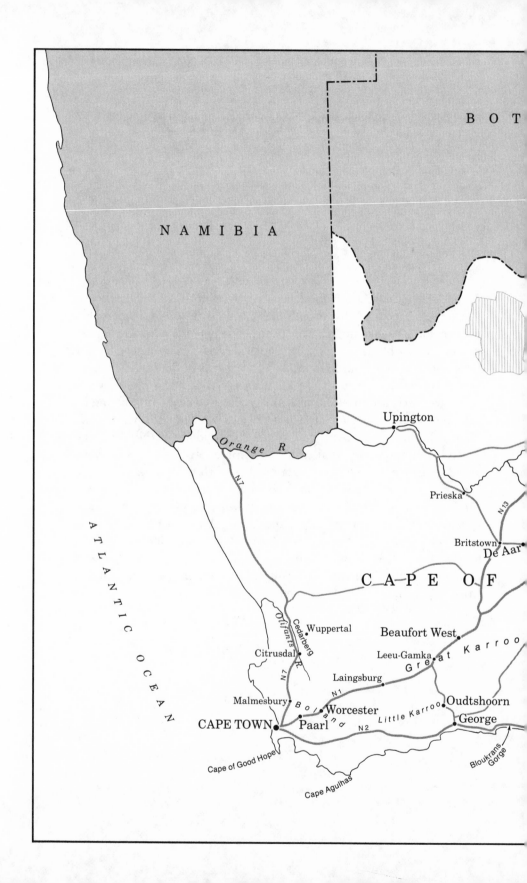

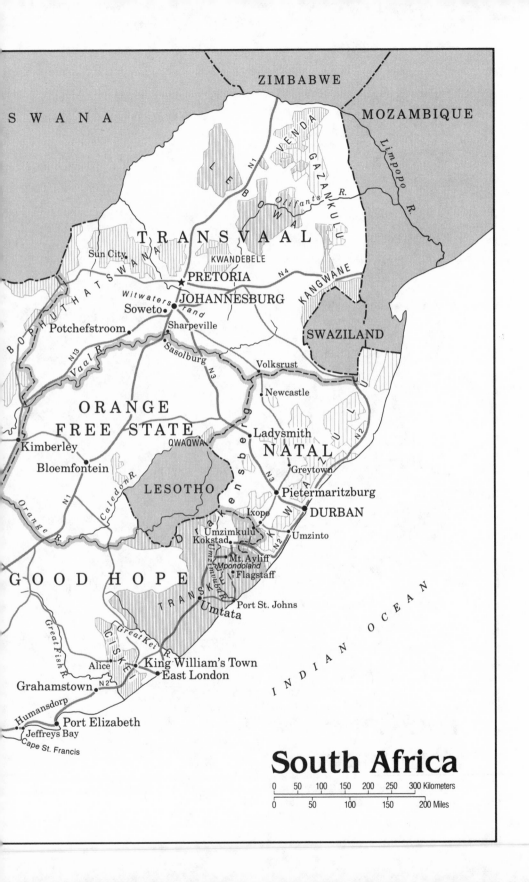

ZIMBABWE

MOZAMBIQUE

S W A N A

VENDA

GAZANKULU

Limpopo R.

L E B O W A

Olifants R.

T R A N S V A A L

Sun City

KWANDEBELE

B O P H U T H A T S W A N A

PRETORIA

JOHANNESBURG

Witwatersrand

Soweto

KANGWANE

N1

N4

Potchefstroom

Sharpeville

Vaal R.

N13

Sasolburg

N3

Volksrust

SWAZILAND

Newcastle

O R A N G E
F R E E   S T A T E

QWAQWA

Ladysmith

N A T A L

Drakensberg

Kimberley

Greytown

N3

KWA

N2

Bloemfontein

Caledon R.

LESOTHO

Pietermaritzburg

DURBAN

Orange R.

N1

Ixopo

Umzimkulu

Umzinto

Kokstad

KZ

N2

G O O D   H O P E

Mt. Ayliff

Mpondoland

Flagstaff

Umzimvubu R.

TRANSKEI

Port St. Johns

Great Fish R.

CISKEI

Great Kei R.

Umtata

Alice

King William's Town

Grahamstown

N2

East London

Humansdorp

Port Elizabeth

Jeffreys Bay

Cape St. Francis

I N D I A N   O C E A N

South Africa

| 0 | 50 | 100 | 150 | 200 | 250 | 300 Kilometers |

| 0 | 50 | 100 | 150 | 200 Miles |

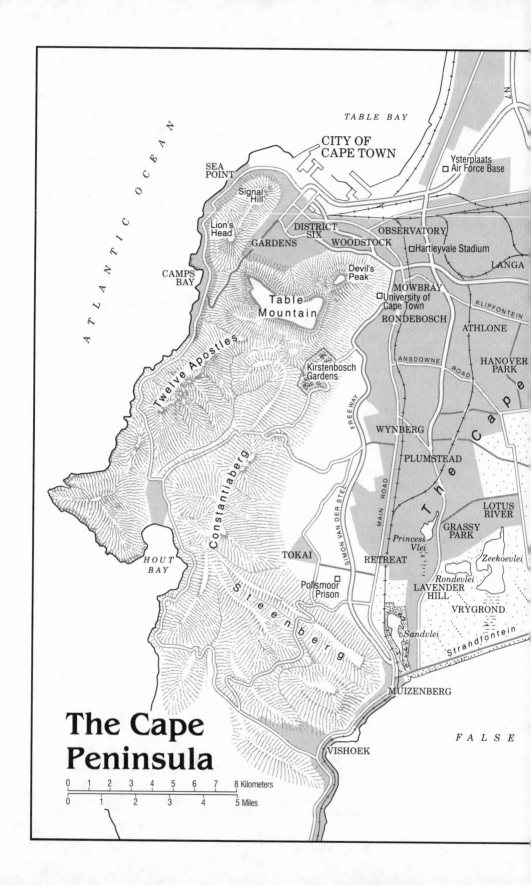

The Cape
Peninsula

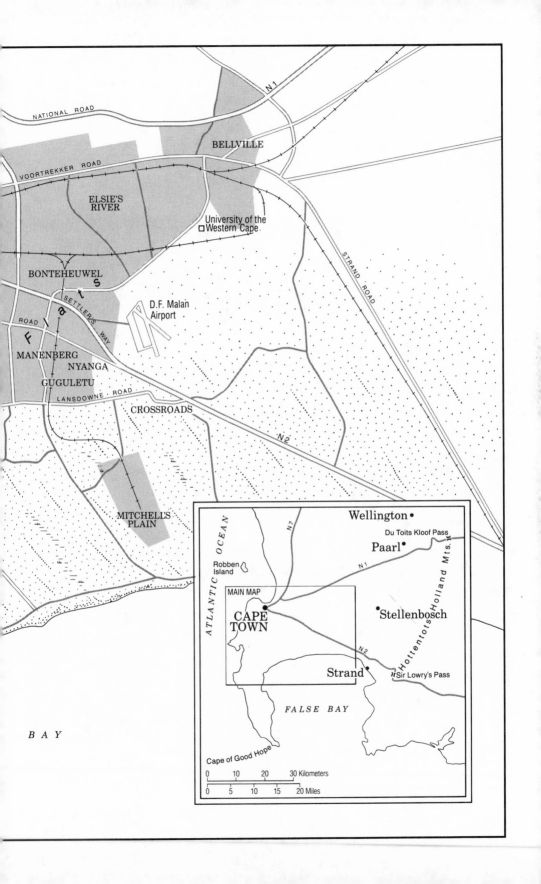

NATIONAL ROAD

N 1

BELLVILLE

VOORTREKKER ROAD

ELSIE'S
RIVER

University of the
Western Cape

STRAND ROAD

BONTEHEUWEL

SETTLERS WAY

F
l
a
t
s

D.F. Malan
Airport

ROAD

F

MANENBERG
NYANGA

GUGULETU

LANDSDOWNE ROAD

CROSSROADS

N 2

MITCHELL'S
PLAIN

BAY

MAIN MAP

ATLANTIC OCEAN

N 7

Robben
Island

Wellington •

Du Toits Kloof Pass

Paarl •

N 1

Hottentots Holland Mts.

CAPE
TOWN

• Stellenbosch

N 2

Strand •

Sir Lowry's Pass

FALSE BAY

Cape of Good Hope

0   10   20   30 Kilometers

0   5   10   15   20 Miles

But to give account of the good which I found there
I will tell you of the other things I noted.

—Dante, *Inferno*

PART I

CROSSING the LINE

1

High above Cape Town, on an otherwise clear day, a snow-white cloud will form, a thin level stripe drawn across the top of the already improbable Table Mountain. Soon the cloud will begin to spill, first in modest cottony puffs, trickling gently over the edge, later in huge silent cataracts, pouring a thousand feet, two thousand feet down the cliffs, as if to inundate the city below. The downward-rushing clouds never reach the city; they burn up as they hit warmer air. But the wave keeps coming, charging off the top of the mountain, out of the strange level cloud, swirling down the great rock face.

The first time I saw this phenomenon I was walking out of a downtown bank. The sight stopped me in my tracks. I pointed, and people on the sidewalk turned and looked, but no one else seemed the least bit amazed. The moment reminded me of a photograph in a book I had owned as a child. In the foreground, people were going about their business on a sunny afternoon on an old fishing pier in California. In the background, a couple of miles offshore, a giant, solid-looking fog bank was rolling toward the pier. The fog bank looked exactly like the wall of white water from a broken wave—"The largest wave in the world?" the caption asked. I was fooled, and spent hours staring at the picture in horror, trying to imagine what happened to the people on the pier. The photograph was like those danger dreams: you're terrified but you're mesmerized, your legs won't carry you away. The cloud falling down Table Mountain had a similar quality. In Cape Town, people call it "the tablecloth," which does not do it justice, and point it out to tourists.

The Cape Town seen by tourists is a stunning place. In any weather, from any angle, the mountain will take your breath away. The city coils around its green lower slopes on three sides, and suns itself on the beaches of two oceans. I have heard visiting yachtsmen, in town for the gala Cape-to-Rio yacht race, pronounce the city's beaches as lovely as Ipanema or Copacabana. On the eastern slopes of the mountain, three-hundred-year-old vineyards, their wineries housed in whitewashed three-hundred-year-old buildings with gracefully gabled facades, carved fanlights, and louvered teak shutters, lie surrounded by forests of oak and pine. Downtown are cathedrals, museums, and public buildings in a profusion of Dutch and British colonial styles, smart shops with signs outside that say SE HABLA CASTELLANO, and a shady cobbled square that was once a slave market. The Cape of Good Hope sits a few miles south, a weathered finger dividing the oceans, now a nature reserve where ostriches, zebras, baboons, and elands roam. Passing travelers have been lavishing superlatives on the Cape since at least the sixteenth century, when Sir Francis Drake described it as "a most stately thing, and the fairest Cape we saw in the whole circumference of the earth."

To the best of my knowledge, no favorable comment of this cosmopolitan type has ever been bestowed upon the Cape Flats. Starting where the greenswards fed by the runoff from Table Mountain end, the Cape Flats is a broad, windy expanse of sand dunes that separates the peninsula from the African mainland. It is an immensely inhospitable area. After the first European settlers had gathered its scant vegetation for firewood, the Flats became so barren that it was nearly two hundred years before a decent wagon road could be built through the dunes to connect Cape Town with the nearby farming districts. The problem was wind-driven sand, and it was only alleviated in the nineteenth century by the planting of hardy shrubs like Hottentot figs and Australian wattle. Still, the Flats remained a bleak, wild place, an almost uninhabited waste—surrounded by rich, fine country.

Today, a majority of Cape Town's population lives on the Cape Flats. Over the past few decades, "government removals" from the older districts of the city have sent hundreds of thousands of people out to live among the scrubby, windblown dunes, in unlikely places with names like Lavender Hill, Grassy Park, and Lotus River. In South Africa it would go without saying that the people who have been removed to the Cape Flats are black.*

The removals were the main component of a grandiose government plan to turn Cape Town into a politically correct city, a model of orderly race relations in an apartheid South Africa. The city center

---

*The majority of those removed were officially classified "Coloured." For an explanation of the racial terminology used in this book, see p. 28.

would be "white." Blacks would live in satellite townships. The bulk of the removals took place in the 1960s and 1970s, but the idea behind them was as old as Cape Town itself. Jan Van Riebeeck, the first commander of the fort built on Table Bay in 1652 by the Dutch East India Company, wanted to build a canal across the Cape Flats in order to cut off the peninsula from the African mainland and from the "savages," as he called them, the "lazy stinking people" whose lands his employers had authorized him to occupy. Van Riebeeck's canal was never built, and the city that grew up on Table Bay became a polyglot entrepôt—the Tavern of the Seas, it was called—and the most racially integrated city in southern Africa. By the lights of the architects of apartheid, of course, something had to be done about that.

Life on the Cape Flats is difficult. Housing is scarce; perhaps a quarter of a million people (in a metropolitan area with an estimated population of 1.5 million) live in illegal shanties. With traditional communities destroyed and all available employment many miles away, families have a tendency to disintegrate. Poverty, hunger, displacement, rage—for a settlement its size, the Flats is said to have the highest murder rate in the world. Rape and robbery are epidemic; alcoholism is a major problem. This is not the Cape Town tourists see.

Some of the old neighborhoods declared "white" were simply "bleached." Others, including a large and densely populated area known as District Six, were bulldozed. The extirpation of District Six cut extremely deep. Among blacks, the neighborhood had associations with the emancipation from slavery. There were families that had lived there for seven generations. People say District Six was the heart of Cape Town. By the time I saw it, the area was a wasteland. Blocks of flats for white police personnel were under construction. There were plans for a whites-only technical college. But most of the district was rubble—extremely valuable rubble, with downtown a brick's throw away. It was as if the heart of the city had been torn out, still beating, and flung onto the Flats.

Beyond the economic explanations, beyond the pitiless specs of apartheid blueprints—and these dictated urban planning in all South African cities—the government's bid for sole possession of the center of Cape Town had a heavy symbolic element. Whites called Cape Town the Mother City. This was where Van Riebeeck first stepped ashore. This was where the House of Parliament stood, here before the humbling face of Table Mountain, which the longtime Prime Minister Jan Christiaan Smuts once called "our national Holy of

Holies." Cape Town was sacred space for white South Africans, and they claimed it symbolically with an army of conquerors' statues, scattered through the downtown streets and parks: Smuts, Van Riebeeck, the Portuguese explorers Vasco da Gama and Bartholomeu Dias, the British empire-builder Cecil Rhodes.

Black people still throng those streets: working, shopping, hawking flowers and newspapers. But they all live far away now, on the Flats, in another world, and merely visit here. Look closely, though, and see more. See the government truck grinding past the elegant pink-colonnaded hotel in its manicured grounds. Hear the faint sound of singing from inside the sealed enclosure on the back of the truck, and when the truck comes to a stoplight, hear the voices rise in a mournful and beautiful African hymn, and see black fists suddenly thrust through the canvas, through the wooden slats into the daylight. And see the gas station attendant in his red overalls turn, and the hotel gardener in his green overalls turn, and the milkman in his blue overalls turn, and the street sweeper in his orange overalls turn, see them all turn toward the truck and raise black fists. The light changes and the truck roars onto the freeway. This is a long-range removal. The people in the truck will be dumped in a semidesert seven hundred miles away.

At an air force base on the edge of the Cape Flats, Mirage F-1 fighter jets in a public display streak past the crowd, flying ninety feet off the ground at six hundred miles per hour. Look closely, and see that this display is related to what happens in the room deep in police headquarters on Caledon Square, the otherwise nondescript room where the torturer works, and that both of these are related to the fact that the new freeways which now penetrate to central Cape Town are never full of traffic. Some taxpayers complain that this shows the freeways weren't needed. Others say, "Look closely; the freeways were not built for commuters." They were built to give the army fast access to the city center in the event of an insurrection.

This prospective insurrection is a consuming preoccupation in South Africa. When the yachts leave Cape Town for South America, they sail past Robben Island, the prison island in Table Bay where potential leaders of the prospective insurrection are jailed. The security surrounding Robben Island is legendary. If and when the revolution comes to Cape Town, though, it will not come from Robben Island. It will come from the Cape Flats. And that is where the authorities intend to contain it, away from Cape Town proper. This is perhaps the uppermost reason for the removals: to rid the city center of the prospective enemy. The streets of District Six were narrow and labyrinthine—easy to barricade, with endless places to hide in house-to-house fighting. The streets on the Cape Flats are wide and straight and the buildings are low, giving the advantage to the side with the heavy artillery.

In 1980 there occurred a sort of dress rehearsal for a mass uprising in the Cape. Two months of organized defiance, led by Cape Flats high school students, erupted in June in widespread violence. Dozens of people were killed by the police—the exact number was never disclosed. In the end, the government's containment strategy was successful in 1980. Both sides did, however, learn some lessons. I was a teacher in a Cape Flats high school in 1980, and I learned a few things, too.

2

At the end of February, when I started teaching, the southeast wind known as the Cape Doctor was still a warm wind. It whistled and sighed through the cracks in New Room 16, and a fine sand infiltrated the classroom while I met my students for the first time. I had been hired to teach, in descending order of work load, English, geography, religion, and vocational guidance to classes spanning five grade levels at Grassy Park Senior Secondary School. In the months to come, the wind would turn cold, and the hundreds of students who poured through the door each day would individuate in my mind to a degree that I would not have thought possible. But on that first day, my students were to me just anonymous waves of maroon sweaters, beige skirts, and shy, curious faces, their ebb and flow controlled by an unsettling siren.

My education began at the beginning, with salutations. Each class would arrive and stand silently in rows, facing me expectantly. I muddled through the first few greetings by introducing myself and urging everyone to sit down. Then, between classes, an embarrassed girl described to me the normal procedure. Following her script, I addressed the next group formally.

"Good morning, scholars," I intoned, feeling absurd.

"Good morning, sir," they roared back in unison.

I paused. They waited. I nodded pompously. They briskly took their seats. It was my first lesson in the local educational atavism, and a quaint first taste of power. The atmosphere reminded me of the mission schools in colonial novels. The students all wore uniforms, the boys wearing white shirts and ties and big black regulation shoes. They called me "sir," and addressed me in the third person—as in, "How does sir like South Africa?" Someone was forever leaping to assist me in the smallest task. Though many of my pupils were fully grown—the oldest was twenty-three—they invariably referred to themselves as "the children."

In deference to our terrific curiosity about one another—and to my unpreparedness to present any of the advertised subjects—my students and I set aside schoolwork for that first day and asked each other questions. I asked them about their parents, their hobbies, their ambitions. I got more giggling than information (topics for essays for future assignment began to suggest themselves). My students' questions were more interesting.

"Has sir met John Travolta?" "Did sir meet Charlene Tilton?" The only Americans many of them had met were evangelists who had come to testify in Cape Flats churches, and I had to admit that I hadn't met Wilma Humphries or the Reverend Glenn Powers, either. My students were especially interested in the lives of black Americans. The less worldly marveled at the news that there were indeed black mayors of big cities in the United States. They were eager to know more about Michael Jackson, Arthur Ashe, "your ghettos such as Harlem," Dr. Martin Luther King, and Pele (time for a quick map of *South* America on the blackboard).

There were two questions that echoed most poignantly for me on that sunny first day at Grassy Park High. The first, which I heard more than once: "Do you find so-called colored people in America?"

What was meant was people of "mixed race," people with both African and European blood in their veins—people, in other words, like my students. In one sense, it should have been an easy question to answer in the affirmative, for there are millions of Americans who could be so described, of course. But what my students were really asking was about where and how racial lines are drawn in the United States, and I found that baneful process anything but easy to describe, even by way of broad historical and political generalizations; for these kids were looking for parallels to their own situation, and racial lines are drawn differently in South Africa than they are anywhere else in the world.

Certainly, the segregation guidelines that had determined the makeup of the student body at Grassy Park High seemed to have been, if nothing else, unique. Student complexions ranged from coal black to a few shades paler than my own Irish-Scottish coloring, while features ran the gamut from East African to Northern European, Malay to Middle Eastern. Neither religion nor language had been the segregationist's criterion. There were Muslims, Catholics, Protestants, and Hindus in my classes, and 30 percent of the school spoke a different mother tongue (English) from the rest (their first language was Afrikaans*). No shared "tribal" past bound Grassy Park students together. The blood of the Cape's indigenous people, the Khoikhoi and the San (called "Hottentots" and "Bushmen" by their European conquerors), ran strongly through the faces and frames of many students, yet the tribes themselves had either been exterminated (Khoikhoi) or had had their remnants driven deep into the interior deserts (San) generations before.

My students' diverse origins were evident, too, in the names on the class lists I had been given. Their surnames were Anglo-Saxon and Islamic, German and African, Indonesian and, in surprising numbers, Afrikaans.† There were names that recalled the slavery their ancestors had endured (most of the people brought to the Cape in the seventeenth and eighteenth centuries from Angola, Mozambique, Madagascar, and Java had emerged from slavery in the nineteenth century stripped, like their counterparts in the American South, of their family names): Thursday, September, February, from the custom of naming slave babies for the month or the day of the week they were born; Hector, Adonis, Achilles, Caesar, Nero, from the custom of naming slave babies after classical figures; Patience, Gallant, and Satisfied, after virtues looked for in slaves by their owners. The number of Afrikaans names—Botha, Cloete, Le Roux, Van Niekerk—and the fact that the majority of Grassy Park High students spoke Afrikaans as a first language, indicated the largest cultural source group for this ethnic bouillabaisse, and the source, too, of most of the European genes on the Cape Flats.

Yet the government had seen fit to classify all these youngsters —to classify some 2.8 million of its citizens—in a racial group it called "Coloured." Hence the ritual local use of the term "so-called," for the

---

*Derived from Dutch, Afrikaans is spoken only in South Africa, where it and English are the two official languages. Students must pass both languages at every grade level to advance.

†Descended from the original Dutch, German, and French Huguenot colonists in the Cape, Afrikaners today constitute 60 percent of South African whites and dominate the country's government. Most of the other whites are of British descent and English-speaking.

classification was the government's creation, and deeply resented as such by the people so called. There were four main racial classifications in South Africa—Africans (of whom there were roughly 22 million); whites (4.5 million); Indians (870,000); and "coloreds"—and four separate educational systems, one for each of these groups. Most "coloreds" lived in Cape Province, where they were the largest of the four "population groups." (The Cape was the only one of South Africa's four provinces where Africans did not constitute the majority.*) "Coloreds" shared with all of South Africa's "non-whites" the basic political deprivation—disenfranchisement—and tended to identify themselves, when a racial term was unavoidable, as "black." In some respects, however, notably the possibility of maintaining secure urban residency, "coloreds" (and Indians) enjoyed options denied to most black South Africans. Hence the plaintive queries about the racial middle ground in America.

The second resonant question came during my last class of the day. The students were seniors. We had already greeted one another and begun our shy, acquainting conversation, when a tall boy with an Afro strode in and took a front-row seat. He offered no explanation for his late arrival. He was not, I noticed, wearing the school uniform. He wore, instead, blue jeans, beige shoes, and no tie. He had a long, serious, light brown face, with a sparse mustache and the thoughtful, fearless expression of a natural-born warrior. His presence obviously made his classmates nervous. They kept giggling and glancing at him. He ignored them. He just sat and stared long and hard at me. After several minutes, he suddenly leaned forward across the battered desk, his dark eyes burning, and interrupted my biography-in-progress of Big John Tate, the heavyweight boxer.

"Why did you come here?"

It was a good question. But a good answer might have taken hours to deliver, so I cast about for something to say, while the other students mumbled apologies and quietly scolded my questioner in Afrikaans. He ignored them except to curl his lip at an English word I caught: "cheeky."

Why did you come here?

I stared into those searching, suspicious eyes for a long moment,

---

*The other three provinces are the Transvaal, Natal, and the Orange Free State. The administrative capital of South Africa is Pretoria, in the Transvaal. Cape Town is the country's legislative capital.

seeking some small inspiration. Finally, I said, "To see for myself what's happening here."

The boy just kept glaring. I glared back. The other students chided him and hissed his name. "Clive!" Nervous giggles. "Clive! Shame!"

Clive began to nod his head slowly. This wasn't really much like mission school at all, I thought. Then Clive sat back and said, "OK. To see what's happening." He half grinned. "Man, you'll see what's happening here."

3

The answer I gave Clive was so true that it could have been my motto. It certainly described my existence at the time, anyway. I was twenty-seven years old. I had left the United States two years before, after finishing graduate school with a singularly useless degree, and had been in transit ever since. My last address had been a little house in the jungle on the southwest coast of Sri Lanka. Before that, Thailand. Before that, Indonesia. Before that, Australia, Fiji, Samoa. I survived by odd jobs and travel writing. If I was doing anything, I was making some effort to see things for myself.

South Africa had not been on my itinerary, exactly. Rachel— Rachel Moore, my intrepid companion, who had left a job teaching college in California to join me in Singapore nine months before—had always wanted to see East Africa. So when we had had our fill of Asia, we decided to head for Kenya. But visas for Kenya had proved impossible to procure in Sri Lanka, and the same went for Tanzania. And no airline would take an American to either place without one. As we were about to get on a train to New Delhi, where there was a Kenyan embassy, Rachel came down with a mild case of hepatitis, and her enthusiasm for further travel in India, which was never very great, vanished. Then an airline clerk told us about a twice-weekly Tokyo-Johannesburg "Gold Exchange Shuttle" which refueled in Colombo. The visa process was easy, said the clerk: it could all be done by airline telex.

After a year in south Asia, such space-age efficiency was bedazzling. The idea of a relatively developed, nontropical country also suddenly had its attractions, because of the hepatitis, for which doctors were already prescribing what seemed like the drastic medicine of immediate return to the West. Perhaps, we reasoned, South Africa might be just the right half-step, a bacterial interregnum between Asia and East Africa, which we could then reach overland, following the fabled "Cape to Cairo" route. By such reasoning, anyway, we tried to put down our misgivings about hying our white hides to the land of apartheid, and applied for visas. Stunningly soon thereafter, we found ourselves on a British Air 747 packed with Japanese businessmen bound for Johannesburg.

Taking a longer view, I see some less immediate, less circumstantial elements in my own motives for going to South Africa. One was the surf. *Endless Summer,* a 1966 surfing movie that profoundly warped my career goals at the age of ten, had its climax in South Africa, where its protagonists, two California surfers, in the course of circling the globe in search of "the perfect wave," found it. I had been pursuing my own endless summer, surfing throughout the Pacific, Australia, and Asia. I was still carrying my surfboard, and "the perfect wave" at Cape St. Francis still possessed a Mecca-like allure.

There was also the matter of pizza parlors. The evidence is there in the journals I kept in Asia, especially in a series of entries made in Indonesia after my second round of malaria: I wanted some pizza. Moreover, I wanted to order it in a modest but air-conditioned Italian restaurant, along with cold beer in a can. At the time I wrote out this desire—while camping in the jungle beside a great surf break on an island a hundred miles west of Sumatra—it had been probably six months since I had seen cheese, much less pizza. The idea of such basic temperate-zone foodstuffs had clearly acquired a terrible force in my mind. So the possibility exists that at some level of awareness I suspected that my little air-conditioned pizza parlor might be found in South Africa and that this hunch, too, served to lure me onto that jet for Johannesburg.

If so, the hunch was correct. Pizzerias abounded in Johannesburg. So did bookstores, supermarkets, first-run cinemas. In fact, the Western-style wealth of the city was an overwhelming first impression, after what seemed like an eternity in impoverished Third World lands. And that culture shock, the psychic dislocation caused by abrupt transit from a world of underdevelopment to one of prosperity, still lingered a month later when I started teaching in Cape Town.

Why did we travel a thousand miles to the southwest to start traveling northeast? Cape to Cairo had something to do with it. So did the surf. So did the fact that we bought a car on our first day in Johannesburg, and dreamed up a great looping route from the Cape up the west coast of Africa, across to the east through the Kalahari

Desert, about which we had read wondrous things, and then north.

We hadn't planned to buy a car. Apartheid made us do it, you might say. That is, none of the buses we tried to catch near the air terminal in Johannesburg would take us. The buses all carried signs saying NON-WHITES ONLY, and their drivers, who were black, refused to let us board. There were taxicabs, but the fares, after Asia, seemed prohibitive. So when an Australian surfer waiting at the terminal told us that used cars were cheap and plentiful in Johannesburg, we were wide open to the suggestion. Johannesburg reminded me at first glance of my hometown, Los Angeles, where life is not possible without a private automobile—and suddenly the thought of getting a car, after a year of oft-horrific public transport, had its own momentum.

I went to buy a newspaper. The teenage girl at the newsstand informed me that the paper I was trying to purchase was "the native edition." Her mien made it clear that she was not joking. "The white edition for today is sold out," she said.

Did the not-sold-out edition, I wondered, contain classified ads?

"How should I know?"

I expressed a determination to buy it and find out.

The girl regarded me for a long, unpleasant moment. Finally, she said, "Suit yourself."

There were, it turned out, classified ads in the paper, and plenty of cars for sale, including a '65 Opel station wagon for four hundred rands (about five hundred dollars at the exchange rate then) that sounded good. We stowed our luggage, hitchhiked to the suburbs and, five minutes after we saw it, bought the car. It was a sturdy, two-tone, sweet old thing. We bought a city street map and went for an inaugural drive. I was in my own little Whitmanic heaven. New car, new continent. *Allons! The road is before us.*

Soweto, the great black township, was the only place in Johannesburg we knew, so we made that a first destination. Yet we could not find Soweto on the city map. The area where one would expect to find it, southwest of the city center—Soweto is an acronym for "South West Townships"—was just a large blank on the map. We found that astonishing. Soweto was, after all, the largest city in southern Africa. Did they have segregated street maps, as well as segregated newspapers? It began to seem surprising that blacks and whites were utilizing the same roads and sidewalks. But then most blacks were walking, while virtually all us white folks were riding in cars. A commuter train rumbled past, filled to bursting with people, all of them black. There were bodies halfway out the windows, even some weary-looking men standing on the cut levers between the cars. The train looked just like many (too many) we had ridden in Asia, except that here we looked at it from across the apartheid abyss. We couldn't ride that train if we wanted to; we were cut off from all that life. We headed for my pizzeria.

So the morbid novelties of apartheid assail one from all sides upon arrival in South Africa. Every form we filled out—to purchase the car, to register at a hotel—required that one identify oneself racially. Even the highway map we bought gave the populations of towns in race breakdowns. The strangest thing of all, though, was how much Johannesburg reminded us of the United States. It was something about the vast, brash wealth of the place, the number of gun and ammunition shops (WHITES ONLY). There was in Johannesburg a simmering, raw atmosphere, laced with invisible violence—Rachel said the city had a "pornographic" quality—that we had not felt since we left the U.S. There were also, as mentioned, the familiar amenities. Delicatessens, cheese, wine, Kentucky Fried Chicken. And other, more loaded, homecoming-like payoffs, such as a wonderful absence of the ceaseless attention the Westerner receives on the street in Asia. Here, nobody gave us a second glance. In white Johannesburg at least, in appearance at least, we fit in.

Of course, the bleak, pointed avoidance of one's gaze by blacks, the eerie atmosphere of formalized racial deference, was scarcely the sort of public anonymity that we had been missing. There was no mistaking these South African blacks for Americans, either. While most were dressed in Western clothes, they moved, spoke, laughed, were built, and carried their babies (on their backs in blankets tied around their waists) in ways that were to us thoroughly exotic. Their most striking feature, though, on first encounter, was simply their numbers. Even in the white suburbs, black people were everywhere: on foot, on bicycles, in buses and delivery vans, in the uniforms of maids and gardeners and municipal workers. The feeling was that *all* the city's work was being done by blacks. Even the Afrikaner housewife who sold us the car, whose husband was a plumber, had commanded a domestic force of maids and gardeners upon whom she appeared to be hopelessly dependent.

The obvious question occurred to both of us more or less immediately: If these blacks were half as oppressed as the rest of the world believed, what was preventing them from withholding their labor, from shutting down this system with a general strike, and making big changes fast? To judge from the newspapers we picked up—"white" and "native" alike—the problem was not that no one was aware of the prevailing injustice. The papers were full of articles and editorials criticizing the government and denouncing apartheid. And the writers seemed to be indicting the South African system in virtually the same terms that we, or any observer with the least partiality to democracy, would have chosen. In Parliament, we read, there was a lively no-confidence debate in progress, with the opposition members storming out amid revelations that the government had been opening their mail and tapping their phones. We had not expected to find such freedom of speech. But what defense could the government possibly offer against these arguments? What defense, for that matter, could be offered against the decades-old, unremitting international chorus of condemnation? This miserable country had even been banned from the Olympics, where every dictator was welcome to send a team. The papers we saw gave few clues to the answers to these questions, and none to the big question about why blacks did not revolt. Everybody in Parliament, of course, was white.

We left Johannesburg for the coast, driving south through a range of weird yellow man-made hills: the slag heaps from the gold mines of the Witwatersrand.* We pushed on into the eastern Orange Free State, where the countryside turned gorgeous. This was late summer and the grass on the highveld was long and a deep green. Great scarlet rimrocks towered over the old Boer† homesteads, with their weeping willows and eucalyptus windbreaks. The fields were full of sunflowers and endless rows of tall, ripening corn. Merino sheep and fat red cattle grazed on the hills. Sleepy little country towns clustered around shady squares and imposing church steeples. Every white farmer seemed to drive a Mercedes-Benz.

In the countryside, though, the black townships were not hidden away as they were in the city. Instead, one or more "locations" sprawled near every white settlement—always with a *cordon sanitaire* of fields, or a river, or a hill between them. And the black towns looked like festering wounds on the lush land. They were treeless, roadless collections of shacks, as wretched as anything in Asia. The

---

*The Witwatersrand—"White Waters Reef" in Afrikaans—is the gold-bearing reef that underlies Johannesburg and neighboring towns; often called simply "the Rand."

†"Boer" is another term for Afrikaner, less widely used now than previously. In Afrikaans, *boer* means "farmer."

houses were built from scraps of cardboard, plywood, and corrugated tin. There was clearly no electricity, no running water. Women trudged along the highway, bent double under huge loads of firewood. Teenage girls carried plastic jugs of water on their heads. And the children, some of them dull-eyed and swollen-bellied from malnutrition, came begging wherever we stopped.

We car-camped our way to the Cape, barbecuing chicken and steaks, drinking good, cheap Cape Pinotage wine, and detouring often. It was easy, almost enchanted traveling. As the *Berlitz Travel Guide* says, South Africa is "Africa on a silver platter, the call of the wild at the end of a superhighway." In Natal, we drove high into the Drakensberg Mountains, then hiked still higher, past thorn trees and antelope, and ate lunch on a rocky peak near a troop of baboons. All around us were sheer purple flat-topped mountains and deep gorges bisected by cold clear rivers. This was too high for white farming. Down the valleys we could see the thatched round huts of Zulu villages, their mud walls covered with strange designs. Rachel's hepatitis had already disappeared, and would not be heard from again.

We descended from the highveld into tropical Natal, reaching the coast at Durban. Then we wandered down through the Transkei, the bantustan* created for Xhosa-speaking people. I surfed. We slept on beaches and at roadside "caravan parks." We picked up hitchhikers, mostly black country people, and plied them with questions about their lives. On the whole, people were friendly, but shy. There was often a language barrier. I was surprised when not one black person I asked had heard of Alan Paton's famous novel *Cry, the Beloved Country,* not even around Ixopo, where the story begins. I was also surprised that no blacks, not even those who asked for our address in America, invited us to their homes. One man did show me his "pass."†

---

*The bantustans are rural areas set aside by the government for Africans to live in. There are ten bantustans, each meant to serve as a "homeland" for a different "tribe." All but one of the bantustans are geographically discontinuous. KwaZulu, for instance, was reported in 1978 to consist of forty-eight separate "fairly large" pieces and 157 "smaller" pieces. All together, the bantustans comprise 13 percent of the land area of South Africa. The Pretoria-supported leaders of four bantustans, including the Transkei, have accepted "independence." No country in the world except South Africa recognizes the bantustans, nor does the United Nations.

†Every African over the age of sixteen is required by South African law to produce on demand his or her pass, complete with employer's validation, certifying his or her right to be in that area. Hundreds of thousands of people are arrested each year for pass law violations, fined, jailed, and "endorsed out" to the bantustans. The policy is

The little green booklet had all the banality of true evil, I thought. But its owner denied that he resented having to carry it. "So long as he is in order, I am right," he said.

In the Transkei, we caught glimpses of the Africa we had come to see. Women in traditional Xhosa dress, their faces made ghostly by masks of white mud, smoked long-stemmed pipes and wore hundreds of copper and beaded bracelets. Blue-black birds with five-foot tails flew up and across the road. At one place, we stumbled into a gathering outside an abandoned homestead, where fifty or sixty people— some in traditional dress, some not—were singing, dancing, and shouting with joy to an extraordinarily compelling *kwela* beat. The energy of the music outpowered any rock band I had ever heard. Later that day, I forced myself to drink a carton of the bitter, sorghum-based Xhosa beer in a rowdy bar where the other customers cheered me on with cries of *"Masisele!"* (Drink up!)

We met few whites, partly because pubs in South Africa were closed to women, and Rachel refused to sit in the strange, sterile "ladies' lounges" to which we would have been confined. We caught plenty of stomach-turning glimpses of local race relations—white children asking their mothers to buy them candy they called "nigger-balls"; a fat white foreman threatening a black railway worker with a metal-tipped rhinoceros-hide whip called a *sjambok*—but the whites we met, who were mostly surfers or fellow campers, were uniformly pleasant. A woman in a caravan park in East London, having noticed collections of Nadine Gordimer's stories and Athol Fugard's plays among our things, said, "You won't go back to America telling people we're all like *they* say we are, will you?" Yet even she was friendly, and fed us our first *boerewors*—a heavy beef sausage beloved by many South Africans. On a hill above that caravan park, a billboard advertised "Texan" cigarettes.

The view from the little bubble of well-being we traveled inside got steadily prettier as we approached the Cape. The coast, sheltered from the dry interior by a range of rain-catching mountains, was a forested, shining series of gentle bays. The sea was warm; the climate grew Mediterranean. The only problem was that we were running out of money. Gas cost nearly three dollars a gallon, food prices were comparable to those in Europe—suddenly, our budget was ten times

---

known as "influx control." Roughly 50 percent of all Africans live in the bantustans, roughly 35 percent live in the cities, and the remainder live in the "white" rural areas. The extreme poverty in the bantustans drives large numbers to migrate "illegally" to the cities, where jobs at least exist.

what it had been in Asia. The months of solvency that we had pro-jected for touring Africa were quickly turning into weeks.

Running low on funds in distant countries was actually nothing new to me. I had always managed before to find work and save. But the South African economy clearly *was* something new. Weeks later, my students would be astonished to hear that I had ever worked as a dishwasher, a gardener, a gravedigger. How could *sir* stoop to such menial jobs! One girl asked if it was true that there were white domes-tic servants in Europe and in America, and when I replied that it was, she and her classmates gasped with wonder—and, I daresay, delight. In South Africa, those sorts of jobs were held exclusively by blacks. In fact, there were no quick, dirty, manual jobs for the likes of Rachel and me. By dint of having white skins, we were considered above such work—as we were too often reminded by blacks who called me *baas* (boss) and "master," and Rachel "madam" and "the lady." Even the whites-only caravan parks, which were strictly for people of modest means, all had, we noticed, special areas for billeting one's "servants."

By the time we reached Cape Town, cash flow was becoming a problem. We were both eager to head north, to see the Kalahari, to get into *Africa* Africa, but if we *had* to stop and work . . . Cape Town, with its mountains and beaches, its wineries and graceful, Old World ambience, was an infinitely more appealing place than, say, Johan-nesburg. Apartheid was still everywhere in evidence, but the atmos-phere was markedly less harsh than elsewhere in the country. The fact that the majority of Capetonians were "colored" had something to do with that, no doubt. There was no drastic break in appearance between different groups. This "phenotypic continuum" gave the city a heterogeneous look, the way I imagined Brazil. There was a greater sense of socioeconomic continuum as well. Cape Town had a reputa-tion as a bastion of liberalism in South Africa. Its red double-decker buses were even newly integrated.

A day or two after we arrived, I wandered into a surf shop, actu-ally considering selling my surfboard. The kid behind the counter didn't want my board, but he did tell me about a desperate shortage of teachers in the local "non-European" schools, as he called them. In fact, his father, he said, was a school inspector.

We went to see his father, who turned out to be an exuberant, avuncular Afrikaner with an armful of postgraduate degrees in psy-chology and education. *"Ag,* man," he said. "These children need help so badly. And their teachers. And their inspectors! Look at this stack of psychological tests I've got from your America, but never have time to distribute! The government simply must give us more money! But I'm sure we can find a place for you."

Rachel decided she couldn't face teaching again so soon, but I found the inspector's enthusiasm contagious. I rushed off to the Cape Flats with a list of short-handed schools. As the school year had started several weeks before, they really were desperate. My interview at Grassy Park High lasted less than an hour. The principal took my word regarding my qualifications, and I started work three days later.

Deciding where to stay was simplified by the Group Areas Act, a piece of legislation under which every residential area in South Africa had been assigned to one or another of the four main racial classifications. With exceptions made for servants, no individual could live in an area not designated for his or her classification. Thus, we were legally forbidden to live in Grassy Park, or anywhere very nearby. So we rented a room in the nearest "white area," a suburb called Muizenberg, on the Indian Ocean coast, five miles away.

4

"Crossing the line" each morning involved a stark transition. I started off on quiet, cobbled beach-town streets, among surf shops and Victorian mansions. Heading away from the coast, I drove northeast, into a wide wasteland of sand dunes. These were the Cape Flats. For a mile or more, there was nothing but sand and scrubby *fynbos,* with the Port Jackson scrub glinting in the low sun. Then the road skirted a large squatters' camp: half-glimpsed tar-paper shanties back among the dunes, underfed children in shapeless old sweaters crossing the road with plastic water bottles. Then came the bleak tenements of Lavender Hill, and the transition was made: from white to black South Africa, from the First World to the Third. Crowds of people tramped alongside the road, pedaled bicycles, and crammed into share-taxis. I was an anomaly; all the other commuters were headed for the white areas. I passed Jessie's Moslem Butchery, the Dandy Cash Store. Then the road curved into Grassy Park.

While it shared the bright, flat, sprawling quality of every place on the Cape Flats, Grassy Park felt less arbitrarily located than some of its sister communities, for it was bounded on three sides by marshes known as vleis. This gave it a rough kind of neighborhood coherence, around a market square known as Busy Corner. Grassy Park looked

nothing like "your ghettos such as Harlem." Where the feeling was
not suburban, it was rural: donkey carts clopping down unpaved
roads, farmers and fishermen selling their produce from wagons,
stock grazing in empty lots. There were a few high-density apartment
blocks, barren brick structures with graffiti-covered walls, unhealthy-
looking stairwells, and little cookie-cutter sections of corrugated tin
slapped on over the ground-floor doors. These places were called,
incongruously enough, "the estates." They had been built in the 1960s
by the Cape Town City Council. The oldest section of Grassy Park was
also council housing—an area called Cafda, after the Cape Flats Distress Association, a private charity that had once administered the
township. Cafda was all tiny red-brick cottages with roofs so low they
seemed to have been built for dwarfs. The people in Cafda were very
poor, but their neighborhood had one great softening feature: fine,
full-sized eucalyptus trees. The rest of Grassy Park sat out in the sun
and blowing sand. There were a few "pondoks," or shanties, built from
scraps of wood and tin and iron, scattered around Grassy Park. But
most of the housing, at least in the blocks around Grassy Park High,
consisted of small, fairly new single-family homes, with electricity
and indoor plumbing. Some of these houses were privately rented, but
most were owned by the people who lived in them.

There were far more prosperous "colored" communities on the
Cape Flats, places where the landscaping, the spacious new homes,
looked much like their economic equivalents in the white areas, but
private home ownership did serve to distinguish the bulk of Grassy
Park from the bulk of the Cape Flats—and, for that matter, from the
great majority of black South African communities. The government
could uproot black property owners, as it had demonstrated countless
times—indeed, it had done so to many people who were now Grassy
Park residents. But it was much more likely to visit its removals on
tenants and on squatters than on black homeowners. Most blacks
lived in government housing of one kind or another. To have one's
own home was a rare blessing, and provided a rare degree of security.
Thus, people in Grassy Park were, as a rule, intensely house-proud.
You could see it in the nameplates that adorned most houses: Our
Haven, Valhalla, At Last. You could see it in the neat front yards and
gardens, the fancy little homemade fences of wagon wheels or terra
cotta, the ornate stained-glass front doors, and well-clipped bougainvillea hedges. The houses weren't precious or pretentious—most had
chicken coops and serious kitchen gardens out back, growing corn,
cabbage, beans, potatoes, beets, tomatoes—as much as they were

cheerful. Given the bleakness of the Flats, the harshness of the policies that had sent people out there to begin with, and the general hard lot of being black in South Africa, this air of sunny contentment struck me as remarkable.

Of course, there was more to it than met a foreigner's first glance. The wide, straight streets which I found so charmingly full of life—people always strolling to or from the shops or the bus stop at Busy Corner, children playing soccer in the quieter roads—were designed to accommodate the armored vehicles known as Hippos, to give the advantage during "times of unrest" to government forces. Some areas were extremely dangerous after dark: street gangs robbed and raped with horrifying freedom. It was many miles to work for most people, first by bus, then by train. Busy Corner had some amenities—a clinic, a pub, a small post office, a fish-and-chips shop, several of the little groceries known as cafés, even a branch of the Standard Bank—but most errands and shopping had to be done across the line. Just as black businessmen were not allowed to trade in the white areas, supermarkets and department stores were not built in black areas. Everywhere were women returning from expeditions to the big shopping malls in the white areas, toting bulging plastic bags. One thing I never saw in the entire year I worked there, though, was a white person on the street in Grassy Park.

The high school was two blocks from Busy Corner. It was one of the most substantial schools on the Cape Flats. There was a core of brick buildings around a courtyard, containing perhaps a dozen classrooms, with three or four smaller buildings out back. In a sandy field adjacent stood the scruffy, gray, two-story, pre-fab "new building," containing another ten classrooms, one of them mine. That was about it, really. There was no auditorium, no gymnasium, no cafeteria, no book lockers, no language labs, no heat. The "sports ground" was a glass- and rock-strewn horse pasture; the library owned fewer books than I do. The classrooms were full of broken windows, broken lights, decrepit desks, and yawning holes in the ceilings.

The contrast with the high schools across the line could scarcely have been more galling. Public schools for whites were vast, immaculate facilities. The new boys' high school in Wynberg, less than five miles from Grassy Park, had six tennis courts, three rugby fields, one hockey field, two squash courts, a swimming pool, a fully equipped gym, five science labs, a geography lab, and four soundproof music rooms.

5

At the end of my first day of teaching, there was a meeting of the
faculty. Forty-odd teachers crowded into the "staff room," jostling and
jovial. Before the meeting began, I was introduced to my department
chairmen, Mr. Napoleon of geography and Mr. Pieterse of English.

Napoleon was a tiny, energetic fellow in his late forties. He had
small bright eyes under high, surprised brows, and a quick, command-
ing air. He wore a baggy brown suit and a pencil-thin mustache. He
had a lisp and admirable posture. "Mr. Finnegan, Mr. Finnegan. Have
you taught geography before, sir?" I confessed I hadn't. Napoleon
harumphed. "Then I must show you how we do it. We'll have a meeting. The other new geography teachers must come, too."

Pieterse was in his early thirties, tall and broad-shouldered, with
a cauliflower ear (from playing lock for a local rugby club) and a
manner that somehow succeeded in being both hearty and ironic.
Pieterse smirked and said, "All the way from America to little Grassy
Park. What part of the States?"

"California, originally."

Pieterse laughed and shook his head. "Well, you'll find life here
boring, man, I can tell you, after Hollywood. And Disneyland."

Pieterse was abruptly carried off by another teacher, who led him
across the room by his cauliflower ear to Napoleon, while onlookers
laughed. Napoleon started pretending to scold Pieterse, flexing a long
thin stick and railing in Afrikaans while Pieterse, who was twice
Napoleon's size, pretended to cower.

I recalled something my predecessor in New Room 16 had told me
during our only conversation. She had advised me to take disciplinary
problems to Napoleon. "The students are afraid of him," she said.
"Sometimes you only have to mention his name to bring them to
order. I let him do all my caning. He's quite good at it, they tell me."

So that long pale stick with which Napoleon was making the air
in the staff room sing was the dreaded "cane." The sight of it made
me uneasy. Coercion, physical violence, suddenly struck me as a terribly crude, inappropriate, almost obscene thing to introduce into the
complex, delicate world of the classroom, where I felt so tentative and
well-meaning, and my students seemed to feel the same, and the
great, ineffable business of education was meant to take place.

I turned away to read a bulletin board, and there found a chart
of teachers' salaries. I had never been told what I would be earning,

so I began to look for my category on the chart. So many years' education, so many years' experience—then I was brought up short. There, spelled out in grubby bureaucratic black and white, were two more salary determinants: race and gender. In every category, a male teacher's salary was roughly 10 percent higher than a female's, and each category of experience, education, and gender was further broken down into four racial categories. In the race breakdown, the differences in salary for teachers of the same qualifications were far greater than in the sex breakdown. Teachers in the lowest-paid classification, "Bantu" (African), were receiving salaries barely half of what their identically qualified colleagues who were classified "white" received. As a "white" male, I saw, I would be earning nearly 40 percent more than a "Coloured" female colleague, and 30 percent more than a "Coloured" male colleague, with the same qualifications.

The principal called the meeting to order. I found myself wondering what racial classification each new colleague whom I could see suffered. Like their students, the Grassy Park faculty were of all shades and physiognomies. Certainly, all four classifications on the salary chart ("Asian" was the fourth, and the second-best paid) seemed to me to be represented. But the truth was that only "Coloureds" and "whites" were legally permitted to teach at Grassy Park High, and that, before I was hired, there were only two people classified "white" on the faculty of fifty. The joke went that the Grassy Park faculty was a so-called colorful group. And they did look eclectic, at first survey. There were debonair old guys in berets, dumpy matrons clutching purses, sleek young women in high heels, and a fellow who looked like O. J. Simpson. There was an eighteen-year-old girl who, it turned out, had graduated from the school the year before and was now back teaching science.

The principal, George Van den Heever, was a big, pale, solidly built man in his sixties who seemed to have a special affection for Americans. When I had turned up unannounced in his office, looking for a job, he had spent most of the interview sharing with me his recollections of the GIs he had met and befriended in Italy during World War II. "Wonderful fellows! They would gladly give you the shirt off their backs!" Now he opened the staff meeting by introducing me to the faculty at large with an extended, acutely embarrassing speech in an ancient oratorical style, ending by dubbing me "our very own Yankee Doodle Dandy."

There was a second teacher starting work that day, a young woman named Elizabeth Channing-Brown, who was also introduced.

I guessed her to be classified "white" (correct). Channing-Brown was an actress, we were told, and she did have the broad, fine, regular features of a leading lady. She would be teaching English, we heard. Channing-Brown looked extremely nervous and was chain-smoking.

As the meeting proper got going, business began to be conducted in Afrikaans. The principal made a long, energetic speech, which became increasingly emotional and dramatic. His voice rose. He pounded on a table. About twenty minutes into it, a bull-necked fellow in a bright green shirt leaned over and asked in a whisper whether I understood the speech.

I shook my head and his face creased in silent mirth.

When I murmured that I wouldn't *mind* knowing what it was about, my neighbor listened closely for a minute, then shrugged and whispered, "There are pupils hanging about who don't belong to this school."

Finally, the principal wound down, and a portly young teacher in an expensive-looking dark blue suit took the floor. He spoke in English and with great fluency, although his elaborate, grammatically impeccable sentences seemed intended only to echo the principal's main points, emphasizing the need for standards and discipline in the school and so forth. This was Mr. Da Silva.

Then a third speech, nearly as long as the principal's. It was given by Mr. Africa, the vice-principal. Africa made great use of his long, graying slab of a beard, murmuring into it with a solemnity reminiscent of the Old Testament prophets he resembled, then lifting his face and raising his voice at key points, to impressive effect. His topic was lost on me, however, as he spoke in Afrikaans. Africa was a tall, thin man, with sad, calculating eyes.

Lulled by the powerful, consonant current of these performances, my attention began to wander. I observed that my colleagues were, on the whole, far better dressed than I. Nearly all the men wore suits, many of them three-piece, while my outfit had been gleaned entirely from the racks of a local Salvation Army outlet. My clothes were clean, but they did not match and they did not fit and, what was more, I was wearing all of the passable items I owned. For my job interview, I had worn my best traveling clothes: some elderly cords, a short-sleeved cotton shirt, and a pair of plastic loafers from Sri Lanka, painted brown to look like leather. Afterward, the principal had gently mentioned the matter of dress. "We're quite casual here," he said, "as you can see from looking at Mr. Tate." But then he went on to mention his expectations regarding a coat and tie.

I looked around the staff room for Tate. He was there, surreptitiously reading a paperback behind his briefcase. Tate had been called in by the principal toward the end of my interview, along with several other teachers, who stood in a row and were told by the principal of my application and of my qualifications and asked for an opinion, while I sat right there and squirmed. They all seemed to squirm, too, until Tate finally spoke. "I think the question is not whether we will have Mr. Finnegan, but whether he will have us." I was very grateful for this Kennedyesque remark, and everyone laughed with relief, and I was hired. Tate was a young, bearded, sweet-faced Englishman (he and Da Silva were the two "whites" on the faculty before Channing-Brown and I arrived), in his second year of teaching history and English at Grassy Park. Tate dressed casually, it was true, in baggy cords and a tweed jacket. He still looked better than I did, though.

The flow of agreeing speeches in two languages which I by now thought constituted a Grassy Park High faculty meeting in its totality was rudely interrupted by a short, handsome young teacher named Nelson October. When he started to speak, the room woke up.

"I'm afraid I must disagree with nearly everything that's been said here this afternoon," October said, in fast, accented English. "The principal, the senior staff, have been talking about making new rules for the pupils as though there were no need to consult the pupils themselves in these matters. This approach has been seen to fail before, and contravenes agreements already reached with the SRC" (Students' Representative Council).

October went on in this vein. I found the tension created by his remarks almost stifling: it so ruptured the consensual mood that I had quickly come to believe prevailed at all levels at the school (*pace* Clive). Yet no one else seemed to share my distress; and then the meeting was suddenly adjourned, precipitating an unabashed stampede for the door.

On the way to my car, I found myself walking beside Elizabeth Channing-Brown. I asked how her first day had been.

"Oh, not so bad, really," she said. "The children were sweet. The only thing I'm afraid about, you know"—and here she laughed nervously and looked around to make sure no one else could hear—"is riots."

6

That first evening, I took home a stack of "schemes" (syllabuses) for each of the subjects I was to teach. These were highly detailed, specifying the content of virtually every lesson all year long. From the moment I opened it, I didn't like the look of the material. It seemed to consist almost entirely of very old-fashioned busywork: memorizing columns of rainfall figures for geography, memorizing columns of obscure animal-gender terms for English (duck and drake, cob and pen, fox and vixen). I especially didn't like the formula for the evaluation of work: everything would depend on a final examination; a student's performance throughout the year would have almost no bearing on whether he or she passed or failed.

Then there were the textbooks. They were old and uninspiring and, upon inspection, revealed themselves to be full of racist mischief. A typical land-use analysis in our geography text: "Because this region is inhabited by the densest White population, we find a great concentration of industry." A sample sentence in the English grammar book: "All the Bantu who had been drinking beer began to fight one another." These sorts of racial stereotypes infested the textbooks. Moreover, there were a number of ways in which the apartheid society was, I thought, being presented as the normal order of things— such that South African geography, for instance, was described as if factors like the Group Areas Act and the pass laws were as common as industrialization or glacial scraping.

It didn't take me long to decide that I would not be doing much teaching according to the schemes. I wondered how many of my colleagues did so. There was clearly a great deal that our students needed to learn about the world they would soon be entering as adults, and precious little of it was being provided by the government's idea of education. I was not really in a position to start teaching the "truth" about South Africa, since I scarcely knew any of it myself. On the other hand, simply conveying the material in the schemes and the textbooks, uncriticized, would have been unconscionable. I was developing a substantial enthusiasm for the "subject" of South Africa. What I could learn, I decided, my students could learn along with me. In geography, I noticed, one of the subjects we were expected to cover was Other African Countries, and the prospect of extracurricular research in this area also suited me fine. Our textbook's gloss on the subject looked to be less than useless, somehow contriving to present the material as though the great wave of decolonization of the past two decades had never occurred.

My introductory announcements to my classes the next day met with blank looks. Exams weren't important? Writing assignments every week? Outside reading?

"That's right."

Lectures, from which they would be expected to take notes? To these kids, it turned out, taking notes meant copying their textbooks, word for word, cover to cover, into notebooks, and using the entire school year to do it. This had, they said, been their main occupation under my predecessor. Their more energetic teachers might put something up on the blackboard for them to copy. But writing and listening simultaneously? Asking questions when they didn't understand? And *disagreeing?* And leading discussions *themselves?*

"That's right," I said. "You'll learn. You'll see."

The children seemed dubious, to say the least. And after my policy announcement concerning corporal punishment—I said I would not be using it—they hardly tried to hide their disbelief.

"Sir!" The children gasped and snickered, pulled faces and made it clear that they thought I was out of my mind. It was, taken all together, not the most encouraging reception. After one class, a girl stayed behind, while three of her friends hovered outside the classroom door. It was the same girl who had told me how to greet my classes. Her name was Hester. She was a big kid, with long brown hair, and a careful, earnest manner. "Will this be how the children in America receive their lessons?" she wanted to know.

I said I supposed so, since that was where I had learned whatever I knew about teaching school. (I didn't mention that I had never taught school before.)

"Thank you, sir," Hester said, very formally. She left and I sat, strangely exhausted, at my squat little teacher's desk and listened to the excited laughter of her friends as Hester joined them and they hurried off down the passage. As self-appointed educational reformer, I clearly had my work cut out for me.

7

This is a digression about terminology. Its importance in South Africa is almost impossible to overstate. Racial terminology can be invidious anywhere, but the uncritical use of the South African government's categories is especially loaded. In the public prints in South Africa, the conventions vary widely, and usages tend to fix the position of a writer or a journal on the domestic political spectrum. A progovernment newspaper will routinely discuss Whites and Blacks and Coloureds and Indians, while an antiapartheid writer will usually take the trouble to hold such concepts at intellectual arm's length, even when the effort requires multiple repetitions of stupefying phrases like "the so-called 'coloured' people." These differences are not just semantic; they reflect a basic dispute about the nature of South African reality. Mere quotation marks may call into question the entire society's legitimacy. Thus, one can say that 15 percent of the population owns 87 percent of the land, or that 15 percent of the population "owns" 87 percent of the land—impugning, in the latter case, the very idea of legal ownership in South Africa, and suggesting, perhaps, that this state of affairs is not only illegitimate, but also temporary.

Government policy is a particularly slippery area. "Apartheid" became an international embarrassment decades ago and has not been used officially since the 1960s. "Separate development" was its successor, and eventually discarded for similar reasons, to be replaced by "separate freedoms," "plural democracy," "vertical differentiation," "friendly nationalism," "constellation of states," "good neighbourliness," and countless other euphemisms for the same policy. Meanwhile, the "bantustans" became "homelands" became "self-governing states" became "black national states," while the "pass laws" became "influx control" became "controlled urbanisation," and so on, *ad absurdum*. Official terms for the country's various "population groups" have also changed with the times. Thus, the "natives" of the 1940s became the "Bantu" of the 1950s became "Blacks" in the late 1970s, while "Whites" replaced "Europeans" after 1971.

Blacks—by which I mean everyone not classified "white"—have tended to reject each of the government's designations for them in its turn, while most opponents of the South African system have continued to call it by its best-known name, "apartheid." The government's reasons for choosing certain terms, and rejecting others, are themselves instructive. As the debate over political rights heated up after the Second World War, "natives" became obviously deficient for its suggestion that only blacks are true South Africans ("Europeans" had the same problem). "Africans," which for many years was what the people the government called "natives" and "Bantu" called themselves, was unacceptable to the authorities primarily because in Afrikaans "African" is *Afrikaner.* The reasoning behind "Bantu" was never clear. The word refers to a large linguistic grouping that occupies most of southern and East Africa; in Zulu, *abantu* means people. "Bantu" was hated by blacks, in any case, and began to be replaced in official usage after 1977 by "Black"—which had actually become the preferred term among black people themselves over the previous decade, in much the same way that it had in the United States.

But South Africans classified "Coloured" and "Asiatic," many of whom had long resented these terms—"Asiatic" was clearly intended to suggest that people of Indian ancestry were not true South Africans, but had a homeland elsewhere—had also begun to refer to themselves as "black" in increasing numbers throughout the 1970s. This was part of a broad-based movement to build a sense of common identity among all sectors of the disenfranchised. As this was a development much dreaded by the government, the introduction of "Black" as a term for the African majority was widely seen as less a capitulation than a subterfuge, a move to prevent those classified "Coloured" and "Asiatic" from calling themselves "black," since that term would now misrepresent their status under apartheid. (Radical "coloreds" had adopted "Non-European" for a period during the 1940s and 1950s as a term to ally themselves with other blacks before the widespread acceptance of "black," but it was now used only by a few pseudo-genteel whites.) The government continued to use "Non-White" to describe all blacks—such that the signs on trains, buses, toilets, liquor stores, and so on still read NON-WHITES ONLY. This term was universally scorned by blacks for the obvious reason that it made "whiteness" the standard of identity. How would whites like to be called "Non-Blacks"?

In this account, I try to use the terms that are most acceptable to the people I am describing. Thus, "black" refers to everyone not classified "white" under apartheid. Where necessary, I distinguish between "colored," "African," and "Indian." Sticking quotation marks around every racial term—and sometimes around the word "racial" itself—can be awkward and tiresome, yet I usually put them around "colored" anyway, out of respect for the great number of people who reject the word. Where a racial term modifies a manifestly un-racial noun—a "white" beach, a "white" cinema—I also sometimes add quotation marks, just to keep clear the legal and arbitrary character of the exclusion involved. Although "African" is not the most progressive term for the people whom the government now calls "Black," I do not usually put it inside quotation marks, because it does not seem to be significantly resented. Neither do I use "Black African," as some writers do, in deference to the feelings of whites (and other blacks) who also consider themselves "African," for nowhere do I credit the suggestion that whites do not belong in South Africa. There are undoubtedly non-racist whites who prefer to see "whites" inside quotation marks, but while one may agree that this is as arbitrary and inexact and insidious as any other racial term, the vast majority of South Africans so classified clearly think of themselves as "white" and believe passionately in the reality of that condition, so I retain the term unadorned. In general, I don't try to impose a didactic consistency in this business of racial designation, but trust to context. Usage changes all the time, and there seem to be no conventions which are both graceful and broadly acceptable.

8

While I struggled to land on my feet as a teacher, my first weeks at Grassy Park High were also, for me, a strange sort of idyll. I loved suddenly having a strict routine, after the unstructured life I had been leading. I also liked the work. It was absorbing and seemed, in some large sense, worth doing. More than anything, though, I enjoyed getting to know my students. Their shyness with me ebbed away steadily. Their initial anonymity began to break up into a prodigious variety of individuals: wry athletes and troubled stutterers, cautious bright kids and jolly fat ones, coquettes, earnest innocents, affable rogues, teachers' pets, and on and on. I had been given no records, no test scores, no files on any of my students, a piece of neglect that was possibly, I thought, just as well.

I saw nine different classes, and each of these, too, slowly began to reveal its own distinct personality. (A "class" at Grassy Park High took most of its subjects together, moving from room to room as a group.) I taught second-language English to three Standard Six classes—6A6, 6A7, and 6A8, they were called. Standard Six (equivalent to American eighth grade) was the entering class at Grassy Park High. Most of the children in Standard Six were thirteen or fourteen, although some were as old as sixteen. I saw these classes more often than I did any others—six periods a week each. Then there were two Standard Seven classes to whom I taught geography—7E1 and 7E2. Their first language was English; we spent four periods a week together. I also saw two Standard Nine classes once a week for vocational guidance, and two Standard Ten classes—seniors, known as "matrics"—once a week, for what was supposed to be religious instruction. Clive Jacobus, the boy who had challenged me on my first day, was a matric. Besides the great range in age and maturity in the classes I taught—there were kids in Standard Six who looked ten years old, while most of the matrics looked like college students—there were subtle differences between, say, all of my English classes. Over time, I found they each required a different touch, which itself changed from day to day, to rouse them to learning.

Our schoolwork went ahead by fits and starts, as my students and I struggled to get used to one another. My inability to speak Afrikaans was in some ways an asset as I went about teaching second-language English—I was not tempted to conduct lessons the easy way, in my students' mother tongue, as some of my Afrikaans-speaking colleagues did—but it became a distinct liability when students would break into Afrikaans to express themselves in a way that they could not in English. Instant translations were usually available, when the Afrikaans in question was not too raunchy, yet I would lose the nuances, especially when they were humorous, which they usually were. My students had, in fact, a highly developed sense of fun, and great comic timing as a group, and before I could understand any of it, I came to admire the relish with which they used and abused the Afrikaans language. (Their dialect was different from that spoken by white Afrikaners—more guttural, musical, and rich with slang.) Their wit worked differently in English, where it had more to do with accents than with phrasemaking, yet it still worked. It's an impossible sort of thing to reproduce in print, but a typical instance occurred one day when I introduced the vocabulary word "bachelor." I asked whether anybody knew what it meant, and somebody piped up, "Like Mustapha." Mustapha was the oldest boy in that class, a sixteen-year-old among thirteen-year-olds. He was deep-voiced, heavily bearded, terribly shy, and somehow, under the circumstances, he was the absolute living embodiment of the word "bachelor." The whole class, teacher included, dissolved in mirth on the spot, and for weeks I could not look poor Mustapha in the face without thinking "bachelor" and having to bite my lip.

To my English classes, I deliberately gave out essay topics that might help remedy my ignorance about my students' lives. And slowly, like images starting to emerge from the clouds of developer in a photographer's chemical bath, their world began to take some shape, to gain some substance, in my mind. Their parents were fishermen and factory workers, stevedores and secretaries, skilled and unskilled laborers. A few were teachers; a very few were successful Muslim businessmen. Their parents were always referred to in respectful, even childish tones, usually as "my mommy" or "my daddy." Organized religion seemed to be a big part of many of their lives. And "church" was clearly more than just Sunday services—it was choral societies, picnics, film shows, fund raisers, youth groups. "Mosque," too, seemed to involve an endless round of Koran classes, special observances, and social obligations. Most of the boys, and many of the girls, were sports lovers. Soccer, cricket, rugby, tennis, swimming, Ping-Pong and "netball" (similar to basketball) were their favorite sports. Hobbies ranged from karate to chess, raising dogs to electric guitar. One boy was a member of the Faking Club, a group that went around staging bloody accidents to test the public's knowledge of first aid.

It was a sanitized version of adolescent life on the Cape Flats that appeared in my students' compositions, of course. There were no alcoholic fathers or pregnant teenagers, no drugs or identity crises. The prevailing writing style was stilted and formulaic, which also tended to reduce the visibility of the real. The pulpit provided the inspiration for a few rhetorical flourishes, as in the essays of one churchgoing girl who liked to end her sentences, "but all forsaken," or "but all in vain," for which touches of color I was grateful. But original, imaginative prose was not something my students had ever been encouraged to write.

Still, their essays were for me a lode of information and ideas about everyday life in Grassy Park. I was struck, for instance, by how often a great, vague creature called "the people" appeared in my students' writing—"the people" not as a political concept or mandate, but as a simple, circumstantial consideration. "The people" were likely to gather at any public event. They were likely to go either way in a pinch. If your house was burning, "the people" might worsen matters by looting, or they might save the day by putting out the fire, you never knew. *Skollies* (hoodlums) and *skelms* (thieves) were also a factor in any public situation. One girl described how she sometimes carried a handful of one-cent pieces with her when she walked in certain areas. If *skollies* came after her, she would throw the coins at them, and while the *skollies* stopped to pick them up, she would make her getaway. The ever-present threat of *skollies* contributed to an overall sense I got of lives being led between some terribly narrow horizons. Many of my students, I discovered, had never even seen the Atlantic coast of Cape Town, though it was less than ten miles away.

Being black in the land of apartheid had something to do with that, but the one great and ongoing narrower of horizons was simple lack of funds. People were poor. Poverty was far from equally distributed among my students, however, and the differences between the situations of some and the situations of others became obvious even in their essays—once I began to understand what I was reading. If a child mentioned "the Primus," for instance—a paraffin, or kerosene, stove—it probably meant that the house he lived in lacked electricity, which in Grassy Park meant he was poorer than most.

My students rarely, if ever, mentioned to me, either in conversation or in their writing, the endless series of humiliations small and large that being black in South Africa involved—such that I could easily have imagined that they lived in a nice tight apartheid compartment where racial slights and insults were not part of their experience. It wasn't so, of course, as I slowly came to see.

My students' writing betrayed no great political awareness of their situation. The acute consciousness of oppression that one might expect to find overwhelmingly among black South African youth, especially among urban students, was simply not in evidence. In fact, their main interests seemed to be thoroughly "normal." When we decided to brighten up New Room 16, my classes brought in posters, handbills, and pictures snipped from magazines until the walls were full of rock bands (Abba, Boney M, Michael Jackson), shiny cars, sports stars, and animals. I contributed a set of maps that I had been carrying when I arrived in Cape Town, which were well worn but useful as visual aids for my chronic digressions about life in distant lands.

What struck me most about my students during my first weeks as their teacher was not the ordinariness of their concerns, though. It was the extraordinariness of their relations with each other. At least *I* had never known high school kids anything like them before.

Basically, it was their lack of nastiness. There didn't seem to be any outcasts among them. The least confident, least likable kids did not appear to lack for friends. Their social life in general seemed imbued with an amazing collective good sense. Not only were there

no class "stars," no in-crowd of popular kids, but there were no couples, no high school romances. Clear friendships existed between the
sexes, but boys generally sat with boys, while girls hung out with girls
(all in a marvelously easy physical intimacy). Heavy romances were
conducted, I was told, only with non-schoolmates. Inside the school,
nobody went steady. It was so sane, it was strange. Strange because
I couldn't help but think back to my own high school experience, to
the semihysterical atmosphere of constant, intense competition—social, sexual, athletic, academic—that had prevailed among the fabulous amenities of our upper-middle-class school. At times it almost
made me envious of my students at Grassy Park High. Their school,
notwithstanding its many deficiencies, somehow had all the warmth,
the healthy emphasis on the group, that my own homophobic, rabid-
individualist schooling had lacked.

This pastoral mood of mine reached its apotheosis at a track meet
a few weeks after I started teaching. Black school sports were mostly
underfinanced to the point of nonexistence, but this was a big annual
event, with about a dozen Cape Flats high schools competing. It was
held at the main "Non-White" stadium in the Cape, which was a few
miles from Grassy Park. We traveled to the meet, the whole school,
students and faculty, in a fleet of rented buses, having canceled classes
for the day. There were a few tricky moments outside the stadium,
where a crowd had gathered of non-students and local *skollies* who
were being refused admission, through whom we teachers had to
shepherd our excited flocks; but once inside and installed in our
Grassy Park section of seats, it was as though the dreary, troubled
world outside ceased to exist.

Facilities on the field were minimal. Many of the runners were
barefoot, and events requiring much apparatus, such as the pole vault
(my old event), could not be staged. Yet the pitch of enthusiasm in the
stands and the intensity of competition on the field were such that the
modest setting seemed transformed. I was thoroughly caught up in
the excitement myself. There were students of mine competing, and
I found myself unabashedly bellowing them on. A Grassy Park relay
team of Standard Six girls won a heart-stopping race, and the pandemonium that followed would have done justice to a world record
effort.

One of my colleagues, a young math teacher named Ivan Grobbelaar, passed me a small bag of tangerines. "For your throat, Mr.
Finnegan," he said, smirking. I was grateful; I had been shouting my
throat raw. I bit into one of the tangerines and gasped. It was satu-

rated with brandy. After he had finished laughing, Grobbelaar informed me that these *naartjies* were standard fare at local sports events. "They don't allow alcohol at the sports grounds here in South Africa," he said. "They even search the people for bottles. So we like to inject these *naartjies,* you know, with our favorite drink." Whole coliseums, according to Grobbelaar, would turn into wild bacchanals, with the revelers leaving behind nothing but a sea of tangerine peels. "And today, you must admit, we do need something to pass the long, boring hours."

I wasn't bored, though, especially as the day wore on and Grassy Park remained in contention for the team title. I had not thought it possible, but the volume of the chanting and cheering rose steadily from its original level. Little red flags had been issued to Grassy Park partisans and each time we won something the flags would all be hurled into the air with a great roar, and a rousing victory song would begin. At one point, Grobbelaar wondered if I wouldn't like to take a walk and relax with some "dagga" (marijuana). But I would not have left the stands by then for anything. Didn't he realize? We had a chance to *win*. He strolled off with Liz Channing-Brown instead.

In the end, we didn't win. But that fact did not seem to matter on the buses back to Grassy Park, where the singing was nonstop. I remember looking out the window at one point, as we passed through some drab Cape Flats township, probably Athlone or Lotus River, where people thronged the dusky roads, and the sun was slipping behind the high purple mass of Table Mountain, and singing students rocked and swayed around me on every side—looking out the bus window and thinking, with a keenly pleasant sense of the irony involved, that it seemed I had finally become infused with something that I had, once upon a time (around the time I was pole-vaulting, to be exact), heard a great deal about, but eventually despaired of ever knowing: I actually had School Spirit.

9

My fellow teachers didn't just dress better than I did. They also drove more presentable cars. Some of them, notably the younger men, could pass hours discussing the fine points of performance in the new Ford Granada, Chevrolet Chevair, or Toyota Corolla. Often, during the lunch recess and after school, one could see platoons of student volunteers deployed in and around some teacher's Mazda, scrubbing the dashboard, polishing the already glistening chrome, and otherwise lost in reveries of abject product worship. My Opel wagon commanded no such devotion. I even began to think that my car, all low-slung and rust-flecked, was considered something of an embarrassment by certain teachers and students. If it was mentioned at all, it always seemed to be by someone remarking the fact that it still had Transvaal license plates—in a tone that suggested that it could at least do without this final indignity. But my vehicular gaucherie was, on the whole, politely overlooked, along with my other eccentricities, by the majority of my new colleagues, who seemed to go out of their way during my first weeks at Grassy Park High to make me feel welcome.

Meryl Cupido was especially unsuspicious. She was the teenage science teacher who had graduated from Grassy Park High the year before. She was a handsome, exuberant girl with long curly black hair and a frank, pealing laugh. Everything I said and did seemed to astound Meryl. She would peer into a sandwich that I had brought from home and exclaim, "Avocado pear! Who else would think to put this in a sandwich? You have such an interesting life, Bill!" Like most of the South Africans I met, Meryl pronounced my first name "Bull," which I found unsettling. And Meryl did so with particular relish, because—as she explained to me—she could not yet bring herself to call any of the other teachers by their first names. I was different because she had not known me while she was a student. Shifting from "Mr. Pieterse" to "Trevor" or "Mr. Tate" to "Alex" would take a while. Meryl and I taught many of the same children (the Standard Sixes), and much of our conversation centered on them. For we found that we shared an unbridled enthusiasm, quite unknown among our more experienced colleagues, for the individual qualities of our individual students, and that we could easily spend hours discussing them, comparing their work, and laughing over their foibles. "And Aubrey September? How will he ever pass his exams? You must help him, Bull! He is not stupid. And that Charmaine? What a wicked girl she is! She just laughs at you. She doesn't care about anything. But she, and some of those others in 6A6 as well, what an *aroma* they have, isn't it, Bull? Someone must show them how to wash!"

John Liberty, the senior physical education teacher, was also friendly. A rumpled, muscular man in his forties, Liberty was an avid baseball player—which was what first got us talking. Liberty had a number of books and magazines about baseball, and drawerfuls of clippings from the sports pages of American newspapers. The club he played for even rented a videotape of the World Series each year, he said, "and we run the thing till it's wrecked!" Although the South African baseball season was just ending as I started teaching, I managed to see Liberty and his team in action a couple of times. They were surprisingly good and serious players. They were also incredibly brave. For they played on badly kept diamonds, where ground balls were forever leaping into an infielder's face, or some outfielder was always going head over heels after hooking his spikes on a tuft of grass. The batters did not wear helmets and the catcher did not wear a cup. When I mentioned to members of Liberty's team that grown men who were not professional players in the United States usually played softball, not hardball, they were shocked. American baseballers were their heroes. "Here, only the *women* play softball." The league Liberty played in was avowedly "non-racial," but everyone in it was black. It reminded me, at first glance, of what I had read of the old Negro Leagues. There were hickory-tough, white-haired catchers in their fifties, who had been playing since the Second World War, trotting out to the mound to calm lanky teenage fireballers. There were leather-lunged wives and friends heckling the opposing team from weatherbeaten bleachers in a creative combination of English and Afrikaans known as *kombuis*. I declined a number of kind offers to join the team, partly because of the excellent chances of injury, and partly because I didn't think I was good enough, but mostly because I could not face the storm of inspired *kombuis* that I was sure would blow every time I stepped up to the plate.

We first met in a strained situation, but Conrad Botha, the school librarian, and I were also soon on good terms. I had gone during my first week at Grassy Park High to remonstrate with him, after having been told by my students that he had decreed that the library would no longer loan out books. Conrad was a slight, boyish fellow about my age, with glasses, a patchy beard, and the habit of calling other male teachers "sir." He apologized for any inconvenience his decree had caused. "But they've asked me to put this library in order. And the only way we can begin is by keeping all the books here, so that we can make a list." I could see his point, and I could also see that his library would not suffice for the purposes of my English classes, anyway. There were so few books, and most of them were in Afrikaans. We would have to use the public library. Conrad and I started talking, though, and I discovered that this was his first year at the school, too. For the past seven years, he said, he had been teaching at a primary school in Wynberg, where his uncle was the headmaster. I was surprised to hear that there was a black school in Wynberg. "Oh, well,"

Conrad said. "You know there's a Wynberg *upper* and a Wynberg *lower*. We live and have our schools in *lower* Wynberg. Quite a number of suburbs are divided that way, since Group Areas. In Wynberg, it's easy to tell the two places apart, because the railway line separates them. There's usually something like that: a highway or an industrial area or some such. But you know you'll always find the property values on our side of the line quite high, and the houses well kept. I don't know why, but people want to live as close as they can to what we call the ruling class. Although they say that if you fix up your place *too* well, and it's just there by the line, they may suddenly decide that your neighborhood must be a white area, and force you out. Oh yes, that has happened. But on their side, it's the opposite. The houses are run down, and they sell quite cheap. Only the so-called poor whites are willing to live so close to the so-called coloreds. You know, if you're interested in studying just how strangely people can behave, sir, you could not have come to a better place than Cape Town."

Soraya Jacobs was another teacher who was friendly to me from the start. She was a talkative, chic, Semitic-looking beauty in her mid-twenties, who drove a new silver Audi and taught sewing. Soraya was engaged to a tall, dashing fellow named Raphael, who had formerly taught at Grassy Park High, and now sold insurance for a living. Soraya and Raphael were Muslims, but not at all devout, and she frequently gave voice to her misgivings about her approaching wedding. She would just as soon not be legally married at all, Soraya claimed. "The things they do to you when you are married in this country, you can't believe," she told me. "For a start, I must give up my permanent teaching post, and become a temporary. Which means they can sack me with just twenty-four hours' notice. Why? Because they believe that a married woman is unreliable. I also must give up my bank account. A married woman is not even allowed to keep her own bank account." It occurred to me that the latter restriction (there was legislation being introduced in Parliament to change it) would really hit Soraya where she lived. For she had the coppery air, and this was very rare in Grassy Park, of someone accustomed to a substantial spending allowance. Her father was a successful businessman who had never let his children want for much. Soraya had taken vacations to Europe; perhaps she and Raphael would spend their honeymoon there, she thought. Soraya's worldliness made her easy for me to talk with.

Ivan Grobbelaar and I also shared a number of students, but his and my conversations about them could not have been more different from Meryl's and mine. Grobbelaar taught Standard Six math, but he never showed any interest in the academic progress of his classes. He liked to regale me with long, smutty monologues on the landing between our classrooms, gesturing toward the students passing below and saying, "These people, I'm telling you, they *like* that thing." Grobbelaar, who was in his late twenties, had a terrible complexion and a disturbing lisp—possibly because he was missing several of his front teeth. He was a flamboyant dresser, given to three-piece lemon-yellow suits, with yellow platform boots and extremely tight trousers. One afternoon, with both liquor and dagga strong on his breath, he boasted to me that he had taken the virginity of a number of girls whom we both taught, none of whom were over the age of fifteen. I was never sure whether to believe him. Although he was hideous, the girls in that class did talk incessantly about how "well dressed" he was.

I was interested in socializing with my colleagues outside school, but I was not sure how to go about it. One Friday afternoon early on, I tried indulging my nostalgia for the afterwork rituals of other jobs I had held by whisking a few people off to a bar I had noticed behind the post office at Busy Corner. My companions were John Liberty, Trevor Pieterse, and another young English teacher, Cecil Abrahams. It wasn't a bad bar—dim, comfortable, with good draft beer and a jukebox full of Motown—but it was a bad idea. I was aware that it was illegal for me to be in there, but I had decided that I would just ignore that fact until someone else brought it up. What I was also ignoring, of course, was the arrogance of my blithely entering a place that was set aside for the exclusive use of my companions, when the equivalent place, set aside for my use—a "white" bar—would have greeted my companions with immediate ejection, if not arrest. With my American chutzpah, I managed to get served in the Grassy Park pub, but somehow the atmosphere never achieved the seamless jollity I remembered from Montana, Australia, and Guam. We all kept glancing at our watches. And when somebody declined to accompany me for a drink the next week by pointing out that it was unwise for a schoolteacher to be seen making a beeline for the bar after work in a community like Grassy Park, I abandoned the idea of unwinding *ensemble* at our "local."

Just a few days later, though, I went to my first staff "braai" (barbecue), which was held at one of the local vleis, and that was a lot more like it. It was a warm, late-summer evening and the braai, when it reached full swing, was as merry as any pub crawl one could have wished for. The *boerewors* was basted with a sweet sharp Cape Malay sauce, and cooked on a makeshift grill in a sandy pit. Disco music blared from a tape deck: Shalamar, Prince, the Spinners, the Commodores, and, most memorably, "Street Life," by the Crusaders. The beer was cold; there was brandy and wine. People danced and, when the moon rose, the waters of the vlei glittered, and a few headlong souls went swimming.

I stood on a little knoll watching the swimmers with Meryl. "You probably never dreamed these teachers got up to such things," she said, laughing. "Well, I tell you, neither did I! Look at Napoleon!"

Napoleon was wearing a tiny, ridiculous straw hat and playing bartender with a manic intensity. As he ran from group to group, ordering people to drink, it was hard to tell whether the self-parody was deliberate. Either way, I was pleased to see teachers who were stern and imposing at school letting down their hair, and especially pleased that, by joining in the general abandonment, I seemed to dissolve some of my colleagues' reservations about me. "Everyone wondered why you came to Grassy Park, you know," Meryl told me. "They thought you might turn up your nose at them."

Around the fire, later in the evening, Trevor Pieterse was telling a joke. "This boy grows up on a farm someplace in the *platteland*. His parents are just laborers, but they manage to send him to school. And he does well in his studies, and gets a bursary, and goes away to boarding school in town, and grows up and becomes a teacher. *Ja*, a teacher. Like Malooi." Malooi was a history teacher, who at that point was passed out in the sand not far from the fire. People laughed. Pieterse went on.

"So the boy comes back one day to the farm to visit his parents. And they're very proud of him, you know. But the Boer who owns the farm is having problems with a troop of baboons who are raiding his mealies [corn] at night, stealing the knobs off the radio in his bakkie [pickup truck], and so on. So the Boer goes to the teacher and he says, 'Trevor, can you help me, man?' (Yes, Trevor was his name.) He says, 'You're an educated man now. Perhaps you can convince these bloody baboons to *voetsek* [scram] somehow. I've tried everything.' But Trevor says, 'What can I do?' But the farmer pleads with him. So finally, Trevor says, 'All right.' He'll try. So he climbs up the *kloof* [ravine] where the baboons live. And the farmer watches him from down below. And he sees Trevor way up there, at the top of the *kloof*, talking to the baboons. The whole troop has come out to hear him, you know. And he sees Trevor saying something, and then the baboons start laughing and laughing. Then Trevor starts talking again. And again the baboons laugh. They're pissing themselves, they're laughing so hard now. Then Trevor starts talking again, and suddenly the whole troop leaps up, and runs off over the mountains like they've just seen a ghost.

"The Boer can't believe it, of course. When Trevor comes back down the mountain, he asks him, 'Man, how did you *do* it?' And Trevor says, 'Well, first I explained to them that I was a colored teacher. They had a good laugh about that. Then I told them what my salary was. That really made them laugh. Then I told them that C.A.D.* was looking for more teachers from this area.' "

Pieterse smirked and poured himself another brandy and Coke while people tried to rouse Malooi by pitching him into the vlei. I drifted over to a group that was arguing about stereophonic sound systems, the sonorous names of Blaupunkt, Magnavox, and Sony filling the air in a rising scherzo of comparison shopping. I wandered on, and came to Georgina Swart, a tall, angular woman in her thirties who taught history, and Chantal Da Grass, a young physical education teacher. Georgina interrupted a story she was telling to ask me, "I don't suppose they have this sort of thing where you come from, Mr. Finnegan—a race-classification investigation?"

Not that I knew of, I said.

"Well, they're quite common here, unfortunately. Especially in Cape Town. We have these people called 'race inspectors,' you see, who are always white, and often very young, and always completely unqualified for this or any other job, who go around at hospitals inspecting babies. They look at fingernails, at hair, at the shapes of noses, and they decide if a baby is white or black. But people sometimes get misclassified. A lot of old scores get settled this way, you see. Someone will inform anonymously on someone else to the Race Classification Board, saying that they have black ancestors perhaps, if they have been classified 'white.' And then there is an investigation. All the relatives are called in and scrutinized, and photographed, and interrogated. Friends are questioned, neighbors are questioned. Family secrets often come out, such as if someone had an illegitimate child at some point. Families are often destroyed, in fact, by these investiga-

---

*The Coloured Affairs Department (C.A.D.), since renamed the Department of Coloured Relations—the administrative body in charge of "colored" education.

tions. What do you think of a system that operates this way, Mr. Finnegan?"

Not much, I said. What could I say?

"Well, perhaps you should think about it," Georgina said. Her arch—and stone cold sober—tone bothered me. But before I could reply, Georgina suddenly started screeching. "Oh! Look at Malooi! On my car!" And she rushed away to shoo Malooi off the roof of her car, where he was quietly dancing in the moonlight. "Leave him," someone called. "He's minding his own business. Anyway, he's *kaalvoet*" (barefoot).

"Kaalvoet and carefree!"

At some point, later that night, I was buttonholed by Pieterse, who was feeling anything but carefree. "Do you *realize,* man," he kept asking, "what it means to be black in this bloody country? Do you *realize* what it is like to work for a government you despise? You can't give up the job, because you have a family, and a house they helped you to buy. But there's no future. There's no opportunity for a black man in this country. You can't possibly understand, man. You're 'white.' You don't know how lucky you are."

Perhaps I didn't. But I did know how embarrassed I was. I offered Pieterse a ride home, but he refused, and drove off into the night, bound for, he said, "the best shebeen in South Africa." (A shebeen is an illegal tavern found in black townships.)

I stayed a while longer there at the vlei, working on some terrible brandy with some other young teachers, who then tried to teach me the rudiments of rugby, using someone's shoe for a ball.

10

My weekly classes with Standards Nine and Ten were an entirely different story from my Standards Six and Seven English and geography classes. The subjects were mandatory, but they were not academic, and no final examination would be administered. The sole textbook in religious instruction was the Bible. For vocational guidance, I had been given a syllabus that included lessons on deportment, hygiene, study habits, the importance of family life, and developing a sense of personal responsibility. About as practical as the lessons got were some instructions on how to use the "hire purchase" system to buy a refrigerator on time. In these subjects, my students themselves suggested that we scrap the syllabus. The class time was normally used, they said, for study and discussion. The Bible was duly set aside. Discussion topics were solicited—the most frequent suggestions were careers, computers, and the pros and cons of premarital sex.

The senior students I saw were a small, serious group, quite unlike the great laughing crowds of the junior classes. In fact, matrics were a truly elite corps at Grassy Park High, for they had survived a ruthless thinning of the ranks. You only had to look at the roster of students: the school's entering class was six times the size of its exiting class. And admission to the school in the first place was a privilege, available only to those who had successfully finished primary school—something that fewer than half of all black South African students do. The matrics were, in short, a very bright, ambitious group, in most cases already far better educated than their parents.

I was therefore stunned to discover that almost none of them had any realistic notions about what they would do after graduation. "Architecture," "medicine," "engineering," "law," they wrote on a questionnaire in the space where I asked them to indicate their career plans. But in the space where I asked what they were doing to further these plans, most of them wrote nothing.

"Where would you like to go to study architecture?" I asked one girl.

She had no idea which universities offered the subject.

"What branch of engineering?" I asked a short, hatchet-faced boy named Hector.

"What branch, sir?"

None of them seemed to know where one actually went for training for these professions, or how one applied and paid for it. None of them seemed to know any doctors, lawyers, architects, or engineers. Grassy Park High had no real career-counseling program. The only career advice most students got from professionals came from their teachers. As a result, the arc of their most concrete ambitions tended to end at the local teacher-training college—where most of my colleagues had finished *their* education—and where the curriculum, I discovered, was merely the high school curriculum done over again, double-time. A few students expressed a desire to go on to "Bush," their name for the University of the Western Cape, the local college for "coloreds."

This all struck me as a great waste in the making. So I undertook to find out what the real possibilities were. Obviously, black advancement was an uphill fight in white-ruled South Africa. "Job reservation" had long been a cornerstone of the apartheid system, protecting the employment and wages of whites against black competition. In recent years, statutory job reservation by race had been largely rolled back in favor of the "floating color bar," which allowed blacks into jobs when their labor was required, and excluded them when it wasn't. But there were very, very few blacks in managerial or supervisory positions in South Africa, or in the professions. Less than 3 percent of the country's university graduates were black. In fact, the percentage of the white population enrolled in universities was the second highest in the world (behind the United States), while for blacks the percentage was lower than that in Ghana.

A great deal of job reservation was not statutory, but simply customary. I noticed that many of the advertisements in the Employment Offered columns in the Cape Town daily newspapers mentioned race classification as a job requirement: "Bantu Chef"; "Coloured Char"; "Junior Salesman (White)"; "African Maid"; "Coloured Office Girl"; "Personality Girls—Europeans Only." Other ads did not need to mention race. Vacancies for cleaners, laborers, and domestic help were simply understood to be open only to blacks, just as advertisers seeking a hotel manager or a production manager for an engineering firm did not have to mention that applicants had to be white. (My first reaction to seeing the race-specific ads was disgust; then a black friend told me that she thought blacks preferred this candor to wasting their time phoning after jobs that turned out to be closed to them.) These were, of course, the same unwritten laws Rachel and I had encountered when we first asked around about jobs.

Government policy still pursued the same objectives that formal job reservation had accomplished in the past. Shortly after I started teaching, Fanie Botha, the Minister of Manpower, had sought to reassure nervous whites by announcing: "There should be no fears in the hearts of our people that they will be squeezed out of their traditional work situation. . . . Still better instruments will be established for protection against unreasonable threats in the work situation."

All in all, the differences between the choices and prospects facing a matric at, say, Wynberg Boys' High and those facing our matrics at Grassy Park High were fundamental. The best universities in the country, every profession—they were all wide open to white children. White South Africans enjoyed full employment, such that even the least capable were guaranteed a job of some kind, at a living wage. Among blacks, on the other hand, unemployment was epidemic, and the vast majority of jobs available did not pay a living wage. What the newspapers did not much advertise, I noticed, were the real career options for most black kids in Cape Town—the docks, road crews, fishing boats, textile mills, and canning factories—employers that loomed large for any Grassy Park students who fell behind in their studies, or whose families needed them to go to work. There was, finally, the terrific educational disadvantage that even our few matrics would carry into any competition for jobs or university spaces with white matrics. In 1980, the government was spending five times the amount on the education of each white child that it was spending on each "colored" child (and *twelve* times what it was spending on each African child),* a disparity that was plain enough in the facilities provided each group, but was also reflected in teacher-to-pupil ratios, the qualifications of teachers, and, inevitably, in student academic development.

Despite all this, I was encouraged by what I discovered in the course of researching the career opportunities available to our matrics. For South Africa was, it seemed, suffering from a serious shortage of skilled manpower. And this was a situation that promised to get only worse in the years ahead. The white population (and government-assisted "white" immigration from Europe and elsewhere) had no hope of supplying the booming South African economy with all the technical, professional, and managerial personnel it required. There was already a call out for five times the number of industrial engineers presently working in the country. Within ten years, the projected manpower shortages in all areas were awesome. Even the government had conceded that its only option was the rapidly increased training of great numbers of blacks. If nothing else, the color bar was going to be floating upward fast, and staying up. If our matrics could just get the education—a university degree or a technical college diploma would certainly be entrance requirements for the technical/ managerial sector where the projected shortages would be most severe—the demand for their skills in the years ahead would be enormous.

I also discovered, in the course of this research, a non-racial careers information service, funded by a private foundation. One Saturday morning, I visited their offices. It was my first encounter with a white liberal organization in South Africa, and I must say I found it delightful. The offices were located in an oak-lined alley in a lovely old

---

*The figures for per capita expenditure on education for the various racial groups during 1979–80: Whites—R1,169; Indians—R389; "coloreds"—R234; Africans in "white areas"—R91.

suburb near the University of Cape Town. They had the ramshackle Victorian-with-xeroxes flavor that one associates with enlightened humanism.

"You're a guidance teacher at Grassy Park High? Oh, that's *wonderful.*"

The staff was friendly, competent, and integrated. After an interview, a nominal payment, and having signed up Grassy Park High for every program in sight, I carried off a heavy stack of notebooks, flyers, new information, and new hope about the "life chances" of my students. The next week, I set my senior students to writing to every university in the country, and to dozens of professional organizations, scholarship funds, and technical colleges.

Most of them, to my surprise, were less than enthusiastic about the assignment.

"Where did you get all these addresses?" Clive wanted to know. (He hadn't even bothered to fill out my careers questionnaire.)

My answer didn't seem to mean anything to him.

I provided sample letters of inquiry, but the students still seemed intimidated. Their real objection, someone finally blurted out, was that most of these institutions "are not for so-called coloreds."

That was true. Still I insisted, arguing that we could work all that out later, that first we simply needed information.

In fact, I had been told at the careers information office that special "permits" were becoming increasingly available to qualified blacks to attend "white" colleges and universities. This was the sort of liberalization, they said, that the government was busy publicizing overseas these days, in order to buttress its claim that apartheid was being dismantled, but which they did not much advertise here at home, where a backlash among the white electorate was always feared. Actually, I was told, the main English-language universities now enrolled four times as many blacks as they had in the 1950s, before higher education was officially segregated. Permits were granted only on a case-by-case basis, but the success rate for applications by "coloreds" had been running very high lately.

So we sent off our letters. And my dubious students, to say nothing of the school secretary, were astonished at the response we got. Brochures and catalogs came flooding back within days. Nobody had known so much free literature existed. We started a file that soon grew into a shelf. We charted application deadlines and began collating requirements. I started holding private interviews to match ambitions with applications for programs and funding. Even Clive seemed to get excited about the possibilities.

11

"Will this be how the children in America receive their lessons?"

My ideas about what might go on in a classroom were quite alien to my students. For kids long trained to a passive, "parrot" role in their schooling, it was no easy matter to grasp what I was doing when I would lecture—stage-whispering to them: *"Take notes"*—but: *"Don't copy"*—because: *"These are for YOU"*—then collect their notes to see how well they were grasping the topic "for themselves." Organized discussions and debate also seemed to cut across the grain of my students' training, making for balky, self-conscious sessions that I was too often compelled to direct myself.

My notions about education were foreign to my students at many different levels. I might, for example, deliberate out loud the merits of two grammatical constructions, and conclude that both were fine, that it was simply a matter of taste. This sort of latitudinarianism has never been in vogue among authority figures in South Africa, and I fear it only confused my students. They wanted to be told what was right and what was wrong, not treated to arcane deliberations. Other strange habits and exactions of mine, like the public library card which I insisted every student procure, or the unheard-of amounts of homework I assigned, at least had the virtue of being straightforward.

In geography, some students seemed to welcome my departures from the syllabus and my criticism of the textbook, while others were clearly disturbed by them. I thought I sensed stirrings of revolt at my presentation on the subject of South Africa's relations with its immediate neighbors. My lessons emphasized the migrant labor system and what I called "economic colonialism," and tended to depict South Africa as a powerful exploiter of the less powerful. These lessons seemed to strike a patriotic nerve in some students, or at least to clash painfully with everything they had heard before on these subjects. "What must we do, sir? The minerals belong to South Africa. There are no jobs in these other places." Other students seemed to understand that I was not criticizing them when I criticized "South Africa." This was risky business, I realized—coming to a country, taking a job teaching in its schools, and telling its young people in so many words that the country's leaders were a lot of racist thugs. But what worried me more were the many students who readily adapted their old rote-learning methods to my alternative syllabus, dutifully inserting FRELIMO into their Mozambique lessons with little apparent comprehension of the material.

Some lessons went wonderfully, others went over like the prover-bial lead balloons. With my English classes, I often misjudged at first my students' proficiency in English. For example, there was a poetry lesson, one that fell squarely in the lead balloon category, during which I read an Ogden Nash poem that I had chosen not only for its nice, relativist message—so appropriate, I thought, to a prejudice-riddled society like South Africa's—but because its subject was one close to many of my students' hearts: African animals. Titled "The Hippopotamus," it went:

> Behold the hippopotamus!
> We laugh at how he looks to us,
> And yet in moments dank and grim
> I wonder how we look to him.
> Peace, peace, thou hippopotamus!
> We really look all right to us,
> As you no doubt delight the eye
> Of other hippopotami.

The silence that followed my reading of this poem's last line might have been deeply gratifying at some other time. As it was, it was merely a function of the fact that nobody got it.

Except Wayan, who was so shy that he nearly choked, trying to hide his snickers in the sleeve of his blazer. Wayan was a dark, deli-cate, deerlike boy, with huge brown eyes and a heartbreaking bow mouth. He was the youngest student I taught, and one of the few real readers. When things got boring, Wayan would try to read science fiction paperbacks under his desk, and when I stunned the bulk of my students by requiring written and oral book reports, Wayan was at a different sort of a loss. He had so many favorite books, how would he choose?

My worst student in English was sturdy, silent little Aubrey Sep-tember. It seemed impossible that he could have passed seven years of English and still have such a poor grasp of the language. But when I met with him privately, I discovered why: Aubrey was a country boy. His family had come to Cape Town only at the beginning of that year. He had previously attended one of South Africa's infamous "farm schools," where his English teachers, he finally told me, blushing deeply, had themselves not spoken English. I started tutoring Aubrey after school.

In between Wayan and Aubrey was a wide range of reading abili-ties and tastes. Most of the girls proposed to read and report on "Mills and Boone books"—the local equivalent of Harlequin romances. Desmond, who raised dogs, chose *Jock of the Bushveld,* by Sir Percy Fitzpatrick. Hester brought in *The Book of Horse and Pony Stories.*

Terence wanted to read the new Wilbur Smith thriller—which looked a bit racy for our purposes. I racked my brain and scoured secondhand bookstores for less regressive literature that would not be beyond my students' ability, and brought in whatever I could find—*Charlotte's Web, The Wind in the Willows,* Eugene Marais's *My Friends the Baboons.* On the whole, the children seemed to regard reading as a chore, an attitude I dearly hoped to revise. But it was difficult to find books that could appeal to them all, for reading in class, and impossible to come up with sets of them.

Class sessions were far too short, I found—less than forty minutes each, on average—to allow me to observe the responses of my students to my lessons properly. For I was experimenting furiously, just winging it really, trying to come up with things that would do more than merely pass the hours, things that would actually *excite* the children. Because that, I believed, was the only way real education ever took place. Of course, there was excitement and there was excitement. I thought that letting my English students teach me Afrikaans might be a fruitful exercise. But these lessons proved almost impossible to control—forty eager teachers trying to outshout each other, with one beleaguered student, whose every utterance absolutely fractured his instructors—and I soon abandoned them.

In geography, too, my attempts to make class time more vivid sometimes went too far. There was one memorable lesson on the solar system, for example, when no amount of description seemed to get the various ideas across. Finally, we just pushed aside the desks and created a working human orrery. That is to say, I stationed students around the room, each representing some celestial body, and set them all to orbiting and rotating at the appropriate rates, while I began dashing back and forth between Earth, Moon, Sun, and Pluto pointing out salient relations, adjusting perturbations, and being fried by an overacting Sun when I flew too close—all for the edification of a class whose screams and sobs of laughter were soon drowning out my narration. The most memorable moment of that lesson, at least for me, was when Napoleon and Africa burst in the door with canes raised and a great crowd of peering faces behind them. They had come to quell the uprising that they had assumed was occurring in my room.

No uprisings did occur in my room. In fact, the feeling in my classes was the furthest thing from the violent, jailbreak atmosphere of the stereotypical American ghetto high school. Some of the tougher boys might have a pack of cigarettes on them and be reputed to use dagga, but hard drugs, weapons, vandalism, open contempt for teachers, and the other symptoms of systemic breakdown that plague so many American schools were nowhere in evidence at Grassy Park High. Neither were there any functional illiterates somehow cruising through school undetected. Which is not to say that the world outside Grassy Park High was not rife with the usual ghetto ills: unemployment, poverty, illiteracy, crime. These woes and their effects were just kept, to a remarkable degree, out of the school itself.

But my aura as "the American" was fading, and with it the overawed, mission-school atmosphere in my classes. For the most part, I was grateful for that. It opened up the possibilities for learning, for real intellectual activity and exchange, and it allowed me to begin to know my students, not as exotic figures in a tourist's pastorale, but as people—people who were just as cruel and just as kind, just as curious and just as opaque, as teenagers anywhere else.

The tide that ran against the sort of thing I was trying to do in the classroom was never really that strong among my students. Among my colleagues, it was more profound. I first felt it clearly when Napoleon held his meeting of the new geography teachers. Napoleon's classroom was the best appointed in the school. There were counters, cupboards, a sink. Old student projects—particolored weather maps and papier-mâché volcanoes—lined the walls. It was an affecting setting in which to hear Napoleon make his pitch for the necessity of hewing closely to the syllabus.

"We must coordinate. If we don't coordinate, we will be lost. What if one of you gets sick, or must leave his post for some other reason, and we can't tell where you are with your syllabus? What if the inspector comes and finds each teacher doing some different thing? What is going to become of these poor children when they must sit their exams? *All pupils must be equally prepared.* It's only fair."

Everyone else seemed to agree: it was essential that we all be teaching the same material at the same time all year long. It was not an auspicious time for me to raise objections to the material itself. So I didn't.

Over lunch in the staff room, I did, however, enter into a discussion of the inadequacies of our textbooks with Alex Tate. And I discovered that my problems were nothing compared to those confronting a history teacher. "One is obliged to teach the government's version of South African history," Tate said. "Which can be quite a problem. Because, in some areas, the textbooks are simply false. Such as on the question of who settled South Africa first. The government likes to put forward the 'open land' and 'simultaneous arrival' theories. This is the idea that the white settlers found an essentially uninhabited South Africa and that the frontier wars were fought against black tribes which had actually just arrived themselves, from the north. These theories are meant to justify white occupation of the land, of course. The problem is that they have been completely discredited by historians and archaeologists for a long time now. Blacks were living throughout South Africa for many centuries before the first whites arrived. In other areas, the texts simply offer the government's rationale for conditions in the country—for very controversial policies like the pass laws, the homelands policy—without mentioning the rest of the world's, much less the black majority's, views on the matter. It's quite bad, really."

So I was far from the front lines, with my junior geography classes, in this battle over the material in our syllabuses. Also, Napoleon's admonitions notwithstanding, I would be administering the year-end examinations to my students myself, whereas Tate taught matrics, and if he wanted them to have any chance of passing their government-administered exams, he had to prepare them to applaud the "civilizing mission" of the European settlers in South Africa, and to use hated terms like "Bantu" and "homeland," and not inside quotation marks either.

12

The principal was determined to transform Grassy Park High into, as he put it, "something more than just a *colored* school"—he pronounced the hated word with violent disdain. His plan: to build a wall around the school. A cheap, plain, cement block wall. It would keep *skollies* and other "elements" from wandering onto the school ground. At the staff meeting where the wall idea was tabled, I was tempted to speak out—in opposition to the wall. I *liked* the fact that donkeys grazed on the sports field, that lovers and street gangs and matrons used the school as a thoroughfare, meeting place, and refuge. I didn't want to see the campus sealed off from the neighborhood, to see it sterilized, as it were. But mine were alien, romantic reasons, I knew, so I kept quiet.

Other teachers were less reticent. Somebody pointed out that our students' favorite record album at the moment was Pink Floyd's "The Wall." Laughter. (It was true.) Someone else pointed out that the record had been banned by the government. (Not true—it was banned two months later.) More laughter. When the topic became fund raising, more substantial objections were offered. The principal thought he could procure the donation of a new car as a raffle prize by a certain charity-minded corporation president. Muslim staff and parents had already consulted their imam. Now they rejected the raffle idea—too much like gambling. Other staff members supported the fund raising, but did not support the wall—the money, they said, would be better used to buy books. The principal kept his dream alive by appointing a committee to devise acceptable fund-raising events.

I found the wall business symbolic in several ways, for I had already come to assume that such supremely local issues represented at Grassy Park High the extent of most people's interest in world affairs.

That assumption was summarily overturned on the afternoon of March 4. I was looking for books in a supply room, and finding nothing but ancient copies of Rider Haggard's *King Solomon's Mines,* when I heard a commotion start outside. I went to the door and saw students beginning to dash back and forth between the buildings. I could hear classes chanting, "Fifty-seven! Fifty-seven! Fifty-seven!" Then kids were suddenly writing "57" on the walls with chalk. Pieterse hurried past, looking flushed and breathless. I asked him what the hell was happening. "Fifty-seven!" he shouted, not stopping. "Mugabe has won fifty-seven seats! ZANU-PF is going to rule Zimbabwe!"

In retrospect, it seems outlandish, but at the time I was stunned. And not by the election result so much as by the powerful reaction it provoked at Grassy Park High. The South African newspapers had been covering the Zimbabwe independence election campaign extensively (if poorly: some had actually predicted victory for the black moderate, Bishop Abel Muzorewa, who was hopelessly compromised by, among other things, his South African support, and was crushed at the polls by the man whom whites in South Africa and Zimbabwe had long insisted was a bloodthirsty Marxist maniac, Robert Mugabe), and I had been talking to my classes about its importance, yet I had gained little sense that anyone else at Grassy Park was really very interested. Now I saw how wrong I was. I also saw how trusted I wasn't: the whole school had been on pins and needles waiting to hear the election results, and no one had said a word to me. The opposition press in Cape Town described Mugabe's resounding victory as evidence "that the government and most white South Africans had no perception of black political thinking," and the accusation could apparently be made, at a local level, against me, too.

My dismay on that score was dwarfed, however, by the excitement of the event itself, and by the realization that seemingly everyone at Grassy Park High understood quite well, thank you, their basic situation, and even felt as one about its ultimate redress. (The government press continued to try to reassure itself. "Rhodesia's situation is not at all analogous with that of South Africa," insisted Cape Town's *Die Burger*. Yet over 90 percent of Zimbabwe's voters had gone to the polls, and that in itself seemed to be analogy enough for the 25 million disenfranchised in South Africa. Those black leaders who were not in jail all publicly hailed the election and its result.)

Politics saturates life in South Africa, that I had already figured out; the idea that Grassy Park was an anomalous backwater had been pure delusion. School let out early that afternoon, and it never looked quite the same again to me.

13

I was groping toward some understanding of South African politics and society. While touring the country and first teaching in Cape Town, I had come up with several tentative answers to the great and obvious question that presented itself when we arrived in the country —about what prevented black South Africans from simply rising up against their outnumbered white overlords. The first was the manifest docility of most blacks. This perception had been shaken by the unexpected response at Grassy Park High to the big news from Zimbabwe, and was further shaken by almost everything I managed to read about the history of black resistance in South Africa. Much of the relevant writing had been banned, but the long, bloody story of strikes, marches, boycotts, revolts, and massacres could be found even in mainstream academic histories. Clearly, not all blacks had been taking their subjection passively. Still, I could not avoid the impression that many black South Africans were shackled by a slavelike mentality, in which self-confidence, self-respect, and conscious, constructive resentment of their oppression were conspicuously lacking.

A second inescapable observation and provisional answer seemed

to be black disunity. From a distance, it might be easy to think of
South Africa's 25 million blacks as a whole and wonder why they did
not act in concert. Inside the country, it was not so easy. People lived
in widely scattered communities, separated by great barriers of ignorance, poverty, language, and culture. There was no national black
political organization; there were no national black political leaders
(other than those in jail or in exile). There was a great range of black
political attitudes. The power of black numbers, as perceived from
overseas, was largely an illusion.

The most ambitious attempts to organize the country's blacks for
mass political action had each been crushed in its turn: the Industrial
and Commercial Union in the 1920s; the African National Congress
(ANC), founded in 1912, and a potent force in the 1950s, but outlawed
in 1960; the breakaway Pan-Africanist Congress (PAC), also outlawed
in 1960; and the Black Consciousness movement, banned in 1977. The
sort of wholesale revolt that I first imagined might work in South
Africa had actually been attempted by an underground movement
known as Poqo (the armed wing of the PAC) in the early 1960s. Poqo
had frightened whites, but inspired few blacks with its violent, ill-
organized program, and it had been easily smashed by the government in 1963. The ANC's first attempts at guerrilla warfare after it
was driven underground were also smashed around the same time,
when a number of its top leaders, including Nelson Mandela, were
captured and received life sentences. An essentially spontaneous national uprising had occurred in 1976, when Soweto high school students protesting educational conditions were attacked by police and
the township exploded. The violence eventually spread to black townships all over the country, continuing for over a year and claiming at
least six hundred lives. "Soweto," as the revolt was known, had been
by far the most serious and prolonged confrontation between blacks
and the authorities in modern times. But it, too, had been handled
with relative ease by the police, who lost not a single man. (The army
was never even called out.) On the black side, there had been no
coherent leadership, no coherent overall strategy.

Of the various ideologies advanced by the succession of black
resistance movements, the Black Consciousness philosophy struck me
as the one most likely to galvanize the greatest number of people into
decisive political action. Its main texts were all banned, but it was still
possible to gather the general theme: aggressive black pride, black
self-reliance, and psychological preparation for majority rule. In

many ways, Black Consciousness had remained a "pre-political" movement, its growth increasingly hampered throughout the 1970s by police harassment, culminating in the 1977 death in detention of Steve Biko, its preeminent leader and theorist, and the subsequent banning of all Black Consciousness organizations and publications. The movement had spread its message widely only among students, and it seemed to have spent more energy rejecting the help of white liberals than it had spent actually fighting the government, but its defiant creed had clearly inspired many participants in the 1976 uprising. Nondogmatic but uncompromising, Black Consciousness had drawn on a wide variety of sources for its ideas, from traditional African nationalism to Marxism to the Black Power movement in the United States.

It was partly the firm line taken against white liberals that appealed to me about Black Consciousness, I think, because the more I read in recent South African history the clearer it seemed that the would-be white allies of black resistance had usually served only to temper black resentment, divert black initiative, and otherwise slow the pace of black emancipation. As Steve Biko wrote, "The biggest mistake the black world ever made was to assume that whoever opposed apartheid was an ally."

My growing disenchantment with white liberalism extended to the white opposition press which had so impressed me in Johannesburg and included both of the English-language daily newspapers in Cape Town, the *Cape Times* and the *Argus*. These papers' critical coverage of the government's behavior remained ferocious, and their editors' conception of the ruling National Party was, in my view, accurate. A typical *Cape Times* cartoon showed a big, brontosaural skeleton, labeled "Nat-Osaurus" and wearing the battered top hat which always adorned caricatures of National Party politicians, with a scientist explaining to a group of museumgoers: "Some time in the late twentieth century it became bogged down in an ideological quagmire and trapped by a political eruption." But just as the major Afrikaans-language papers were all openly linked with the National Party and uniformly supportive of government policy, the opposition papers were all closely identified, I soon realized, with the Progressive Federal Party, the largest white opposition party. Both the papers and the party were controlled by the same South African English business interests. Along with making a profit, getting the Nats' goat was the opposition papers' *raison d'être.*

➤ This lack of "objectivity" did not bother me, once I understood its particular bias. What did bother me was the bias itself. The opposition press subscribed to the PFP's platform, which boiled down to a call for "power sharing." This call was entirely ignored by the government, but it was actually less sweeping than it sounded. The envisioned power sharing was limited; it was decidedly not one-person one-vote. As a January 1980 editorial put it, "No sensible person these days is dogmatic about constitutional forms or puts forward extreme solutions such as separate development or universal franchise in a unitary, Westminster-style constitution." (The "sensible person" in question here was clearly white, since even opinion polls carried out by *government* commissions showed that an overwhelming majority of black South Africans favored exactly that "extreme solution": one-person one-vote in a unitary state.)

The editors of the opposition press avoided this definitive, "constitutional" question when they could. They preferred to concentrate in their editorials on the government's responsibility for the countless "unsavoury incidents" caused by apartheid—deploring the eviction of a "colored" athlete from a "white" steak house, or the enforcement of beach apartheid. They were not above squeezing political capital out of these stories—sending, for instance, a *Cape Times* reporter to the beach with three PFP politicians to record their high-minded horror at police harassment of black beachgoers. The real concern of the white opposition over such incidents was pragmatic, however. The constant insults and humiliations being dealt out to blacks could all too easily become, as one of the beachgoing politicians put it, "the cause of violence to come in this country." More substantive oppression was viewed from the same perspective. The essence of the white opposition's view of the need for amelioration of black misery seemed to me contained in the well-worn observation, made in a *Cape Times* editorial about hunger on the Cape Flats: "If they do not eat, we do not sleep."

South Africa's "international image" seemed to be of special concern to the English-language papers. Each instance of the continued virulence of apartheid, they complained, only "confirms this country's critics in their belief that South Africans are a weird breed of race-obsessed bigots." (Again, it was only white South Africans whose reputation was thus imperiled; but this confusion, of South Africa *in toto* with its white minority, was extremely common among whites, even among liberals.) They would often fret in print about South Africa's image as a "police state," and point out that it looked very bad to people overseas for the government to be continually "banning" persons,* jailing its opponents, withdrawing passports, outlawing political parties, and so on.

None of this is to say that the protests of the opposition press against such practices were not sincere, and even sometimes useful to their victims. Neither is it to say that the opposition press did not itself suffer any government strictures. There were over one hundred laws containing press curbs on the books in 1980, proscribing coverage of everything from national defense to prison conditions, energy policy to police operations. There were also some extremely broadly worded laws in among the stacks of "security legislation," laws that, for example, defined "terrorism" as anything that served "to embarrass the administration of the affairs of the State." Such laws naturally resulted in a high degree of "self-censorship" among journalists; but there was also direct censorship. In 1980, the *Rand Daily Mail* of Johannesburg began to indicate just how restricted was its reporting by inserting a picture of a pair of scissors alongside portions of stories which had been censored. I thought Louis Le Grange, the Minister of Police and Prisons, captured the government's attitude toward the press perfectly when he said, "The State and the press must have a pleasant relationship, but, when it is necessary, we talk to them with a sword in our hand in great friendship."

On some key issues, the position of the white opposition was even in agreement with the preponderance of black opinion (insofar as that could be canvassed). The PFP and its newspapers advocated, for instance, the repeal of several of the legislative mainstays of apartheid, including the Group Areas Act.

Still, the white opposition's endless talk of "change" and "intergroup reconciliation" came to seem hollow to me, and I began to mistrust its newspapers. My problem, I realized, was that I was beginning to view the white opposition, and by extension its mouthpieces,

---

*"Banning orders," which usually run for five years, are served on opponents of the government without warning or explanation. Banned persons are usually placed under some form of house arrest. They may not write for publication, be quoted in print, have their photograph published, meet with another banned person, or even be in the same room with more than one other person. They are usually forbidden to enter any educational institution, library, printing establishment, factory, or hospital. Sometimes they are banished to remote parts of the country. Banned persons are effectively erased from society, and are often served with new banning orders when their original orders expire. Between 1950 and 1974, the South African Institute of Race Relations estimates that 1,240 persons were banned. In May 1980, there were 146 banned men and women.

from the perspective of those South Africans with whom I was spending most of my time—from, that is, the Cape Flats. And my awareness
of their irreducible "whiteness" was becoming obtrusive as a result.
I still read the daily papers, but more and more I read them with an
eye for their unwitting irony, for their self-serving piety and their
peculiar self-absorption. Seen from that angle, they could be terribly
obtuse. There was a *Cape Times* editorial reviewing the findings of an
official inquiry into the 1976 uprising, an editorial that ended: "The
lesson to be absorbed, then, is that a gap in understanding between
black and white existed in Soweto and elsewhere around the country
before the upheaval. We may draw our own conclusion that this gap
is still in existence." I remember laughing over this "conclusion" with
a colleague in the staff room at Grassy Park High. Said my companion: "That means the nanny just won't open up to madam the way she
used to!"

Such are the fissures in South African life that I was coming
around to seeing the value of what had seemed beyond comprehension
on my first day in the country: separate newspapers for blacks and
whites. The only black paper in Cape Town was a weekly, the *Cape
Herald,* which was widely read on the Cape Flats. If black people
wanted to see a daily paper, though, their only options were the white
papers—which were "white" not only in the relatively subtle politi-
cal-editorial sense I have been describing, but in every department, in
every detail. I've mentioned some glancing instances of this, but I first
ran into it squarely when I heard that the *Cape Times* had published
a list of all the high school graduates in the Cape the previous year,
and I looked it up to see what the results had been at Grassy Park
High and neighboring schools. I found the Senior Certificate Pass List
—but Grassy Park was not among the dozens of schools listed. I was
baffled until, in the *Cape Times* of three days later, I ran across the
Coloured Senior Certificate Pass List. In the world of the white papers, there were high school graduates, and there were Coloured high
school graduates.

The argument for separate newspapers for blacks was partly practical. What use were the entertainment pages of the *Cape Times* when
the cinemas listed were all whites-only? What use were the ads for
housing, when the flats and houses were all, or nearly all, in the white
areas? Here was an ad for dancing lessons—it was against the law for
blacks and whites to dance together, so the lessons were presumably
being offered to whites only, although the ad never said so. Blacks and
whites did live in such rigorously separate worlds—did it not make

sense that, would it not be easier all around if, they should have separate daily journals?

There was a psychological argument for black papers, too. Seen from the perspective of the Cape Flats, the outstanding quality of the white papers was that of *exclusion.* They were produced by the white minority for the white minority. Black life was at best a shadow in the background of the "real life" being led in the white areas. The Cape Flats was covered like a police beat. Every Monday, there was a body count—so many assaults, so many rapes, so many murders—and that was the week's news from the nether regions. Blacks remained spectators, strangers in their own land.

Black papers tended to adopt editorial positions that were far more hostile to the government than those of the white opposition press—such that, in 1977, the government simply banned the nation's largest black paper, *The World,* and jailed its editor. Any black paper that was *not* openly defying the government would have been in an impossible position in the black community. This I eventually understood—some time after I began to see the extremely limited relevance of even the white opposition press to the lives of black South Africans.

But before I grew too sensitive to the hypocrisy of it all, I found the back and forth of white politics which dominated the white papers fascinating. The PFP could be terribly eloquent in its denunciations of the government. It had, after all, little else to do except polish its technique. The Nationalists, meanwhile, regularly skewered the PFP on the contradictions of its position as well-heeled protester. For the most part, the government employed a surprisingly cool, social-scientific rhetoric on even the most inflammatory issues of race and subjugation. Its spokesmen were constantly reaching out fraternally to "other groups." "The more we are prepared to sweat together in peace, the less likely we are to bleed in war," as the Minister of Cooperation and Development (formerly "Bantu Affairs") put it. Gone was the rhetoric of naked white supremacy; the government now worked hard to convey a neutral, managerial attitude toward the problems of the country. The PFP made the most of the ruling party's occasional slips, such as when the Minister of Posts and Telecommunications informed Parliament that blacks had "slower thought processes" than whites did. The opposition press had a field day with this remark—although the minister said he saw no reason to retract it. But this was all a far cry from the days when a Nationalist MP had felt free to say in public that he wished more blacks had died at Sharpeville—"Sharpeville" being a famous massacre in 1960, when police opened fire on a peaceful demonstration, killing sixty-nine blacks and wounding hundreds, most of them shot in the back while attempting to flee.

The torch of unadulterated white supremacism had not been extinguished in South African political debate; it had just been passed to the various white parties to the right of the government, notably in 1980 the Herstigte Nasionale Party. These parties were the refuge of whites who, alarmed by the government's recent reformist gestures, had begun defecting from the National Party. The HNP advocated the restoration of job reservation; it rejected the principle of equal pay for equal work. At its convention in 1980, the party called for all-out war against Angola, which was providing bases for black South African guerrillas. It was essential to show blacks "who is boss in this white man's country," the party leaders declared. In a way, I found I actually preferred the outrageous policy statements of the HNP to the more measured positions taken by the Nationalists and the PFP. At least the leaders of the HNP stated in public exactly what they stood for. The problem was that many members of the National Party apparently saw things the same way—the far right was growing stronger with every by-election.

What exactly were these alleged reforms that the government was introducing that were alienating so many apartheid-loving whites? I had a hell of a time trying to answer this question during my first months in South Africa. Certainly, it was all still a matter of far more talk than action. Prime Minister P. W. Botha had told the country's whites the year before that they would have to "adapt or die." This was the kind of statement that appalled the *verkrampte*, or unenlightened, wing of his own party. At the same time, the government remained committed to the basic apartheid program, including the ultimate "denationalization" of most of the country's blacks. A seemingly endless series of consultative bodies were forever being appointed in the government's effort to formulate some broadly acceptable plan for the country's future. But these councils and commissions, most of them launched with a great deal of fanfare, all seemed then to drift slowly out of view, their charter incomplete or overly restrictive, their purpose forgotten, their recommendations ignored. In time, I learned to look upon this level of official activity with some of the skepticism that most black South Africans did.

The bottom line was not hard to discern. The white minority imposed its will on the black majority by force. The South African police and military were massive, highly motivated, and extremely well-armed organizations. Blacks were unarmed and unorganized. The eyes and ears of the Security Police* were everywhere, and there were few constraints upon the state when it moved against its opponents. This was perhaps the simplest and most complete answer to the question about the failure to date of blacks to throw off the yoke: the whites, though few, were just too strong. The African National Congress, operating from exile, fielded a small guerrilla force, known as Umkhonto We Sizwe (Spear of the Nation), estimated to contain between two thousand and seven thousand fighters, most of them based in training camps in rural Angola. Returning clandestinely to South Africa in tiny bands, ANC guerrillas attacked power stations, railway lines, government offices, township police stations, and other economic and symbolic targets on a regular basis—averaging six or seven incidents a month in 1979. The ranks of the ANC had been bolstered by the exodus of thousands of young blacks from South Africa after the 1976 uprising. Still, the military threat it presented to the government was negligible.

But the press coverage of these "terrorist" attacks, and of the numerous "terrorist" trials being held (usually *in camera*) continually around the country, did serve to highlight the true location of the battle lines in the ongoing South African crisis. For when it came to the prospect of violent black resistance, the sentiments of whites, pro- and anti-apartheid, converged, and the white opposition took a position indistinguishable from that of the government. The sentiments of blacks on the same issue were rarely revealed in the press, but when they were, the effect was stunning. In January 1980, for instance, four young men from Soweto seized a bank in a white suburb of Pretoria, took twenty-five hostages, made demands including the release of Nelson Mandela, and were killed in a police assault. Four days later in Soweto, twenty thousand people gathered to give one of them a hero's funeral.

Other issues that provoked a similar convergence in white opposition and government positions were South Africa's banishment from the international sporting community, and the disinvestment movement in the Western democracies. The whole spectrum of white politicians opposed this sort of "foreign meddling." Again, it was difficult to know exactly what most black South Africans thought about these

---

*Often known as the Special Branch, or the Security Branch, this plainclothes wing of the South African Police deals exclusively with "political" crime. Its exact size is a state secret, but its power and influence have grown immensely in recent years.

issues—in the case of disinvestment, it was a treasonable offense to advocate it. But there were many signs that blacks appreciated any form of international pressure that made whites squirm.

I've said that the overwhelming power of sheer black numbers in South Africa was largely an illusion, which dissolved upon closer inspection. Nonetheless, there were statistics, particularly population projections, which unavoidably revived the idea that simple arithmetic doomed white rule. Blacks were multiplying at a far faster rate than whites. Within twenty years, it was estimated, there would be over 40 million black South Africans, with only 5 million whites. Blacks were also moving to the cities. The fraction of the black population living in urban areas, which in 1946 stood at less than 30 percent, representing 2.5 million people, was in 1980 over 40 percent, or 10 million people, and was expected to reach 75 percent, or 28 million people, in the next twenty years. Blacks, finally, were going to school. While there were fewer than four black high school students for each white high school student in 1980, it was estimated that within three decades that ratio would exceed *nineteen to one*.

The government was furiously trying to juggle these numbers by declaring bantustans "independent." Thus, 2.4 million blacks assigned to the Transkei had vanished overnight on October 16, 1976, and another million or so disappeared the next year as a scatter of impoverished settlements called Bophuthatswana became a "black national state." Yet such manipulations seemed to me to do little to change the real balance of forces—whatever that actually was—in South Africa.

14

6A6 was my "register class"—like American homeroom. I spent more time with them than with any other class. In some ways, 6A6 was the most difficult group I taught. It was a big class—forty-one children—with a limited attention span. If the pace of a lesson flagged even for a moment, they could be lost in space for the rest of the period. They were a disparate, only modestly talented group, almost visibly suffering from a lack of solidarity. While my other Standard Six classes were already forging coherent class identities, 6A6 remained an unsynced welter of individual wills. This, I became convinced, affected their concentration. At any given time, most of their attention was being consumed by the search for a group identity. They were impatient with each other, and could not sit still when I slowed things down to attend to the problems of one of their classmates.

Hester was in 6A6. She asked me if she could be the class monitor, taking attendance and so forth, and was immediately pushed aside by three or four other children who wanted the job themselves. Hester was obviously the best choice for monitor, the calmest, neatest, most organized of the candidates. But 6A6 did not exert the kind of joking, generalized pressure on the others to withdraw the way I believed my other classes would have done, and in the end I had to make the appointment myself. Hester turned out to be not only a reliable taker of attendance, but a valuable source of information about the moods and problems of her classmates.

6A6 was "immature," Meryl said. I thought of them as lost and unfocused. They responded best, I found, when I broke them up into small groups, gave each group a specific assignment, and circulated among them, observing and advising. But even then, some children fussed endlessly about which group they wanted to be in and had trouble getting anything done.

6A7 revolved around a core of stylish, outgoing girls: Natalie, Angela, Mieta, Desiree. Their raciness set the tone for the class. Natalie and Angela were gum-chewing, brisk, flirtatious, given to carrying perfume and makeup in their schoolbags. Desiree was a horsey, appealing girl with silky eyelashes and great aplomb. Mieta was short, soft-spoken, bright, and probably quite spoiled—her family's house, I noticed, was named after her. 6A7 was with it. If a classmate failed to answer a question correctly, some wag would be heard tapping out the drumbeat to Queen's "Another One Bites the Dust," a then-current pop hit. There were a number of boys in 6A7 who, perhaps inspired by the flashy girls in the class, also cut striking figures. Philip, a long-limbed, velvet-voiced boy with jet-black skin, was said to be a gifted cricketer. Terence was a handsome, fast-moving kid whose character seemed to alternate daily between supercilious mischiefmaker and vulnerable young sensitive. 6A7 had none of the identity problems 6A6 had; but class discussions were difficult. There were just too many kids with too much to say. (6A7 reminded me of another Top Forty song then popular on the Cape Flats: the Sugar Hill Gang's "Rapper's Delight.") On the other hand, having students write on the blackboard worked well in such a voluble, appearance-conscious group.

6A8 was the smallest of my English classes, and the easiest to teach. Meryl called them "mature." They were a brainy, cheerful, well-behaved group who seemed as if they had been together for years rather than weeks, they were so close. When one of their classmates landed in the hospital with an infected leg, I ferried the whole class over to see him in my car, ten or twelve at a time, on different afternoons, and each time I was amazed anew at the way they collected around his bed, chattering and laughing, showering the boy with sweets and fruit and visibly raising his spirits. 6A8 had its share of cutups and screw-ups, but it had a rock-solid center. There were several quiet, precocious girls, who at fourteen seemed to have the poise and judgment of grown women. These included Amy, a broad-faced, light-skinned, top student with a lovely, gentle sense of humor, and Shireen, a stocky, beautiful girl who always wore an ancient black school blazer. There were also a couple of brilliant boys—Malcolm, who got by far the highest marks in all my English classes, and Josef, who had just turned thirteen and consistently beat matrics at chess.

But it was a stolid, drawling boy named Oscar who really emblemized 6A8 for me. Oscar's father was a fruit seller who was causing his son to miss whole weeks of school by taking him off to Pretoria to help him peddle Cape produce. Oscar was struggling to stay in school, and I tried to help him by giving him his assignments ahead of time. Oscar's composition book was battered and stained from life on the road; his exercise papers were often smeared with dried citrus slime; but he kept up with the rest of his class, at least through the first term.

7E1 was a big, noisy group that was also self-conscious and easily intimidated. Perhaps it was only because their first language was English, but both my geography classes reminded me more of American schoolchildren than any of the others I taught did. 7E1 contained a number of goody-goodies, most but not all of them girls, whose dedication to behaving properly often lured them to the edge of what was considered ludicrous at Grassy Park High—mincing to the front of the classroom to pick up a praised assignment, standing too primly to answer a question. The class as a whole seemed somehow more "middle-class" than the others I taught. The children in 7E1 loved an uproar—they had created the human orrery that was quelled by Napoleon and Africa—but they always seemed *aware* of themselves as being uproarious, and they could be brought to order in an instant. 7E1 had been together for a year, but they lacked the kind of "class" (in the Marxian sense) cohesion that helped to mute overt competitiveness among my other classes. They responded more readily to both the carrot of teacher's approval and the stick of teacher's irritation.

7E2 was exactly the opposite. They were rowdy and reprobate. They were clearly the bottom half of the English-medium Standard Sevens. Nearly all of them had failed at least one year; some had failed several. The boys were tough guys, the girls were permanently auditioning for roles as gangster molls, and they all seemed to take a sort of battered pride in being a notorious troop whom teachers were never pleased to see. The size of 7E2 shrank steadily, because of fresh dropouts, but the improving teacher-student ratio did not seem to improve the remaining students' ability to concentrate. They exhausted me, especially on the days when I saw them in the late afternoon. And yet I got a kick out of 7E2. Their jaunty, stylized roguery reminded me of home even more than 7E1's individualism did. And 7E2's dead-end teen-rebel attitude provided a strange sort of relief from the smothering sense of responsibility that many of my other students caused me to feel.

I tried to uncover some of my students' sense of their larger situation—to clean off the connection, as it were, between the Cape Flats quotidian and its national context—by assigning essays to my English classes about their family histories. To one group, I even suggested that they use factors like the Group Areas Act and the Population Registration Act* as specific points of reference.

This assignment got abysmal results. I had guessed that there might be some strong traditions of oral history within my students' families, explaining how they came to be where they were, and I was not wrong. An English composition for school, however, was just about the last place in which these personal, usually very bitter histories would ever normally—or prudently, or indeed decently—be shared. Neither was I the most reassuring solicitor of such volatile material. Because who *was* I really, and what were my *motives* for gathering information about my students' families, their experiences with government policy, and, by implication, their thoughts and feelings about such things? Had I not discovered already how trusted I wasn't? Did I not realize that we were in a country where a teenage boy had recently been convicted of "terrorism" for writing an anti-white poem?

In Grassy Park, moreover, the question of ancestry was a vexed one. In the handful of essays that arrived on the date they were due,

---

*The Population Registration Act (1950) requires that every South African be classified racially.

I found several that seemed to struggle to underline the "European" relatives in the writer's family tree. There were others, from Muslim children, that emphasized the exclusively "Malay" character of the students' backgrounds. I was struck by the high percentage of those compositions I got that mentioned families' having moved to Grassy Park from District Six—this was the sort of information I was actually looking for—but the unwisdom of the whole assignment was already so obvious that I abandoned it then and there, without ever seeing anything on the subject from most of my students.

Informal discussions, especially some that took place during the lunch period and after school, were far more successful. There were a number of students who had taken to hanging around New Room 16 after class on occasion. Among these were an inseparable threesome from 7E1—Wayne, Nico, and Shaun. Nico was short and slim, with long straight hair and huge, dark, serious eyes. Wayne was tall, light-skinned, and goofy, with wavy reddish hair. Shaun, the leader of the group, was small, dark, thin, and officious, with watchful yellow eyes and terribly stiff posture. These three all owned skateboards and said they were interested in surfing. Shaun seemed to have an inexhaustible fund of questions; I soon figured out that most of these were prepared beforehand and represented the trio's pooled curiosity. I had a lot of questions myself, and as we grew more comfortable with one another, the boys from 7E1, as well as other students, slowly opened up and told me some of what they thought and felt and knew.

"Some people call this 'the wilderness,' " Shaun said once, when I had asked how he and his friends liked living in Grassy Park. "They would prefer that they still lived in town. But we're used to this here. We don't mind it."

"My mommy calls it 'the desert,' " Wayne said. "She says she can't hang out the washing because of the blowing sand."

" 'Siberia,' that's what my father calls it," Nico said. "He hates it out here. He's always telling about how life was better when we lived in town."

"Lots of old people say that," Shaun said. "They say they miss their friends, and the neighborhoods they lived in. Most of the houses in Mowbray* had stoeps [front porches] where people used to sit. In District Six, they had balconies. So the roads were much livelier."

"Some people committed *suicide* after they got their so-called 'love letters,' " Nico said, suddenly speaking with vehemence. "And

---

*A Cape Town neighborhood that was decimated by Group Areas removals.

some old people they just climbed in their beds, and they wouldn't get up, and they just died there. They didn't want to live anymore."

Shaun: "The old people, when they first came out here, they used to get lost. They couldn't find their own houses."

Wayne laughed. "You might find some old *toppie* just sitting there in the road crying. He had taken some drinks, you know, and now he couldn't find his house!"

"They're still removing people, to this very day," Nico said darkly. "Sometimes one part of a family must go one place, and the other part some other place, and they lose contact with one another."

"The same thing happened when they brought us 'population registration,'" Shaun said. "Some family members might have straight hair and fair skin and be classified so-called white, while others may be darker, and classified so-called colored. These are brothers and sisters I'm talking about! They must live apart. It's the law."

"They put a pencil in your hair," Wayne said. "If it falls out you're white, if it stays there you're colored."

Nico: "In Mowbray, *die boere* was staying out of the sun, and the whole family getting crew cuts, just to be safe!"

My students sometimes distinguished between Afrikaners and English-speaking whites. They called Afrikaners *die boere,* and used the term to mean both the Afrikaner people and the authorities in general, particularly the police and the government. When I asked who it was that stuck pencils in one's hair to determine one's race, they answered, *"Die boere."* "The English" were a more distant group —they lived in big houses and owned businesses.

Most of the time, though, my students simply spoke of "the whites," as in "The whites drive some *lekker* [literally, "tasty"] cars" or "The whites don't like to see black faces on TV." At first, they were tentative around me when mentioning "whites" at all, and I was quite sure that they never showed me anything like the real extent of their resentments. Yet they slowly relaxed, and I was eventually able to make a few observations—notably, that my students seemed to know few if any white people personally. Collectively, of course, in some deep sense, they knew whites intimately, in the way that servants always know their masters, employees their bosses, the exploited their exploiters: from long and careful observation. But in my students that knowledge all seemed to be secondhand, as if gleaned entirely from friends and relatives who worked with whites, from popular mythology, and from ideas gathered at a great distance.

"Apartheid" means "apartness," and I became convinced that grand
apartheid, particularly the Group Areas Act, had succeeded, at least
in Cape Town, in digging great new abysses of ignorance between the
various "population groups."

The range of attitudes held by Shaun, Wayne, and Nico toward
apartheid and removals seemed to have its origins in their families'
different experiences. Wayne was by far the mildest when the subject
was the government and the destruction of District Six, and the least
sympathetic toward the suffering of the poor and uprooted. "Have you
seen Cafda, sir?" he once asked me, snickering. "It's a terrible place.
We never go in there. Cafda is worse than the estates. We don't like
those subeconomic people. They don't even have proper toilets!" Another time, while we were talking again about forced removals,
Wayne said, "People complain, but most people like it better here
than in town. Out here, they own a house, and the houses are new,
a lot of them, not all falling down and old like you had in town."

"How should you know?" Shaun asked suddenly. "You don't remember any place in town. And has sir seen the pondok this boy lives
in? His mommy don't own it, she rents it. And they better watch out
it don't get bulldozed! That's how new *it* is."

"We're not council renters, we're private renters," Wayne said in
a crushed voice. I later saw his house, where he lived with his mother
and several sisters—it was a two-room tin-walled shack—and thereafter understood some of Wayne's compulsion to distinguish himself
from "subeconomic people." At the time, noting his misery, I lamely
tried to change the subject.

"They don't bulldoze in Grassy Park, do they?"

"Yes, sir, they do," Shaun said. "In Klip Road a couple of years
ago, they knocked down a lot of pondoks. And the people put them up
again, but *die boere* just knocked them down again."

"When did that happen, exactly?"

"We was in Standard Four. Remember, we went to watch?"
Shaun said to Wayne. Wayne nodded, but he did not, I noticed, laugh
in his usual brainless way about how funny the people looked, standing around crying while the government bulldozers turned their
homes into rubble. Fourteen-year-olds are not known for their com-
passion—at least my schoolmates at that age found nothing more
amusing than the plight of the rejected and degraded—but one's own
shame can be sobering, at least temporarily.

Nico displayed more political awareness than his friends, and he
obviously got much of that from his father. Nico's father was a bricklayer who made sure his children understood the bitterness of his own

experience. "When my father answers an advert for a bricklayer, there might be ten okes [guys] show up for one job, but if one of the guys is white, he gets it. They don't ask him his qualifications. He is hired for the color of his skin, not for his skills, that's what my father says. Once, he had a job as a messenger in an office, when he couldn't find building work. That was the worst, he says. He was the only so-called non-white in that office. They wouldn't let him use the same teacups as everyone else. He had to take his own teacup to work. My father says we mustn't hate the whites, but we must turn our backs on them. He calls himself a black man, and he says our future is with the Africans, not the whites."

Although he had been too young himself at the time to remember it, Nico knew by heart the story of his family's forced removal from Mowbray. "This Boer came in our house, one of the department inspectors, and he started looking around the place, taking note of everything, you know, all the improvements my father had made, and he was very rude to my mother. Then he went outside and we heard him talking with one of his *boets* [mates], another inspector, and saying how he liked our place, and thought he might just buy it for himself. Because they could get our places very, very cheap, you see, because we were forced to sell. And he didn't actually buy our place, but some other people on our road did sell their places to the very same inspectors who threw them out. It was an architect that bought our house. And he turned it into one of these so-called Chelsea cottages, with the *dingus* [whatchamacallit], the carriage lamp, beside the front door. My father says they built a swimming pool as well, but we only saw what they did to the front. We used to go there sometimes on our way into town, just to look."

Many Grassy Park families apparently went back on occasion to their old neighborhoods in the city center, even when those neighborhoods no longer existed. A Standard Nine girl named Annette told me, "On Sundays, we go to the cemetery where our granny is, there by our old place. All the shops and houses in that area have been knocked down. It's mostly all rubbish, and what a lot of *rats*. Just a few churches and mosques are still there. But now they say they want to move the cemetery. It's been declared 'white' as well. They want to dig up the people and move them, and if we won't agree, we just won't be allowed to visit our granny no more. My mommy is very upset about that. Already her *losie* [funeral society] is in trouble because of the removals, with the members scattered all over now, in Bonteheuwel and Athlone and everywhere. Now she doesn't know where she will be buried."

The Group Areas Act had virtually created Grassy Park. Whether people wanted to talk to me about it or not, it did not take me long to understand what a bitter, bitter foundation that was. Sometimes the easygoing, laugh-a-minute atmosphere at Grassy Park High would seem to dissolve before my eyes and reveal a sea of pain and anger so terrible that I simply had to look away. At such times, the fine gradations of "political awareness" suddenly seemed unimportant. Even the most unconscious children could not help but understand their basic situation. The school itself sent an unambiguous message: this government considers these children to be of inferior material. That message was so clear and harsh that I thought it rang in the air like a broken alarm all day every day at Grassy Park High. The fact of exclusion from the city's best facilities—schools, cinemas, restaurants, neighborhoods—was certainly not something that anyone needed to have pointed out. Even Wayne, when we talked about surfing, told me, "The whites keep all the best beaches for themselves. We are only allowed to go where the waves are dangerous and the sand is not nice and the sharks come. There are no facilities for us. We must *kak in die bundu* [shit in the bushes] like animals."

Aubrey September saw Cape Town differently from most of his classmates. To Aubrey, newly arrived from the Boland—the farmlands of the Western Cape—the city was one vast, if intimidating, field of opportunity. He rode the train into town on a Saturday not to see what the whites were doing to the old neighborhood, but to walk through the open-air market on the Grand Parade, or to gawk at the great modern shopping mall known as the Golden Acre. I asked Aubrey to tell me about going shopping where he had lived before— simply getting him to speak in English had already become the main part of our after-school tutoring sessions.

"There was just the one shop, sir," he said. "On the farm itself. It gave not much things. Only bread, paraffin, sugar, soap. But there was no bus to some other shop. Prices was high, sir, but we must buy there. The *baas* gives credit, so the people borrow. But they must not leave the farm when they are borrowed. People, they want to leave. But they must not. The *baas*, he will send the police after them."

I enjoyed our tutoring sessions far more than Aubrey did, I think. I was fascinated by his descriptions of life on a farm. When I asked about the primary school he had attended, he said, "The school is small, with only few teachers, and few books. All the standards go together, up to Standard Five only. For high school, we must go to boarding school. But only few children finish Standard Five. Most, their parents tell them they must stop, and go to work on the farm, to earn them money. They cannot afford them still in school. They say, 'Why must a big child who can read and write still be at school?' The old people, they can't read and write."

Aubrey's own parents were literate, he said. His father had been a foreman on the farm, and his mother came from the Boland town of Oudtshoorn. They had moved to the city mainly so that he and his brothers and sisters could get a better education. "But everything is better here," Aubrey said. "The food, the houses, the clinic. Over there, when a person gets sick, they must just lie in their house. Maybe the *baas* comes, or his wife. But they only go to doctor when they is very, very sick. Over there, in winter, so many children is sick in the lungs, sometimes there is not one in the school. Also the people got rickets, and tuberculosis. Here you can just go to clinic every time."

I asked Aubrey what farm workers ate. "Bread," he said. "And soup for supper, in the wintertime. The people cannot afford meat and vegetables and fruit, like we have here in Cape Town."

I asked about drinking, and Aubrey looked uncomfortable. "On Saturdays, some people are drinking. Even on Sundays. The wine is very cheap on the farm. The young wine. The men who are working in the fields are drinking wine all day while they work as well. They must have a *dop* in the morning, first thing, before they will start. And another one at supper, and another at teatime. That is how they work on a farm. My daddy says it is bad, but even the children who start working must have their wine, or they won't work." This was the infamous *dop* system, by which Cape farmworkers were partly paid in drink, and as a result kept hopelessly alcoholic, unhealthy, and docile.

Although he claimed to be pleased in every way to be living in Cape Town, the only times I saw Aubrey really animated were when he spoke about his playmates in the Boland, about hunting birds with slingshots, trapping hares, and diving from a high rock into a pond. Once, he told me about how his father had used to catch baboons that were raiding the farmer's crop, and Aubrey's eyes grew wide and his words tumbled over one another in his eagerness to tell the story.

There was something I began to notice about Aubrey: he was always alone outside class. The idyll of my first weeks at Grassy Park High was passing, and exceptions to the rule of mass fellowship had begun to appear as the multitude of my students continued to in-

dividuate. Aubrey, the impassive little country boy, was clearly one
of them. Wayan, whose long thin limbs seemed to grow at least an
inch a week and who seemed to be in a permanent state of mild shock
as a result, was another. After our tutoring sessions, I would watch
Aubrey walking across the field beyond the new building from my
classroom window, with his green canvas book bag slung over the
shoulder of his ill-fitting blazer, and I would find myself aching at the
thought of the universal hardship of a lonely adolescence.

15

I may have been starting to look at South Africa from the vantage of
the Cape Flats, but that was not where I lived. I lived in "white" Cape
Town and, for months after our arrival, I continued to take a prodi-
gal's delight in its amenities. I loved shopping in the vast, immaculate, abundantly stocked supermarket. I gloried in the beautifully
landscaped highway that carried us around the mountain into the city
center. The downtown park known as the Gardens, surrounded by
museums and a cathedral and affording a front-row seat at the epic
movie screen of Table Mountain, was a near-perfect place to read
away a Saturday afternoon. And the oceanfront promenade at Sea
Point, on the Atlantic coast, with its shining high rises, its scalloped
little beaches, its Porsches and pensioners taking the sun and stylish
women walking afghans, had a crisp, sea-washed density of wealth
that, in some strange way, did my soul good. It actually reminded the
well-traveled less of Rio than of Nice; it reminded me of every rich
cold dessert that did not exist in the malarial jungles of Asia.

Of course, the sense of disporting oneself in a roped-off preserve
rarely left me. My consciousness of the line as a geographical barrier
was acute, thanks to my job. When I saw my students in the supermarket—as I often did, for the market was equidistant from Muizenberg
and Grassy Park—when I saw them with their mothers piling shopping carts high with all the items that cost twice as much in the cafés
at Busy Corner, I was always aware that they had had to cross the
main north-south railway to get there, and that the line there consisted of electrified double tracks with chain-link and barbed-wire
fences, and that the bridges and tunnels across it were few and, if
necessary, easily blocked off.

The line also had a million smaller segments, scattered throughout the white areas, dividing lavatories, liquor stores, trains, sealing
off pubs, restaurants, cinemas. While inside places flagged by WHITES

ONLY signs, I often wondered what the other people were thinking. No one seemed uneasy. They were eating, drinking, watching a movie; few of them had ever known another arrangement. The tension, the sense of historical siege, that often fills descriptions by foreigners of white South Africa seemed vague and farfetched there in Cape Town. If white housewives did practice weekly at the pistol range, their laughter in Sea Point supper clubs did not seem less vigorous and blithe for the exercise. If the air in white Cape Town was suffocating, it was due more to complacency than to fear. My own sense of the substructure of this racial beau monde was clearly not shared by its denizens. Once, standing at a hotel counter, trying to get the attention of a rude and incompetent white clerk, I acknowledged the friendly grumbling of some other frustrated patrons about the service by saying, "That's job reservation for you." Their jocularity turned at once to incomprehension and cold hostility.

Blacks glided around the fringes of these all-white venues in uniforms. Most of them seemed to be in Invisible Man mode, when they were not actively self-abasing. At a student bar, I ordered a certain brand of beer from a black waiter. He took the trouble to inform me, "We call that beer 'Soweto,' sir."

"Why is that?"

"Because the kaffirs* all drink it," he cackled.

My unamused stare seemed to bring him up short and, once I had discarded the possibility that he had picked me out as a liberal and was giving me a shrewd twist of the racial tail, I decided that his remark was as good a clue as any to what was going on in the minds of my fellow drinkers. We did not become regulars at that or, alas, any other bar in Cape Town.

Apart from my job, Rachel and I were leading a rather reclusive life. Muizenberg was a terribly quiet, genteel place. There was a lawn-bowling club near the small shopping district, and the discreet cries of the elderly players in their brilliant whites were often the only human sounds to be heard on the entire main street. The room we rented was in a crumbling turquoise mansion, clinging to a hillside overlooking False Bay. There were two other people living in the house, both young men whom we rarely saw. The house had a neglected air. There was no furniture in the long, high-ceilinged living room, and nothing on the walls.

The house commanded a fantastic view, including everything

---

*"Kaffir" is the South African equivalent of the American "nigger."

from the Hottentots Holland Mountains to the Cape of Good Hope itself. Cecil Rhodes—Rhodes of Rhodes scholarships, Rhodes of Rhodesia—had built a huge, thatch-roofed "cottage" immediately below, and more big houses blanketed the hillside in each direction. At the foot of the hill, commuter trains snaked along the coast between red-brick Victorian stations. Rachel and I got to know this view well, because we each set up desks on the spacious, picture-windowed balcony that overlooked it. She had begun quarrying articles from the lode of her doctoral dissertation. I spent most of my time on the balcony planning lessons and reading in my students' blue-covered composition books. We ate our meals in an alcove between our desks.

In the early evenings, when the beach was deserted and the sky still bright above the mountain, Rachel and I liked to take walks along the water's edge, starting below our place and heading east. The first half-mile or so was the Muizenberg waterfront. This was a "white" beach. Brightly painted cabanas, a miniature golf course, an arcade of shops (all closed for the season), stood alongside small, orderly parking lots and the sugary expanse of sand. Then there was a river mouth, after which the beach became a wide, scruffy, undeveloped shore known as Strandfontein. This beach was, according to several signs, reserved for the exclusive use of the Coloured Population Group.

If we walked far enough, it was possible to pretend that we were in no Group Area at all. Focus closely enough on the autumn twilight, the changing weather—the evenings were getting shorter and chillier now—the sea, the dunes, the various shore birds—sandplovers pitter-pattering in the shorebreak, gulls and terns and Cape cormorants wheeling and screaming overhead—and you could almost imagine the *strandloper* Khoikhoi padding along this littoral, wiry and dark in these deep blue shadows, wearing skins, carrying spears, perhaps pausing for a pipeload of dagga. The Khoikhoi cultivated dagga and bartered it throughout the Cape. Those were the ancestors of my students. They were nomadic pastoralists, keeping sheep and long-horned cattle, and their land tenure was communal. The Dutch arrived in 1652, and within a few years' time territorial segregation between the races was officially established. The line was first a stream. A year later, when the Europeans took some more Khoikhoi land, it was "a bitter almond hedge" planted by the Dutch fort commander.

16

In my classes, formal debates were generally flops. My students did not seem to take to the idea of argument for its own sake. I discovered that I could sometimes rouse certain classes to spirited discussion, though, by playing devil's advocate. One day, with 6A8, I began class by saying what a great thing it was that the South African national rugby team was about to include its first black player. I asked Marius Le Roux, who was a rugby player himself, whether the new Springbok, who was a Boland "colored" named Errol Tobias, would be likely to acquit himself well.

Marius stood and shifted from foot to foot. He had a slight stutter. "He's a good player, yes, sir. But—but some people are saying they selected him only because he's black."

I asked Marius if he thought that was true. Marius shrugged and looked miserable. Another hand shot up. "Elroy?"

Elroy, a chubby exuberant boy, stood. "It is true, sir!"

There were murmured objections. Shireen spoke. "It is true they were looking for a black player. But Tobias still must prove himself."

Why were they looking for a black player?

Koos, a small, hoarse-voiced boy with a fighter's flattened nose: "Because they want the Lions to come!"

The British Lions were scheduled to tour South Africa in June, playing provincial rugby clubs as well as the Springboks. Anti-apartheid groups in England and elsewhere were already protesting the planned visit.

"Will the Lions come?"

Nobody seemed sure.

"If they do come, will any of you go to see them?"

Murmurs, laughter. Neville, a hulking, curly-haired boy, stood. "When the Lions came to South Africa before, sir, some people went to watch, but they shouted against the Springboks. Black people did this. They wanted South Africa to lose."

"Shame," a girl named Zainul said, and the class laughed.

Neville: "This makes the whites very angry, sir."

Elroy jumped up. "Also Amy, sir, because she loves Rob Louw!"

Amy began to protest, amid general laughter. Rob Louw was a dashing young Springbok. Koos called out, "She keeps a big photo of him by her bed!"

What about Tobias? Would people still boo the Springboks with

Tobias on the team? Opinions were divided on this question.

"Nothing is different. Tobias is only window dressing."

"Tobias is the first. There will be others."

Were sports being integrated in South Africa?

"In a few places, they are. In some codes, such as cricket."

"They are *not,* sir. The whites only say so because they want other countries to play sport with South Africa again."

Had the international sports boycott of South Africa had much effect?

"Oh yes."

"Window dressing!"

Shireen: "If *die boere* allow a few so-called non-whites to play sport with whites, it is only for one reason. They want to get back in the Olympics. They want to play international cricket and rugby again. They don't plan to change anything else. You must understand this, sir."

What would South Africa have to do to be readmitted to the Olympics?

"We must have no more apartheid in sport."

"We must have no more apartheid full stop."

"SACOS must approve it."

"SACOS will never approve it. All SACOS knows to do is boycott."

SACOS was the South African Council on Sport, the leading organization of the non-racial sporting movement. It enjoyed extensive international recognition, and did have effective veto power over the readmission of South Africa to the Olympic Games. SACOS was powerful on the Cape Flats—it sponsored the baseball league John Liberty played in, and most of the sports leagues the children played in —and everyone in 6A8 seemed to have something to tell me about it. Criticism and support were expressed in roughly equal measure. I was struck by the deep ambivalence many children seemed to feel about South African sports in general, and the Springboks in particular— spontaneous pride in the home team, coupled uncomfortably with resentment. It was much like the mixed feelings of patriotism and black solidarity that seemed to surface when we talked in geography about southern Africa. Clearly, an Errol Tobias was never going to provide the deep rush of pride and hope to black South Africans that Jesse Owens and Joe Louis had once done for black Americans. The British Lions did tour South Africa in 1980, but the black stands in the stadiums where they played were empty.

* * *

Good discussions also sometimes sprang from unlikely beginnings. One day with 6A7, I was letting the children tell me more about one of their favorite subjects: *skollies.*

"They like a *chalunga,* sir!"

A *chalunga* was a broken bottle neck full of dagga.

"Or a white pipe!"

A white pipe was a mixture of a barbiturate called Mandrax and dagga.

"And they also drink some alcohol, and then they go out attacking the people and robbing them."

Did *skollies* carry guns, I wondered?

"Some of them, yes, sir. But mostly they use pangas" (machetes).

"And I and J knives. Those are fish knives, sir! Very sharp!"

Were *skollies* not afraid of the police?

"No! They call them *mapuza.* They are not afraid."

"The *police* are afraid. They hide from the gangs if they see them."

Did the gangs ever attack the police?

"No. They just keep away from them. They're only interested in what watches and radios and CB sets they can steal."

Why did young men join gangs?

"Because they are . . . *deurmekaar*" (confused).

"Because they leave school and have no job."

"Because they like to be in a big group. Then they feel strong. They get the tattoos that says they're in the gang, on their arms, sometimes even on their necks. They wear the hats."

What could be done about the *skollies?*

"There must be more police."

"Except nobody likes to join the police."

"The Peacemakers was putting a stop to them."

Who were the Peacemakers?

"Vigilantes, sir. The people just stopped waiting for the police to help them, and they organized themselves."

"The Peacemakers wore orange coats. They carried sticks and whistles. They were very well liked. They walked about at night, and if they saw something, they whistled, and the others all came."

"The *skollies* were frightened. They was just disappearing after a while."

"But then the police tried to make the Peacemakers into reservists. And they wouldn't do it."

"If they went with the police, the people would stop respecting them."

"Nobody here respects the police, sir. That is why they can never get enough men for their training. Because the police here are not just for stopping crimes."

"That's why you will never see a television program here like 'Chips.' Because the people here *hates* the S.A.P. Nobody would watch."

What else were the South African police used for?

"For politics, sir. They watch people."

Nobody seemed inclined to elaborate on this point. So what happened to the Peacemakers, I asked.

"They broke up."

"The cops broke them up."

"And the *skollies* came back worse than before."

Somebody began drumming out the beat to "Another One Bites the Dust." But nobody laughed.

Few of my students read the daily papers. I tried to encourage them to start doing so, by bringing in articles they might find interesting, and urging them to do the same. Marius Le Roux surprised me by bringing in a clipping about a furor in the Transvaal over the inclusion of a rugby team from a "colored" school in a tournament that had always been whites-only. National Party leaders were condemning this modest bit of integration in Parliament, a fifteen-thousand-member Afrikaans teachers' organization had denounced the idea, and white schools were withdrawing from the tournament in droves. "Now you can see, sir," Shireen said. "This is how things really are. And all over a bit of schoolboy rugby."

Late in March, I brought in an article from the *Cape Times* about Zenani Mandela, daughter of Nelson Mandela, who had addressed a thousand students at the University of Cape Town and called for her father's release from prison. I asked 6A6 if they knew who Nelson Mandela was. The children all avoided my gaze; no one answered. I asked Hester. She stood and said, very quietly, "Yes, sir. They know."

In geography, I tried to use the newspapers to flesh out our classwork. While we were studying Namibia (also known as South West Africa), I brought in news items about the bush war that South Africa was fighting there with the guerrillas of the South West Africa People's Organization (SWAPO). I was amazed to find that many children seemed to know absolutely nothing about it. News coverage of the war was heavily censored, certainly, but "the boys on the border" were a constant refrain in South African public life—on television and the radio, as well as in the papers. "We hear about 'the border,'" Shaun said. "But you never hear where it *is.*" Some of my geography students, however, clearly grasped the basics of the Namibian conflict. Nico put me on the spot in front of 7E1 one day when he said, indicating the *Cape Times,* "They call SWAPO 'terrorists,' sir. But some people call them 'freedom fighters.' Which is right?"

"Would anybody else like to try to answer that?"

Nobody volunteered. The class watched me closely.

"Well," I finally said, "that's the big question. *The* big question. The government here in South Africa calls them 'terrorists.' But what do the people of Namibia call them? Why is the government unwilling to allow elections in Namibia in which SWAPO may participate?"

7E1 seemed disappointed that I would not declare myself more clearly; but that was as far as I thought I should go.

I was determined to involve my students more actively in their own education than they seemed accustomed to being. This meant, in my English classes, a writing assignment every week, and in all my classes a diminished emphasis on examinations, an increased emphasis on student projects. To convince the children that I was serious about my many small assignments, to convince them that they would not be able to pass my class simply by cramming for the year-end examination, as many of them seemed in the habit of doing, I kept careful records of their work, which they were welcome to review, and penalized them for late papers.

I tried to encourage more original writing by having the children write "tall tales"—and got back some surprisingly long and vivid compositions, full of monsters and witches and angels, *doekoms* (witch doctors) and djinns (Muslim spirits) and student derring-do. I brought in all the dictionaries I could find and broke classes up into groups and taught them dictionary games. The dictionaries were also useful for etymology lessons. Etymology seemed to fascinate many of my students. Being bilingual, they grasped it quickly, though they had apparently never been shown how to unearth the roots of words before.

Teaching the children to speak clearly and confidently in English in public, and not to mumble or blurt or break into *kombuis,* became a special project of mine. The dreaded oral book reports were this project's main event. I would stand at the back of the room and instruct the reporter, if he or she seemed very nervous, simply to speak to me. Then I would nod encouragingly, signaling like a stage director for more voice, better posture, less crazed twisting of hair around finger. Some natural actors took to speaking before their classmates wonderfully well, and even hammed it up. Others suffered pure agonies of stage fright and stuttering.

Wayan's report on *The House at Pooh Corner* was a particular ordeal. He was terrified and spoke only to me, in a tiny, lisping, not-yet-deepened voice. Wayan tried to tell me the entire story, and got hopelessly lost in the adventures of Pooh, Tigger, Eeyore, and Christopher Robin. He obviously knew the book so well, and loved it so much, that he didn't want to leave out a single detail. It was impossible that the rest of the class was following his narrative, it became so jumbled, but I didn't have the heart to stop him, with his huge, liquid eyes fastened on mine, and his high, soft voice droning on. Fortunately, the class full of teenagers between us stayed quiet, perhaps hypnotized by their classmate's voice, which they had rarely if ever heard before, until we were all rescued by the siren.

17

The turquoise house was up for sale. I estimated its market value at a million dollars. But I am from Los Angeles. The asking price for the house was less than forty thousand dollars. I asked one of our housemates, an apple-cheeked boy with a shore job in the navy, why it was being offered for so little. He said Muizenberg was no longer fashionable, that the prime Cape Town property was all over on the Atlantic coast now. But our other housemate, a teenager named Peter who worked in a bank, rejected that explanation. All real estate prices were profoundly depressed, he said, and had been since 1976. "It's this bloody revolution they're expecting."

The owner was an author who lived nearby. One evening, he came by with some prospective buyers, then stayed after they had left. He was a vivid, thick-set, hassled-looking fellow. He wore an Irish sweater and spoke with a strange, rolling burr.

"I sometimes wonder if anyone will ever buy this poor old place," he said. "I should never have put my son in charge of it."

The owner's son, a drug-addled wastrel, had rented out the house to a long line of transient foreigners, school friends, and dubious characters who had contributed greatly to its present disrepair. The owner ran through a convincing litany of paternal and landlordly miseries, then shifted to a topic that we soon came to know as his favorite: the bloody government.

"They're mad. Simply mad. They carry on with these insane policies. They're determined to bring Armageddon down on all our heads. And the worst part is, more and more of these so-called English are throwing in with them now."

In reality, the worst part, in the eyes of our landlord, was what the government was doing to him personally. For, besides being an author, he was in the publishing business. And although he neither wrote nor published political works (his oeuvre consisted of children's books, travel books, and a popular history of the Bushmen), our landlord was convinced that the government was systematically obstructing his business ventures. This occurred, he said, because he was English-speaking and because he had refused to join the Afrikaner-led National Party.

To understand our landlord's complaint, to understand anything at all about South Africa—to *get anywhere in* South Africa, our landlord might have added—one must know something about the Afrikaners. Today they dominate the country's government. But this hegemony is a relatively recent state of affairs. During a century and a half of Dutch colonial rule, and particularly during the ensuing century of British imperial rule, Afrikaners themselves lived as restive subjects of alien authorities. In fact, the settlement by whites of much of present-day South Africa came as the result of a mass flight, begun in 1834, into the interior by Afrikaners determined to escape British rule in the Cape. Known as the Great Trek, and largely triggered by the abolition of slavery, this migration led to the founding of the two Boer Republics, the Orange Free State and the Transvaal. When British interest in the big gold strikes in the Transvaal led to an attempt at annexation, Afrikaner resistance culminated in the bloody Anglo-Boer War of 1899–1902, which the outnumbered and outfinanced Afrikaners lost.

Independence from Britain, achieved in 1910, did little to improve the Afrikaners' position. Compared to English-speaking whites, Afrikaners remained poor, uneducated, and unskilled. Drought and depression forced hundreds of thousands of them off their farms in the 1920s and 1930s. In the towns and cities, destitute Afrikaners were sinking to the social and economic levels traditionally occupied in South Africa by blacks. The ownership and management of the South African economy were almost exclusively in the hands of English-speaking whites. How the Afrikaners managed to turn this situation around is an ethnic success story possibly without parallel in recent world history. The watershed year was 1948, when the National Party came to power on a platform they called apartheid.

In 1948, Afrikaners finally united as a bloc to elect a government specifically dedicated to the uplifting of the *volk*. By remorseless gerrymander, the Nationalists consolidated their position and within a few years had become unbeatable electorally—a situation that has not changed since. Our landlord's contention that English economic ascendancy had been systematically checked under "these bloody Nats" was easily verified. Since 1948, the percentage of Afrikaner workers in white-collar jobs had more than doubled. Where the per capita income of English-speaking whites was more than twice that of Afrikaans-speaking whites in 1948, they now approached parity.

This "national" economic advance was achieved in large part by a great expansion of the public sector. Public corporations known as "parastatals" were created for everything from the manufacture of steel to oil exploration, and these organizations were staffed at virtually all senior levels by Afrikaners. While loudly resented by the English private sector, state favoritism toward Afrikaner businesses became a fact of South African life. It was here that our landlord's interests were being most clearly prejudiced. In 1977, for example, the Department of Information had awarded 98 percent of its publishing budget to the Perskor group, an Afrikaner publishing house that had several cabinet ministers, including the Minister of Information, on its board.

Neither was our landlord wrong when he complained that increasing numbers of English-speakers were joining the National Party. Since 1948, Afrikaner nationalism had gradually taken heed of the geopolitical realities of its rule, and relaxed from its earlier, near-religious exclusivism, until it now actively sought to include all South African whites in its dispensation—under Afrikaner leadership, of course.

The usual view of apartheid is as a system of racial oppression, and this is obviously its definitive feature. But apartheid can also be seen as a system of ethnic patronage, representing the triumph and utopia of a long powerless and insecure group.

Certainly that was how our landlord saw it, as we sat sipping local cream sherry on late summer evenings in his crumbling investment, hearing about his woes. And our two housemates, while they lacked his experience, education, and status, shared his view, for they, too, were English-speaking whites. The sailor would come off duty railing bitterly about his Afrikaner superiors, repeatedly distinguishing "Dutchmen" from "white men" in his remarks. His father was a government clerk in Durban, and the sailor had already come to understand that real opportunities in the military and the civil service, both unusually large and influential establishments in South Africa because of the special requirements of administering apartheid, were effectively restricted to Afrikaners. And Peter, the young bank clerk, who had vague aspirations toward a socially respectable racial liberalism, when he heard where I was working, declared himself sympathetic with the curious remark, "I'd sooner have a colored friend than an Afrikaner!"

Afrikaners repaid these sentiments with interest when it came to *die Engels*. The collective memory of British devastation of Afrikaner farms and homesteads during the Anglo-Boer War was very much alive; indeed, there were still people who could remember the concentration camps built by Lord Kitchener's imperial forces, inside which twenty-six thousand Afrikaner women and children perished. Afrikaners called the English *rooineks* ("red necks"—burned because unaccustomed to the African sun) and *soutpiels* ("salt penises"—with one foot in Europe and one foot in Africa, an Englishman's *piel* dangled in the sea) and constantly questioned their ultimate commitment to South Africa. As an Afrikaner policeman in a popular song put it, "You've got the big mouths, you've got the degrees, but when things turn sour, then you run overseas."

The determination of Afrikaners, on the other hand, to remain in South Africa was rarely questioned by anyone. There was no European homeland to which they might return. This truism, along with the sheer size and wealth of the white population, the industrial economy, and the military, was what made South Africa seemingly an exception to the postcolonial historical rule. The domino theory of decolonization, which assumed that because white settler rule had been replaced in every other country in Africa it would inevitably disappear in South Africa as well, simply did not take into account the unique strength of the Afrikaners' attachment to the land they occupied.

They were undeniably a remarkable people. They were, after all, only 9 percent of the country's population (roughly the same number as those classified "Coloured"). Inevitably, the other 91 percent spent a great deal of its time contemplating this small group that somehow ruled the South African roost. An English-speaking surfer in Muizenberg offered me what seemed to be a widespread perception of the

Afrikaner character: "You can't go through a Dutchman," he told me. "You must go around him. He is as solid as a brick shithouse. And exactly as intelligent."

Black people naturally tended to focus on Afrikaners' racial attitudes. One of my colleagues at Grassy Park High once tried to explain these to me. "You simply can't imagine how the Boer sees things," he said. "He honestly believes that blacks are not human beings like himself. They call us 'things.' All the time, they talk of 'these black things,' and that's exactly how they think of us—as 'black things' that do their work for them and cause them trouble sometimes and must be controlled. The idea that we are human beings, equal to them, that we deserve the same rights as them, that we could be bosses and leaders over them and run the country, seems absolutely absurd to them. It must be a joke, and not a very nice one, they think. To them, that would be like having baboons run their beloved country. They will never allow it. And their attitudes won't change for many generations, no matter what happens here. They won this land with the Bible and the musket, and they still think that way. They believe they are the Chosen People, and God gave them this land."

Whether or not these generalizations amounted to a fair description of modern Afrikaner racial attitudes, they certainly represented the view of most black South Africans, a view based on long and hard experience. And the religious convictions of Afrikaners clearly were crucial to their outlook. The great majority of Afrikaners belonged to the Dutch Reformed Church, which preached a puritanical Calvinism that stressed the ideas of predestination, obedience to authority, and an elect chosen by God for salvation. In South Africa, Dutch Reformed theology had long become entangled with Afrikaner ethnic nationalism. Thus, the Great Trek was extravagantly identified by Afrikaners with the biblical flight of the Israelites from Egypt, the defeat of the Zulus in battle was attributed to the divine plan for Afrikaner hegemony in southern Africa, and God's elect were believed to be the Afrikaner "nation." Dutch Reformed theology was racist; it had long occupied itself with providing scriptural authority for apartheid. Membership in the main Dutch Reformed sect, which was virtually a state religion, was restricted to whites. (There were "daughter churches" for blacks.) It has often been remarked that Afrikaner political and religious thought developed without benefit of the Enlightenment in Europe. Certainly, a deep hostility to liberal democratic ideas emanated from every corner of the Afrikaner establishment, and not least from the synods of the Dutch Reformed Church.

Afrikaans literature was another matter, I discovered. A dissident literary movement known as the *sestigers* (sixties-ers) had produced a number of independent-minded writers, including the novelists André Brink and Etienne Leroux and the poet Breyten Breytenbach. The cosmopolitan vitality of these writers' work and their determination to confront Afrikanerdom's true legacy and significance were departures from the norm as radical, in many ways, as those of the handful of courageous Afrikaners who had identified themselves with the cause of non-racial democracy. Indeed, the literary and the political—like the religious and the political—tended to converge rapidly in South Africa. In 1980, Breyten Breytenbach was in Pollsmoor Prison, which was a stone's throw from our local supermarket near Muizenberg, serving the fifth year of a nine-year sentence for "terrorism."

It was easy to see the truth of much of what other South Africans said about Afrikaners. Their ethnic nationalism was plainly advanced at the expense of their countrymen. Their spokesmen seemed obsessed with Afrikaner "identity." Their leaders' idea of serious debate was pathetically limited. Afrikaner "cultural" groups like the powerful secret society known as the Broederbond (the Brotherhood), from which virtually all the leaders of the government were drawn (including every prime minister since 1948), expounded the most dubious ideas about "racial purity." The government tried to force Afrikaner cultural holidays on the nation as a whole. (How could blacks be expected to celebrate occasions like the Boer pioneer Paul Kruger's birthday? Or Van Riebeeck Day, or Settlers Day, or the Day of the Covenant? The latter marked the date when trekking Boers massacred three thousand Zulus. These were all national holidays.) The great public monuments in the country all seemed to be dedicated to Afrikaans culture and heroes, from the tremendous, glowering Voortrekker Monument outside Pretoria to the unsightly modernist spire of the Afrikaans Language Monument outside Cape Town, which Breyten Breytenbach once called "a finger in the eye" of every non-Afrikaner in South Africa. The utterly dour, unanimously male, and almost totally Afrikaans character of the government's upper echelons provided the final brick in the impression of brute ethnic domination.

And yet I soon became skeptical of the complaints of English-speaking whites, partly because the ethnic distinctions they sought to draw were blurring all the time. There *were* many English-speakers in the National Party. Conversely, the new leader of the PFP, Frederick van Zyl Slabbert, was an Afrikaner. The clear differences between English and Afrikaner business enterprises were also disappearing as the economy became more complex. I found it got difficult, moreover, to credit the wailings of people who were benefiting from the system as it was being run, and making no effort to change it. The idea, which seemed to be extremely popular among English-speaking whites, that things in South Africa had only become objectionable since 1948 seemed to me entirely fraudulent. Although the National Party's program of dispossession and repression was more systematic, blacks had been dominated and exploited by whites no less energetically under earlier governments. The foundations of the bantustan policy had been laid long before by the system of "native reserves" established by the British colonial authorities. English-speaking whites had not been slow to profit from the opportunities afforded by post-1948 policy, either. The Durban City Council, which was exclusively "English," implemented Group Areas with unparalleled ferocity throughout the 1950s, uprooting thousands of Indian traders and property owners from the newly "white" central business district, where English businessmen who had long coveted Indian holdings were suddenly able to acquire them at distress prices, thanks to National Party policy.

The only National Party member I knew during my first months in Cape Town was, in fact, a British immigrant. He was an older man named Harold, who ran a secondhand goods shop in Muizenberg. Harold's shop was a big, dark, dusty place, full of useless gewgaws and overpriced Victorian furniture. Hanging in the front doorway was a motheaten old scuba-diving outfit, complete with a bulbous helmet with a wire-grilled face window. On the wall inside hung a South African flag and a framed photograph of P. W. Botha. I went into Harold's now and again in search of household odds and ends. Harold, who was a swarthy, heavyset fellow, lived above his shop with his wife and her mother. One afternoon, when he heard my accent, Harold said, "You Americans could learn something from us."

I asked him what he meant.

"I mean about how to keep these baboons in their places. Over there, you've got your Muhammad Alis and your Martin Luther Kings, but over here, we never let them get that far. We give them their own places, and make sure they mix among themselves only, and we have far fewer problems. You must admit this is a much safer country for a white man than America is."

I asked Harold if he wasn't worried about the "changes" P. W.

Botha was always announcing were imminent.

"Not a bit of it. I have complete faith in the man. He's not going to give away the country. Everybody knows what has happened to all the other countries in Africa after the blacks got hold of them. They've went bankrupt. The whole system in those places has broken down. There's no public order. And there's no democracy neither. The Prime Minister knows all this. He knows what he's doing."

Harold was not a typical government supporter, in that he came to the National Party not through long-standing ties of culture and community, the way most Afrikaners did. Neither was Harold the most polished spokesman for the Nationalists, with his continual surly references to "baboons" and "kaffirs." The well-educated Nationalists I eventually met spoke very differently, emphasizing "group identities" and their belief that most of what was worth owning in South Africa rightfully belonged to whites because, in their view, whites had *created* the wealth. Yet the same themes ran through every defense of apartheid, I found: racism and "public order" and a deep determination not to "give away the country," lest it go the way of the rest of Africa.

It was largely from the newspapers, I gathered, that "everybody" knew how bad life was in the rest of Africa, for horror stories about "Black Africa" were standard fare in all South African newspapers. If it wasn't forty-seven people suffocating in a Lagos police van, it was a witchcraft trial in Tanzania, or Joy Adamson, author of *Born Free,* being murdered by one of her assistants in Kenya. Cape Town's *Die Burger* was especially ardent on this theme in its editorials: "Africa north of the Limpopo is a ghastly scene which is getting worse almost daily. Economies, and with them civilized norms, are collapsing." Even Zimbabwe, *Die Burger* reported, was "reverting to jungle."

I relied on the local papers no less for my ideas about strange lands—particularly during those first months in Cape Town, when I probably knew ten times as many blacks as whites, and the strange land that interested me most was white South Africa. I could follow white politics on the front page; I could study white weddings and cocktail receptions on the society page. It was through the daily papers that I became aware of the seemingly boundless concern among whites for the welfare of lost puppies and kittens—small animals rescued from the sides of roads seemed to make the front page nearly as often as the Prime Minister did. Another white obsession involved breaking obscure world records. Somebody was forever "disco dancing" for four hundred hours, or "snake sitting" for eight weeks. This all struck me as a rather miserable ploy to evade the international boycott of sporting contacts with South Africa, a boycott that did not yet extend, apparently, to the *Guiness Book of World Records*. (What is "snake sitting"? It's spending twenty-three and a half hours a day in a glass cage with dozens of poisonous snakes. My favorite snake sitter was given to dramatic comments to the press during his breaks. After a tense weekend: "Saturday and Sunday were dreadful nightmares of hell!")

The real nightmares of hell occurring around the country sometimes surfaced in the papers, too. There were always farmers being hauled into court for torturing their workers, sometimes to death—these cases were so common that it became clear that some white farmers went about such business routinely, *without* much fear of being criminally charged.

One news item that illustrated for me exactly the distance between the South Africa I saw from New Room 16 and its counterpart across the line which I was not seeing was a report that schoolchildren in Bloemfontein, the capital of the Orange Free State, were being taught "hate songs" about Zimbabwean Prime Minister–elect Robert Mugabe. They were being encouraged, apparently, to sing "Kill Mugabe" to the tune of "Singin' in the Rain." While that melodic transposition sounded rather twisted, I thought it was nothing compared to the thinking of the director of education for the Orange Free State who explained to newsmen that "positive indoctrination was necessary to prepare youth to withstand the onslaught of communism and the total onslaught against South Africa."

18

"Playing the fool," as my students called it, was an age-old local game, favored by blacks when dealing with whites: the fawning, false sincerity, the elaborately silly English, the knowing winks. I was never faced with real, angry defiance in my classroom, nor even with the rank, malicious misbehavior that had been visited upon teachers in *my* high school. But I did have children start playing the fool with me. And it was difficult to know what to think when it happened, much less what to do.

My students did not share my uncertainty. They would urge me to *beat* any of their fellows who seemed to be playing the fool. "Here,

sir, you may use this ruler! He is a wicked boy!" "Sir, let me go find
a cane!" The children would invoke the example set by my colleagues.
Mr. Erasmus, the phlegmatic, pipe-smoking young fellow who taught
in the classroom next to mine? When his female students misbehaved
or did not do their work, he was given to pinching them on the fatty
part of the upper arm—so hard sometimes that it bled, they claimed.
And the children clearly respected him for this ferocity. "You must
be *streng* [strict], sir," they would tell me.

Yet I wasn't really tempted to such measures, nor to invoking
Napoleon's dread name. I was wary of the cycle of intimidation and
defiance that seemed to consume much of my colleagues' time with
their students. There were teachers who spent whole class periods
nearly every week administering mass canings, and seemed to feel
obliged to put on unfortunate, quasi-military airs betweentimes. No,
I was determined to treat my students as if they were capable of
studying without physical threats, as most of them certainly were.

Charmaine might have been an exception. She was a sleepy, hapless, overweight girl, bright but sloppy and strange. Her classmates
in 6A6 called her *pampoenkop*—"pumpkin head"—and her head did
sometimes seem too heavy for her body to support. Charmaine had a
distracted, anarchic manner that was unusual at Grassy Park High.
She was also a past master at playing the fool. Once, when I called her
up to the front of the room to hand in an assignment, Charmaine
danced up the aisle rather than walked—not a quick, jivey, teenage
dance, but a slow, subtle, profoundly African dance, shuffling two
steps forward, one step back, twisting her heavy hips rhythmically.
In some way that is difficult to explain, it was the most subversive
thing I had ever seen in a classroom. It absolutely electrified her
classmates, and left me, the "European" object of her insolence, completely flabbergasted. Charmaine deposited her assignment on my
desk, and plodded back to her seat in triumph, making it clear that
she was now restraining herself from dancing while "master"
watched.

On another occasion, I insisted upon seeing whether Charmaine
had a missing textbook in her schoolbag, and she opened the bag to
reveal not books, but a reeking mess of garbage that turned my stomach and caused students nearby to change their seats. Charmaine
drove me crazy, she was so inscrutable and immovable, so clever-but-
lazy. Maybe a few lashes with a cane or a ruler might have motivated
her more than all my speeches and antics and good intentions. I didn't
know. But I wasn't about to send her to Napoleon to find out.

Both of the times I did take my discipline problems to someone else backfired. The first instance occurred when a boy punched a girl in 6A7 just before class started and just as I spotted Grobbelaar, who was their register class teacher, passing by outside. I didn't want to take the time to deal with them, so I quickly delivered the wrangling students over to Grobbelaar, explaining what had happened. Before I returned to my class, I paused, however, to hear Grobbelaar's first words to the children—which I found horrifying. He ignored the girl, who was crying, except to tell her to be quiet, and addressed himself instead to the frightened, shamefaced boy. "Now you must know better than this," he said. His tone was kindly and paternal. "In this country, the laws are on the female's side. Even after you marry them, they may still go to the police and lay a charge against you if you beat them. A man has very few rights in this country. So he must be careful." When the two children returned to class a few minutes later, I noticed that the boy was smiling and that the girl's tear-streaked jaw was set.

The second instance came when I tried to put a stop to a rash of unexcused absences in 7E2. I sent a girl named Mareldia, who I knew had been cutting class, down to the principal's office to explain herself. The principal showed his appreciation for my involving him in such a matter by insisting that I meet with Mareldia's parents before she be readmitted to class. With waning enthusiasm, I asked Mareldia when her parents could come in.

"They can't, sir," she said, pouting. "My daddy is blind and my mommy is crippled. You must go to them."

This seemed too awful to be true. But it was. So off we went, Mareldia and I, after school, to see her parents. They turned out to live in a tiny, trim house set back from a sandy road near the Princess Vlei. Mareldia's parents were an older couple, who both looked hard-used by life. Her father had a crestfallen face and sightless eyes, and wore a straw hat with a green band. Her mother wore a tentlike blue housedress and limped painfully. They were both visibly distressed and excruciatingly polite. I felt like a perfect twit marching in to announce their daughter's misbehavior.

Mareldia's parents gave me tea, and we sat and talked about Mareldia, who sat apart and looked nearly as miserable as her parents. It was the first student's house I had been inside. The living room we sat in was small and dim and overfurnished. There were photographs—family photographs, wedding photographs, graduation photographs—on the walls, and photo albums on a coffee table. On the mantel were commemorative plates, two porcelain dogs, and a bouquet of plastic roses under glass. A framed print of *The Last Supper* stood on a bookshelf near a brightly colored picture of a green-eyed Jesus gazing passionately toward a throne on a cloud.

"She's our only daughter," Mareldia's mother lamented. "And she's normally a very good girl."

I assured her parents that Mareldia was a good student, too— which she was. She had just fallen in with a wayward crowd in 7E2.

"I'll whip her," Mareldia's father promised.

I swallowed hard and gazed bleakly out the louvered window at the bamboo and kikuyu grass leading down toward the vlei. As soon as it seemed decent to do so, I took my leave. And I never sent another student of mine to the principal. Absenteeism was not a real problem in my classes, anyway.

Among my senior classes, discipline itself was not a problem. The matrics had not reached their exalted status by waiting for someone else to motivate them, and now that we had tapped into a vein of information about opportunities that few of them had believed really existed, their energy for planning their futures suddenly became boundless. Hector wanted to be an *industrial* engineer. Michael wanted to be a *marine* engineer. Jillian decided to study architecture at the University of Cape Town. Ishmail would study medicine at the University of Natal. A number of matrics simply wanted to go to the University of Cape Town, with no particular professional goal in mind, the same way so many white students did—I did not discourage this approach. A few thought they might apply to Stellenbosch University, the leading Afrikaans university in the country, located in a small town within commuting distance of Cape Town, or perhaps to one of the other Afrikaans universities upcountry. After all, they were Afrikaans-speaking themselves. Again, I encouraged this can-do attitude.

But some of my colleagues looked askance at me when they saw all the applications that the matrics and I were amassing. One day in the staff room, Georgina Swart said, "I understand that you've started a letter-writing campaign, Mr. Finnegan. Who was the young fellow in America? James Meredith? Do you plan to make another James Meredith here, Mr. Finnegan?"

19

The first time Clive Jacobus turned up after school in my classroom gave me a start. Clive and I had become reasonably friendly in the weekly class sessions we had together—when he bothered to show up, which was not always—but I had had no sign that he wanted to know me. Then, one windy Thursday afternoon, he strolled into New Room 16 and made himself comfortable sprawled across the top of a desk.

"So tell me," he said. "What do you think of this country, now you've been here a few weeks? Are you convinced Biko killed himself, just to make the Special Branch look bad?"

Steve Biko's death had been in the news that week. After a lengthy inquest, the three doctors who had treated Biko in jail had just been absolved of blame by the South African Medical and Dental Council.

"I think it's a crazy place," I said.

"Why? Haven't you been anyplace else in your travels where the black cinema usherettes are forbidden to look at the screen while films for whites are shown?"

I laughed. I hadn't heard that one before.

"Separate development, we call it here," Clive said.

With Clive, there was no question about his political awareness. Indeed, there was not much to talk about with him other than politics. The government had just released the report of its commission of inquiry into the 1976 uprising, so we talked about that. "According to them, it was all just 'outside agitators,' " Clive said with a snort. "What do you think of that?"

"I wasn't here. But it sounds like they're dreaming out loud."

"That's exactly what they're doing. And do you know what they say about the teachers in the Peninsula here?"

I did know. The report claimed that Cape Town teachers "played an important role in creating an atmosphere of dissatisfaction and unrest among youngsters."

"Do you think that's true?" I asked Clive.

He shrugged. "In some cases. At some schools." Then, watching me closely, Clive said, "Actually, some people say that's what you're trying to do."

Now I knew why Clive had come to see me. He had heard something about my deviations from the syllabus and wanted to see if he could sound out my political views. "Not me," I said. "I'm just trying to find out what's going on."

Clive snorted. He had heard that one before.

But Clive took to coming around regularly to talk. He was interested in my background, it seemed, especially my family and my experience in the American student anti-war movement. One day, I asked him about his family, and Clive surprised me with a long reminiscence about his childhood. His father, he said, was a school principal in the northern Cape town of Upington. "That's on the Orange River, quite near Namibia. It's a strange place. Completely different to here. We only came down here when I was starting high school. Before then, I was a real *plattelander*. I had never seen really big buildings, or great masses of people. . . . Up there, I would say people are a lot closer to the earth. Everybody keeps goats. In fact, if you have a lot of goats, people reckon you're rich." Clive laughed. His face had a faraway look.

"Actually, the location in Upington, the so-called location, used to be quite a wild place. There's so many types of people up there. Xhosas, Damaras, Sothos. There's people from Zimbabwe, and quite a few Bushmen. And these people they call Basters, who wear their hair long, and look like so-called whites, some of them. Just about everybody speaks Afrikaans. You don't really hear anybody call themselves 'colored,' even though that's how a lot of people are classified. There used to be a lot of mixing, a lot of intermarriage, but the Boers have fairly well stopped that now. *Wrywing tussen bevolkingsgroepe,* the government calls it—'friction between the races.' They say apartheid is meant to prevent it, but it's really meant to make it worse. Divide and Rule, we call it. . . .

"People are so poor up there. They'll go along the railway line for hours, just hunting for little bits of coal that fall off the trains. Otherwise, they must go out in the veld, looking for firewood, and that's even harder to find. If they find a cow that's been killed by a train, that's like Christmas. They just butcher it right there, and carry the meat home. I used to go out in the veld with my friends, and hunt hares with these little weapons we made. Like catapults. But my family was well off, compared to most other people. Especially after my father was made principal. He's still up there. We only see him during holidays.

"I remember the first time we heard the Beatles. It was in a cafe, along there by the river, on a wireless. I don't remember what song it was, but my brother, he was there, and he said he would go to England himself when he got older, and play his guitar, and all that. And he did. He went about six or seven years ago now, and he's still overseas. Now he lives in France, but he's traveled all over Europe.

He sends us letters, and snapshots sometimes. He had really long hair for a while. He's had quite a few different jobs. He reckons he'll come back here to visit one day, but he says he could never live under apartheid again. I always looked up to him quite a bit, but it's been so long now, I haven't seen him since I was in primary school.

"You probably think this is all really boring." Clive, who had been speaking slowly, and clearly savoring his memories, had suddenly become self-conscious and gave a nervous laugh. I assured him that I was not bored, and he seemed to believe me.

The wind was piling sand up on the landing outside my classroom door as we locked up and left. "The weather's going to change," Clive said, and pointed to the mountain. From Grassy Park, one looked upon the east face of Table Mountain, where the great butte ran back into rocky heights known as the Constantiaberg. Black clouds were gathering along the summit that afternoon. "Everybody here just looks at the mountain to know the weather," Clive said. "They say the best place to see what's going to happen is out here, on the Flats." Clive laughed and I offered him a lift home in my car.

Late that night, while I was marking papers at my desk on the balcony, it began to storm. Soon there was thunder and lightning and rain so fierce that the windowsills sprang improbable leaks: little jets of water shooting horizontally into the house.

20

Nothing highlights the peculiar contradictions within apartheid quite like the plight of those people classified "Coloured." The concept is a grab bag; there are no fewer than seven official subclassifications under the heading "Coloured." These include "Cape coloured," "Cape Malay," "Griqua," and "Other coloured" (a number of my colleagues and students at Grassy Park High were, I eventually discovered, "Other coloureds"). Even more than with the other race classifications, it can be argued that "Coloured" is a bureaucratic fiction, an administrative convenience, that there is no such "race." On the other hand, a certain amount of group identity is created simply by the fact of classification, particularly when the law mandates forced segregation, and in other ways treats one group differently from others. Furthermore, it must be said that "coloreds" did not simply spring into existence *ex nihilo* with the passage of the Population Registration Act. Though its edges might have been blurred, there was clearly a large, Cape-based group of people with a cultural tradition distinct from those of their Xhosa, English, Afrikaner, and other neighbors. And while avoiding apartheid-serving notions of "ethnicity," this tradition merits some description here, for it was the heritage of the people of Grassy Park.

"Coloreds" are sometimes called "brown Afrikaners," and they do share some common ancestry and many traits with the people who enslaved their forebears. Nearly 90 percent of them speak Afrikaans as a first language; they are the only group in the world besides the Afrikaners themselves who do so. Many belong to the Dutch Reformed "daughter" church for "coloreds." At the same time, many "coloreds" repudiate all cultural connections with *die boere*. Once, when I said something about how expressive the Afrikaans language seemed to me, an Afrikaans-speaking student of mine denied it bitterly, saying, *"Nee, meneer, dis 'n bobbejaan se taal"* ("No, sir, it's a baboon's language"). I even met a few royalists on the Cape Flats, all of them older people, who expressed their rejection of Afrikanerdom by embracing its traditional enemy, hanging the Union Jack and photographs of the Queen on the walls of their homes. Though "colored" farm workers were often said to prefer Afrikaner employers, whose rough-and-tumble ways they understood, to the chillier English "gentleman farmers" of the Cape, few if any "coloreds" had ever shared the political views of most Afrikaners.

"Coloreds" are often compared to American blacks. It has been pointed out that, under the South African race classification laws, the majority of American blacks would be considered "colored." The two groups share a history of slavery, and the absolute deracination that slavery entails—a historical experience unlike that of most black South Africans, who were conquered and largely dispossessed of their lands, but were never actually bought and sold, with their languages lost, their societies atomized. I was frequently struck by similarities between the mannerisms of "coloreds" and those of American blacks, such as the way certain scapegrace "coloreds" called each other *Gam*, Afrikaans for "Ham," the biblical figure whose descendants were made "hewers of wood and drawers of water," and short for *Gammat*, a pejorative for "colored"—which reminded me of black Americans calling each other "nigger": neutralizing the hated epithet by expropriating it. Certainly, black Americans had long been a source of inspiration for "coloreds" in Cape Town. In the nineteenth century, a group of black American sailors off a visiting ship so impressed the locals with their singing, dancing, and banjo playing that attempts to emulate them during the traditional two days of liberty at New Year's (a tradition that dated from slave days) soon turned into a vast annual parade and festival known as the Coon Carnival, in which the entire center of Cape Town was turned over to "coloreds" in top hats and satin minstrel outfits, playing guitars and saxophones, banjos and cellos, snare drums and tambourines in troupes calling themselves the Hollywood Palm Beach Serenaders, the Dahomey Minstrels, the Famous Richmond Gentlemen Coons, and the Spes Bona Nigger Minstrels.

But the Coon Carnival illustrates well the difficulty of describing "colored culture," for by 1980 the "coon" idea had been widely rejected by "coloreds" as an insulting stereotype, so that, although it was probably still the first thing many South Africans would think of if asked to come up with an example of "Cape colored culture," the Coon Carnival was actually in sharp decline, and would probably cease to exist altogether soon.

Do the leading writers, artists, and musicians classified "colored" represent "colored culture"? The most successful of them—Dollar Brand, Dennis Brutus, Alex La Guma—all seem to leave South Africa (as do their African counterparts—Miriam Makeba, Hugh Masakela, Nat Nakasa), and undoubtedly never refer to themselves as "colored," although their lives were largely determined by the "colored" experience. Do the "cultural organizations" found among "coloreds," such as the Eoan Group, a well-known Cape Town ballet, opera, and theater company, represent "colored culture," or merely a "white aspirant" aspect of black South Africa? The choral societies, the sports clubs, the "benefit societies" (private cooperatives intended to help members build homes, buy property, and so forth; these societies, like the funeral societies known as *losies,* were affected especially badly by Group Areas removals), the many and prominent churches, were all these not the warp and woof of a "culture"?

Perhaps this is simply to indicate the obvious, that despite the political protestations that no such thing as a "colored" people existed, there did exist a full-blown network of organizations and relations among the people so classified.

₀ "Coloreds" are often said to be "Westernized," compared to their African countrymen. And it is true that "coloreds" observe few if any of the traditions of preconquest South Africa, some of which survive more or less intact among Africans. "Coloreds" have no traditional headmen or hereditary chiefs, no traditional land tenure practices or marriage practices, such as bride price, and no strong traditions of witchcraft or animism. Many South African whites believe that because "coloreds" lead lives they consider "civilized," they deserve better treatment than Africans, who remain comparatively foreign. Other whites believe that "pure-blooded" Africans possess stronger personalities and more innate "dignity" than people of "mixed race" —a form of racism not unknown among Africans themselves.

The white South African obsession with "racial purity" has surely had its most devastating effect on "coloreds." Interracial unions were common in the early days of the Cape Colony. A popular saying has it that the Europeans arrived at the Cape on April 6, 1652, and "the color problem" was born nine months later. The first official interracial marriage was celebrated in 1658. In 1672, five hundred of the six hundred European colonists resident in the Cape were adult males; the genealogical results of such a population structure should be self-evident. Two distinguished early governors of the colony, Simon and Willem van der Stel (after whom Stellenbosch, the second town founded by Europeans and a major cultural center of Afrikanerdom, was named), would have been classified "colored" in modern-day South Africa. Before very long, however, the good Cape burghers, progenitors of the Afrikaners, developed an intense racial self-consciousness, and a phobia about the mixing of the races. This obsession became a first principle of modern Afrikanerdom. As Dr. Niklaas Diedrichs, the State President of South Africa in the 1970s, wrote, "One of the outstanding achievements of this *volk* is that in the midst of an overwhelming barbarism, it succeeded in remaining white." Genealogists whose research has indicated that the Afrikaner gene pool is composed of significant amounts of African blood have found their results attacked hysterically by defenders of the *volk*—while being greeted with mirth and appreciation by other South Africans.

Some of the National Party's most offensive post-1948 legislation was included under the 1950 amendment to the Immorality Act (scheduled for repeal at the time of writing), which forbade sexual relations across the color line. The purpose of this law was, as a Cape Town magistrate recently explained, "to prevent the mongrelization of the races." A member of the Johannesburg Coloured Management Committee gave this view of the law and its reasoning: "The so-called Coloured is the product of racial mixing as affirmed in the law that declares us Coloured. This self-same law, the White man's law, also declares that this sort of mixing is illegal and therefore abhorrent . . . the specific law outlawing the activity that created us is called the Immorality Act. This repugnant law makes us feel that we as Coloureds are immoral creations."

Many whites clearly shared this feeling. The existence of "coloreds" was often still attributed to "passing sailors" mixing with black women, rather than to local residents. Along with the belief that "coloreds" were "immoral creations" went a conviction widespread among whites that most "coloreds" were alcoholic, promiscuous, dependent, and violent. In the time I was in Cape Town, I lost count of the number of whites who, hearing where I worked, made sad or leering or contemptuous reference to one feature or another of this stereotype. A favorite pronouncement among white males: "There's not a girl over the age of thirteen in those colored townships who's still a virgin." The fact that a strikingly high proportion of the "colored" population is in South African prisons seemed to have escaped no white's notice. The historical burden of white attitudes was embedded in people's very names. Getting out from under images and ideas like these, fighting their internalization, was a dilemma faced in some ways by "coloreds" alone.

Which is not to say that "coloreds" had a more difficult time of it than other black South Africans. On the contrary, "coloreds" were not subject to influx control, as all Africans were; which meant that "coloreds" were not being constantly arrested under the pass laws and "endorsed out" to a bantustan. They could legally own property in "colored" areas of "white" South Africa. These, and numerous other incremental advantages, such as statutory preference over other blacks in certain areas of employment and the higher per capita allotment for education than Africans received, amounted to greater opportunities for advancement and a significantly more secure existence for many "coloreds" than was available to their African compatriots. The distance between Grassy Park and one of the barren, overcrowded, absolutely impoverished bantustans like Qwa Qwa simply could not be measured in kilometers.

Of course, the distance between Qwa Qwa and the more established sections of Soweto was not much more vast. And for sheer deprivation the living conditions of many "coloreds" rivaled those of any other sector of black South Africa. There were an estimated 150,000 "colored" squatters on the Cape Flats in 1980, most of them living in tin and cardboard shanties among the dunes, without roads or laws or sanitation. On Cape farms, "colored" workers were notoriously underpaid and underfed. Kwashiorkor (malnutrition), rickets, tuberculosis, and severe gastroenteritis were all widespread, and the "colored" infant mortality rate nationally was nine times that of white infants. (Life expectancy was actually lower for "coloreds" than for Africans.) Again, this sort of stark misery seemed far away from

Grassy Park. Even within Grassy Park, however, a great range of socioeconomic status was obvious at a glance. Between someone like Soraya, contemplating a honeymoon in Europe, and the toothless illiterate janitor who cleaned my classroom after school, there yawned a gulf of privilege almost as deep and wide as that which separated most whites from most blacks.

The legal and political status of "coloreds" was in as much doubt and flux as everything else. It was an irony of history that much of the most notorious apartheid legislation introduced after 1948 was actually directed at "coloreds." The 1949 Prohibition of Mixed Marriages Act and the 1950 amendment to the Immorality Act were certainly so, for sex and marriage had long been forbidden between whites and Africans. The Group Areas Act also hit "coloreds" hardest (along with Indians). Many Africans suffered from Group Areas, of course, but most Africans had always been forced to live outside the "white" towns. The Population Registration Act had its most destructive impact on mixed-race families and communities. And it was the limited "colored" franchise in the Cape that the Nationalists attacked and sought to abolish in the 1950s—finally succeeding in 1956, after a battle which was still recalled with an abiding bitterness in Grassy Park in 1980. The international disapprobation of apartheid has often seemed to focus on these "grand apartheid" laws as if they were the main body of institutionalized racism in South Africa, but the truth is that they merely consolidated and extended a great deal of existing legislation. The limited "Native" franchise in the Cape had been abolished, for instance, in 1936. But if the targeting of a minority group like the "coloreds" for a whole new barrage of legal discrimination was really intended, as one Nationalist member put it in Parliament, "to make our colour sense clear before the world," it seemed to succeed.

The provision for "coloreds" in the apartheid master plan was never clear. The centerpiece of apartheid planning was always the bantustan scheme, the ultimate denationalization of all Africans by assignment to one of the ten "homelands." As Dr. C. P. Mulder, then Minister of Cooperation and Development, put it in a 1978 address to the House of Assembly: "If our policy is taken to its logical conclusion as far as the Black people are concerned, there will be not one Black man with South African citizenship." But government policy toward "coloreds" and Indians has had nothing like this ruthless logic. In the early 1970s, the government unveiled a plan to build an entire "colored" city, to be called Atlantis, thirty miles north of Cape Town. This

instant metropolis would have its own industrial base and a population of between 800,000 and one million by the turn of the century.
It was a preposterous scheme, and by 1980, with construction grinding
to a halt, Atlantis was clearly going to thrive only as an example of
Nationalist pipe-dreaming about the great unsolved "problem" of the
"coloreds." A number of elected "colored" councils were established
to represent "colored" opinion to the government, but all of these had
been rejected, discredited, and forced to resign by their constituencies.
In March 1980, the government announced the formation of an *appointed* body of representatives, to be called the Coloured People's
Council, but popular "colored" reaction was so disdainful—the body
was immediately dubbed the Coloured Puppets Council—that the
names of the appointees were never made public, and this idea was
also quietly abandoned.

There was a long-standing debate within the ranks of the government about whether to devise "homelands" for "coloreds" and Indians or to grant these groups some form of limited parliamentary
representation. I often heard bitter jokes made about the idea of a
"colored homeland." "What did they imagine District Six was?" "Who
they going to dream up for our tribal chiefs?" The Atlantis project was
widely regarded as a failed attempt by Pretoria to create the nucleus
of such a "state," and a vast new "colored" housing development
called Mitchell's Plain, located far out on the Cape Flats, was sometimes referred to around Grassy Park as "the homeland," even
though most of it was still under construction. "We will be forced to
move to our very own bantustan soon," a fellow teacher once said to
me about his family's pending move to Mitchell's Plain. (The government's blueprint called for 250,000 "coloreds" to be living out at
Mitchell's Plain by 1982.) The intensity of this debate within the
government grew throughout the 1970s, and was a key factor in a
major faction split in 1982. The aforementioned Dr. Mulder, who
today leads the breakaway Conservative Party, continues to advocate
the creation of "colored" and Indian "homelands." But the *verligte,* or
"enlightened," wing of the Nationalists led by P. W. Botha has prevailed.

A tri-parliamentary constitutional plan was first announced by
the government in 1977. Then still ill-defined, it was rejected by even
conservative "colored" and Indian groups, for it completely excluded
the African majority. P. W. Botha's response was unintentionally
eloquent. He said that "even if the Coloureds and Indians do not
accept the new constitution, the government will go ahead and imple-

ment it until they do accept it." In 1983, a referendum on the plan was finally held among white voters, who approved it, and elections for segregated "colored" and Indian chambers of Parliament were held in August 1984. These elections were widely boycotted, but just as Botha, who is now State President, promised it would be, the new plan was instituted anyway. The "junior chambers" of the new parliament have jurisdiction over only what the government determines are their "own affairs," which do not include national policy, foreign policy, or any other area that could conceivably also concern white South Africans, who effectively retain all power. Africans continue to have no representation, although there is talk of yet another chamber of Parliament being created to represent those "urban blacks" for whom no "homeland" can be found.

The government's primary motive for granting "coloreds" and Indians limited parliamentary status, over the objections of the vast majorities of those very groups, was, according to one view, military. The South African armed forces were suffering from a manpower shortage. Industry was being hurt by the ever-increasing amounts of time white draftees were being required to serve in the military, and the shortage was expected to worsen. Military leaders, who were often said to be ahead of the country's politicians in their strategic thinking, and who were believed to have a great influence over P. W. Botha (who served for many years as Minister of Defense before becoming Prime Minister), had reportedly concluded that the only solution to the manpower problem was the introduction of conscription of "coloreds" and Indians. This could hardly be done while these groups enjoyed no political rights; hence the tri-cameral parliament. P. W. Botha and his military advisers often talked about the mobilization of a "total strategy" to counter what they called "the total onslaught" being mounted against the South African system. Clearly, that long-range strategy involved winning "coloreds" and Indians over to the side of the white minority, as it strove to defend its hegemony against the African majority. (At the time of writing, conscription of "coloreds" and Indians has not been introduced.)

It was this situation, as much as their racial and cultural background, that caused "coloreds" to be seen as "the people in-between." For many years, there had been speculation about whether "coloreds" would ultimately throw in their lot with the Africans or with the whites. By 1980 that speculation had abated, for most "coloreds" had been profoundly alienated by their treatment under apartheid, and the time had clearly passed for political alliances with whites. The

Black Consciousness movement, with its emphasis on the unity of Africans, "coloreds," and Indians, had been instrumental in the development of a "black" self-image among an entire generation of "coloreds." The turning point in that process was the 1976 uprising, when thousands of "colored" students took to the streets in solidarity with the students of Soweto, and many lost their lives.

But "colored" political protest had a lengthy tradition, dating back to the founding of the predominantly "colored" African People's Organization in Cape Town in 1902. Early protests focused on discrimination in education. The creation of the Coloured Affairs Department spawned the Anti-C.A.D. movement, which merged with the predominantly African All-African Convention in 1943 to form the Non-European Unity Movement. The Unity Movement was a Marxist, but anti-Soviet, organization that stressed the need for unity among Africans, "coloreds," and Indians, rejected white leadership, and in other ways presaged later movements like the Pan-Africanist Congress and Black Consciousness. The Unity Movement commanded the attention of many "colored" intellectuals in the 1940s and 1950s, while the South African Communist Party exercised a strong, if indirect influence over "colored" workers through certain trade unions before its suppression in 1950. "Coloreds" were active in the Congress Movement through the Coloured People's Organization and the South African Congress of Trade Unions, and there are today many "colored" members of the exiled liberation movements. I often heard reverential mention on the Cape Flats of local "coloreds" who had left the country for military training, men like Reginald September, a major figure in the ANC, or James April, a captured ANC guerrilla sentenced to fifteen years, or Basil February, who was killed in a ferocious battle with the Rhodesian Army while attempting to re-enter South Africa.

Of course, support for black liberation was not unanimous among "coloreds." There were those who professed indifference, either convinced that the government was too strong to be swayed, or believing "coloreds" to be in a no-win situation, as well as a few who believed that a black government might not necessarily prove better for them than the white government. Yet these were nearly all older people. Younger "coloreds" called themselves "black," and even the most conservative "colored" opinion to be heard in public was vehemently anti-government.

21

In a pharmacy near Busy Corner, I saw a bottle on a shelf: "Hi-Lite Special Complexion Cream—Lightens, Brightens, Smooths." Near it was another: "Karoo Freckle Cream—with special bleaching ingredient." I had read somewhere that twenty million units of skin lightener had been sold in South Africa in the past ten years—this during the heyday of Black Consciousness with its slogan Black is Beautiful. Black physicians were calling for the outlawing of skin lighteners, which had caused permanent damage to millions of people. How acute, I wondered, was this neurotic consciousness of tint among my students? In a composition titled "Falling in Love," I noticed that they invariably fell in love with someone with "light skin, fair hair and sexy blue eyes." A friend who taught art to Cape Flats primary-school children told me that, when they drew self-portraits, the children usually drew blue-eyed blonds and got furious if the inaccuracy was pointed out to them. I guessed that Kenneth and Mamie Clark's famous 1940 doll experiment—in which five-year-old black American children, given the choice between black and white dolls, consistently chose the white dolls, showing that they already understood the inferior status of black skin in American society: the finding helped to win the landmark desegregation case, *Brown* v. *Board of Education* —would reveal the same attitudes if conducted among the children of Grassy Park.

But the truth was, I couldn't see it. I often heard from whites that skin tones were everything in "colored" society, that lighter-skinned "coloreds" looked down upon their darker neighbors; but I never heard the same thing from "coloreds," and never got any sense of its being so in Grassy Park. Among whites, on the other hand, such attitudes were obviously rampant. A surfer I knew slightly, who had kinky light brown hair, once confided to me in a husky voice that the other kids at his junior high school had called him *kaffirkop* ("nigger head"). "You simply cannot imagine how heavy that is here in South Africa, how painful it was for me," he said. There were always stories in the newspapers about dark-skinned whites. One man claimed to be unable to get work because of his complexion. Employers lied to him, he said. One security firm told him he was too small, then turned around and hired his friend who was smaller, but whiter. His life was an "unbearable hell," he said. "My wife is fair, my child is fair, yet I am treated like dirt." Blacks I knew were often perversely amused by such stories, particularly by the suggestion that whites were out-raged at being "treated like dirt" when they did not *deserve* to be. "He means 'treated like a black,' " a fellow teacher said to me.

That whites should be hysterical about the possibility of falling out of the privileged caste that their racial classification gained them was understandable. That blacks should be persuaded by life under apartheid to believe that whiter was in a myriad of ways—aesthetic, social, financial—more desirable would have been just as understand-able. But beyond the skin lighteners and the children seeming to wish themselves or their lovers blond, I never, as I say, saw anything to indicate this. Perhaps I was just a poor social scientist and missing all the clues, but the blacks I knew seemed infinitely more sane about "race" than did South African whites. A light-skinned, freckle-faced boy in one of my Standard Nine classes was nicknamed "Boer" by his friends—loaded as the term was, the children seemed to disarm it with the easy, joking way they used it. I winced when I read that Charlene Tilton, the honey-blond star of "Dallas" and one of my students' favorite actresses, was coming to Cape Town, and that a Charlene Tilton look-alike contest would be held to welcome her. Then a girl in 6A7 told me, "They must have a Donna Summer look-alike contest, because we think Natalie can win." People in Grassy Park often talked about "play whites"—"coloreds" who tried to "pass" as whites—and there was even a teacher at Grassy Park High who was said to be one. But such people seemed to be more pitied than envied. I remember a light-skinned colleague telling me of his joy the first time he saw a photograph of Malcolm X. "I said to myself, 'Man, if this paleface can be a great black leader, then there's hope for me yet.' "

22

I was wary of Nelson October initially. His performance at the first faculty meeting I attended had been a rude surprise, and then he had pointedly boycotted the intermural track meet at which I had had my late-blooming epiphany of school spirit. Somebody said it was some-thing about the stadium management's having broken the rules of a sports federation he belonged to. Whatever it was, October had stayed behind alone when the rest of us boarded the buses for Athlone. Yet his personal manner was not prickly and off-putting, the way this sounds. On the contrary, October seemed to be a singularly good-natured fellow. He had bright, dark eyes of great intensity, a ready laugh, seemingly boundless energy, and an athletic grace that left me unsurprised when someone said he had been a top local soccer player before a leg injury ended his career. He was twenty-four, but seemed older. Heavy-bearded and thoughtful, he had been teaching at Grassy Park High for five years and his presence, his influence, seemed as broad and deep as any senior teacher's.

As I tried to make his acquaintance, though, I began to see that October was also wary of me. He was perfectly pleasant, but my attempts to strike up conversations with him all went nowhere. Unlike some other teachers, October was in no hurry to know the Yankee Doodle Dandy. I finally managed to break the ice one day when I noticed October in the staff room reading a collection of Pablo Neruda's poems. I asked how he liked them, and he said they were marvelous; he only wished he could read them in the original Spanish. I speak Spanish, and I had soon agreed to translate the lyrics from a record October owned and cherished, but could not understand, containing the murdered Chilean revolutionary Victor Jara's songs and poetry.

Nelson and I began to talk a lot. He was amazingly well read and well informed, not only about South African issues but about international affairs. I was chagrined to find that, although he had never been overseas, he frequently knew more than I did about countries I had visited. We agreed about most things, including, to Nelson's obvious pleasure, the American role in the Vietnam War and the behavior of the United States in Latin America. I thought Nelson was painfully romantic on some subjects, though, notably the course of the Cuban Revolution, and we argued away a number of free periods on the subject. Finally, Nelson slipped me a United Nations pamphlet containing a six-hour speech by Fidel Castro, entitled "We represent the immense majority of humanity . . ." I skimmed the pamphlet and decided that it was no use disputing a fundamental tenet of what was obviously a well-developed belief system.

Our conversations always came back to South Africa. Nelson was interested in my impressions of the country. I mentioned that I found the ubiquity of the color line in Cape Town daily life oppressive, and he laughed heartily.

"You're just not used to it! The funny thing is, petty apartheid is basically there as psychological reassurance to whites, who are insecure because they know they are so heavily outnumbered. White liberals want to scrap petty apartheid, because it's unfashionable, and it makes them feel guilty. But nearly all of them are wealthy. They know they can simply *buy* whatever distance *they* want to keep from the masses. They just want to redecorate the place. Would you be more comfortable if it were redecorated?"

"Probably."

"Well, the oppressed are not interested in redecoration."

One day, I put to Nelson the rudimentary question I had been asking myself since arriving in South Africa, about what prevented blacks from simply rising up. Nelson's reply confirmed my own impression—that deep disunity was the main obstacle—as he described the success of what he called "the regime's long-range strategy: Divide and Rule." Nelson talked about "the apartheid theory of nations" (which tried to cast "coloreds" as a "nation-in-the-making") and the "retribalization" that was the goal of all the "tribal" segregation foisted on blacks by the government. He also mentioned "the sheer savagery of the state's repression." I suggested that the passivity of so many blacks and the obvious willingness of others to collaborate in their own oppression were also major factors, but Nelson dismissed the point, saying, "In every system of colonial occupation, there are collaborators." He mentioned the South Vietnamese government under the Americans, the Indian troops and administration under British imperial rule, and the thousands of blacks who fought for the whites in the Zimbabwe independence war. "Consciousness has to be raised, of course. But the contradictions within the system will eventually destroy it for purely objective reasons."

"But surely people have to first shake off this huge inferiority complex they seem to carry around," I said.

"That's the BC line," Nelson said, and I blushed. He meant "Black Consciousness" and he was right; that was exactly where I had found my few ideas about the black liberation struggle. "BC made an important contribution at a certain point," Nelson said. "But it was a response to a special set of circumstances. You see, the 1960s were a very quiet time in South Africa. The repression was intense, after the banning of the liberation movements. A lot of white liberals came forward, and more or less filled the political vacuum. They were the only ones who dared to talk about black liberation just then. BC arose partly in reaction to that situation, which was obviously unacceptable. BC got things moving again, and its message had a big effect among students. But most of them were unaware of what had occurred in the 1950s."

"Which was?"

"Which was some very progressive mass action. It was a different atmosphere then. It was still possible to hold big outdoor rallies. Here in Cape Town, you would find open meetings taking place on the Grand Parade during lunchtime, with many of the workers in the city attending. They might be addressed by people from the ANC, the PAC, the Non-European Unity Movement. The Unity Movement was especially strong here, and had quite a progressive analysis. All this was before the crackdown, of course, which came in 1960, after Sharpeville. Many of the strategies used at that time now seem naive. People underestimated the ruthlessness of the state. But just because the struggle was forced underground in the sixties didn't mean that people were less aware of their oppression. Just as it doesn't mean that now. Because the struggle is largely underground right now, too.

"People are capable of rising up together spontaneously. We have seen that they are, here in Cape Town in 1960, and again in 1976. But the state is ready, now more than ever, for spontaneous mass uprisings. They can contain them militarily. They can cut off the townships very easily, and starve people out in the event of a general strike, as they have done. No, man, the only strategy open to the liberatory movement has been what we call *hamba khale*—go carefully."

For the first few months we knew each other, Nelson went carefully with me. I learned almost nothing from him about his personal life, his family, his past, his activities outside school. I did discover that he had studied civil engineering for a year and a half at the University of Cape Town before dropping out to become an unqualified teacher. I found this news exciting, which seemed to amuse Nelson. When I wondered why he dropped out, he shrugged. "It seemed irrelevant," he said. Another teacher told me that Nelson was active in the non-racial sporting movement and that his father was a major figure in that movement. Nelson's father was a foreman on a poultry farm, who—according to Mr. Pasqualine, the oldest member of the Grassy Park faculty—had suffered for his political activism during the crackdown on dissent in the 1960s. "He was a highly skilled craftsman in the furniture trade," Pasqualine told me. "But he was blacklisted and could get no work at all for years. He and his family had to live on charity. That's how he comes to be out on that farm today!"

Pasqualine was a strange, hook-nosed, bottom-heavy old fellow who actually talked constantly about people who had suffered at the hands of the government in years past. His main theme was the persecution of his own father, who had been deported many years before to Goa. "They crucified him!"—this ejaculation was Pasqua-line's repetend. One often heard it mimicked around Grassy Park High. Everyone had heard the story too many times.

Another favorite tale of Pasqualine's concerned two former teach-ers at Grassy Park High, a husband and wife. The husband had been a leader in the Unity Movement. "One morning, with no warning, into the staff room they came, the Special Branch! They grabbed them and dragged them off to Caledon Square, just like that! Eventually, they sent him to Robben Island for ten long years. She served several years herself." I later met the main character of this story, who didn't recall the staff room drama that Pasqualine did, but confirmed the rest—Grassy Park High, the Unity Movement, his ten years on Rob-ben Island, his wife's time in prison. What crime had they committed, exactly? "We were foolish, that's all," the man said, and changed the subject. I was later told that Pasqualine himself had been politically active in his younger days, but that he had been picked up for "inter-rogation" in the early 1960s. He had talked rather freely to his inter-rogators, it was said, and had never been the same since.

I had been reading South African history and whatever I could find about the black resistance to white rule, with a notion about passing on what I could learn to my students. Slowly, the sheer pre-sumption of this plan was becoming apparent. People in Grassy Park knew exactly what had happened between blacks and the government over the years. In fact, the Cape Flats had seen some terrible violence in the 1976 uprising. Over one hundred people had been killed in a long series of bloody clashes with the police, and there were few people in Grassy Park who had not known somebody who was killed or injured. To this day, one local boy, who attended the next high school over, came to class with a colostomy bag, having lost his lower intestine to a police shotgun blast. My coming to see the ludicrousness of a white foreigner's trying to instruct black people in the history of their own resistance did not dim my interest in the subject, however. I continued to study and to soak in all I could, if only to be less in the dark myself. And my conversations with Nelson were a source of constant insight and come-uppance.

On one occasion, Nelson and I stood looking at a pale blue police bakkie—a pickup truck with a big steel cage built on the bed—which was parked across the street from school. The cops often parked there. They liked to watch the schoolgirls. Inside the cages on the bakkies there were usually prisoners: Africans found on the streets with their passes not in order. They would be jailed and then shipped to the

Ciskei, or the Transkei, or some other distant bantustan. The bakkies sometimes sat there for hours, with the prisoners baking silently in the cages, while the policemen smoked and called to the schoolgirls. From my classroom window, I could see them, and I often had to force myself to ignore them to be able to concentrate on my lessons. Now I pointed to the bakkie—Africans called it a *kwela-kwela,* or a "nylon"—and asked Nelson what he thought the cops would do if I went over and told them I would report them if they didn't immediately deliver their prisoners to wherever they were taking them.

Nelson shrugged and began to talk quietly about "structural violence." Those cops in their bakkies weren't simply enforcing some unjust laws, he said. They were engaged in "counterrevolution." "There's a war being fought in this country, you see, a war between the government and the oppressed. Whites never see it. The outside world never sees it. But it's being fought, in the alleys of the townships, inside the jails. This "—Nelson nodded at the bakkie—"is just one more scene, one more skirmish, in that war."

I thought that was pretty dramatic, although I realized that Nelson was really suggesting that I be less dramatic myself, in the personal sense, that I try to see local events in a broader context. This was a basic difference between us. I saw things in particulars. I was interested in why the police trucks were called "nylons"—it apparently had something to do with the mesh that covered the cages. I was riveted by the suffering of the people inside the cages. Nelson, on the other hand, seemed to try to see everything analytically, "structurally," strategically. This was, in fact, only one instance of a more general tension that I felt between my way of looking at the world and the way things were in South Africa. Everything here seemed to force one away from the specific, toward the general, away from the local, toward the national (even the international), away from the personal, toward the political. The pressure was relentless, and I was aware that I was not holding my ground especially well.

23

South African life, the spectacle of racial repression, was upsetting in a more or less straightforward way. This other, almost ontological discomfort was not so obvious, though it became more marked every week I was in Cape Town. The problem of racial terminology, which rendered the simplest remarks self-conscious and clumsy, typified the larger dilemma. It bedeviled me especially when I wrote letters, because it went against my notions about how to move and live in other people's countries. I realized I had developed, in the course of my travels, a certain passivity—or perhaps impassiveness is a better word. I tried to take the world on its own terms. I had become loath to pass judgment on, to project my values onto, almost any aspect of other cultures. This was partly an achieved humility, partly intellectual exhaustion and retreat, and partly simple expedience. How much pleasanter it is, after all, to roll with, rather than disapprove, all the odd customs and anachronisms one falls upon in faraway places. But living in South Africa undermined this easy exoticism. It might be colorful and "local" to toss off remarks about having spent the afternoon in a Coloured cinema or a Bantu township for the folks back home; it might seem unduly formal to be slapping quotation marks around every third phrase. But there was no way around it. No matter how awkward, obvious, and adolescent-sounding it made one's prose —the sense of using so many words only "under protest"—the alternative, using them *without* protest, was worse. Ungainliness seemed to come with the territory, along with that coarsening of perception that often surrounds highly politicized times and places. Nothing is simply what it is; everything stands for something else, some social or political or economic force or objective, some ideology. There was a corresponding vulgarization of social life, in which the consciousness of race, of people's assigned slots under apartheid dwarfed individuals—whites were *Whites,* blacks were *Blacks,* and all attempts just to forget about race for a while were foredoomed.

With language, everything had to be decoded. "Self-determination" was apartheidspeak for white domination. "Total strategy" was apartheidspeak for the maintenance of white domination. Language was often debased to the point of meaninglessness. Thus, the legislation that had closed previously "open" universities to black students was called the Extension of University Education Act. And the pass laws were contained in the Abolition of Passes Act. "War is Peace. Freedom is Slavery." Language was being used in South Africa as a type of totalitarian weapon. Resistance, vigilance, no matter how tedious, was obligatory.

Of course, all the vigilance in the world could not keep daily life from beginning to seem "normal." Nelson had said I was just not used to petty apartheid, and he was right. The longer I stayed in Cape Town, the less I noticed the WHITES ONLY signs. This was partly desensitization, and partly my growing understanding that the elimination of every WHITES ONLY sign in South Africa would not necessarily change anything. The issue was power, not park benches. I even started to think of petty apartheid as a tourist attraction. It appeared to titillate light-skinned foreign tourists, anyway, whom I often saw photographing a big WHITES ONLY sign on the beach at Muizenberg. The thrill was similar, I figured, to that provided by the torture chambers that are the perennial favorites on tours of old castles and prisons. Apartheid was good, old-fashioned, unapologetic evil. It was a form of social organization that tapped a certain nostalgia in many Americans and Europeans, conservatives and liberals alike.

But South Africa was not the stable, repressive place that tourists saw—that Rachel and I had seen on our car-camping tour. It was not "totalitarian" in the way that a country like the Soviet Union was. Besides the parliamentary opposition and the opposition press, there was the true opposition, the forces of black resistance, which were largely invisible to the untrained eye in March 1980, but were always there, regathering themselves. Despite the oft-noted similarities in their techniques of repression and official doublespeak, South Africa was less like the contemporary Soviet Union than it was like prerevolutionary Russia. The Soviet Union today was a relatively static society. Power was centralized and not up for grabs. South Africa was a different story. Everything here was politics, the evanescent vagaries of factions and programs, movements and alliances, and the great search among the powerless for a unifying ideology. Oppression was palpable. No detail was neutral. Local geology and ostrich farms and puberty rites among the Xhosa might be fascinating topics, but to write about them was a political act—an act of omission, a tacit acceptance of the apartheid status quo. Conventional travel writing about South Africa was out of the question. My way of traveling, of venturing through "the world," was itself insufficient.

24

As with other aspects of my initial idyll at Grassy Park High, my sentimental envy of my students' school experience soon faded. Inferior education was, after all, inferior education. Its effects could be amusing, as in the answers that came back on a geography quiz. The religion of most Swazis? "Swastika." The religion of most Botswanans? "Optimist." An African colony for freed American slaves? "Pretoria." The states that border Zimbabwe? "Paris," "France,"

"Rhodesia," "New Zealand," "Sweden." Eventually, though, the not-so-funny side of such ignorance had to be faced, and the frustrations of working inside the system that allowed it had to be felt.

The problem began everywhere. I found myself focusing on little things that no one else seemed to notice. Such as the unpredictable class schedule. There were no clocks in the classrooms, which meant that the siren kept catching me unawares—in the middle of a lesson, in the middle of a sentence. I bought a watch and learned the normal schedule, down to the minute, so as to be prepared. Yet I still kept getting blindsided by the siren, which seemed to go off at odd times more often than it did on schedule. It sounds minor, but the damage done was major, to my way of thinking. The great lesson aborted, the terrible dead time when a lesson was finished but the siren failed to wail—the cumulative effect was time and effort wasted, and a sloppy, apathetic attitude toward what went on in a classroom.

The traditions of apathy, of inferior work, ran deep. When I assigned essays to my English classes from the list of innocuous topics provided by the syllabus, I was invariably struck by the sameness of all the compositions produced. It was as if the writers, while not exactly copying each other's papers, were all working from the same Ur-essay. This occurred even when I gave them a free choice of topics. Dozens of papers would come in with the same title—"Falling in Love" or "A Night on the Mountain"—and the same basic story. These essays were all, I eventually realized, traditions in themselves. They were heirlooms—updated versions, very often, of essays once turned in by older brothers and sisters. There *were* Ur-essays. The only way to get more original writing, more "real work," was to assign quite specific, unlikely topics, and when I did so the fluency of my students' writing suffered noticeably.

It did not help that a number of my fellow teachers seemed to share the government's view of their pupils: as expendable, as predestined low achievers in the larger society. I saw this attitude in the way some teachers boasted that they never took work home with them. "For what I'm being paid here, do you think I'm going to give them more of my time? Not bloody likely," one told me. "You must give them something to keep them quiet during class, and get your marking finished then." I thought I saw it, too, in the way some teachers treated the students like servants, sending them off to the shops on errands, over to domestic science for a cup of tea, out to their car to fetch some item, without ever saying "please" or "thank you." Some teachers were said to carry their exploitation further, such as one fellow who was often accused behind his back of extorting sexual favors from his female students in return for passing marks. The school administration knew what he was up to, it was said, but the teacher in question had gathered enough damaging information about each of his superiors to destroy all of their careers, and thus kept his job through blackmail. I was never sure what to make of these stories, but I was certainly unimpressed with this teacher's commitment to his work. He planned to move to the United States as soon as possible, he told me, "to get away from this damn apartheid."

Such individuals were exceptions, to be sure, on the Grassy Park faculty, which had its share of dedicated professionals and, from what I could tell, truly gifted teachers. But the shortage of higher educational experience among my colleagues was serious. Only a handful had university degrees, and nearly all of those were from "Bush." While Meryl Cupido was the youngest, she was far from the least qualified teacher on the staff. There were others who had never finished high school. Pasqualine was said never to have *gone* to high school. And he was teaching vocational guidance to matrics. Many people, both students and faculty, openly complained that Pasqualine was "senile." Yet the shortage of teachers was so severe that he was never asked to retire. (Indeed, it was so severe that they had hired the likes of me off the street.)

A number of teachers were going to night school, or correspondence school, working slowly toward degrees that would increase their job qualifications—and, not incidentally, their salaries. At first, I was impressed to see them all studying their university textbooks during their free periods and lunch breaks. When I sat in on their discussions, though, I was quickly disenchanted. The courses sounded at least as exam-oriented as our syllabuses. There was virtually nothing else *to* them, and no material was ever discussed in my presence in terms of anything except how it might appear on an exam. Napoleon, as a veteran of the medieval history course that a couple of younger teachers were assaying, would hold forth enthusiastically about "my feudal monarchies" with no greater apparent interest in the meaning of the words he spoke than my students had when they pronounced most Swazis to be Swastikas. I found this depressing— that the same profound irrelevance seemed to cling to higher education as that which threatened to render everything we taught here in high school absurd. What was more, all the time and energy that went into this extracurricular study by teachers was probably being subtracted more or less directly from the time and energy they gave to their students at Grassy Park High.

To an outsider, especially one educated in well-funded institutions by well-trained, more or less conscientious professionals, these various chains of apathy, incompetence, and pernicious tradition were all painfully clear. Perhaps that was one of the only advantages to being an outsider. But none of this was unique to black South Africa, of course. The vicious circle of inferior education, academic retardation, and low expectations was also, I knew, a perfectly virulent reality among the poor in many, many schools in the United States. But that awareness changed nothing at Grassy Park High, and the clear view I had of the system's action upon my students was unnerving. We teachers were hired to prepare these children for lives of subservience, pure and simple. If we produced a few exceptions, that was wonderful. But the permanent psychological damage being inflicted every day by apartheid, the sheer waste and destruction of human potential in a society rich enough to do far better, would not be notably lessened.

25

To be a white teacher in a black school in South Africa, no degrees or certificates were required. It was essential, however, to own a quantity of native diplomacy. Alex Tate was obviously blessed in this regard. He was the best-educated member of the Grassy Park faculty, and was always being consulted on points of history, procedure, and administrative judgment (such as my hiring), and yet he wore his erudition lightly and kept a judiciously low profile in most school affairs. His classroom was decorated with pictures of his own favorite writers—D. H. Lawrence, Bessie Head, Wole Soyinka, and others whose books were certainly unknown to nearly everyone who ever entered the room—yet Tate somehow managed to avoid creating the stuffy, "aspirant" atmosphere that might easily have collected around him. He was very popular with his students, and when an intramural soccer tournament was held, one of his senior classes honored him by naming themselves "Tate United."

Mario Da Silva was not so blessed. For a start, he made no secret of his desire to move as soon as possible to a position at a white school. Da Silva had perfectly good reasons for wanting to make the change. There was the distance he had to drive each day to cross the line.

There was the fact that he could never fill more than a "temporary" post at a black school—this restriction was government policy, declaredly to hasten the apartheid goal of totally single-race schools, though also used to eliminate white teachers whose motives for teaching in black schools became politically suspicious: temporary staff could be dismissed on twenty-four hours' notice, with no explanation required. For a family man like Da Silva, this lack of job security was understandably irksome. Finally, to be a white teacher in a white school *did* require both a degree and a certificate, and Da Silva had earned both. The certificate, a B.A. (Ed.), was awarded only after the successful completion of a one-year postgraduate course. Da Silva took obvious pride in his education, and regularly opined that the dearth of jobs at Cape Town white schools would not last forever.

In Grassy Park, however, having passed the government's white teacher training course was not perceived as a badge of distinction. In fact, people said it only meant that a person had been successfully brainwashed by the government. The rigor of the program was not academic, it was believed, but ideological. The tenets of something called Christian National Education were drummed into candidates, whose enthusiasm for these ideas was then closely monitored by government officials. Only candidates whose enthusiasm was convincing, it was said, passed. I heard this précis of white teacher training from a number of different teachers at Grassy Park High. It provided, indeed, the first occasion for me to hear words like "racist" and "fascist" used by my colleagues.

Neither was Da Silva's cause in Grassy Park aided by the fact that he had served in the South African Army, and continued to serve several weeks a year as a reservist. Such duty was far from voluntary; yet it had a potent symbolic significance in black South Africa. (Soldiers on active duty were sometimes used as teachers in black schools, and soldier-teachers were required to file a form each week with the local authorities giving the names of any students who seemed to harbor politically subversive ideas. I heard about one soldier in Natal who was court-martialed for refusing to fill out the forms and served a year in military prison.)

These institutional associations constituted two strikes against Da Silva at Grassy Park High. His personal manner—which was an odd combination of nervous scurrying and an almost magnificent arrogance—and his tactlessness in advertising his desire to teach racially privileged children rather than those in his classes at Grassy Park earned him his third strike. He was widely hated and had constant problems with his classes. Though less violent than many of our colleagues, he was very strict, and given to pouting when his pupils misbehaved. These classroom conflicts would occasionally escalate, until Da Silva would find his car's windows smashed or his briefcase stolen, and the principal would be compelled to intervene. These troubles only contributed to Da Silva's desire to get a job elsewhere as soon as possible.

My fellow newcomer, Elizabeth Channing-Brown, began having her troubles, too, within a few weeks after we started teaching. While she apparently had little success in controlling or inspiring her classes, neither did she seem to antagonize her students, so it was not that the "riots" she feared came to pass. It was the other teachers who gave her a hard time. Channing-Brown was given to tardiness, absence, ill health, and chronic disorganization, and those of our colleagues who disapproved of her job performance did not long hide their feelings on the matter. She was lectured and snubbed, and even had parts of her paychecks docked.

I felt sorry for her. From our few getting-acquainted conversations, I had learned that she had some terrible problems outside school. Her boyfriend had been paralyzed by a motorcycle accident. Her home life seemed to be an unending series of rip-offs, disasters, and evictions. One night while hitchhiking she was raped, and a number of her absences from school were occasioned by the necessary court appearances. True to her luck, the trial of the alleged attacker, whom Channing-Brown swore was the guilty man, ended in acquittal. Finally, a heavy drug habit seemed to be taking its toll on her health. I was shocked to learn that Liz was only twenty-one years old, because the lines around her mouth, the expression in her big sunken eyes, made her look at least ten years older.

One thing that could be said in Channing-Brown's favor was that she was not a racist. She took an almost ostentatious pride in the fact that many of her friends were black. Unfortunately, a number of those friends were also hoods. She seemed to be always recounting adventures in which her "friends" were featured stealing her roommate's stereo or burglarizing a neighbor's flat. Channing-Brown's speech itself reflected her familiarity with certain "elements," as the principal would have called them, on the Cape Flats. She was a graduate of an exclusive private girls' school in Pietermaritzburg, Natal, but her upper-class English was weirdly seasoned with crude drug slang and *skollie taal* Afrikaans. Her dramatic training (at the University of Cape Town) only heightened the incongruities when she opened her mouth.

Still, the vehemence of people's dislike for Liz Channing-Brown puzzled me, until one of our colleagues explained it. "You see, Bill, we've seen her sort before. Not so much just lately, but quite a lot through the years. These white varsity dropouts, they don't know what to do with themselves, so they go teach in a 'colored' school. They're not trained. They're not professional. They quit in the middle of term. They don't care about the children. They only come here for the hardship pay."

This "hardship pay," or "inconvenience pay," was something the government had awarded to whites teaching in black schools in previous years, ostensibly to compensate for the "hardship" of having to use the same toilets as everyone else. It had been discontinued in the drive toward single-race schools, but not everyone knew that, and it remained a focus of the local mistrust of the motives of whites who crossed the line to teach.

I was exempt from a good proportion of that mistrust because I was American. Tate was, too, because he was British (Kenya born, actually, and educated in South Africa, but a British subject and thus exempt from the South African military draft). But the more time I spent in Grassy Park, the harder it became to imagine how a typical, government-supporting Afrikaner could have functioned there as a teacher. Channing-Brown was seen as a *joller,* a disreputable dropout, privileged but not representative. Even Da Silva was spared the full onus of ethnic oppressorship, for he was seen as Portuguese, a much-resented group itself, but nothing compared to *die boere.* None of us could really serve as an example of the true Afrikaner apartheid mentality. Anyone who could have done so, it eventually seemed to me, would have been in an impossible position. We were "whites," yet we were given the benefit of the doubt in Grassy Park, given the opportunity to prove that we were not the enemy—which, considering the suspicions built into the situation, was rather amazing. The diplomacy, clearly, cut both ways.

26

Clive and I had the catalogs, brochures, and prospectuses from nearly every university in South Africa spread out on the round table on the balcony at our place in Muizenberg. It was a solemnly beautiful afternoon outside, with a light north wind brushing dark blue strokes across the pale surface of False Bay. We were drinking beer and finding the catalogs amusing, in a strange sort of way. Those for the

Afrikaans universities were full of pictures that looked as if they were taken somewhere in northern Europe in the late 1950s—groups of strapping, clean-cut white students strolling in the mountains or laughing it up at a "coffee and rusks party" in a dormitory room. There wasn't a black face anywhere.

"Look at *this,*" Clive said. It was the prospectus for the University of Pretoria. He was pointing to a photograph showing a group of students dragging a covered wagon across a sports ground—"the symbolic transfer of student authority, the Voortrekker Oxwagon," read the caption. "You know it's a true Boer religious ritual when they drag in the Great Trek," Clive said.

I laughed, but not hard. This was strange amusement because what we were really doing here was pronouncing some fond hopes, at least of mine, dead.

Clive tossed aside the catalog for the Rand Afrikaans University. *"Ag,* none of these 'white' unis have these facilities for black students. Why don't they just say so? There isn't one integrated university residence in South Africa, you know."

I did know. I had been looking further into the possibilities for Grassy Park High students to gain admission to various universities around the country, and my initial optimism, based on the increasing availability of "permits," had been hosed down thoroughly by what I had found. The University of Pretoria, for example, had turned out to have 16,584 students. Every last one of them was white. And the enrollment figures for the other Afrikaans universities were not much more edifying. The complete absence of black faces in their catalogs was not simply insensitivity, as I had assumed at first; it was reality. Permits were available everywhere, theoretically, but they were obviously not being issued everywhere. Georgina Swart's crack about my trying to create a South African James Meredith by encouraging our matrics to apply to any university in the country had obviously been on the money. And the more I thought about what it would be like for any of our students if they were actually to gain admission, a permit and, from somewhere, the necessary funds to attend one of these Afrikaans universities—the loneliness, the hostility, the housing and transport problems, the *danger*—the less inclined I felt to encourage them to apply. In fact, I was sorry that I had ever persuaded my students to send away to some of these schools in the first place—only so that they could feel the sting of exclusion.

Clive seemed to sense my distress. "But it's interesting," he said, and shrugged. "It's funny to see what *die boere* do at varsity. Nobody at Grassy Park would ever go to Potchefstroom, anyway. Nor to one of these bush colleges."

That had been another unpleasant surprise. I hadn't even realized, when we sent away for their literature, that some of these schools—the University of the North, the University of Zululand, Fort Hare University—were "ethnic" colleges. But it seemed they were all located far out in the bantustans (hence the origin of the term "bush") and that each one was designated for the exclusive use of Zulus, or Vendas, or Ciskeians.

"These places are the weirdest-looking of all," I said.

"They're like detention camps," Clive said. "The students have to get permission to invite anybody into one of them. They don't have SRCs. They're not allowed to discuss anything in their classes."

The students in the pictures all looked like they had been cast by the government for roles as grateful, God-fearing natives.

"The professors are all Boers who couldn't get jobs in the 'white' unis," Clive said. "They're meant to be real *verkramptes.*"

I sighed. "I suppose we should just forget all these schools."

"And Durban-Westville as well," Clive said. The University of Durban-Westville was for Indians. Its catalog made it look like it was in India: young men in Nehru caps, young women in saris, Hindu shrines in the background. Clive said, "They couldn't get them on the boats back to the old country, so they sent them to Durban-Westville." He pushed another prospectus toward me.

"Let's face it," he said. "UNISA is the answer." The University of South Africa was a correspondence college, based in Pretoria. Clive tapped their brochure. "This is the only way the whites can handle non-racial education—through the post. It's the perfect university for South Africa. Nobody has to see anybody else."

Actually, all that was left, in the way of universities, were the four English-language "white" universities. These were obviously the only places for which black students were receiving all the permits that the careers information service had told me about.

"These are clearly the only real universities in the country," I said to Clive. "At least the students in the pictures *look* like students."

Clive said sourly, "They've even got a few token blacks in the photos."

"And it's time they had a lot more on their rolls!"

I had already admitted it to myself—that I would have to narrow the focus of my enthusiasm down to the possibilities for getting Grassy Park graduates into the "English" universities, particularly the University of Cape Town, to which they could commute. It was true that none of these schools had a student population even 10 percent black, but their administrations had at least declared themselves in favor of "open" admissions, and some, such as Witwatersrand University in Johannesburg, were offering "bridging programmes" for "students who, while qualified to gain admission to the University, find themselves at a disadvantage due to shortcomings in their educational preparation."

"That means the victims of Bantu Education," Clive said. "The victims who survived."

"That's right."

"But these English unis, they're no good, either, you know."

"Why not?"

"Because they're completely . . . 'white,' really. They're part of the system."

"Sure they are. But they offer a better education than UWC does."

Clive sighed and shook his head. "Whatever that means," he said.

I walked Clive down to the train station. We arrived on the station platform and sat on a bench in silence for a while. The sun had dropped behind the *berg*, leaving the station and the shoreline in warm, blue shadow. A train entered the station, headed in the wrong direction for Clive. When it came to a stop, its engineer sat immediately opposite the bench we occupied.

"I used to work on the railroad in the States," I said.

"You're joking."

"I was a brakeman. I loved it."

"I can't believe it."

"Why not? It was great work. All up and down the country. Good pay. That was how I paid for graduate school."

"What about the people you had to work with?"

"They were fine, most of them. In fact, some of them were wonderful."

"Then they must be very different from the railway workers in this country. Here, they're the thickest people around. You can't even talk to them. They're the so-called poor whites. They wouldn't have jobs at all if it weren't for job reservation."

The engineer opposite us glanced our way. I gave him a wave. He did not respond. Clive laughed.

"See what I mean? He's just staring at you because you're sitting with me."

The engineer looked away, and he pulled the train out of the station without looking in our direction again. Clive's laughter was raucous. "Did you see what a rock that guy was? Do you see what I mean? Railway workers are the worst. They and the white miners. And their fucking trade unions."

"Don't tell me you're down on *unions.*"

"The white trade unions in this country? They're the most reactionary racist group there is. Haven't you heard of Arrie Paulus?"

"Who?"

Clive stood up. His train was coming. He shook his head. "He's the head of the Mine Workers Union. He says all blacks are baboons. You should start reading up on these things."

Clive started hurrying down the platform toward a knot of black people. That was where the "Non-White" cars tended to stop. I followed him. We shook hands at the door of a crowded, third-class carriage. Clive gave me a funny grin, then pushed his way into the car. As the door shut and the train started, he called out something to me in Afrikaans, which I couldn't understand but which made the people around him, all of whom were staring at me, laugh slyly.

27

My research into university admissions had revealed much about the educational system that employed me, the system Clive called "Bantu Education." The great disparity between the funding of black schools and white schools, the tremendous dropout rate in black schools, the chronic shortages of textbooks, classrooms, and qualified teachers— the numbers alone told the story. But apartheid in education was both grand, in the sense of broadly devastating, and petty: white schools even got free wastebaskets and an unlimited supply of toilet paper, while financially strapped "colored" schools were obliged to pay five rands for every wastebasket and were allotted only one roll of toilet paper per student per year (creating hardships of which I had personal experience).

The numbers reflected present conditions; black education also had a history that bears mentioning. Black schools and white schools in South Africa have always been separate and unequal. The white attitude toward black education was once described as "too humane to prohibit it, too human to encourage it." The early Cape colonists recognized the danger that allowing slaves access to education might inspire inconvenient aspirations, and accordingly restricted such access. The 1905 School Board Act made racial segregation in education *de jure,* and in 1910 the ratio of government expenditures on white to African schools, per capita of population, was reported to be 333 to 1. "Mission schools," funded by overseas churches, were responsible for virtually all black education. That changed, along with so much else, after the National Party came to power in 1948.

The Afrikaner Nationalists knew well the political importance of educational administration. In the nineteenth century, the British colonial authorities had made English the sole medium of instruction in South African schools, forcing Afrikaners who were determined to resist the empire's campaign of anglicization to start up schools of their own. These schools were seriously inferior to those the English could afford to support. The large-scale immigration of British teachers, especially after the Anglo-Boer War, increased the pressure toward extinction of the Afrikaners' language and culture. Thus, when the Afrikaners gained power, they immediately instituted a new educational system, one that emphasized *their* language and *their* culture—this was the program known as Christian National Education. Besides rewriting the history textbooks to emphasize the achievements of the Boers and revising the syllabus to include instruction in apartheid, the new system segregated English and Afrikaans "white" schools. The traditionally English schools bitterly protested Christian National Education, but the Nationalist government in Pretoria eventually swept all before it.

On black education, the Institute for Christian National Education had made the National Party's position terribly clear in a manifesto issued only months before its accession to power.

> Native education should be based on the principles of trusteeship, non-equality and segregation; its aim should be to inculcate the white man's view of life, especially that of the Boer nation, which is the senior trustee.

The Bantu Education Act, passed in 1953, took away responsibility for African education from the churches and the provincial governments, and relocated it where "the senior trustee" could better control matters—under the national government. Three separate education departments were eventually established: one each for "coloreds," Indians, and Africans. The previous education system had done the black man a disservice, according to then Minister of Native

Affairs (later Prime Minister) Hendrik F. Verwoerd, when it "misled him by showing him the green pastures of European society in which he was not allowed to graze." While he often invoked this preposterous idea—that the Nationalist shepherds were merely concerned that their black flocks not be led astray—Verwoerd did not dissemble about the new program itself. As he explained it to Parliament in 1953, "The natives will be taught from childhood to realize that equality is not for them . . . The Bantu must be guided to serve his own community. There is no place for him in the European community above certain forms of labour."

Under this sort of "trusteeship," the quality of black education plummeted. While the black population grew rapidly, African high schools and vocational colleges in the cities were actually closed down, as the government sought to use the lure of education to implement its bantustan scheme. By 1980, 75 percent of all high schools for Africans were located in the bantustans. Another feature of the drive to "retribalize" Africans was the introduction of compulsory "mother tongue instruction" for the first eight years of schooling, a policy that deeply damaged black education. Not only were the African languages used unsuitable for teaching certain subjects, but eight years of instruction in Xhosa could in no way prepare pupils for high schools in which they would suddenly have to begin studying in English or Afrikaans, any more than it could prepare them for life in South Africa in any but the most menial capacities. (Mother tongue instruction was not an issue in Grassy Park, nor was education used there to steer people toward a "homeland." People did say, though, that the quality of "colored" schooling had also deteriorated since the takeover of education from the churches by the government.)

Bantu Education was applied to universities in 1959 with the misnamed Extension of University Education Act, which closed the English-speaking "open universities" to blacks, while establishing "tribal colleges" for Zulus, Xhosas, Sothos, "coloreds," and Indians. The black, church-run University of Fort Hare at Alice, which had produced a generation of southern African leaders, including Nelson Mandela, Robert Mugabe, and ANC President Oliver Tambo, was taken over by the central government, and went into a rapid decline. According to Professor Ezekiel Mphahlele of Witwatersrand University, Bantu Education has achieved many of its anti-educational objectives. As Mphahlele told an interviewer, "We've lost a whole generation since about 1960, when it really began to take effect. All that generation of people can hardly articulate themselves. They can't hold conversations for long. They can't initiate things. Their dependence on white people is remarkably high."

At the same time, Bantu Education generated so much resentment that it became a mobilizing issue in itself. The 1976 uprising was sparked by student protests against a government attempt to impose Afrikaans as a medium of instruction in Soweto high schools. In its wake, government policy made some adjustments. The Afrikaans requirement was quietly dropped, and the Department of Bantu Education was renamed the Department of Manpower and Training. The economic pressure created by the shortage of skilled manpower—and by violent protest, which both hampered production and frightened off foreign investment—made some liberalization of the black educational system begin to seem desirable to some government policymakers and, in certain forums, the rhetoric of reform began to replace the Verwoerdian rhetoric of "trusteeship." In other forums—notably, before the white electorate—the old rhetoric was retained, as voters were assured that none of the funds traditionally used for white education would be diverted to black education. In fact, nothing substantial was changed. In 1980, the disparity between government spending on black and white education was actually greater, both proportionally and absolutely, than it had been twenty-five years before.

Two weeks after I started teaching at Grassy Park High, I read in the paper a typical example of the ambivalent rhetoric then in use on the subject by government officials, when Punt Janson, the Minister of National Education, told the Parliament: "We want to give White education the very best, and then we want to give the other peoples the best possible in the shortest possible time." Janson went on to elaborate this Panglossian position. According to the newspaper's summary of his remarks, "It was the task of the white man to speed up the closing of the gap in the level of civilization between white and black in South Africa. . . . Whites had to ensure that they maintained their advantage in education in the interim period as the task of educating and training the other groups would be their responsibility . . . it was wishful thinking to expect this gap to be closed within ten or fifteen years."

28

Rachel and I went on a moviegoing binge. We took what black friends later called "your cowboy approach" to movie house apartheid and went to whichever films we wanted to see. Though we never saw anyone else try to cross this aspect of the line, in either direction, no theater refused to sell us a ticket. It wasn't a bad way to get to know the city. We saw films in wretched Cape Flats townships, in snooty English suburbs, in spooky working-class Afrikaner neighborhoods (row after row of little white houses with plaster gnomes in the little yards; stolid, ill-dressed audiences with seemingly massive appetites for cinematic schmaltz), and in a couple of great gaudy old-time picture palaces in the once-"mixed" districts. Nearly all the movies were Hollywood product—some had been made for American television, but most were the usual studio features—and the distribution pattern gave us a chance to catch up on films we had missed while living in Asia. The "white" cinemas showed films that had seen their first U.S. release a few months before, while black cinemas, which got the same films a few weeks later, if they got them at all, also played a hodge-podge of odd and older films that had somehow stayed in circulation. We saw *Tom Horn, Cleopatra Jones, Blind Fist of Bruce, Apocalypse Now.*

Sometimes we saw my students—one warm, dusty Saturday afternoon at the Princess Cinema, for instance. The Princess Cinema was a hulking old brown barn of a place in the heart of black Retreat. (Retreat was one of those schizoid suburbs that straddled the line. White Retreat was little more than a vast shopping mall, but black Retreat, on the other side of the railway and across some empty fields, was a big sprawling township, with a ramshackle, old-style main road full of greengrocers, fish peddlers, bottle shops, and barbershops.) Saturday matinee tickets at the Princess were thirty-five cents. That particular day, we got there late, when the steeply rising tiers and balconies were already jammed with kids. We sat down in front, where the floors were sticky, the seats were broken, and the stench of urine, dagga, and spilled beer was intense. It was a rowdy crowd. After a boy had crashed into me twice, I escorted him by the collar out of our row and announced to our immediate neighbors that nobody else would be permitted past our knees. (That was not, I reflected, the sort of thing I would have tried in a black ghetto back home, but it went down all right at the Princess.) The film that afternoon was *National Lampoon's Animal House,* which vaulted us into a faraway world—early-sixties college fraternity life, a revised version of—from which we were untimely yanked when the picture ended some minutes before it should have, and the house lights went up.

Nobody else seemed to notice or care that we had not seen the whole movie. But Rachel and I bounded straight up to the projectionist's booth, barged in, and demanded of the startled little man working there that he show the rest of the film.

"That's it!" he told us. "There's no more. Look!" He showed us the film on the reel. "That's how they send it to me, hey. They don't care."

The projectionist offered us cups of tea in consolation, and we sat and chatted with him while he prepared the next session's reels. He was a middle-aged man in a knitted Muslim skullcap, and we soon discovered that I taught one of his daughters at Grassy Park High.

"Just tell me one thing, man! Will she pass?"

I predicted she would, from what I had seen of her work. We wondered if his children got free admission to the movies.

"You must be joking," said the projectionist. "I wouldn't let my kids come into this place. Don't you see the things these *skollies* get up to down there? They smoke dagga right in the cinema! You people must have courage to go in there, especially for the Saturday matinee!"

The windows in the projectionist's booth looked out on the Retreat main road. As we sipped our tea, I watched the people down on the street. In the crowd of kids outside the cinema, laughing, stretching, blinking in the sun, I recognized several of my students. There was Amy, from 6A8, and Terence, the quick, handsome Young Werther from 6A7, wearing a leather jacket. The children looked different from the way they did in their school uniforms, especially the girls, who now wore skintight pants, platform shoes, and heavy makeup. The projectionist's views notwithstanding, we hadn't found the atmosphere inside the theater the least bit threatening. Still, it was worthwhile to be reminded that my students, when out of school, often mixed with kids whose lives and futures were nowhere near as promising as their own. At the sprawling pub and disco next door, I saw there was a sign announcing, in alarmist lettering, that two local bands, Bloodshed and Revolution, would be providing the evening's entertainment.

The "cowboy approach" to petty apartheid had obvious limitations. As I had realized in the Grassy Park pub, it could work only one way, and for that reason could easily be taken as an insult by blacks whose separate, unequal facilities were lightly being entered by scoff-law whites like us. But it was a constant conundrum. You didn't have to seek it out. Say you're a light-skinned person standing on a suburban train platform in South Africa. A train pulls up. The car that stops in front of you has plenty of seats, but a sign on it says NON-WHITES ONLY. Do you run down the platform like a good apartheid citizen and jump into a WHITES ONLY car? Or do you reject this vicious nonsense and show your rejection by boarding the car that's in front of you, thereby flaunting your privilege before all the black people on the train, and risking being thrown off up the line by the conductor as well? Furthermore, once you get to know your local train station, do you go wait in that part of the platform where you know from experience the WHITES ONLY cars customarily stop, thus softening the car-that's-in-front-of-you quandary, or not? All South Africans face choices like these every day, and for them the options virtually always come in the more "experienced" form: they all know the layout of the station platform, as it were, all too well. But "face" is probably the wrong word—"avoid" is more like it—and for the foreigner, such evasions come less naturally. So you squirm, and twist, and try to act as if apartheid does not apply to you; you try to make your separate peace by going to any movie you please.

But it all got much trickier when it involved other people.

Shaun, Nico, and Wayne had professed themselves interested in surfing. So I invited them over to our place one Saturday morning, and we went down to the beach. They wanted to proceed to Strandfontein, the "colored" beach beyond the river mouth. But the best waves were breaking at the "white" beach. I told them not to worry about it, that I thought it would be all right.

They conceded that at Muizenberg beach apartheid was normally enforced nowadays only during the holidays—"when *die Transvalers* come down to *die Kaap,* and they want their beaches all lily-white," Shaun said, putting on a heavy Afrikaans accent and getting a nervous laugh. Like many Capetonians, Shaun, Nico, and Wayne were terrific chauvinists about their city, convinced that it was the only civilized place in a barbaric land, that if Cape Town were only left alone by Pretoria, it could turn itself into a non-racial utopia in short order. *"Ja,"* Wayne said. *"Die boere* wants to be able to get a good tan without being reclassified."

It was overcast and windy, not beachgoing weather. We went to the "white" beach. We hurried across the sand and into the water and, as I had predicted, we had no problem. We splashed around in the surf for an hour or so. The boys were nimble and fearless and were soon tottering toward shore, arms windmilling. They screamed with laughter at one another's efforts. There were few other surfers in the water. One boy about the same age as my students shouted a few obscenities at us from a distance. But it began to rain, and by the time we came in the beach was deserted.

29

Replacing the apartheid propaganda in the syllabus with material presumably more useful was only one part of my deviation from the pedagogical norm at Grassy Park High. I was also trying to change my pupils' study habits, their approach to information and authority, even their ideas about themselves and their own potential. These ambitions, too, began to draw fire from some of my colleagues, who made pointed remarks within my hearing about "American-style education." Trevor Pieterse surprised me with a comment passed lightly, but clearly in his capacity as chairman of the English Department. He said, "You know, I can see from the number of composition books you take home each night that you're a hard worker, Bill, but I hope you won't start giving great heaps of homework to your pupils, because you should realize that many of them live in places, terrible little pondoks, with ten or twelve people in them, where they can't possibly do it."

I did realize this. At least some of my students had already told me the same thing: that they lived in crowded, ill-lit places, which was why they hadn't done their homework. But the real question for me was less the conduciveness to schoolwork of each student's home situation than how much I should allow that consideration to determine my academic expectations. The assumption that poor children (black children) could not be expected to work as hard in school as better-off children (white children) was an extremely insidious one, I thought, and one that too many teachers used simply to save themselves work.

I made no special effort to find out where or how my students lived, but over time various errands took me to many of their homes. Koos, I discovered, lived with at least eight other people in a tiny, tin-walled shack in the back blocks near Rondevlei. Terence lived in a low-roofed old row cottage half smothered by bougainvillea, with a front room the size of a closet. Hester lived in a cinder-block house surrounded by a forest of rusting cars and trucks—her father was a mechanic who worked from a pit dug in their backyard. Elroy lived with two older sisters and an ancient grandmother in a cavelike house near Busy Corner. The walls inside Elroy's house were painted a shiny blue and yellow and were so heavily spackled that they seemed to bulge and recess like the walls of the catacombs. Mieta lived in a brand-new Spanish-style house ("Mieta") and had her own room. Shireen lived in "the estates" in Lotus River. Marius Le Roux lived in Cafda.

I went to see Marius after he missed a week of school with the flu. It was the first time I had been to Cafda. There were barefoot children shooting each other with imaginary six-guns in the dirt road outside the tiny brick cottage. When I climbed from my car, the children stopped playing and stared. A group of men in undershirts played checkers on a nearby tree stump, and a tape deck near the checkers game played Sister Sledge's "We Are Family." Riding past on the back gate of a coal truck were two men wearing burlap sacks like headdresses and shouting their prices to the housewives who stood in doorways or backyard gardens. Cafda had a sleepy, earthy feeling that reminded me of villages in Asia and the South Pacific. Everywhere one looked, there were people: weeding, cooking, visiting, sponge-bathing at a tap, emerging from a privy, smoking in the sun.

I knocked on the Le Rouxs' door. A tiny face appeared in a window. I smiled, but the face darted away and a hubbub of shouts, bangs, and scurrying started up behind the door. Finally, the door opened. An older woman with thick glasses, wearing a heavy housecoat, confronted me. She had a mustache and a suspicious expression, and her gray-black hair was pulled back into a tight ponytail.

"Ja, meneer?"

I explained who I was and why I had come. The woman seemed to relax. Behind her, the cottage was dark, but I could make out Marius's bicycle, which he rode to school, hanging from the ceiling above an iron bedstead. The odor of years of kerosene cooking wafted out through the doorway. At my first mention of Marius's name, several children had run hissing into the cottage's second room. Now Marius appeared, looking waxen and frightened, wearing a coat over pajamas.

I asked how he was, and Marius stammered that he would be back in class the next week. I gave him some homework I had brought. Behind Marius, the woman who had answered the door was shooing children away. One ran out the back door. The woman began dusting off the bedstead. Clutching the folder I had given him, Marius came outside and shut the door behind him. "Sir," Marius said, "my auntie wants to give you tea, but her cooker is not working. Can sir wait a bit? She has sent to the neighbors."

I made Marius call his aunt and I thanked her. But, I said, I had to be going. She studied me closely for a second, then nodded. We sent Marius back to bed. Before I left, his aunt asked me how Marius was doing in school and I told her he was doing fine. "He must pass," she said. "All he cares for now is the rugby, but he must pass his Standard Eight. Then he can live better than this." But her gesture, indicating the neighborhood around us, conveyed no shame or disgust. Marius's aunt was a woman of formidable dignity, and I now wished I had accepted her offer of tea. But after I'd glimpsed the lack of furniture inside her house, the cramped and lightless space, the newsprint wallpaper, I had not wanted to embarrass her by going in. We shook hands and I left.

Marius always did his homework. So did Shireen, although she complained. The building Shireen lived in was a hideous six-story, pink-and-gray cement block of flats standing in an open field. I went by there one Friday afternoon after finding in my classroom something I guessed belonged to Shireen: a booklet of vouchers for a "fun fair" being held that weekend in Athlone. My Standard Six students had been so excited about this fun fair it seemed worth it to try to deliver the vouchers. Graffiti proclaimed Shireen's building to be in the territory of the Born Free Kids. The stairwell stank of urine. I found Shireen's door on the fourth floor. She answered it herself, and her eyes opened wide when she saw me. "Sir! How could you find me here?" Yes, the vouchers were hers. She was very glad to see them— and glad to see me, too, it seemed, once she got over her shock.

Shireen invited me in and introduced me to her family: brothers and sisters, her mother, a brother-in-law who drove trucks cross-country for a living. It was a tidy, crowded little apartment, made dim by heavy drapes. On the walls were Pre-Raphaelite prints, a sampler stitched with "Home Sweet Home," and some old family photographs tinted so that even the men seemed to be wearing lipstick. There were elaborate brass candlesticks on the table, and brass fire irons, although there was no fireplace. In the next room, a radio announced what had been said that day in Parliament. I drank a beer with Shireen's brother-in-law. Shireen showed me her pet rabbit which she kept in a cage by her bed. Shireen seemed to share her bedroom with at least three other people. I asked her where she did her homework, and she indicated the table in the front room, the only table in the apartment. "I am sometimes there all night," she mugged. "While everyone in here is sleeping, I must listen to the people fighting outside when the men come home from drinking. I have so much homework for English, I may have to stay home from the fun fair!"

In general, I thought my students could do their homework. Few if any of them were reduced to studying under streetlights, as the children in the poorest townships were. In some cases—Oscar's, for instance—I tried to be flexible. Yet I continued to expect more work, particularly more writing, from most of them than they had been used to doing.

Still, Pieterse's caveat worried me.

Other aspects of my little reform program were also starting to give me pause. I found myself, for instance, in the interests of improving my students' English, having to reject at every turn the pithy, charming pidgin that they were used to having accepted as English (*colored* English). I also found myself, while trying to encourage academic ambitions, seeming to reject the life of manual labor that the government so clearly expected most of them to accept, and which most of their parents and older relatives led. Stigmatizing these things was hardly my intention, but the possibility of such unwanted results flowing from my efforts to raise the sights of my students helped raise, in turn, the larger question: What kind of people was I trying to turn these kids into, anyway?

In moments of faith, my answer to this question leaned heavily on adjectives like "critical," "articulate," "informed." At other times, I knew "middle-class achievers" to be equally true. In pursuit of that teacher's grail, student motivation, I found myself falling back increasingly on my own schooling for models. I tried to foster academic competition, both explicitly, with class rankings, and implicitly, with regular praise for the neat, bright, bookish kids like Mieta and Wayan and obvious disapproval of the devil-may-care like Charmaine. These are the age-old strategies and preferences of teachers everywhere, of course, but I worried that my "whiteness" gave them an edge, an undertone, they would not have in the classes of a local teacher—as if I were rewarding the children who could act "whitest." And I underlined the alienness of my expectations with my careful record-keeping and inflexible penalties for late papers. This helped to "spread out" and identify my students by performance, making it very clear who was doing well and who was not—as opposed to the prescribed system, which let everyone go through the year relatively unevaluated and then be decisively passed or failed by the final examination, long after classes were over.

It was ironic that what my colleagues considered overly permissive, personalized, "American-style" teaching would have seemed anything but progressive in the United States. I did allow a level of free-form activity in the classroom that, by Grassy Park High standards, bordered on anarchy. I was willing to experiment with assignments and teaching arrangements. I was even willing to solicit alternative suggestions from my students. But the emphasis I placed on performance, on production, on turning in all work on time, was nothing less than reactionary. I knew that; it was my reaction to the system as I found it. What I didn't know was whether this was the right reaction, or whether it was actually no better than clinging to the syllabus, for the way it avoided any real surrender to the children's instincts. I was intent upon developing a conventional type of academic discipline and "maturity"—but toward what end?

There was, I decided, an essential contradiction in my goals. I, like any teacher, wanted hardworking, attentive, disciplined students. On the other hand, I wanted to encourage a critical, independent habit of mind among my students toward all received ideas. This contradiction is probably inherent in the concept of a liberal education, but in New Room 16 it began to seem preternaturally sharp. What my students really needed, I was eventually convinced, in the way of preparation for life in South Africa, was nothing less than a *radical* skepticism, a rigorous, across-the-board, *combative* approach to all forms of vested authority, particularly "white" authority. And here I was, a white authority figure. Yet I could hardly give them high marks for defying me. At one level, I believed in my lessons and assignments. At another, I could see the value of my students' rejecting them—and me. I was not enamored of the harsh, dictatorial "authority" that many of my colleagues seemed preoccupied with maintaining in their classrooms. It lent itself to a stagnant, unhealthy kind of education, where the students were expected to serve as passive receptacles, being filled with undifferentiated, largely irrelevant knowledge. This passivity, I believed, could only encourage a more general disposition to accept the world as it was—surely a disastrous attitude in the circumstances of black South Africa. At the same time, a quiet, orderly classroom was a serious form of bliss.

My confusion often led me onto doubtful ground with my students. I would find myself trying to untangle two deskmates too absorbed in each other to pay attention to a lesson. "Jasmine! Zainul! What is this, parts of speech or parts of the body?" What, I might well have asked myself, was *I* doing? I still admired my students' capacity for a kind of lovers' delight in one another, complete with doting silliness while without romantic or sexual focus; yet I began to consider banishing all cuddling from the classroom, as inappropriate to an academic atmosphere. It wasn't that I was getting stiff-necked or discipline fixated à la Da Silva. A few of the implications of my ambitions for my students were simply starting to make themselves felt. The paradox was that I should be trying to transform my students into exotic versions of my old college-bound schoolmates, when I liked them so much the way they were.

Of course, there were always little incidents to remind me that there was really no danger of my effecting such a transformation of the great majority of my students. One Monday, for instance, three girls in 7E2 showed up for class missing all their upper front teeth. It seemed that one of them had gone to the dentist to have a tooth extracted, and had then and there decided to have *die vier voorste*—the front four—all removed. Her friends had simply decided to keep her company. It was fashionable, they said, to have *die vier voorste* out. "It makes kissing sexier," one girl giggled. I was horrified. Yet I was the only one in the classroom who was shocked. Everyone else was amused, even admiring. "The whites think it looks *skollie, sir*," somebody explained, laughing. "But we think it looks *lekker.*"

This collision of middle-class attitudes with ghetto values and style could have been happening just as easily in an American inner-city school. Likewise the problems associated with teaching standard English to ghetto children, and the contradictions contained in "upward mobility" generally. Cape Flats reality sometimes intruded upon the grounds of Grassy Park High in forms that were familiar to an American, too. There was, for instance, the time I ran afoul of the Vlei Monsters. They were a young Grassy Park street gang, given to shaved heads ("eggshells") and earrings. The Vlei Monsters were said to be pushovers compared to the big, well-organized gangs: the Weekend Spoilers, the Hardlivings, the Genuine Schoolboys, the Panorama Kids. Still, it was generally agreed that I had made a very foolish move when, in my second month of teaching, I chased a bunch of Vlei Monsters off the landing outside my classroom. Afterward, I was told that, as a result of this rash act, my life was no longer worth "a tin continental." But I actually found it more agreeable to be fretting about the Vlei Monsters than about what deleterious effect my teaching might be having on my students.

30

There were shantytowns everywhere on the Cape Flats. Most of them were hidden away in the dunes—illegal, lawless, shadowy places. I picked up a hitchhiker one afternoon while heading south out of Grassy Park. He was a middle-aged man wearing old denim overalls, and he said he was going to Vrygrond. Vrygrond was one of the shantytowns between Grassy Park and Muizenberg. I asked my rider how long he had lived at Vrygrond. He looked unhappy about having to speak to me, but he replied, "Couple of years now, *meneer.*"

I asked how long he had been in Cape Town.

"All my life, *meneer,*" he said.

I was surprised. I had assumed that the squatters were all recent arrivals from the rural areas. I asked where he had lived before Vrygrond.

"Manenberg."

Manenberg was one of the older townships on the Flats. Why had he left there?

My rider looked more reluctant than ever to answer. Finally, he spoke. "We was in a council flat there. They got rules about who may stay in the flat, you know. My wife's parents came to stay, because they had no other place. But when the inspector finds out they was there, he put us out. We couldn't find no other place, so now we's at this Vrygrond."

"How is it, living there?"

"If you must know, *meneer,* it's no good. Especially in the winter-time, when it rains, and the wind tears the roofs off the houses. We got no running water, no electricity, no protection from the *skollies.* It's an unhealthy place, so we sent our children to live with my sister. But we got no other place for ourselves. I must travel to Bellville each day for my job, and it's bloody far. Excuse me, *meneer.*"

I wondered if many people at Vrygrond had jobs.

"Most have jobs, yes. Most people there is like us. They're Capeys themselves. They just can't find a place to live. There's some squatter camps where the people is all from Transkei and so, and they come here looking for work. But most of us, we just lost our places to live. In town, or out here somewhere."

The man gestured vaguely toward the Flats. He had a dirty, exhausted, after-work look that *deserved,* I thought, a shower, a beer, and his feet up in front of the television—and he seemed to know it. I asked if the children at Vrygrond went to school.

"A few of them, they go to primary school. The older children, they don't go. That's why we sent our kids to my sister. They's all in school there at Bonteheuwel. You can let me down here, *meneer."*

I wanted to ask the man if I could go with him to Vrygrond. But leaving my car at that spot would have been unwise. Besides, the man would probably have refused. I watched him trudge across the sand and into the bush.

Later, I read what I could and discovered that there were some 200,000 people living in squatter camps on the Cape Flats. Most of the adults were, in fact, employed, had been so for years, and came from Cape Town. The shantytowns were the product of a massive shortage of black housing in the Cape, a shortage that every black I asked believed the government had created deliberately. In the case of the African townships, this had a straightforward purpose: to discourage immigration. In "colored" areas, it seemed to stem from a combination of removals, inadequate housing budgets, bad planning, sheer indifference, and the authorities' awareness that an insecure group was an easily controlled group. There was a great deal of talk about the housing shortage, but little action other than the construction out at Mitchell's Plain, where the rents would be far higher than most "coloreds" could afford. The rents in Grassy Park, for that matter, were extraordinarily high, because of the housing shortage. Clive once asked me what we paid for our place in Muizenberg, and when I told him twenty-five rands each, he exploded. "You couldn't rent a *shack* in Grassy Park for that amount! People pay a hundred and fifty rands for rooms!"

I never did find anyone to take me into Vrygrond. People in Grassy Park looked at me like I was crazy when I mentioned it. "You don't want to go traipsing out to such a place, Bull, I can assure you." Finally, I just went there myself one day, parking some distance away and hiking across the dunes. When I reached the edge of the settlement, I stopped on a high dune and stood looking down. Shanties were scattered through the hillocks and troughs of sand and brush. The community looked formless. Was this the result of decimating raids?

Or was the random, scattered layout a defensive tactic against raids? The shanties had been built with scraps of wood, iron, plastic, cardboard, and sheets of corrugated tin. The nearby dunes were strewn with garbage. The stench of open sewage rose on the afternoon air. Some little children were playing in a stack of old tires beside one pondok. An old woman labored along a twisting trail with a load of firewood. A man wearing what looked to be half a volleyball as a hat pounded a sheet of tin flat with a post. With the afternoon sun at my back, nobody noticed me. After a while, I decided against going into the camp. If this was the alternative, it no longer surprised me that people in Grassy Park were willing to pay criminally high rents, or let themselves be forced out to Mitchell's Plain and struggle to pay them there.

Mitchell's Plain was the reverse image of Vrygrond. It was an eerie place, located far out on the Flats, some twenty miles from the city center, at the end of a brand-new railway line. Monotonous rows of small, neat houses stretched for miles between awesomely wide thoroughfares. The houses were dreary but, by black standards, "middle-class"—the government liked to show off Mitchell's Plain to overseas visitors. Like apartheid itself, the huge, half-finished project had the slightly dazed, unlikely quality of cheapskate futurism.

Patrick Abrahams lived in Mitchell's Plain. Patrick was a young assistant manager in the supermarket where we shopped. He and I had started talking one Saturday morning. Patrick was a dark, slight, eager, good-looking man, who did not try to hide his glee at discovering I was American. He declared his devotion to American entertainers ranging from Earl Klugh to Steve McQueen, and asked me for my phone number. We later made a date to play squash at a multiracial sports complex in town. When we met there, Patrick exclaimed over my "casual" outfit—old shorts, old T-shirt, old running shoes. He was in spotless whites himself. But we had some good games, and we began to play together regularly. Eventually, Patrick invited me out to his house.

"It's not much, but it's my very own," Patrick said when I arrived one evening. His house was small, immaculate, and rather blandly modern, much like its owner. There were travel posters on the walls, jazz rock on the stereo, and photos of Patrick's two little daughters tucked under the glass of the coffee table. We drank brandy and Coke while Patrick's wife, Irene, a soft-spoken secretary for a big corporation, ironed clothes in the kitchen.

"It's not so bad out here," Patrick said. "The commute is hell of a long, but what can you do? We were all crammed in with Irene's parents before this. They keep the roads quite clean out here, and it's very safe, compared to other places."

Patrick had been working for the same supermarket chain since graduating from high school. "They've been good to me," he said. "We're a company that's growing very fast, you know, so there's lots of opportunity. I've had a pay rise every year I've been there. Advancement is on merit, which is not exactly the case everywhere in this country, as you might have noticed. We're even thinking of expanding into some overseas markets now. Perhaps I'll be sent to help open a new hypermarket in California, and you can show me some of the sights over there, Bill!"

Patrick kept jumping up to change the music while we talked. His tastes were an odd combination—George Benson would be followed by Jessie Colter. He asked me what sort of music I collected, and was amazed to hear that I did not collect any. "Not even a music system at home! That must be the traveling life, is it? I don't think I could enjoy that myself. I enjoy collecting things."

Patrick did enjoy collecting things. He was a long-distance runner, so he collected the badges and ties of running clubs from all over the world, a box of which he got out to show me. He had several "pen pals" overseas, who helped him collect stamps. He had a collection of pipes, although he did not smoke. All these things we looked through over the course of the evening.

When it came time for me to leave, Patrick said, "You know, Bill, I'm very happy you came to see me. This government is so stupid, the way it tries to keep people apart."

This remark caught me off guard. I enjoyed Patrick's company partly because being with him was like taking a vacation from South Africa. He was a sort of person you might find anywhere, a hardworking family man, a jock, a bit fastidious, but decent and sweet. "I'm not interested in politics," he liked to say—in fact, he said it constantly. Patrick struggled to avoid the obsessions and distortions that seemed to attach themselves ineluctably to the personalities of oppressor and oppressed in South Africa. Every conversation with him did not slide inexorably into the maelstrom-topic, "apartheid." But as we stood in his front yard there in Mitchell's Plain, I could not resist asking, "Well, what are you going to do about it?"

Patrick gave a short bark. *"Do* about it? What can be done? The bastards are far too strong." He sighed, and ran a hand along the fender of his car. "Things are getting better. South Africa is joining the modern world slowly. Some of your American firms here are leading the way. You come from a great country, Bill. You are very lucky. May I come visit you there someday?"

"By all means," I said, and we said good night.

I set off and promptly got lost in the huge labyrinth of Mitchell's Plain. All the streets looked the same, and only one of them left the township, connecting it to the outside world—this was a security measure, rendering the whole area easy to seal off in the event of unrest. I wandered the maze of identical houses for what seemed like hours. And though we continued to see each other occasionally for squash, I never did visit Patrick again.

Ephraim was a small, tousled-looking African handyman in his thirties. Our landlord had begun fixing up his house as part of the effort to sell it, and Ephraim had come to do the work. He took up residence in a tiny room outside the back door, in a place that we had thought of as a shed, but now realized was the servants' quarters without which no house in white South Africa was complete. Ephraim painted and varnished and patched floors and walls. At night, he listened to an old plastic radio in his room and received visitors. I could hear their laughter and ringing Xhosa speech from my desk on the balcony.

I was interested in Ephraim, if only because he was the only African I came into contact with each day. But he was not an easy person for me to talk to. His English was poor, and his manner with me was distant, especially after I asked him to stop calling me *baas*. There seemed, moreover, to be nowhere for us to talk. Ephraim was obviously uncomfortable sitting down anywhere inside the house, and he never invited me into his room. Finally, on a series of warm evenings, I supplied the beer and we met on neutral territory, out behind the house, where we would sit around on upturned buckets, or stand around while I barbecued steaks, and talk.

"My wife and children are in Transkei," Ephraim told me, after I had asked. He spoke very softly. "I send them money, but I didn't see them for two years now. They want to come to Cape Town, but I tell them no, there is no place for them to stay here."

Though he never told me so, I soon guessed that Ephraim was in the Cape illegally. Ephraim never told me much, really. His wariness of me remained profound, and he preferred to listen to me talk, or better yet to Radio Bantu, than to speak himself. He would translate the songs and messages on the radio when I asked, and he taught me to count to ten in Xhosa—and struggled to hide his amusement at my attempts to make the explosive "click" sounds that characterize the language. But his English was easily exhausted. What I mainly got from Ephraim was just a glimpse, no more, of Grassy Park from the other side, from the perspective of one of the millions of less privileged black South Africans.

"Grassy Park has many Muslims," he said, when I told him where I worked. "Malays. They are very rich. They own all the cafes and shops."

While this was a great exaggeration, it was true that the people of Grassy Park enjoyed advantages that Ephraim had never known. Being classified "Coloured" rather than "Bantu" was part of it. The 200,000 Africans in Cape Town were considered, moreover, to be the worst-off urban blacks in South Africa. Since the Western Cape was officially designated a "coloured labour preference area," it was especially difficult for Africans to gain permission to live there legally. In other major cities, Africans could, at least in theory, acquire ninety-nine-year leases on certain properties in the African townships, but Cape Town continued to practice "old style" influx control (this was finally changed in 1984). There were three long-established African townships on the Cape Flats—Langa, Nyanga, and Guguletu—but there had been no new housing for Africans built for many years. At least half the Africans in the Cape were there illegally, most of them living in shantytowns. The radical insecurity of African existence in the Cape militated against normal family life, making for a viciously high proportion of single men, like Ephraim.

One evening, Ephraim informed me, "The Muslims here in Cape Town keep slaves. Colored children from upcountry, they buy from their parents." I had heard other versions of the same story. Well-to-do Capetonians supposedly offered to take the children of penniless farm workers from the Cape hinterland to town, where they promised to care for them and send them to school, in exchange for housework or work in the family store. Such an arrangement would give the children the chance in life they could never get on the farm. But the unscrupulous city folk supposedly gave those desperate parents who agreed a false Cape Town address, took the children away, and put them to work, keeping them under lock and key and never sending them to school. This was probably not the common practice people claimed it was, yet the story seemed to illustrate well the world of difference that existed between the situations of city and country blacks.

Ephraim refused to talk politics with me. When I asked whether he thought the Transkei was an independent country, he looked at me as if I had threatened his life. He would say nothing about white people. After a few beers, he would, however, offer opinions about the failings of various blacks: the gangs in the townships, the non-Xhosa Sowetans who thought themselves better than migrant workers (Ephraim had done two "joins," one-year stints as a contract laborer in the gold mines near Johannesburg, living apart from the local residents in the migrant workers' compounds known as hostels), and the "rich Muslims" of Cape Town. I couldn't tell if the remarks about other blacks were for my benefit, or if they were sincere. Perhaps Ephraim thought I, like most whites in South Africa, simply liked to be reassured that there really were still serious interethnic rivalries among blacks, that the destruction of the various traditional societies had not in fact created a single vast laboring class in the country.

It was clear, in any case, that if I was ever going to have a halfway candid conversation with Ephraim, I would have to do something different. It was no good trying to hang around the barbecue with him as if we just happened to be neighbors. At school, I got to know people by working with them. Here, I was firmly stuck on one side of the great South African sociocultural divide: oceans of mistrust seemed to separate me from Ephraim. In a half-dozen conversations, he never once looked me in the eye. I tried to imagine his experience, in which it seemed likely that no "white" had ever tried to talk to him as a human being. It was a daunting thought. And before I had come up with any bright idea about how to bridge the gap, Ephraim disappeared.

He was picked up by the police for not having his pass in order. His sister came by and collected his radio, blankets, and paraffin heater while I was at school. Rachel said the sister hadn't seemed particularly upset. I was stunned myself, though I shouldn't have been. Hundreds of thousands of people were arrested each year for pass law violations. *Kwela-kwelas* full of African prisoners were common sights. Ephraim would pay a fine, and/or spend a few weeks or months in jail, and/or be sold to a farmer for convict labor, and then be transported in shackles back to the Transkei. As starvation is a powerful goad to travel, Ephraim would almost certainly be compelled to pick up and leave his family again before too long.

Some months later, I had occasion to visit the "bachelors' " living quarters in Langa, and I thought again of Ephraim. A middle-aged African woman named Lillian, whom I knew only slightly, had asked me for help in finding her brother. He had a friend who lived in a Langa workers' compound. We went out there on a cold, gray Saturday afternoon. At the entrance to the township there was a big sign warning all "Non-Bantus" that they needed a permit to enter. I decided against going to the police station for a permit. If I was stopped, I would just act the ignorant foreigner.

Conditions in the residential sections of the African townships on the Cape Flats were not as appalling as one might expect. Parts of them resembled Cafda: neat rows of tiny brick houses with gardens and detached privies. But the workers' dormitories in Langa were another story. There were dozens of them, and they looked less like living quarters than like temporary warehouses. They had tin walls and tar-paper roofs, concrete floors and no interior ceilings. Thirty to fifty men lived inside each one, and as we began our rounds, poking our heads inside one barracks after another to ask the residents whether they knew the man we sought, I could see that there was no privacy to be had in any of the buildings. The dormitories were all exceedingly dark and airless, and filled with an overpowering stench of old cooking and unwashed bodies and clothes. The men who lay on the bunks staring suspiciously at Lillian and me ranged in age from their twenties to their sixties. I asked Lillian how long she thought some of them might have lived in these places.

"Many, many years, the old ones. For as long as they have been working for their firms."

"Their firms? The government didn't build these compounds?"

"No, the companies build them, for their workers. That's why the people call this 'slave housing.' "

I asked if any of the men living there might actually be married.

"Oh, yes," she said. "Most of these men, they have wives and children in Transkei or Ciskei or somewhere. They just call them the bachelors because they cannot bring their families here."

In one building, there was a group of men playing cards near the doorway. An older fellow, who looked to be drunk, saw me and said, "What is it, my *baas*? What brings you to the pig sty?"

The others chuckled and shushed him. In the courtyard outside there was a large lavatory that obviously served several nearby dormitories. Inside the lavatory, I could see two men squatting over an open gutter.

I left Lillian to her search and returned to my car. It was parked near a small, dilapidated shopping center. Outside the shops there were tables set up with hawkers selling everything from sofas to summer squash. One table was covered with sheep's heads, bundles of tripe, and pink piles of liver. Stout women brewed traditional sorghum beer in big oil drums. Skinny chickens darted about in the mud. A blind man played an accordion, and people nearby swayed to the music. I sat in my car and tried to make myself invisible. It was a dreary day, and an extremely dreary setting, yet the people of Langa seemed, on the whole, lively and gay. I wondered how many of them had their passes in order. I wished Lillian would return.

31

Qualified, married, "permanent" male teachers at Grassy Park High were eligible for low-interest housing loans from the government. Most of them took out the loans and bought new houses in and around Grassy Park. Liberty's place had a garage, a study, and wall-to-wall carpet; Pieterse's had a tile roof, Italian tile in the kitchen, and stoeps both front and back.

The unmarried teachers nearly all lived with their parents. Nelson October was an exception. He lived alone in a tiny old row house in lower Wynberg. It was a crumbling neighborhood of cracked sidewalks, kerchief-sized yards, and concrete bungalows with small verandas and corrugated metal roofs—remnants of the Indian colonial architecture brought to the Cape by the English.

Inside, Nelson's place was dusty and bare. There was little furniture and nothing on the walls but a few team photos of soccer clubs. Books took up most of the space. One day I wondered aloud how many of the books on his shelves were banned.

"None," Nelson said.

He pulled down a large loose-leaf volume: *Jacobsen's Objectionable Literature.* He was a subscriber to this index, he said. Every month they sent him a few more pages, and every month he went through the list of newly banned books and pamphlets, combed his shelves for newly illegal works, and threw out any he found. "The police like to raid certain people's houses and go through their book-shelves," he said. "That would be a pointless reason to go to prison."

I leafed through *Jacobsen's*. It was a very funny book, in a horrifying sort of a way. Thousands of items were listed as proscribed—the Publications Control Board outlawed some 1,200 publications a year. In the most recent supplements, novels by John Irving, Jerzy Kosinski, Carlos Fuentes, and Alex La Guma had been banned. The enemies of the South African state seemed to lurk anywhere and everywhere. Here was a history of the Palestinian struggle, something by Tanzanian President Julius K. Nyerere, a compilation of the World Council of Churches' "statements and actions on racism." Many, many academic works were listed, although it was hard to tell from the title what could have been objectionable in *Problems of the History of Philosophy*. The whole spectrum of erotica was covered, from how-to manuals like *The Joy of Sex* to a myriad of calendars for a myriad of Clutch and Brake Specialists. (Postcards showing bare-breasted black women were available in every corner shop, but images of bare-breasted white women were forbidden in any form. *Playboy* and *Penthouse* were not allowed into the country.) All old-fashioned spicy fiction was also out. Alas, and adieu, *Wicked Is My Flesh*, by Stephanie Blake. The output of entire publishing houses, both leftist and pornographic, in Scandinavia, the United States, Eastern and Western Europe, had been barred.

By far the most voluminous Objectionable Literature, however, consisted of works about South African politics. It seemed that every book, pamphlet, and magazine ever put out on the subject must have been banned. Inflammatory tracts and landmark works of scholarship, trial transcripts and campus weeklies, the possession of all alike was prohibited. Rare was the month that the National Union of South African Students or the International Defence and Aid Fund in London had not had something outlawed. Reading down the endless lists was very unsettling. It was as if, before your eyes, a whole country was being deprived of the information and intellectual tools with which to understand its own situation. Titles like *Basic Facts on the Republic of South Africa and the Policy of Apartheid* were consigned to nonexistence. *Works about the banning process itself were banned.*

Besides all the books and pamphlets, there were innumerable posters, T-shirts, buttons, films, and "objects" listed. All this censorship at least had the dubious virtue, I thought, of being non-racial. But Nelson corrected that notion. Some films, he said, were approved for viewing by some population groups, but not for others. The main

concern there, he said, was that only whites should see foreign films
that featured blacks and whites in roles that were not clearly hierar-
chical—that is, with blacks subservient. Whites were believed to have
the sophistication necessary to understand that these were other cultures being displayed on the screen; black audiences might be confused by seeing black people in positions of power. I thought of *Animal
House.* The only blacks in the film had been stereotypes—in a bar, in
a rhythm and blues band, and, in a scene that had made me squirm,
in a small group of African exchange students who were shunted off
to a dismal corner of a frat party: the nerds whom nobody could be
bothered with. The South African censors had chopped up the movie
pretty badly, but they had obviously had no problem with its racial
attitudes.

I later realized that this two-tiered censorship applied in other
areas as well. From the news, one could easily gain the impression
that the thought control in South Africa was as pervasive as in the
most absolutely repressive countries. An apprentice mechanic in the
Transvaal was sent to prison for eighteen months for drinking tea
from a stainless steel mug with faint, crude scratchings on it saying
things like "Release Nelson Mandela" and "P.W., we want our land
back." Two men were sentenced to four years for singing freedom
songs at a music festival in Johannesburg. But these people were
black, and a vastly different set of standards applied to, say, white
intellectuals than to black industrial workers. Where the slightest
murmur of political awareness could get a black worker fired and
shipped off to a bantustan, I found that left-wing sociologists at the
University of Cape Town were not afraid to suggest that "armed
struggle" might be the only path to democracy in South Africa. Of
course, such suggestions were made only in obscure scholarly journals. I assumed it was the unwillingness of the government's censors
to brave those frozen wastes of prose that allowed these academic
journals to print what they did. But again, Nelson offered some am-
plification.

"Naturally, the government hates these academics who attack
the system. But they're very dependent on the English universities for
white manpower. And there's a brain drain of English-speaking academics going overseas already. They don't want to increase that. So
they try not to force confrontations with the 'white' universities. In
any case, they know that whatever these lecturers say is purely symbolic protest, with no popular movement behind it. And individuals
can always be banned, if necessary. In the last analysis, the universi-

ties are all dependent on government financing."

I wondered if Nelson had ever been in jail. I asked him.

"No," he said, looking thoughtfully at his bookshelves. After a minute, he said, "Some people seem to believe that if you haven't been inside, then you can't possibly be serious about struggle. But I reject that. The point is to stay *out* of jail. If you go in, you've probably blundered somehow. And what can you contribute from inside?"

Nelson changed the subject.

In many ways, it occurred to me, Nelson, although unjailed, had already forsworn the ordinary pleasures of society. He lived like a monk. There was rarely anything more than peanut butter, biscuits, and tea in his kitchen. He didn't drink. He didn't have a girl friend —although there were female teachers at school who clearly yearned for his attentions. He seemed to spend all his spare time reading. Once, when I invited him to accompany Rachel and me to a multiracial theater in town to see a show featuring "the Nkoma Zulu and 'Gum Boot' Dancers," Nelson stared at me in embarrassed astonishment. "There is a total boycott of that venue, in the first place," he said. "In the second place, I wouldn't go to see that group of retribalized puppets dance to the regime's tune if they were the only entertainment in South Africa."

We decided to skip the Gum Boot Dancers ourselves. I was less easily persuaded, though, when it came to faculty braais, which Nelson also shunned. When I pressed him, he said, "Drinking, dancing, acting the fool—why should I? I would rather read a book."

I thought that was pretty elitist and said so.

Nelson laughed. "There is simply no time for that nonsense," he said.

Although he struck me as being religious by nature—his political commitment was clearly his religion—Nelson had no more patience with conventional religion than he did with conventional merriment. We sometimes argued about the potential role of organized religion in a political struggle. Nelson scorned religion as the popular opiate and that was that. I argued that black churches had made a great contribution to the civil rights struggles in the United States, that the Christian base communities in Nicaragua had been crucial to the success of the revolution there, and that some churches in South Africa seemed to be doing important anti-apartheid work and helping to politicize their congregations.

Nelson would have none of it. "These so-called activist churches are run by diversionary liberals," he said. "Most black churchgoers belong to reactionary sects, anyway, where the priests and dominies tell people just to accept their lot in life. That's their message. God will take care of everything. You'll be happy in heaven, not here on earth. For most of the oppressed in this country, particularly the youth, the first step to politicization is the rejection of their parents' religion. There is no place in the struggle for these so-called holy men."

I thought Nelson's attitude was rigid and unrealistic, although, when he directed his criticism at the government's "Christianity," it got hard to argue.

32

Clive had said that no Grassy Park High matric would really think of going to an Afrikaans university, and in a way I hoped he was right, since I now realized that it was probably not possible for any of them to do so. There were the few who had expressed interest, though, and I had encouraged them. Now it was backtracking time. I met with Warren, a pockmarked, serious-minded matric who had taken home applications for Stellenbosch and for the University of the Orange Free State. Warren planned to become a minister in the Dutch Reformed Church.

"My father says I'm mad to think about going off to the Free State. He says it's too expensive, and the people there isn't nice. But he's never been there himself, and he doesn't know about bursaries."

"What does he say about Stellenbosch?"

"He thinks I should rather go to Bush."

"What do you think?"

"I don't know, sir. I'm not interested in Bush. I already know what is there. These Afrikaans universities, it might be a bit difficult, in terms of the social life, but they have more to offer, academically, and I might be accomplishing something else as well, going to one of them. It would be getting out of this little world we're put in here, and perhaps helping some of these Afrikaners see that we're not all drunken 'hotnots,' as they think."

How could I backtrack with Warren? I didn't even try, beyond making it clear that I would not endorse defying his parents, which he would not have dreamed of doing, anyway. I said I would help him with the applications.

Other matrics who had mentioned applying to Afrikaans universities were more easily nudged toward the University of Cape Town, which in nearly every case could also provide the courses they wanted. But I had made some further disconcerting discoveries about my students' career prospects. A boy named Adam had said he wanted to be a commercial airline pilot. But there were no black airline pilots in South Africa, it seemed, and no plans to train any. A girl named Glynnis had expressed a desire to become a veterinarian. There were no black veterinarians in South Africa. There weren't even any black airline *stewardesses*, I was told, after a girl named Shahieda wrote "air hostess" on my careers questionnaire. I wondered if these students were aware of these facts. And if they knew that there were no black pilots or vets, how much had my cocksure encouragement influenced them to want to be the first to break the color bar? Or were they perhaps deliberately challenging me, throwing my great confidence about their great futures back in my American face? Fortunately, none of these cases was urgent—would-be vets and pilots first had to go to college.

That apartheid was riddled with irrational features, I had never questioned. But running up against these continuing institutional obstacles to training for blacks at a time when South Africa was suffering from a dire and worsening shortage of skilled manpower was enough to make me start to doubt my assumption that the authorities operated with even a basic ration of enlightened self-interest.

"Verwoerd was an economic illiterate": this was the conventional wisdom by 1980—meaning that the original apartheid blueprint had contained no understanding of the requirements of a growing industrial economy. Liberal businessmen were constantly pointing out that apartheid and free enterprise were incompatible philosophies, and predicting that economic growth would destroy apartheid. Even before I saw it spelled out, the second part of this argument made sense to me. For someone coming from southern Asia, the vitality of the South African economy was unmistakable. In southern Asia, as in most of the Third World, the Malthusian specter still haunted the villages. Populations grew faster than economies and there was simply no prosperity *to* share. The South African dynamic was clearly the opposite. Despite gross inequalities and widespread poverty, a modern, high mass consumption economy was coming into being. The country was industrializing; proletarianization was already far advanced.

That industrialization meant increased economic opportunity for blacks was the assumption that underlay my counseling our Grassy

Park High matrics to seize the initiative, to get aggressive about their careers. But the further assumption, that industrialization meant democratization, that each black kid who managed to grasp the brass ring and become a fully credentialed member of the modern society hastened the ultimate collapse of apartheid—everything I was seeing in South Africa belied this idea. While black wages were definitely rising, black political freedom had been just as steadily shrinking for thirty years. With the ongoing implementation of the bantustan scheme and the creation of the police state with its permanent emergency powers, the regime's population control had only become more thorough. South Africa was not England. Because industrialization had forced the rulers of nineteenth-century Britain to introduce universal education and extend the franchise to avoid a revolution did not mean industrialization would force the same changes in South Africa. The system here had a historical logic all its own.

33

George Van den Heever, principal of Grassy Park High, often seemed a bit of a buffoon. He wore a gray fedora and drove an old green Chevrolet very badly. He had a strange, distracted, saurian air about him, such that in a conversation one was never sure whether he was listening. "He's mad" was the pronouncement one heard about him from teachers and students alike. I once watched him crossing the school courtyard, headed for the faculty rest room. Obviously unaware that he was still thirty yards from his destination, he was blithely unzipping his fly as he walked. When I disloyally mentioned this bizarre sight to a colleague, she shrieked with laughter. "That is exactly how Van should be remembered," she said.

The principal was sometimes not seen around school for days at a stretch. At other times, he seemed to be everywhere, popping into classrooms to observe lessons, surprising unwary students smoking cigarettes behind a building. One day after school I was sitting in the staff room with half a dozen other teachers while Ivan Grobbelaar entertained us on the guitar. Grobbelaar being Grobbelaar, he began to improvise the dirtiest lyrics he could around the already smutty Chuck Berry ditty "My Ding-a-ling." Our catcalls and laughter were abruptly cut off when the principal stormed into the staff room. He had been standing outside near an open window, listening, and he was in a rage. He ordered Grobbelaar to his office and began berating the rest of us violently. What kind of teachers were we? Did we have no respect for ourselves, for the school, for the pupils? How could we sit enjoying such filth *in mixed company?* People were edging toward the door, but Meryl Cupido and I were trapped, cornered together on a small couch. When the principal's tirade was finally over, we were in shock. Grobbelaar would be sacked, that was certain. Perhaps we would be, too. We had definitely lost face forever with the principal.

But Grobbelaar was not fired, and colleagues laughed at Meryl's and my concern. "In a week's time, he won't even remember who was involved," one teacher said. Another told me, "Van remembers what he must remember, and that is all. He has a long history himself, you know. He used to be quite a drinker in his younger days, and he caused plenty of trouble for himself. He used to get drunk at parties, all that sort of thing. Once, some other teachers got him very drunk and took him and dumped him on the lawn of the inspector's house. That was almost the end of his career. But he managed to keep his post. And he remembered who did that to him. And over the years, he has revenged himself on each and every one of them. When it comes to that sort of thing, Van does not forget."

In fact, the principal's manner toward me did not seem to change. He continued to assail me with tales of the wonderful GIs he had known at Monte Cassino. "They had Lucky Strike cigarettes. They had Hershey's chocolate. They had everything except racial prejudice!" Van also liked to talk with me about the American civil rights movement. Dr. Martin Luther King, Jr., was his greatest hero, he said. He surprised me with all the black American political leaders he seemed to know—he mentioned Ralph Abernathy, Joseph Lowery, Jesse Jackson, Andrew Young. When I said that I had worked in Tom Bradley's first unsuccessful mayoralty campaign as a boy in Los Angeles, the principal was delighted.

Now and then Van even brought Americans around to New Room 16: vice-consuls who eyed me strangely and suggested I come around to their offices and "register," black bureaucrats who told me pointedly that they had administered aid programs in *Black* Africa, touring educators who gushed over the good work I was doing among the world's needy. The principal was obviously showing off the extent of his connections in the great world to me, and I was impressed. They did seem considerable. He also seemed to be showing me off to his visitors, like some sort of prize pet, which I wished he would not do. It was not Van's attitude that I minded. I just didn't want my cover blown. This was partly because I simply enjoyed anonymity; it was my *mode de voyage.* But it was also because I was working illegally. I had applied for a "work permit" from the Department of the Interior, but had not yet received a reply, and to work in the meantime was against the law.

34

Rachel and I decided to throw a party. Our turquoise mansion had seemed from the start like a great party venue. One of the reasons staff parties were held at the vleis was because the houses in Grassy Park were so small, while here we were, living in twelve cavernous rooms all by ourselves (by this time, Peter had been drafted and left for the army, and the sailor had left for the sea). When our landlord came by one night and announced in triumph that the house had been sold, and that we would have to vacate in a month's time, our thoughts about a party were perforce kicked into gear. We settled on a date and I invited all of my colleagues. Most of them said they would come. Except Nelson. He had better things to do that night, of course.

But as the date of our party drew near, other teachers also began to make their excuses. This one had a rugby club meeting. That one had "pickanin trouble." It was apparently an intimidating prospect, being on the wrong side of the line after dark. But I chided and lobbied shamelessly to get people to come anyway. It was touch and go until the afternoon of the party itself. Then I smelled the great pots of curry being cooked up by the girls over in domestic science, and saw the traditional staff room liquor kitty finally starting to grow, and I knew we were over the top.

People started arriving as it got dark. Nobody could believe the size of the house. The vast, bare living room with its fifteen-foot ceiling, the hundred-windowed balcony with the million-dollar view, all the rooms upstairs—it was all fairly galling, while showing the first people to arrive around the house. But soon enough the house was full of people, and music too loud to permit any of the more delicate forms of chagrin. The senior teachers like Napoleon, I noticed, did not turn up, but nearly everyone else did, and they all seemed to bring friends and family, music and food. The night turned into a *lekker jol,* as everyone said. In my language, the joint rocked.

Moments stand out:

The arrival of Dorian Nero, a lanky, fey teacher of Afrikaans, with five women in tow who looked like they had all just come from the Hookers' Ball—great, strapping, extravagant creatures in fake furs and jewels, high heels, heavy makeup, streaming flamboyance through our kitchen. To my surprise, everybody seemed to know them. "Dorian's females," someone called them. They were fabulous dancers. One of them turned out to be the older sister of a girl whom I taught.

Cecil Abrahams, inspired perhaps by our view of False Bay, holding a small crowd on the balcony in thrall with tales of his exploits as a scuba diver in the cold dark Cape deeps, including a reenactment which allowed the talents of a biology teacher and aspiring actor named Cornel to shine in the role of a big fish—stalked under tables, behind desks, and between startled dancers before being speared by a mop handle.

Rachel teaching a group of hardened disco dancers some of the moves in her own neo-flamenco style of Southern California rock-'n'-roll dancing.

A young English teacher named Andre angrily explaining to me that the personnel for the Cape Coloured Corps in the South African Army was drawn entirely from the *platteland.* "It's because they're so poor and so ignorant, they don't know any better. They just want the uniform. They think it looks nice. And the pay—to them, that's a fortune. You won't find a single *ou* [guy] from Cape Town who would ever join the army!" (I found this speech highly embarrassing, because Meryl was standing nearby with her boyfriend, who was in the navy.)

By popular demand, an a cappella performance by the evening's disc jockey, a dapper young Muslim woodworking teacher named Moegamat, of "Unchained Melody." Moegamat hunched his shoulders, closed his eyes, and filled the house with the deep, corny, ultraromantic tune, drawing long sighs and even sniffles from the temporarily hushed assembly.

The landlord's son showed up, along with a number of his friends, including the school inspector's son who worked in the surf shop. Though I had mentioned the party to the surf shop clerk, I was surprised to see these louts, and thought they would be ill at ease in this company. I was wrong. One of them informed me that they had specifically come "for the Coloured chicks," and *mirabile dictu* I soon saw them ensconced in an upstairs room smoking dagga with several of "Dorian's females."

But the most surprising arrival was that of Mario Da Silva and his wife, Alison. I had invited them but, again, I had not really expected them to come. Then suddenly there they were, overdressed, nervous, gulping wine and thanking me repeatedly for inviting them, while dark looks were shot their way and some people openly grumbled. Leading the grumblers was Georgina Swart. I had heard her in the staff room at school describe Da Silva as "a fascist," and express her wish that he had "stayed in Mozambique" and got what the Portuguese there had coming to them; Georgina began to flutter with malice when he walked into the party.

But I had talked with Da Silva myself, and didn't believe that he was really all the terrible things people said he was. I didn't even believe he was a refugee from Mozambique. He was, however, undeniably part of the Cape Town Portuguese community, which had, along with other recent immigrants from southern Europe, such as Greeks and Italians, a terrible reputation on the Cape Flats for racism—for "overconforming," as it is said, to the white South African norm. Thus, Da Silva's personal curriculum vitae tended to be obscured, I thought, by communal passions. It didn't help matters that his young wife was Afrikaans, or that they had met while she was working, as Georgina informed me, "as a secretary at C.A.D.!"

Somehow, Mario and Alison got through the evening unscathed. They seemed to be unaware of the general hostility toward them, a blissful ignorance I found fascinating. In retrospect, it seems no greater than my own naiveté, my own earnest belief that a nice big non-racial party was by definition a gesture in the right direction in South Africa. It was a great party, though, one that I was even led to believe went down in Grassy Park High social history. What was more, everyone managed to get home without being arrested, even the handful who did not leave before dawn. The house sustained some minor damage, and some major clutter, but was still salable.

While slowly cleaning the premises the next day, however, I ran across one memory from the night before that clanked unpleasantly: Meryl saying that some of our mutual students had mentioned to her my syllabus innovations. They sounded wonderful to her, she said, but she had heard that they did not sound so wonderful to some of our senior colleagues. If Meryl was hearing that, my status at school was shakier than I had supposed.

35

Meryl was right. The tide of objection to my little classroom reforms was definitely rising. One teacher took it upon herself to tell me that there were "paid police informers" among the children in every class at Grassy Park High. I found that hard to believe. Yet I did seem to be on a collision course with the school administration over my neglect of the government syllabus, and I was not at all sure how I should handle that confrontation.

One thing I could *not* do, I decided, was quit. Apparently, some terrific percentage of the white teachers at black schools did so in the course of the year—and a good number of black teachers did as well. For the children, the short-term result of all these departures was, of course, a major disruption in the presentation of a subject, even when a replacement could be quickly found, which they normally could not. All the projects and assignments undertaken by a class, all the monitoring of individual problems and progress, were tossed into the air —and generally out the window. This was why Napoleon said he was so intent on the standardizing of teaching, to minimize this problem. The more widespread effect of these random interruptions was more diffidence, more alienation, on the part of the students. Why work very hard for, or get very involved with, a particular teacher, when he or she might disappear tomorrow? The message received by the students was: Nobody, not even our teachers, takes our education seriously.

It was a particularly insidious syndrome, I thought, and it forced me to decide, quite soon after being hired at Grassy Park High, that, no matter what, I had to teach the year out. My resolve on this point was redoubled when the teacher in the classroom next to mine quit, and his classes spent the next two months doing nothing, because no new teacher could be found. In time, too, I had another incentive to finish the year. Because they were not learning the prescribed syllabus, my students would be in serious trouble if I were not around to prepare, administer, and mark their final examinations.

36

Rachel, having met by now many of my colleagues and students, marked my enthusiasm for my work, and discovered no more interesting employment in Cape Town, found her aversion to teaching much eroded. She paid another visit to our kindly school inspector and the next day went to work in a high school near where Nelson lived. She seemed to hit it off well with her students. Yet she did not last a week. The principal of the school where she was teaching suspended her with the explanation that her papers were not in order. Though she had applied for a work permit, she had not yet received one. The principal would try to keep the job open for her while she waited, he said.

Mr. Van den Heever had been less sticky, and less self-protective —he knew I didn't have a work permit either. But as the weeks passed and no response came from the government to my application, I had begun to worry. Rachel's suspension only increased my nervousness. Then, one day in April, I received a summons from the Coloured Affairs Department, relayed by a glum-faced Van den Heever, to an immediate appearance at their offices in town. Yes, said the principal, I should simply leave my classes without a teacher. I drove into the city with an unquiet heart.

C.A.D.'s offices were out on the reclaimed land known as the Foreshore, a bleak place of empty freeways and gigantic new government buildings of a blockish, minatory architecture. I rode the elevator to the tenth floor of one of them, and proceeded, as instructed, to the office of a Mr. Loubser.

Loubser was a bureaucrat, middle-aged, not unfriendly, with the pencil-thin mustache still favored by many Afrikaners and a thick Afrikaans accent. I sipped instant coffee from a Styrofoam cup and he asked questions. His questions were wide-ranging. He wanted to know not only why I had come to South Africa, what I thought of the country, how I liked teaching at Grassy Park High, and so on, but all about my family, my previous jobs, my education, my taste in films and music. I began to think I was really in trouble. Then, without warning, Loubser lowered the boom: "Mr. Finnegan, do you have a work permit?"

I looked him in the eye and said, "Yes."

He paused for a second, then went on with his questions. I couldn't believe he believed me. I hadn't found my desperate little lie the least bit convincing. Now I expected a deputation from the Security Police to come through the door any moment to take me off for some *real* questioning. But it turned out that the purpose of this interview, apart from Loubser's desire "to meet this American *ou* who wants to teach in our colored schools," was simply to help C.A.D. evaluate my professional qualifications so that they could determine my salary.

Loubser had received my transcripts from the American colleges I had attended, and needed some of the information translated into South African terms. Dazed with relief, I was happy to oblige.

But convincing Loubser that "Studies in the Romantic Imagination" was equivalent to the local English I, or that the courses I had taken in oceanography, astronomy, geology, and so on amounted to something like Geography I, proved hopeless. He was completely nonplussed by the colorful farrago of American higher education. I left the C.A.D. offices resigned to a lousy salary.

A week or two later, I finally heard from the Department of the Interior. I went back to the Foreshore, to the Immigration Office, and presented my passport. The obese young woman behind the window perused some papers, then stamped them all violently and handed back my passport.

"Your request for work visa is denied," she said. "You must leave the Republic within six days from today."

Remonstration was useless. When I asked to speak to her superior, the woman behind the window offered to call a guard to throw me out. I left, feeling stricken. I did not want to leave my job, leave my classes, just like that, not at all. I spent the evening drinking heavily. At some point, I made a resolution not to take this thing lying down. The next morning, while feeling slightly less indomitable, I started phoning Pretoria.

Again and again, I got lost in endless telephone labyrinths, shunted from clerk to clerk to dial tone. Nobody had ever heard of me, and they never told work permit applicants the reasons their applications were denied, anyway. Then, just when all had begun to seem lost, I was connected with someone who described a little-used appeals process in these cases. If I could get certain forms completed and letters written by my prospective employer (former employer was more like it, I thought—my classes were at that very moment no doubt shrugging their collective shoulders and figuring I was history, one more jive-ass vanishing teacher), testifying to my absolute indispensability and their extensive unsuccessful efforts to find a qualified South African for the post, then I just might be allowed to appeal the department's decision. This was my straw, clearly. I clutched at it and sped to the Foreshore for the forms.

To my great surprise and everlasting gratitude, Mr. Van den Heever went along with the appeal. He signed a letter, which he had me write, all about how wonderful I was and how desperately these poor children needed me. He also said, with an air of weary, Machiavellian authority, that he would see that C.A.D. did not interfere with me.

My luck held as I returned to the Immigration Office and found on duty behind the window a different young woman, who accepted the appeal forms without a snarl and said they would let me know. Did I still need to be out of the country by Tuesday, I wondered? No, she said, that would not be necessary. I left before she could change her mind and managed to teach my last class of the day.

But now everything felt different. Surely C.A.D. would discover any day that I didn't have a work permit and sack me. Or Immigration would find out I was already working and chuck me out of the country. Or my appeal would simply be denied, and I would be sent packing that way. It made for a type of insecurity that undermines one's life at every level. You're reluctant to turn in a roll of film for processing because you may not be around to pick it up. You don't buy the big jar of mayonnaise because you may not be around long enough to eat it. I had sent for a box of clothes from home, and now I worried that it would arrive too late. Most important, it was difficult to plan weeks and months of coordinated lessons for my classes when my tenure suddenly felt best measured in days.

As it turned out, I was still around when the box of clothes arrived. They weren't brand-new, and they didn't all fit, but they instantly quadrupled the size of my professional wardrobe and were a big hit with my students, who loudly noted every new article, right down to sir's sleek new socks. I was still around, too, to receive my second month's paycheck. When the principal was handing out the checks in the staff room, John Liberty turned to me, looking up from his check, and said archly, "Taxation without representation! You Americans wouldn't stand for this, would you?" I grimaced in sympathy, and thought about how nasty it truly was to feel at the mercy of a faceless, unfriendly government, slight and self-inflicted as my own predicament was.

PART II

BOYCOTT

37

One cool sunny morning in the middle of April, everything at Grassy Park Senior Secondary School was summarily turned upside down. The spectators became the actors, the authorities stepped aside. In Paulo Freire's famous formulation, the objects became subjects. When I arrived at school that morning, I felt like I'd passed through the looking glass. Homemade banners and painted slogans festooned the walls and fences: WE WANT OUR DEMOCRATIC RIGHTS; DOWN WITH GUTTER EDUCATION; RELEASE ALL POLITICAL PRISONERS. The entire student body was marching in a great solid phalanx around the campus, chanting, carrying placards, singing freedom songs. "A PEOPLE . . . UNITED . . . will never be DEFEATED," they roared, over and over, as they paraded. They gave clenched-fist Black Power salutes, and thundered out this Zulu call-and-response:

"*Amandla!*" (Power!)

"*NGAWETHU!*" (To the people!)

"*A-man-dla!*"

"*NGA-WE-THU!*"

The Grassy Park faculty trailed behind the children in a knot, looking nervous. As I approached, Pieterse looked at me sheepishly, shrugged, and mouthed, "Boycott."

The word had been in the air for weeks. My younger students had pronounced it with a guilty relish. I had privately doubted that they knew what it meant. Now I saw differently. Students of mine waved excitedly from the midst of the marching column, as though they had just boarded a train bound for somewhere wonderful and I was on the platform seeing them off. There was Hester, there was Shireen, and Oscar and Mareldia. I waved back, and soon found myself murmuring along with the rollicking refrain of "Freedom Is Not Free"—*You've got to pay the price, you've got to sacrifice. . . .* A colleague pointed out a white car parked across the street from the school. "The Special Branch," he hissed. One of the two men in the car was taking pictures.

After a few circuits of the school's perimeter, the procession turned into the courtyard. A small platform was set up, with a microphone. The principal was accorded the honor of speaking first, and for a few moments it was as if things had suddenly returned to normal. The principal launched into one of his gusty, bilingual sermons about his own long history of dedication to improvement in education. But the students did not behave normally. At first, they were strangely hushed and attentive. Soon, they were openly restive. The principal saw the trend of things and quickly drew his remarks to a close with heated, oblique admonitions to maintain order "lest the tragedies of 1976, when the police killed hundreds of schoolchildren, be repeated!"

A succession of senior students then mounted the platform and gave us progress reports on simultaneous boycotting at other Cape Flats schools. There was a complete stayaway at nearby Parkwood High. There was a mass meeting at the local teacher-training college, with a decision likely to shut it down. More schools were walking out every hour. The boycott had apparently taken the authorities by surprise. These bulletins were crisply delivered, and each drew passionate cheers from the twelve hundred students filling the courtyard —as well as some conspicuous applause from the teachers milling at their flanks. The student speakers displayed a striking poise and seriousness. They did not discuss the planning of the boycott, although it had clearly been extensive, and its architects were now emerging from their anonymity. Notable among these, and obviously a leader, was Clive.

Clive spoke forcefully, articulating the situation in both English and Afrikaans. The boycotting pupils' demand, said Clive, was for full equality in education. Short-term, that meant an end to the drastic disparities in funding among the various racist school systems. Long-term, it meant an end to apartheid in education. The pupils would settle for nothing less than a single, non-racial educational system. These remarks each elicited a tremendous roar from the Grassy Park student body.

Clive urged his audience not to lose perspective, however. These goals would not be achieved overnight, not without struggle and sacrifice, because the government—"the regime," he called it—was deeply committed to their frustration. The boycott of classes was simply a tactic, he said, not an end in itself. The tactic's effectiveness would have to be reappraised continually. For now, it seemed to be the best available way to focus public attention on the problems of schools. *"This is not a holiday from school,"* Clive insisted, driving each word home. "It is a holiday from brainwashing." Pupils, Clive said, should come to school each day, on time, but they should refuse their normal lessons. Leaving the school grounds, which would provoke confrontation with the police, would not be constructive. Did everyone agree with this plan for the boycott?

A deafening acclamation endorsed the plan.

"Amandla!"

"NGAWETHU!"

After the convocation in the courtyard broke up and the pupils had resumed their marching and singing, I stood and watched my colleagues, who now mostly loitered near the staff room, smoking and chatting. Many of the teachers, I thought, looked *smaller* today, as though the theft of their authority had physically shrunken them. Napoleon, particularly, seemed lost inside his baggy brown suit. Da Silva and some of the senior teachers looked profoundly disturbed and disgusted; but most of the others just looked uneasy or bored. A few, notably Nelson and Meryl, appeared quietly elated. I joined them. Nelson asked me what I thought, and I said I liked the bit about a holiday from brainwashing.

In fact, I liked a lot more than that. This jubilant, organized defiance was easily the most exciting thing I had seen since coming to South Africa. It was nothing less than life rising up against death. It was also, for me, rather redemptively déjà vu. For I found the badly aged battle cries from my own student days—for "relevance in education" and "power to the people"—rang here in Grassy Park with a fresh significance. And when, later that morning, somebody produced a guitar in a classroom where several dozen of us, students and teachers, had gathered after the principal had dismissed school for the day, I found I could even link arms with my companions and sing Pete Seeger songs without feeling even slightly absurd. It was the sweet African lift and twist that these kids put on the most self-serious liberal lyric. I didn't tell Nelson any of this, though. I asked him what he thought. He said a great deal would depend on how many schools joined the boycott.

38

As it turned out, a very large number of schools indeed joined the boycott.

But the walkout at Grassy Park High would not have been such a bolt from the blue for anyone who had been watching the forces gather for the previous couple of months. At the beginning of February, two thousand parents and pupils had gathered at Regina Mundi Cathedral in Soweto and called for a boycott of schools. That call went unheeded, but two weeks later, one hundred pupils at Mount View High School, a "colored" school on the Cape Flats, did boycott classes for a day to protest their school's poor condition and lack of stationery. Two days after that, eight hundred students at Fezeka High School, in the Cape Flats African township of Guguletu, walked out to protest a textbook shortage, an increase in school fees (and the fact that they had to pay such fees, when white pupils did not), the rules that compelled them to buy and wear "expensive and unnecessary uniforms," and the lack of student representation. The Fezeka principal rejected the pupils' demands, but the community's School Committee was more sympathetic, and after a week of talks the children returned to class.

Then, in the second half of March, pupils and parents from Mount View and Crystal High Schools—both located in an especially desolate section of the Cape Flats known as Hanover Park—held two mass meetings, protesting a number of abuses, including textbook shortages, "teachers' drunkenness, lack of qualification and unreliability," misuse of corporal punishment, and the fact that one of the principals had summoned the Security Police after he found "SWAPO" written on a blackboard. The condition of the Hanover Park schools was infamous—they had simply never been repaired after the 1976 uprising, and resembled, in their pupils' words, "bombed sites." Pleas were made for their reconstruction, along with calls for the resignations of both principals and several "inept" teachers. After attending these meetings, three white teachers at Crystal High were dismissed. On the next school day, students staged a wildcat boycott protesting the dismissals.

All the ferment in February and March in Cape Flats schools occurred around relatively local issues at individual schools. But in the first week of April, after the Hanover Park boycott had been crushed, representatives from a number of Cape Flats high schools— the press reported nineteen, but it was apparently fewer—met and

produced a list of grievances. These still focused on textbook deliver-
ies and the reinstatement of the dismissed teachers, but by the next
week, when representatives from twenty schools gathered, the grievances included such items as the disparity in teachers' salaries according to race. At this second meeting, held on April 12, a statement was
issued threatening a mass boycott if the pupils' grievances were not
redressed within three weeks. Neither the authorities nor the public
seemed to take much notice. Two days later, a host of Cape Flats high
schools, including Grassy Park High, elected to wait no longer.

39

"We want the same education the white children get," Wayne said.
"That's why we're boycotting."

"Has sir seen their schools? They've got swimming pools and
tennis courts," Shaun said. "And tuck shops [school stores] like supermarkets."

"And bioscopes!" (cinemas)

"They learn the truth," Nico said. "They don't get brainwashed
like we do."

On the second day of the boycott, when it became obvious that
marching, singing, and speeches were not going to be enough to fill the
hours, the student leaders at Grassy Park High asked the teachers to
join them in establishing an "alternate curriculum." After some hem-
ming and hawing, the faculty decided to accept the offer.

The "alternate curriculum" consisted of a great hodgepodge of
subjects suggested by both pupils and teachers. Liberty and Chantal
offered to lead workshops on the non-racial sporting movement. Conrad Botha would teach something about computers. Trevor Pieterse
volunteered to lecture on the *sestigers*. Soraya would present a class
on women's issues. Meryl would offer some direly needed education
on sex and contraception. Nelson, Alex Tate, Georgina Swart, and a
fiery little math teacher named Jacob would offer a variety of topics
in history and politics, including the French Revolution, the Bol-
shevik Revolution, the fall of Allende's Chile, and divers aspects of
South African history, from Khoisan culture to the bantustan policy
and the tradition of black resistance. Tate would also teach a student-
requested course on rock-'n'-roll music. I was asked to lecture on the
United States Bill of Rights.

But working out a schedule for these "awareness sessions," as they were called, took much longer than necessary, I thought. The faculty was clearly glad to have some organizing to do. But just as some teachers seemed ineffably shriveled by the students' boycott of their classes, so the same people at times appeared to have contracted an instant dotage and become incapable of basic organization and decisions. In the end, I got so impatient that I jumped up and started assigning people topics and venues myself, and drew up a comprehensive schedule of lectures and workshops. This schedule was ratified immediately by all concerned, and run off on the staff room mimeograph. That it was not my place to impose my solutions in such a situation, that anything else might have been going on in those meetings besides a simple act of scheduling, seems not to have occurred to me at the time. I was just eager to get to work. Naturally, my Swiss-clock schedule was followed for less than one day, and I don't think I saw a copy of it other than my own after the second day.

As "awareness sessions" got under way, those teachers who could adjust to the newly unstructured environment—and they were by no means all of the Grassy Park faculty—found themselves flattered by classrooms full of children rapt with the much-repeated conviction that only now, finally, were they receiving something that could legitimately be called education, only now were their teachers revealing to them the *important* things they knew. If anyone became bored, they were free to get up and leave, and if they distracted their fellows, the teacher was free to send them away. There was always a march, a meeting, or a sing-along which they could go join. Education had been liberated on several fronts at once.

During the first days of the boycott, I taught, besides the Bill of Rights, mass vocabulary lessons. For a whole new political lexicon was filling the air, in speeches, manifestos, and pamphlets, and I had discovered, upon questioning, that few of our students could define *oppression, racism,* or *class.* It was a strange sensation, looking out across a room full of eager young faces in South Africa and saying, "What do we mean by 'liberation'? Koos?" Or, "Mieta, can you give us an example of 'indoctrination'?" Or, "Amy, use 'democratic' in a sentence, showing that you know what it means." From definitions we went on to the functions of inferior, "gutter" education. "Cheap labor!" Elroy cried, parroting the phrase on many a placard. "It is to make us stupid," a boy whom I did not know announced. Many children seemed to agree with the dubious proposition that the education provided at "white" schools was something wonderful that they were being denied. I tried to suggest that white schoolchildren were also receiving a narrow, passive, and politically censored schooling, but ran into a wall of vaguely resentful skepticism. Our students did not want to be told what they wanted, not this week.

One problem I did not face, though it bedeviled a large number of my colleagues from the beginning of the boycott, was the reproach implicit in the constant denunciation of the normal school curriculum issued by boycott leaders and quickly picked up by the mass of students. How *could* their teachers have conspired to waste their time with that government propaganda? At Grassy Park High, there were few cases of direct confrontation, but the humiliation of individual teachers was reportedly common at other Cape Flats schools, and the atmosphere everywhere was thick with newfound faculty conscience. Needless to say, I heard no more about my previous deviations from the syllabus. The confrontation with the authorities that I had been dreading had been postponed indefinitely by the advent of this infinitely more serious confrontation.

A whole new version of South African history was available in the awareness sessions. Had the children been taught that blacks and whites arrived in South Africa at more or less the same time? Now they were free to learn that the Khoisan had lived in the country for thousands of years and that the Bantu-speaking groups had arrived fourteen hundred years before the first whites settled at the Cape. Had they learned that the indigenous people were in a state of ceaseless tribal warfare before their conquest by the Europeans? Now they could discover the actual contours of the various societies and their conflicts in preconquest South Africa, with the "bloodthirsty despots" and campaigns of destruction that dominated the official history now counterbalanced by the facts—facts that showed, among other things, that autocratic leadership was virtually unknown south of the Limpopo before the arrival of the Europeans, and that low population densities had actually made violent confrontations between tribes relatively rare. It seemed to interest our students especially to hear that the 200,000 Cape Khoisan had not passively suffered their extermination by the Europeans, but that the indigenes had in fact kept the Portuguese off their coasts for 150 years with their ferocity, routed a would-be English convict settlement at Table Bay, and waged a war against the Dutch East India Company's fort at the Cape which very nearly succeeded in destroying it in 1659.

There were so many myths to explode! That the Great Trek had been the result of the Afrikaners' resentment of British colonial rule at the Cape, for example, was true, but the key element of that resentment was all but invisible in the history textbooks. The fact was that the Boers refused to accept, even in principle, legal equality between blacks and whites. They trekked, in the words of their leader Piet Retief, "to preserve proper relations between masters and servants." Of course, no black South African could be jarred by the revelation that the Boers treasured white supremacy. Still, it seemed important to be setting the historical record straight right there in a government school.

There were also many local myths that came in for debunking. In Cape Town, even black people were prone to talking about the good old days before 1948. But apartheid's roots went much deeper than mere National Party policy. The Native Lands Act, for instance, passed in 1913, before the National Party even existed, had been arguably the single most devastating piece of legislation in South African history, forcing the evictions of millions of black tenant squatters from white farms and directly causing mass starvation. And it had been tacitly approved by the British crown, which ignored deputations of black South Africans protesting this "sickening procedure of extermination." One could keep going back through South African history: to the systematic slaughter of the San in the eighteenth century, to the segregationist edicts of the Dutch East India Company in the seventeenth century. White supremacism had been born in South Africa not in 1948, but in 1652, with the arrival of the first permanent European colonists.

The story of black resistance—in tribal units until the late nineteenth century, and in modern political organizations since the early twentieth century—a history that was entirely ignored or misrepresented in the prescribed history textbooks, also became the subject of many an awareness session. The forbidden names and acronyms were spoken, loudly and often: ANC, PAC, BPC, Bambata, Dube, Gandhi, Abdurahman, Plaatje, Kadalie, Sisulu, Luthuli, Mda, Mandela, Tambo, Mbeki, Ngoyi, Sobukwe, Biko. These sessions were always led by the same few teachers and tended to draw the same few older, more sophisticated students, yet they seemed to me to be the most essential kind of education, taking place exactly where it was most needed, and I found them strangely moving. An understanding of the tradition that this boycott advanced was absolutely critical, I believed. In a situation like South Africa's, history is no lifeless palimpsest; it is the chart of possibilities.

Scrawled on a blackboard: "The classrooms of the oppressed are not for intellectual cowards." On another blackboard, a famous statement by the Cape Town "colored" leader, Dr. A. Abdurahman, in protest against the 1905 School Bill: "We are excluded not because we are disloyal, not because it has been proved we are inferiorly endowed and unfit for higher education, but because although sons of the soil, God's creatures and British subjects, we are after all black." Alongside this quotation, in blistering contrast, was scribbled one of H. F. Verwoerd's infamous dicta: "If the Native in South Africa today is being taught to expect that he will live his adult life under a policy of equal rights, he is making a big mistake." And beneath that, from a former administrator of the Transvaal: "We must strive to win the fight against the non-White in the classroom instead of losing it on the battlefield." At Grassy Park High, for the moment anyway, the white supremacists seemed to be losing this historic struggle.

"So what do you think of it so far?" Clive asked me.

"It's amazing."

Clive had been in constant motion since the boycott began. (Before that, I realized in retrospect, he had not been around school much.) We had just run into each other in the courtyard outside the staff room. In an upstairs classroom, children were singing "Solidarity Forever" and "We Shall Not Be Moved."

"Have you been getting many people at your awareness sessions?"

"Standing room only."

Clive laughed. "They all want to listen to your American accent." He grew serious. "But we're quite concerned that some of the Standard Sixes and Sevens may start bunking [playing hooky]. So we really must keep them busy. Simply explaining the issues is not always enough. You teach Sixes and Sevens. What is your impression of their level of awareness of what's going on?"

"It's hard to say. Some of them seem a bit lost. Most of them seem to grasp the basic issues. They're all looking to you and the other matrics to tell them what to think and what to do."

Clive shook his head. "It's so strange. There's all levels. From little kids who think this is a holiday, to some others, even including a few on the SRC, who think this is *it*, that everything will just snowball from here. You know, the workers will come out next, the country will be paralyzed, and the regime will fall. Just because we don't have the cops storming in here, they think the cops are *afraid* of us."

We both snorted, then both glanced reflexively at the entrance to the school, where the riot police had still not gathered.

40

The boycott spread rapidly all that week. By Friday, thirty high schools and 25,000 students in the Western Cape were refusing their lessons, and on Saturday representatives from sixty-one different Cape Town black educational institutions met to discuss strategy. This meeting resulted in a list of specific demands for equality in education, the formation of the Committee of 61 (later the Committee of 81), and a call for a national schools boycott. The following week, that call was heeded by some one hundred thousand students throughout the country. In Cape Town, the boycott was a complete success almost immediately. Every "colored" high school on the Cape Flats went out on strike, as did all the teacher-training colleges and the University of the Western Cape. And in the weeks that followed, the boycott continued to spread, even into black primary schools, until it finally involved an estimated two hundred thousand students in every corner of South Africa.

The government's first reaction was cautious. "It is not necessary for them to go into all these hysterics," said Coloured Affairs' chief inspector of schools on the first day of boycotting. "If they want student councils, they only have to ask their principals." A disinformation campaign was quickly started up, however. Within three days, anonymous pamphlets condemning the boycott began to appear at Cape Flats schools.

As the boycott continued, official statements became both ominous and placatory. Marais Steyn, Minister of Coloured Relations, told Parliament that "agitators" and "propaganda agents" were behind the boycotts, yet he also professed to understand that the students had legitimate grievances. "Agitators are using the problems that do exist for their own political purposes," he said. Steyn's own relations with the "Coloured population group" of which he was nominally minister were foredoomed by the fact that he held a second cabinet portfolio, as Minister of Community Development. That post made him the chief enforcer of Group Areas. Steyn's protestations of sensitivity to the pupils' grievances were undermined, in any case, when the pupils stayed out a second week and Steyn abruptly threatened to close the schools. This threat was widely condemned, and by the time the Minister was prepared to offer to meet with student representatives, the Committee of 81 was refusing to talk to him because he was "not elected democratically."

Prime Minister P. W. Botha began to get in on the act after the second week of the boycott, and his threats had a distinctly heavier tone. "No self-respecting State can allow agitators to misuse school-children's uniforms to challenge the authority of the State," Botha said. "If the State is challenged and it hits back, it will use all the power at its disposal."

The white opposition displayed more sympathy and comprehension. On the same day that Botha's menacing remarks were published, the *Cape Times* declared—quite accurately, I thought—that the school boycott was simply "the community giving notice that the rising generation will not work the machinery of their own oppression." In Parliament, an opposition spokesman warned the government that a "powder keg" was developing on the Cape Flats, a situation comparable to Soweto's in 1976.

The government, despite its leader's bellicose talk, clearly did not want that powder keg to ignite. When student marches ventured off school grounds, they were dispersed by the police with tear gas and baton charges. But the children for the most part stayed inside their schools, and the police showed an uncharacteristic restraint. Neither side wanted a repeat of the massacres of 1976.

41

Although teachers conducted, for the most part, the awareness sessions at Grassy Park High, the boycott remained the students' show. It was curious that their great activation should have come in the form of a refusal; it was wondrous to see the energies that refusal liberated. Student government—formerly a pallid bureaucratic exercise—was suddenly a vital reality. Most of the meetings were held *in camera,* but the extent of grass-roots participation was obvious from the number of reports being delivered to classes from delegates to various committees. It was democracy in action, and full of pleasant surprises. I was struck, for instance, by the way 6A6 chose one of their least prepossessing classmates, a sickly, cozening boy named Myron, as their envoy to the schoolwide Students' Representative Council. It was not easy for a Standard Six student to follow all that was said at an SRC meeting, and some junior delegates apparently did not understand that they were expected to make a complete report back to their classmates. But Myron seemed to rise to the occasion, taking his responsibilities very seriously and doing a creditable job. This, I thought, was a fine example, too, of the great and sane socializing process that went on at Grassy Park High, in which the least agreeable kids were almost instinctively drawn into the center of the group for rehabilitation.

In the great cracks of free time provided by the boycott, and watered by the prevailing excitement, a guerrilla theater bloomed. Plays written and produced by students were performed in the classrooms, in the courtyard, and out on the playing field. Broad humor at the expense of the authorities was a favorite theme, and certain student actors were much in demand for their roaring, pantagruelian imitations of Security Police officers. These buffoons, who saw "communists" behind every bush and schoolbook and lived to torment noble, quick-witted boycott leaders, were invariably destroyed by The People—a part usually taken by the audience itself.

I learned a lot from watching these productions. One play, for example, was about what would happen in downtown offices and factories on a "rainy Monday"—the local euphemism for a general strike. The white bosses stumbled around helplessly, cursing the "hotnots." They could not even make themselves a cup of tea. One obnoxious woman's misery seemed to be a source of special glee for the audience. I asked someone about her.

"She's the Jewish lady," I was told.

I was shocked. Someone else explained that Jews owned most of the textile mills in which Grassy Park women worked. Jewish women were often put in charge of factories owned by their husbands, I was told, and they had acquired terrible reputations in the black community as ignorant, tyrannical, and unfair bosses. "They're even worse than *die boere*," my informant claimed. Hence the cruel caricature. I still didn't like the sound of the taunts thrown at the "Jewish lady," especially those thrown by some Muslim students, but the play was a smash hit which ran in various forms for weeks.

Another popular play, put on by 6A6, depicted the travails of a boy from the *platteland* whose family had just moved to Cape Town. His new classmates refused to sit beside him, claiming they could still smell the cow dung on his shoes. He was thoroughly miserable. Then he saved one of his classmates from a burning building, and the other children came to see the error of their attitudes. Although a peroration about the need for "solidarity of the oppressed" followed this drama, it was not the play's message per se that I found interesting, so much as the fact that it was conceived and staged by 6A6, in a spirit of cooperation and creativity that I would never have imagined my poor register class could muster. 6A6 seemed to have found, through the boycott, the solidarity *it* had so conspicuously lacked. "All the children are proud to be in 6A6 now," Hester told me. "The other classes ask to see our play."

Yet I noticed that Aubrey, who should by rights have been playing himself as the country kid, was not even in the play, but stood off at the edge of the laughing audience, tight-lipped and ignored. The depth of local prejudice against rural people was no fiction, and the healthy process that drew a Myron into the bosom of the group was clearly still not working for an Aubrey, despite the catalyst of a rising political consciousness.

Student discussion groups thrived. These were generally not open to teachers, although I was sometimes drawn into groups that were meeting in my classroom. One day, some pupils were debating whether to demand the abolition of school uniforms. As I had gone to schools that did not require uniforms, I was consulted. I said I thought the abolition of uniforms might backfire, in that the children from more prosperous families would be able to wear a different outfit each day, while poorer kids would have to wear the same cheap clothes all the time, which might embarrass them. This notion set off a storm of argument. The group began considering a demand that uniforms be kept compulsory but provided free to the students by the school, since the cost of uniforms was already prohibitive for poorer families. When they could not seem to reach a decision on sending this idea to the SRC, I suggested they take a vote. This suggestion—which I made often, in various situations—went, as usual, nowhere.

I seemed to be the only person in Grassy Park who regarded voting as the ideal way to weigh issues and make decisions. It was, after a certain amount of debate, my answer to nearly every tactical question. "Come on, let's *vote* on it." Sometimes students would try to oblige me. But if two-thirds voted one way, they would invariably raise their fists and intimidate the other one-third into voting the same way. No amount of my explaining the sacred principles of direct democracy could dissuade them from this behavior. The principle involved, *I* was told, was simply the protection of their "unity." At the time, I wrote off this attitude to the lifelong conditioning of an anti-democratic society like South Africa's. Later, I started to see how, under the boycott circumstances, "consensual" decision making might actually have its advantages over the opinion poll model I had brought with me intact "all the way from California." In the face of their overwhelmingly powerful foe, a high degree of "unity" was indeed a sine qua non among the striking students.

That unity was represented throughout the Cape Peninsula by the Committee of 81. The Committee's membership was perforce anonymous, though it was well known that our school's representative was a small, quiet matric named Elliot. Elliot seemed a curious choice for the job, as he was not among the natural leaders in his class, until one realized that that was precisely his qualification. Charismatic students like Clive were already drawing enough government attention to themselves. They did not need any more. The Committee of 81's deliberations were a subject of terrific interest not only to the tens of thousands of students they directly concerned, but also to the press and to the government—particularly to the Security Police. Remarkably, the Committee managed to continue functioning effectively through the first several weeks of the boycott.

"We learned our lessons in 1976," one member of the Grassy Park High SRC told me. "That was an uncoordinated revolt. Now we take every precaution we can to avoid bloodshed and arrests, especially the arrests of our leaders. The Special Branch tries to infiltrate every group that opposes the government, and learn their plans and tactics. Well, we have studied the government's methods and learned their tactics."

I got a glimpse of the resultant countertactics one evening during the first week of the boycott, while giving Clive a lift to a meeting. He was very mysterious about our destination and kept an eye on the rearview mirror. Suddenly, he told me to pull over, jumped out of the car, yelled "Thanks," jumped in another car going in the opposite direction, and was gone.

From the beginning, the more sophisticated students among the boycott leaders tried to stress that the boycott was not directed primarily toward the government, and was not ultimately interested in "concessions." Rather, they said, it was directed toward the black community, as education and encouragement. The boycott's main goal, according to this view, was to lift the mass political awareness and morale. The students carried their message directly to the community at mass meetings.

The first such meeting in the Cape was held in Grassy Park after the first week of boycotting. Seven hundred parents and pupils filled an old church hall on a chilly Thursday evening. I went along with Alex Tate, although we had been warned that the Security Police would surely have observers present, and that if we were identified we would lose our jobs. We saw only a handful of our colleagues at the meeting. But I would not have missed it.

The atmosphere in the hall was urgent and purposeful, though the defiance in the air was far more shadowed and nerve-racked than anything we saw during rallies at school. A stage full of students and a few community leaders ran things. After a brief, solemn welcome from the chairman of the local ratepayer's association, the meeting was opened to the floor.

A heavy, nervous, middle-aged woman in a flowered *doek* (head scarf) rose. She began to describe, in halting *kombuis,* the anguish suffered by the mothers who worked with her in a factory in town, as they worried about the safety of their children. "We don't know what might happen to them. There's nothing we can do. I tell my daughter to be careful, but she only tells me the children know what they're doing. How can they know, when they're so young? She says we must take chances to win our freedom, but I don't like to see my children take the chance of being hurt. The other mothers feel the same way. We respect what the pupils are trying to do with their boycott, but we are afraid."

For the next hour, a parade of other parents expressed similar feelings. Some blamed themselves for the situation. "If only we had fought harder ourselves," one man said, his voice shaking with emotion. "If *we* had not let the government get away with apartheid all these years, our kids would not be in this danger today. We let keeping our jobs become more important than winning our freedom."

The fears of parents notwithstanding, support for the boycott among those at the meeting appeared to be unanimous. Testimonials to the courage and maturity of the pupils were offered up by speaker after speaker. Some of the remarks were very moving. Slowly, discussion turned to the statement that would be issued after the meeting. Calls for everything from classroom repairs to a universal franchise in a non-racial democratic South Africa were proposed, and their merits debated.

"If we demand too much, we will be ignored."

"If the people speak with one powerful and resolute voice, they will not be able to ignore it!"

"They can accuse us of using the children's boycott for our own political ends."

"This boycott is *about* political rights, not new dustbins. It is a disgrace that these poor children must lead us!"

Some of the participants in this parley, none of whom I recognized, began to display an extraordinary eloquence in English. Bejeweled phrases, packed in tremendous Victorian sentences, tripped off their tongues. Who were these people, I wondered. They were obviously not humble laborers, nor was this the first time *they* had declaimed in public about the iniquity of apartheid. One old fellow, with an immaculate white mustache and a professorial manner, proposed the most high-flown, antique rhetoric of all, richly studded with phrases like "our inalienable rights and irreducible dignity" and "the sectionalist oppression of this illegitimate neo-colonialist regime." The bulk of his pronunciamento was ultimately adopted. While I didn't know who stood for what, it was clear even to me that these highly polished speakers represented constituencies larger than just themselves and any children they happened to have in school. The government's allegations about the boycott being the work of "agitators" were stabs in the dark, but the truth was that virtually all avenues of black political expression had been closed off by the government, that schools were one of the few places where blacks could even congregate, and that class boycotts for that reason did express the frustration and anger of not just the students, but of their parents and of the black community as a whole. The anonymous orators who rose at the mass meeting in Grassy Park were actually some of the old-style politicians of the Cape Flats—some of those, that is, who were not banned, dead, in prison, or in exile.

Yet the night belonged, as the season belonged, to the students. They explained the issues and boycott strategies to their parents. They put out the most affecting pleas of all to the community at large to join "the struggle," as they called it. Their self-confidence, their idealism, were so impressive that you could literally see it bring tears to the eyes of their elders. And before the meeting broke up, several student speakers, in an effort to reassure worried parents, took the trouble to emphasize again the point that this was not 1976. *"We know what we're doing this time,"* a frail boy from my religious instruction class declared. "Nineteen seventy-six was *reactive.* That was just an explosion, a response to the government's provocations. This boycott, this uprising, is *proactive.* It's as well planned and well controlled as we can make it."

As if to throw a cloak of safety over this fragile-sounding proclamation, someone in the back of the hall began just then to sing, in a

high, clear voice, "Nkosi Sikelel' iAfrika" ("God Bless Africa"), and
seven hundred voices immediately rose into the slow, beautiful pan-
African anthem of the liberation struggle.

The statement issued to the press after the Grassy Park community meeting was a strongly worded endorsement of the pupils' boycott. And an avalanche of expressions of "total support" for the striking students followed over the next two weeks, issued by black civic,
religious, and teachers' organizations throughout the country.

I found this unanimity, and the militancy of many of the resolutions passed, surprising and exciting. Then I began to notice, in the
remarks of various "moderate" black leaders, a recurring concern
that "no one should be able to point the finger and say we did not do
our part." That didn't strike me as the most inspiring motive for
involvement. It made it sound like supporting the students was simply *de rigueur* in black South Africa at the moment.

Certainly, not everyone in Grassy Park had been at that first
community meeting singing "Nkosi Sikelel' iAfrika." The next day at
school, while watching some kids marching around the campus perimeter chanting, I noticed a tiny old lady suddenly cross the street, wade
into the crowd of students, and pull out a little girl by the hair. The
old woman began slapping the girl, calling her "cheeky" and
"naughty." The other students tried to intervene, hastening to explain to the woman that this disobedience was an important part of
the struggle. But the woman just glared at them all with a vast
disgust, turned on her heel, and set off in the direction of home,
dragging her weeping granddaughter behind her.

No teacher at Grassy Park High spoke out publicly against the
boycott during its first weeks, although there were a number who
were obviously not pleased by developments and took little or no
interest in "awareness sessions." Mario Da Silva sat in his empty
classroom reading. Ivan Grobbelaar began spending his time at the
racetrack in Kenilworth. A Muslim teacher of Afrikaans named Khatieb passed his days selling car insurance on the school phone. Two
older ladies who taught religion and sewing ensconced themselves
with their knitting on a couch in the staff room, where they could be
heard muttering darkly about the way things were going.

Senior staff with somewhere to hide generally hid there. The
principal retreated to his office and was not seen for days at a time.
Vice-principal Africa disappeared into *his* tiny office under the steps

of the new building. Pasqualine buried himself in the back of the dark, narrow book room which was his responsibility and lair. (And students did cruel but hilarious imitations in their ubiquitous street-theater groups of a mad old man groping fearfully out of a cave of books, quickly bewailing his father's crucifixion, and scurrying back in his hole.) Napoleon was perhaps the most pathetic figure of all. The former lion of geography now darted from his classroom to the staff room, and seemed plagued by a host of new nervous tics. The awareness sessions he offered were suspiciously close to normal geography lessons, and were not well attended. Napoleon's extensive collection of canes was nowhere in evidence these boycott days, and no one seemed to want to hear about his medieval monarchies, either. I was later told that, during the 1976 uprising, Napoleon had been assaulted by a matric who ran amok with a panga. He had escaped that attack uninjured, while the student ended up in a mental hospital; but Napoleon's present uneasiness was certainly understandable, as he moved among hundreds of newly "empowered" students who remembered the pain of his beatings.

"No one expects anything different from some of these reactionaries," Nelson said. "But I'm very disappointed in Grobbelaar."

"You are?"

I couldn't imagine why Nelson would ever have expected anything more from the man I considered the original sleazemaster. We were interrupted by a student request for help with a poster. Nelson's classroom was a veritable factory of posters, placards, and banners these days. Jars of blue, red, green, black, and yellow paint lined one wall; children knelt on the floor over squares of cardboard, long rolls of butcher paper, and sheets of white cloth, writing THE SYSTEM STINKS and BE REALISTIC NOT RACIALISTIC and SKIN COLOUR ISN'T EVERYTHING and BIKO LIVES and FREEDOM NOW. In one corner, a portable phonograph played Nelson's well-worn Victor Jara album (¡Un Pueblo Unido Jamás Será Vencido!). In another corner, some students were planning a collection to finance the rental of a film. We had already seen The Story of Miss Jane Pittman, about an American slave and her emancipation, and If, about a student revolt in England. Which film did I think they should get for the next showing, Viva Zapata or Nicholas and Alexandra? Both had proved extremely popular at other boycotting schools. I voted for Nicholas and Alexandra. No, I didn't think I wanted to teach an awareness session on the life of Zapata. I hadn't even seen the movie.

My awareness session on the Bill of Rights had mainly drawn

older students, and had been less a lecture than a discussion. Some interesting things had come out, as we talked about the meaning of each amendment and its relevance, if any, to the South African situation—notably, one boy's comment, "I think the whites will one day wish they had made something like a Bill of Rights here, because they are going to need it themselves." I had since led awareness sessions on the disinvestment campaign in America and Western Europe, and the anti-nuclear movement. Meanwhile, my daily vocabulary lessons had evolved into newspaper-reading sessions. A group of students and I would gather in my classroom each morning and read that day's *Cape Times* together, taking time to analyze and criticize articles and editorials. This was a wonderful way to combine lessons in vocabulary, reading comprehension, and "current events"—especially since we ourselves constituted much of those very events these days. That is, the boycott did. I urged students to consider other ways, other perspectives from which, certain stories could be covered, and they seemed quick to grasp the concept of news selection and its ideological elements.

Nelson returned from his poster conference. I asked him, "What did you expect from Grobbelaar?"

"That he would show some solidarity with the students. After all, he's not one of these teachers who only cares about keeping his job, not with the way *he* behaves."

Nelson had a point.

"He's almost as temporary here as *you* are," Nelson said, and laughed. "Have you still heard nothing from Pretoria?"

I hadn't.

"Well, I'm sure the students will add your reinstatement to their demands after you're thrown on a plane going to Miami."

Nelson laughed. I didn't. The three white teachers whose dismissal had sparked protests at Crystal High had not been reinstated. In fact, the more I learned about their case, the more nervous it made me. The Crystal High principal had fired them at a Friday afternoon staff meeting, in front of forty-eight other teachers. According to the *Cape Times,* "He said that the school had been a happy one last year but this had changed when these teachers arrived." The principal alleged that the teachers had been "subverting the minds of pupils with politics and ideologies to bring about chaos and instability in South Africa." Coloured Affairs' local office told the teachers they were fired because qualified "colored" teachers had been found for their jobs, but when two of them applied for new posts, Coloured

Affairs' head office unwittingly offered them their old jobs back! After this mistake was discovered, the offer was hastily withdrawn. But no teachers had yet taken their places at Crystal High. As if all this were not enough, much was being made in the press over the fact that one of the teachers involved was "English." Although she had graduated from the University of Cape Town, had a three-year-old child who was born in South Africa, and owned a house in Cape Town, this foreign political agitator carried a British passport. A few weeks after her dismissal, the government abruptly revoked her temporary residence permit and ordered her to leave the country.

I wandered out of Nelson's room and across the courtyard. A group of children was singing "This land is your land, this land is my land" in the corner of the courtyard, transposing South African geography onto the original lyrics: *"From the great Limpopo to Robben Island . . ."* As I passed, Charmaine suddenly stepped from the group and into my path, singing "This land is *my* land," staring me straight in the eye, and pointing to herself on the *"my."* I pushed past her and continued on to New Room 16. There was only one person in my classroom when I got there: Wayan. He had his face buried in a science fiction paperback, and he started sharply when I entered. I motioned to him to relax and keep reading. Wayan had been mostly hiding in books since the boycott began.

42

The boycott was a time-honored tactic of black resistance in South Africa. Bus boycotts, school boycotts, consumer boycotts—some of the best-known episodes of the freedom struggle had been boycotts. When I arrived in Cape Town, people were still talking about the successful boycott the year before by black consumers of the products of two local firms—a pasta manufacturer that had fired workers for joining a union, and a potato chips maker that had sponsored "racial" sporting events. Black school boycotts had been part of the South African scene since the first slave school was established in 1658 and its students ran away and hid in a cave on Table Mountain, refusing bribes of rum and tobacco to return. In 1955, the ANC had organized a school boycott to protest the introduction of Bantu Education. Some seven thousand students were expelled during that boycott, and over one hundred teachers were dismissed. Alternative schools were established, but to avoid prosecution under laws that prohibited unregistered schools, these had to be called "cultural clubs," and no chalk or blackboards could be on the premises. The ANC schools were harassed by the police—there were raids, beatings, arrests, and bannings—and chronically short of funds. The schools collapsed completely after Sharpeville.

"Boycotts are exercises in non-collaboration," Nelson said. "They increase the self-awareness of the oppressed *as* oppressed." This was no doubt true, but there were also glaring problems, I thought, with the boycott as a tactic. For one thing, its repeated use only underlined the weakness of blacks in South Africa. People could refuse their schooling, they could deny themselves potato chips or transport, but these were such passive gestures, and in themselves exerted nothing but the most localized pressure. School boycotts were especially problematic. Despite the seemingly widespread recognition among blacks that the education provided by the government was flawed, that it was designed not to teach people to think but to teach them to obey, there was a tremendous desire for education, *any* education, among the broad mass of black South Africans. This desire had been built up through generations of poverty and illiteracy in the midst of Western-style prosperity, and even if it was not being expressed publicly during the first weeks of the 1980 boycott, it formed a heavy undercurrent of anxiety, especially among parents, who desperately wanted their children not to waste their chance to get the education most of them had never received. Education was seen as the ladder to a higher standard of living. By many blacks, it was seen as the freedom road itself.

The boycott leaders were, I discovered, way ahead of me in their thinking about the limitations of the boycott as a tactic. Although strategy meetings were held in secret, their content could often be inferred from the dozens of broadsheets and pamphlets, anonymous and otherwise, that circulated throughout the boycott. These pamphlets—one imagined the feverish, clandestine writing and wrangling, the midnight printing on school and company mimeographs, the bundles hidden in the trunks of cars, the children with packets carried under their jackets, the thudding of hearts as police cars passed—made interesting reading. "The boycott is not an end in itself," one of them declared. "The boycott can achieve short term victories. These are important because they give students confidence in themselves, teach them through practical experience the basic lessons of organization and create the climate wherein political consciousness can flourish."

Many of the pamphlets dealt with the shortcomings of "gutter education," and advocated an alternative, "education for liberation." "We must be prepared to fight for a just and equal society. We must become actively engaged in the fight for liberation as part of our educational process."

As the boycott continued, the pamphlets seemed to emphasize increasingly an economic analysis of the South African system. Thus, one pamphlet asserted that

> the struggle in South Africa is not against apartheid "pure and sim-
> ple," not against white domination ALONE, but ALSO against the
> whole system of class exploitation which underlies it . . . TO MAIN-
> TAIN AND DEVELOP THE EXPLOITATION OF THE WORKERS
> IS THE BASIC PURPOSE OF THE APARTHEID SYSTEM.

The problem in South Africa was not, according to this pamphlet, "some special evil in white people," but "an economic system in which the wealth of our country, the mines, the factories and the big farms, are owned by a tiny minority. This ownership enables them to exploit the labour of the working people for their own profit."

At Grassy Park High, too, the politically correct line soon became a "class analysis." In our discussion groups, especially those with older, more sophisticated students, we no longer spoke of black people and white people when we talked about apartheid. We spoke instead of "the ruling class" and "the oppressed," even occasionally of "the proletariat." It was a peculiar twist. Rejecting the government's terminology, rejecting the whole question of race as racist, and replacing all that with tough-minded terms that implied a systematic, radical, and constructive approach to the problem of liberation, was an exhilarating exercise; it was more than semantics, it was like the intellectual annihilation of the entire apartheid worldview. But in South Africa, of course, the dichotomy was false. "Class" is not some eternal structure, but something that happens in time, a historical relationship, and in South Africa that relationship—once defined by things like Christianity, literacy, and participation in the money economy—had become defined almost entirely by "race." The two concepts were not extricable.

And yet I myself took to this new way of talking about apartheid with enthusiasm. The system was not as it was because whites were inherently wicked, I told my students, but because apartheid was *profitable*. That was the reality; the rest was illusion, "false consciousness," in Marxist argot. The truth, of course, was that framing the issues in terms of *something* other than skin pigmentation simply made my own position more comfortable. What I did not know was that this gambit—deflecting resentment onto some vague "economic" group—was a hoary tactic of the white left in South Africa. In Grassy Park in 1980, for reasons of local ideological evolution unknown to me at the time, this "non-racial" terminology was simply back in fashion.

Marxism seemed to be making a comeback among the black resistance nationwide, a development noted with alarm by the white newspapers, whose polls showed that blacks tended to associate capitalism with greed and exploitation and communism with equality. There had been influential communists among the black intelligentsia in South Africa for sixty years, and the Communist Party itself had played an important, if ambiguous, role in the freedom struggle until it was outlawed in 1950. Many blacks were said to continue to have mixed feelings about the ANC because of its links with white, Moscow-oriented communists. But in 1980, I often heard criticism of the Black Consciousness approach to South Africa's problems as being insufficiently "socialistic." Black Consciousness had been, as Nelson said, an important influence on many young people, including some of our matrics, who now seemed intent on graduating from an analysis that emphasized "race" to one that emphasized "class."

Personally, I found I learned more from talking with groups of senior students these boycott days than I did anywhere else. Once or twice, a number of them gathered in New Room 16, and I sat in on their discussions. Their energy for debate seemed inexhaustible. Their curiosity, their independence, their eagerness to figure things out were light-years ahead of anything I had seen before among high school students. When they applied their "class analysis" to the government's current reformist talk, they defined the state's long-term outlook about as well as anyone I had heard. "The regime is preparing to drop 'race' as the only standard for membership in the ruling class," a Muslim boy named Omar said. "They've realized they can afford a few black faces among the oppressors. That's what they mean by 'total strategy.' It will still be minority rule, but the rest of the world will leave off condemning the system here just as soon as they see a few token blacks sitting in that minority."

I found this perception especially shrewd because it contained the awareness that government spokesmen were right when they complained that South Africa was judged internationally by a different set of standards with regard to human rights than were other countries, particularly Third World countries. It was true: the world would abide a hundred different kinds of tyranny, but in the late twentieth century the one thing it would not abide (at least not *silently*) was legal discrimination by race.

"What we must get rid of is capitalism!"

"First apartheid, then capitalism. This whole so-called free enterprise."

"Is it free enterprise when the law forbids the oppressed to own property in the central business districts?"

"And they won't even allow us to have a shopping center where we live?"

"How can you have free enterprise with Group Areas? Private property is meant to be the basis of capitalism, but here the government can just take away your property and tell you to move. They say they hate communism, but that *is* communism."

"That's not communism! Under communism, the people own everything. Here, some so-called ruling class liberal can speculate in the property that's confiscated by Group Areas, and make his fortune while he's crying in public about how terrible apartheid is."

"Free enterprise is what they have in America. Do they have laws saying where people must live and where they may trade in America?"

As the resident authority on things American, I confirmed that they did not. I also confirmed that the South African government's anti-communism, and especially its self-description as a free enterprise economy, went over big in the United States. American corporations that did business in South Africa regularly echoed this claim, in the course of their argument that their operations here provided jobs and opportunities—when their spokesmen were quite aware that South Africa had probably the most strictly regulated, government-dominated economy in the non-communist world.

"Do all Americans think capitalism is best?"

I guessed that most of them did.

"Do you think so?"

"I think it works pretty well in some forms in some places."

"And here in South Africa?"

This was the kind of question that could get me into several different kinds of trouble. "I agree with people who say that apartheid and a free market economy are not compatible, that you can't have both. Because of Group Areas, and because of job reservation, but even more because of influx control. Never mind all the disadvantages of poverty, and lack of education and training. When you can't freely sell your labor, you're missing the most basic element of a free market."

"Does a free market mean freedom?"

"Not necessarily," I said. "Capitalism certainly doesn't equal democracy. Look at all the countries that are supposedly capitalist—Taiwan, Chile, South Korea, Zaire—and are also dictatorships. In poor countries, capitalism has a tendency to make a few people rich, and leave out the rest."

"Just like here in South Africa."

"Capitalism just appeals to people's greed," one girl announced.

"And their ingenuity," I demurred.

"What about in America? Is it just a few rich there?"

"Quite a few, and a very big middle class. But capitalism and democracy go together differently there than they do in a poor country. Not so many people get shut out."

"What about the blacks?"

"Most of them are shut out."

"And the rich blacks there, the ones we always read about?"

"They're not typical. They've escaped the ghetto."

"It's just like here!"

"Not altogether," I said.

"It *is*. There are a few blacks with some money and some power. And they're the Buthelezis and the Thebehalis* of America."

"No," said Omar. "Somebody like Andrew Young in America probably has a lot of support among black Americans. Here, the question is not really whether some guy with black skin, some Thebehali, is allowed onto the board of some corporation, or even into the government. The question is who that black man *represents*. Does he represent the people? Truly? Has he been democratically chosen?" A number of students laughed in derision, and Omar concluded with a flourish: "Where *are* our true leaders?"

Everybody knew the answer to that one, and a number of students murmured it. "On Robben Island."

"Out in Table Bay."

"On the Island."

"Murdered."

There was a heavy silence.

---

*Chief Gatsha Buthelezi, head of the KwaZulu bantustan; David Thebehali, then-mayor of Soweto.

"Democracy is what we want, not capitalism."

"Nor communism."

"And democracy is what the regime will try to stop us from getting, at all costs!"

And so it went, on and on. As can be seen, our senior students were well on their way to acquiring a deep skepticism toward every aspect of the society in which they lived, and particularly toward its masters. They no longer needed to have the government's rhetoric translated for them. They could do it for themselves. Separate development meant continued white domination. Total strategy meant continued white domination. I often tried to steer their discussions toward the situation of the millions in the bantustans, and the millions of migrant workers, for whom apartheid was not restrictions on downtown business ownership, but pass raids and starvation. Rural Africans and their problems were, I realized, in some ways more foreign to my students than were the whites of Muizenberg. And they were highly receptive to new information offered about "the masses"—crowding into awareness sessions on Xhosa culture, bantustan politics, worker safety (and the lack thereof) in the gold mines, and the feudal conditions that prevailed among black workers on white farms.

But note how, in the heat of discussion, the niceties of "nonracial" terminology tended to fall away, and the "ruling class" again became "whites." Of course, if one were to listen in on unguarded conversations among blacks anywhere in South Africa, one still heard, as one had always heard, and as it will continue to be for as long as apartheid exists, the authorities described as "whites."

Did the matrics and I ever find time these days to discuss what they were going to do, individually, with their lives after high school? No—nor the inclination. I tried to avoid thinking about the implications the political ideas that now filled the air held for the kind of career counseling I had been doing before the boycott began.

43

The time had come for us to move out of the big house on False Bay. Because we were still waiting for our work permits—still waking up each morning wondering if we would be expelled from the country that day—we were in no mood to house-hunt. Rachel, moreover, had received news that her mother was ill, which raised the possibility that she might have to return to America soon. Thus, it was a godsend when Alex Tate said that two of his roommates were leaving, and we would be welcome to take over their room in the flat he rented in Rondebosch.

Rondebosch was the university district. It was a much livelier place than Muizenberg and just as pretty. The splendid brick-and-ivy campus of the University of Cape Town occupied the wooded lower slopes of the east face of Table Mountain; Rondebosch fanned out onto the fields further down, beneath a lush green canopy of oak and plane trees.

Our new address was the second floor of an old manor house beside the railway line. The grounds of the estate had been broken up and given over to four or five small apartment blocks, all handsome two-story buildings painted pale green and disposed around a court-yard full of well-tended rose bushes, asphalt walkways, and royal palm trees. Just across the railway line were the playing fields of one of the oldest private boys' schools in South Africa. One block in the other direction, between our place and the university, was an impos-ing new theater complex where plays like Athol Fugard's *The Island* (about Robben Island) played. There were cinemas, supermarkets, bookstores, and several student pubs within a couple of minutes' walk.

Alex lived with Fiona, a thin, shy, attractive woman with big sad eyes and thick blond hair. Fiona was an architect by training, but she spent her time these days designing and constructing not buildings but fantastical skirts and dresses—moody, brilliant garments, mostly of African and Asian material—a few of which she managed to sell in the more adventurous Cape Town boutiques.

Alex and Fiona had met at Witwatersrand University in Johan-nesburg, and had come to the Cape in their old Volkswagen two years before. Their flat they had turned into something of a fairy bower. Tapestries and mobiles and great Chinese paper butterflies hung from the ceilings; walls were painted burgundy, doors were painted blue with silver stars, oversized tarot cards adorned the risers on the stairs. The first time I walked into the place, it was like being transported back through time and space to apartments I had frequented in Berkeley as a teenager ten years before.

Living there produced many more of the same echoes. The house-hold belonged to a "vegetable co-op," which membership involved long, slow meetings with other group households, early morning trips to a commercial produce market, wrangling with lazy fellow co-op members, and sundry other experiences reminiscent of our own efforts, when we were students, to beat the supermarket out of its profit margin. Fiona was a vegetarian, so our communal suppers also tended toward the rice-based, highly spiced, quasi-Asian casseroles that I will always associate with the Northern California of another era.

The living in Rondebosch was easy. The rent we paid was preposterously low, just as it had been on the coast. Our room had a fireplace, we each had a desk—mine had a great view of the mountain. Fiona and Alex were delightful roommates, considerate and witty, and the four of us got along famously. In the evenings, we would sit in Alex's study, sip sherry by the fire, and play Scrabble. Once, Alex asked me where, in all my travels, I had found to be the most romantic place. Bali? Tonga? The highlands of Sumatra?

"Right here," I said, and it was true. The walls were lined with good books and Picasso prints, the fire burned bright and fragrant, the furniture—the rosewood desk, the Oriental rugs, the lamps for which Fiona had made beautiful beaded shades—was all so perfectly tattily elegant. A guitar stood in the corner, medieval folk tunes played on the stereo, the windows were leaded and looked out on the courtyard and a towering mountain. Nowhere in the real world, in all its dust and glare, could possibly be this romantic. Tonga, by comparison, was a bore. The others laughed when I said so—and the peculiar, sandblasting harshness of South African life seemed to me to edge closer at that moment outside the leaded windows and burgundy walls.

Moving to Rondebosch soon doubled and then redoubled the number of white South Africans I knew. Our neighbors were mostly students and pensioners, and were quite unrepresentative of white South Africa as a whole—there were very few Afrikaners around, for a start, and I never met anyone there who was willing to defend apartheid—but that did not stop me from finding the people of Rondebosch a fascinating new group to watch, and to generalize freely from.

At first, the shrill cries of the schoolboys at rugby practice on the playing fields across the railway line would fill me with unease, as I sat preparing the next day's awareness session on foreign investment in South Africa, or on the government's refusal to sign the Nuclear Non-Proliferation Treaty. What went on at white schools, anyway? Were the pupils, or for that matter their teachers, even aware of what was occurring among their counterparts across the line? When I put these questions to graduates of white schools whom I came to know in Rondebosch, they usually laughed in my face.

"They don't know, and they wouldn't give a stuff if they did know," a chemical engineer with a punk haircut told me. "The boys are interested in rugby and girls, the girls are interested in clothes and boys, and they're all true believers in The South African Way of Life. Check the scene in the white school in Herbstein's book. That's exactly how it is."

Denis Herbstein's *White Man, We Want to Talk to You* was an account of the 1976 uprising by a former South African correspondent for the BBC. The scene in question took place in June 1976, in a white middle-class English-speaking high school classroom in Johannesburg, where a teacher was trying to discuss with his students the carnage then occurring ten miles away in Soweto. The students' suggestions for handling the uprising: "Shoot them," "Kill them all," "Teach them a lesson." Their analysis: "They are savages," "They are straight out of the jungle." The teacher's attempts to explain black grievances met a wall of incomprehension, and even self-pity. Teacher: "It can't be very nice to have no say in the running of your own life." Students: "We haven't either, no one listens to us."

"It's a conspiracy of ignorance," one UCT student said to me. The more I learned about white education, the more apt that description seemed. Contrary to what many of our students believed, white schools used virtually the same textbooks we did at Grassy Park High. They learned the same historical myths and untruths, plus a few more. "We were even told that blacks had a far better life than the English press would lead us to believe. Their rents were low. They paid no income taxes. They were really quite happy with the homelands policy. All complete bullshit, and we all believed it!" White schools used the same rote, exam-obsessed educational methods as those in our syllabuses. Their students' access to the world of ideas outside apartheid was, in short, no greater than that of black students, despite their vastly superior facilities.

Of course, the training given white students differed fundamentally from that offered to black children, in that whites were being prepared to *rule* the country. Undereducated, overprivileged white kids were simply not permitted to consider any other possibility. A compulsory subject in white schools was something called "Youth Preparedness," the Standard Six text for which contained the following passage:

> Our forefathers believed, and we still believe today, that God himself made the diversity of peoples on earth. . . . Inter-racial residence and intermarriage are not only a disgrace, but are also forbidden by law.

It is, however, not only the skin of the white South African that
differs from that of the non-white. The White stands on a much
higher plane of civilization and is more developed. Whites must so
live, learn and work that we shall not sink to the cultural level of the
non-Whites. Only thus can the government of our country remain in
the hands of the Whites.

I began to think that white schoolchildren needed our awareness
sessions at least as badly as our students did.

Yet this generalization shortchanges some white schoolchildren.
The teenage daughter of a UCT lecturer confided to me that many of
the girls at her private high school were distressed when their teachers forbade them to hold discussions of the black schools boycott.
"What can we *do?*" she asked me, her pale cheeks flushed with good
intentions. "If one of our teachers were to let us discuss what we liked,
they would be sacked."

Also, I began to notice that when the whites I got to know in
Rondebosch—working people in their twenties and thirties, as well as
UCT students—got together and talked about their school days, a
striking pattern in the careers of their old classmates emerged. The
top students from the top schools—the South African Etons and Har-
rows—all seemed to be banned, in prison, in political exile, gone
underground, or dead. This was greatly exaggerating the case, of
course—only a minority of top students had actually suffered these
fates—and few white radicals had developed their politics while at
school. But this impression did serve to underline the shattering seriousness, even among the elite of the white elite, of any real commitment to black liberation.

The English-medium white universities were not, in any case,
party to the "conspiracy of ignorance" that prevailed at white schools.
If anything, they were places where a good number of students blos-
somed in the relative intellectual freedom, and social conscience flour-
ished. However one might gauge the depth of their political commitment—and nearly everyone in South Africa tended to dismiss it as
fairly shallow—white English-speaking university students made a
good deal of anti-apartheid noise. Thus, when the black school boycott
began, the Students' Representative Council at UCT promptly sent a
message of solidarity. "Although we do not share a common experience with the pupils," their resolution read, "nevertheless our commitment to a just and free society demands that we support their
demands for the abolition of discriminatory education." Students at
the University of Natal began to boycott their lectures in solidarity

with black students, and in the third week of the boycott, four thousand UCT students, nearly half the student body, refused to attend classes for several days. Then, after they had returned to class, the campus SRC organized, in response to a call from the Committee of 81, an "international day of solidarity" in which more than two hundred overseas student unions and universities took part.

As for the teachers in white schools—here, Herbstein's chilling transcription was apparently misleading. For the government's teacher-training program weeded out, according to the people I talked to about white schools, nearly everyone who might prove as sympathetic to the suffering of blacks as the teacher in Herbstein's classroom seemed. Liberal teachers existed, but they were besieged.

While I sat preparing awareness sessions, I would sometimes try to conceive the outlook of my counterpart, my adversary across the line who was wholeheartedly delivering the government propaganda that I was busy trying to disassemble. But the mentality remained dauntingly foreign. The year before, I read, two high school teachers in the Transvaal had helped tar and feather a Pretoria historian for having written a revisionist essay about the Great Trek—and they were still teaching. Those teachers' organizations that had protested the inclusion of a "colored" team in a school rugby tournament were now reportedly considering forming a nationwide whites-only sports body to resist integration. These people, I thought, were *teachers?* And it wasn't only Transvaal Afrikaner teachers who thought like this— or Free Staters struggling to set "Kill Mugabe" to "Singin' in the Rain." Right here in Cape Town, just as the boycott was starting, a high school teacher named Trevor Robertson was leading a campaign to prevent the opening of one of the city's beaches to all races. Of the open beach proponents, Robertson declared, "Their object is to erode the Group Areas Act—the cornerstone of apartheid, and the salvation of the white man in South Africa."

In the early winter evenings, trying to collect my thoughts, I sometimes liked to stroll around the old school across the railway line. It was a beautiful campus, all oak trees and graceful Cape Dutch buildings, bell towers and perfect emerald lawns. The boys on the playing fields, with their blue and white uniforms, their grass-stained knees, their ardent cries in the deepening gloom—they did not much resemble oppressors. But to make sense of anything in South Africa, to keep clear of the deadly vleis of the traveler's inchoate nostalgia, I had to be, like Nelson, cold and dry—analytic. One of the images we used at school to illustrate the functions of the different racial educa-

tional systems involved funnels. The funnel of black education was
jammed at the top with far too many students, most of whom were
spilling out to land on the ground outside a factory, while a very few
popped out the bottom to land at lower clerical posts. The funnel of
white education had the same number going in the top as came out
the bottom, and those emerging landed straight in the head office of
the factory. This, here, was that white funnel.

44

While many teachers participated in the awareness sessions at
Grassy Park High, few were willing to draw the attention of the
authorities to themselves by speaking in public. During the third
week of the boycott, at a mass rally at school, three teachers—Nelson,
Georgina, and Jacob—abandoned this cautiousness and consented to
address the student body as a whole. The rally was held in the courtyard. Nelson gave a quiet, intense speech about the systematic violence of the apartheid state, urging the students not to be distracted
by all the talk about how the boycott might become "violent," but to
remember instead that relations between the state and blacks were
already extremely "violent," by any reasonable definition of that
word. What this boycott, what the freedom struggle itself was all
about, he said, was the creation of a nonviolent society, a consensual
democracy in which state violence would be unnecessary. Georgina
talked about the need for solidarity between students, teachers, and
parents. Then Jacob took the microphone, and proceeded to assail the
government, the Security Police, C.A.D., the Prime Minister, and any
other apartheid target that occurred to him, in rapid colorful bursts
of phrase that had the students screaming with laughter and roaring
with applause.

Afterward, Nelson was furious with Jacob. "That guy needs to
learn to think before he speaks. Whose purpose does he serve by
exposing himself like that? If I'd known he was going to get up there
and beat his breast and dare the Security Police to come and get him,
I would never have shared the same platform with him. Who is he
working for, anyway?"

Whomever he was working for, Jacob was a ubiquitous figure at
school during the first weeks of the boycott. A tiny, dark, quick-mov-
ing man with gold-rimmed glasses, a chipmunk laugh, and a ragged
goatee, Jacob hailed from the Eastern Cape, where he had been as-

sociated with Steve Biko's since-banned Black People's Convention in the mid-1970s. Jacob had not been teaching long at Grassy Park High, but his tireless work in the "alternate curriculum" had quickly made him a solid favorite among the students, and his awareness sessions were usually standing room only.

I went to one of Jacob's lectures. It was billed as a history of the resistance in South Africa. It was that, and several other things as well. Again, Jacob lit into the authorities with manic glee. He called the Prime Minister "Pete Wapen"—"wapen" means "weapon" in Afrikaans, and this was in fact P. W. Botha's nickname in the government—and imitated mercilessly the South African leadership's angry, foolish reactions to every challenge. He scribbled the names of black resistance heroes on a blackboard, shattering stick after stick of chalk with the force of his writing (each time drawing a short burst of laughter from the eighty people crammed into the first-floor class-room—and then a long burst when he suddenly whipped an offending piece of chalk out the window, cursing C.A.D. *sotto voce* for always providing inferior materials). Jacob's exegeses of the various move-ments, ideologies, organizations, and leaders in the struggle were vivid and, in all cases, sympathetic. His own thinking clearly owed most to the current of black nationalism represented first by the Pan-Africanist Congress and later by the Black Consciousness move-ment, but he avoided the temptation to criticize other factions of the liberation struggle, eulogizing the martyrs of the African National Congress and the South African Communist Party along with his own political mentors. It was a freewheeling bombardment of a perform-ance, full of one-line summaries of complex historical forces, quick character sketches, bizarre asides, apocryphal anecdotes, and more than a few dubious facts—I was actually tempted several times to interrupt to set the record straight on one point or another, but the freight train of Jacob's monologue had always hurtled on to the next point before I could decide whether or not it would be worth it.

The highlight of the lecture was an extended demonstration of the techniques of torture employed by the Security Police. Jacob had personal experience of some of these practices, since he had been detained for seven months without charges or trial in 1976. There was "the airplane"—the prisoner was forced to hold his arms straight out at his sides and rotate them and was beaten when he could no longer continue. There was "the refrigerator"—a very cold room into which a prisoner was thrown naked and wet for hours and sometimes days. There were hoods, electric shocks, fists, boots, truncheons, the "wet cap," "the helicopter," solitary confinement. There was starvation, sleep deprivation, suspension by the feet, suspension by the wrists, partial suffocation. There was the tenth-floor windowsill at police headquarters in John Vorster Square, Johannesburg, from which so many political detainees had "jumped." As he relived these nightmares, Jacob's performance reached its highest pitch of enthusiasm. He whirled and danced, acting out everything, playing all the parts in a high, theatrical voice and laughing crazily. To my horror, his audience laughed right along with him.

Jacob's lecture shook me, and not only because of the brutality he described, or the idea (not true, in retrospect) that our students somehow found torture funny (they laughed, actually, to relieve tension). It shook me because it made me wonder what I was doing. Some of Jacob's dates and figures might have been doubtful, but his effect on an audience was undeniable: *he got to them.* It was an old-fashioned, holy-roller kind of speaking, more exhortation than education. Yet it worked. And it suddenly showed my own lecturing style, my careful pursuit of the precise phrase, the nuance of meaning, in what I found to be a very unfavorable light. What did it matter whether these kids knew that the latest research showed that the rate of infant mortality in some areas of the bantustans was 282 per 1,000 live births, not 90 as the government claimed, and not 400 as some demagogues said? Who cared whether the number of people hanged by the state last year (133) was more or less than the number Iran had executed? The point here was mobilization, "conscientization," not fact-check hair-splitting. Was my dilatory, academic approach even remotely appropriate here?

45

Another incident that shook my self-confidence occurred a couple of days later, when we received word at school that the riot police were on their way to Grassy Park High. The students all hurried to their register classrooms, where we quickly took attendance. I had never been given instructions on what to do in case of police attack, and there seemed to be none forthcoming now, so I told 6A6 that we would simply stay put. If the police came, I would lock the door. The children would keep their backs to the windows. If a tear gas canister came through a window, we would pick it up and throw it back out. Okay? The children, some of whom looked terrified, all seemed agreeable to this plan. While going over it again to make sure they all understood it—looking out into forty young faces, all looking worriedly back at me—I felt in my chest a distinct *clunk* of responsibility for their welfare. "It'll be all right," I said.

I poked my head out the classroom door. The school seemed deserted. Nobody here but us revolutionary banners, baas.

Further down the landing, I saw Ralph Pereira stick his head out of his classroom. I told 6A6 to stay seated and quiet and went to confer with him. Pereira was an affable, middle-aged science teacher whose company I usually enjoyed. Today, he looked grim and a little wild-eyed.

"Any sign of the storm troops?" I asked, half-kidding.

Pereira stared at me. "What did you tell your kids?"

"I said I'd lock the door if the cops came."

"Serious? They'll just knock it down."

It was my turn to stare. "Why? Why would they break into a classroom to get at kids who are just sitting quietly?"

"They'll throw tear gas in."

"We'll throw it back out. What did you tell your class?"

"I told them, if the cops come, they should run in every direction." Pereira gestured across the fields.

I was shocked. "But the cops will chase them. And that's when they start shooting, when people run away. They're much safer in their classrooms."

Pereira shook his head. "I don't think you understand, Bill," he said. "First of all, I cannot tell these children just to sit quietly and wait for the riot police to come in and attack them. And I'm sorry, but I don't think you understand *how much these Boers hate these children.*"

The kids in Pereira's classroom had started making noise. He gave me a tight nod and went in. I returned to New Room 16, still convinced my contingency plan was preferable to Pereira's. Fortunately, neither of our ideas was put to the test, for the riot squad did not turn up that morning. But Pereira's words—and the sad, vehement way he had spoken them: "how much these Boers *hate* these children"—stayed with me for days, and disturbed me deeply.

Did I know anything about the sort of hatred that existed in South Africa? *Did* I understand the risks our students were running when they defied the government? People in Grassy Park talked about 1976, about the kids who had died. They talked about secret mass burials at night near Soweto. Though nearly all the books and articles written about the 1976 uprising were banned, the government's own commission of inquiry into the unrest had turned up Cape Peninsula police sergeants who ordered their men "to fire at the rioters because it would be easier to arrest them if they were wounded," and intrepid souls who testified that they had heard the Cape Town riot squad "boasting among themselves how many people they had shot and in what ways they had shot them." Even in liberal Rondebosch, a neighbor had told me about other neighbors who acted as vigilantes in 1976, taking high-powered rifles out to vantage points near the townships and returning with tales of having "killed plenty of kaffirs." And there were cases in which children *had* been attacked in their schools by police, *and shot to death*—in "colored" Cape Town high schools just like ours.

For me, these were only stories—and casualty figures did not convey real violence or real peril. For our students, on the other hand, official violence, white violence, was an imminent potential. It constituted the immediate horizon for their boycott. Many of them had seen it unleashed before. This realization caused me to think again about "conscientization," which I usually conceived of as a more or less rational process, having to do with knowledge and analysis. During the first week of the boycott, Jasmine of 6A8 had asked me, in all earnestness, "if sir was ever conscientized." Feeling silly at first, I had told her how, when I was about her age, I had been awakened to the immorality of the United States' role in the Vietnam War. No one in 6A8 had heard of Vietnam, so I ended up telling them a long story—about the war, about the anti-war movement, about student radicalism and the political sociology of the suburbs where I grew up. They seemed to understand quite well how my political awakening, such as it was, led to rifts with friends who were not similarly "conscientized," and how children even broke with their parents over the issue. But they were uncomprehending when I explained that, for me personally, Vietnam was always a disembodied event, that in those days I didn't even know anyone who had been there. To these children, I realized, "conscientization" did not have to do with coming to understand something they saw on TV or read in the papers. It had to do with things happening in the streets, to their families and neighbors, and to themselves. And the pivotal experiences that "conscientized" them were very likely to be violent. After all, which would make the greater impression on anybody—never mind a young teenager—a teacher's lecture on United Nations arms sanctions, a self-conscious discussion of inferior education, or the violent hatred of the white authorities made manifest by guns, dogs, and tear gas?

In the first days of the boycott, I had argued with Georgina Swart about "conscientization." Georgina had emerged, as soon as the boycott began, as a hard-line leftist with a devoted clique of senior students. I had never taken Georgina seriously before, partly because she was in the habit of wearing toxic amounts of sweet perfume, but mostly because her conversation seemed to be made up exclusively of gossip about other people's private lives and personal defects. Georgina's conversation had changed after the boycott started, though, and now featured constant references to the year she had spent studying in Lusaka, Zambia. This sojourn had great cachet in the newly politicized climate, since virtually no one else at Grassy Park High had spent any time at all in "independent Africa." Lusaka, moreover, was the headquarters in exile of the African National Congress—a point that no one ever mentioned, but of which Georgina and her listeners were all very aware.

Our little argument had occurred after I heard Georgina talking in the staff room about the difficulties she was having getting students to remember the differences between the Third and the Fourth International. "They tell me what Marx wrote on the national and colonial question when they mean Lenin! Some of them must be drilled endlessly before we can really call them conscientized." I tried to suggest that "conscientization" was less a matter of indoctrination, of drilling children in a dogma, than it was of awakening people from passivity and unconsciousness, of rousing them to a critical, confident view of their situation. Georgina had dismissed my view as "very idealistic," and I had wondered if I were not in fact underestimating the importance of discipline, of unanimity, in political mobilization. But now it began to seem that I had not gone far enough. A "critical, confident" approach was only a start; real opposition to the government in South Africa required nothing less than old-fashioned courage.

The boycott had been nonviolent so far, and students and police were both taking care to avoid confrontation. Yet the climate was beginning to darken. A number of people—including high school students and teachers in the Cape—had been detained under the security laws since the second week of the boycott. All our students knew what "detention" meant. It meant solitary confinement in a prison cell. It meant utter helplessness, uncertainty, and terror. It probably meant many hours of interrogation by the Security Police. It probably meant torture. Jacob might be able to make the experience sound unreal and slapstick, but everyone knew it was all too real. Since the early 1960s, at least fifty "politicals" were know to have *died* in detention—with official explanations like "fell out of tenth floor window" (Mathews Mabelane), "fell six floors down stairwell" (George Botha), "application of force to neck" (Joseph Mdluli), "suffocation" (Fenuel Mogatusi), "bronchopneumonia following head injuries sustained in a shower" (Nichodimus Kgoathe), and "brain injury" (Steve Biko).

As much as anything else, "conscientization" involved helping people to overcome their fear of the authorities. The "socialization of courage," someone had called it. At Grassy Park High, you could almost see it being nurtured and developed among our students, in their rallies and songfests and discussions, in their ceaseless talk about "sacrifice." I wasn't crazy about the more kamikaze side of this mentality, but the constant repetition of slogans and catch phrases had begun to make sense to me. These were the signs and symbols and passwords of a subculture that was flourishing in the boycott atmosphere. It was really more a culture than a movement, because it had no apparent connection to a formal political organization. It was a very potent formation, nonetheless. It was the subculture of revolution.

I felt sorry for parents who had to watch their children becoming members of this fervent and perilous new subculture. There was a tailor with a shop at Busy Corner, a man whose son was a Standard Nine student whom I knew slightly. I was in the tailor's shop one afternoon during the third week of the boycott, having a torn pair of pants repaired, when the tailor suddenly asked me what I thought of the boycott. I said something about how it was all very "interesting." The tailor harumphed. He was a stooped, balding man with very thick glasses. "Oh, it's all very well, but I'll tell you true, I don't know what will become of these children," he said. "They are becoming strangers to their own parents. They talk all this language we never heard before, and accuse us. They say they don't care about their education, and they're not afraid of the police. They are becoming rude and foolish. Here are your trousers, sir." I took the pants from the tailor and paid him. He stared me in the face, and in his magnified, unhappy eyes, I saw more pain than I was ready for. "My boy was doing well at school. He didn't give a hang about politics before. I wish someone would talk some sense into him. He won't listen to me."

Our students were talking more and more now about how they might link up with "the workers" in some sort of joint protest. There was even talk of calling a general strike, although it was soon realized that such a call would go unanswered, if not unheard. The only large-scale action attempted by the students off school grounds during the first weeks of the boycott was a march that took place on Tuesday, April 25. That day, very few children showed up for school. It seemed that students from a number of schools had decided en masse to ignore the Committee of 81's order to stay on school grounds during school hours, and had assembled instead in the Cape Flats community of Athlone for a march on the city center, seven miles away. At Grassy Park High, we sat numbly, listening to the radio for news. An estimated eight thousand students had gathered in Athlone. They set off for town, singing and clapping, blocking traffic. Before they reached even the first white area, the riot police attacked, with tear gas and batons. The marchers scattered. Some were trapped in a parking lot. Others were helped to escape by sympathetic motorists. I had visions of my students running, dodging clubs and bullets, being hurt, maimed, and worse. Hester, Mieta, Nico, Mareldia, Shireen—I felt like a parent with two hundred missing children. But no shots were fired, said the news. There were no serious injuries. Still, my anxiety scarcely diminished until the next morning, when all of our pupils showed up at school and awareness sessions resumed.

The Athlone march had been seemingly patterned after another march, one that had deeply impressed itself on the South African political memory. That march occurred on March 30, 1960, nine days after the Sharpeville massacre. A large crowd had gathered in Langa, on the Cape Flats, and began marching toward the city center. The march was headed for the buildings of Parliament, but was diverted to Caledon Square, outside police headquarters. The size of the crowd has been variously estimated, from fifteen thousand to thirty thousand, and its revolutionary potential much debated. Certainly, it was an unprecedented gathering of blacks in the heart of a "white" South African city. The closest thing to a leader the crowd produced was a twenty-three-year-old UCT student named Philip Kgosana. Kgosana was persuaded by the police commander to lead the crowd back to Langa, in exchange for an interview with the Minister of Justice. Had he refused the deal, some observers believe South African history might have been different, but Kgosana accepted it, and the crowd dispersed peacefully. Kgosana was arrested when he turned up for his interview, and the African townships on the Cape Flats were sealed off by the police and military. Food supplies were halted for a week, until the popular will to resist was destroyed.

This was the kind of thing being discussed at Grassy Park High these days—should Kgosana have negotiated? how could the regime be caught off guard again?—so that it was sometimes easy to begin to believe that "the community" was poised for insurrection. This was far from true. On another trip to Busy Corner, I was standing in a small, family-run fish and chips shop where I often went for lunch. While I waited for my food, I listened to the shopwoman gossiping with another customer.

"Have you seen Crystal lately? She dresses quite smart now she's got that job."

"I reckon they gave her a Barclaycard."

"I reckon so. And she'll be able to buy whatever she likes on very good terms."

"She was talking about a washing machine or else a tumble dryer."

"I thought perhaps a motorcar. Oh, look, the mister's waiting for his lunch while we stand here skindering. Shame. How's things at the high school, sir? They still boycotting?"

I said they were, indeed.

"Shame."

Oppression, I thought, was domesticating. And it was necessary to recall that most of "the community" still had its mind on Barclaycards and tumble dryers. Not that a major showdown was not approaching. It was on the last day of April that the Prime Minister made his ugly threat: "If the State is challenged and it hits back, it will use all the power at its disposal." I found myself studying the glowering oval of his face in the newspaper, wondering what exactly he had in mind.

46

It had become my habit each morning on my way to school to buy a *Cape Times* from one of the little barefoot newsboys in ripped shorts and castoff jackets who worked the intersections throughout the Peninsula. One Tuesday, during the boycott's fourth week, while driving slowly through a cold tule fog which stood that morning on the Flats, I happened to glance at the paper where it lay on the front seat, and caught sight of what looked like Mr. Van den Heever's face on the front page. I pulled over and snatched up the paper. It *was* Van den Heever. The photograph showed a group of business-suited men striding past the Parliament buildings downtown, with our very own Grassy Park High principal in there striding with them. This, the caption said, was the delegation from the Union of Teachers Association of South Africa (UTASA), which had met yesterday with the Prime Minister. I was flabbergasted.

I had heard of UTASA only vaguely—it was a "colored" organization, that I knew, and definitely not a trade union, despite its name. I had not known Van belonged to it. Apparently, the UTASA leadership had been summoned to the Prime Minister's office to explain what it was the boycotting students wanted. According to the accompanying article, "The coloured teachers put to him their grievances in discussions both sides said had taken place in a spirit of goodwill."

Well, well. I drove on into Grassy Park, where I spotted Chantal Da Grass just leaving her house for work. I stopped to give her a lift. When she got in the car, I dramatically presented her with the morning paper. To my surprise, she seemed nonplussed.

"It was in yesterday's *Argus,* too," she said. She read the *Cape Times* article while I maneuvered through the ghostly ground fog at Busy Corner. I parked in a sandy field next to school and Chantal handed back the paper.

"I didn't know the principal was such a bigshot," I said.

"He's a moron," Chantal said bitterly, and climbed out of the car.

I was flabbergasted anew. Chantal, who was usually gregarious and forthcoming, declined to expand on this execration. I followed her into the staff room, where we were told that the principal had just called a staff meeting. The occasion, of course, was his report from the meeting with the Prime Minister.

The principal arrived, as ponderous and unreadable as ever, and gave us a surprisingly modest, tough-minded account of the meeting, with none of the overawedness I would have expected. In truth, I was a little awed myself at the thought of his having just been in the innermost sanctum of the power structure, eye to eye with the most powerful man in the country (the most powerful man, for that matter, in the whole of Africa)—a harsh, humorless figure with an infamous temper and a marked taste for repression—having, in P. W. Botha's own words, "frank discussions." I wanted to hear what the office looked like, what the etiquette had been, what the principal himself had said, whether Botha had become angry or been charming. But the principal stuck pretty well to the press release script. UTASA had presented a list of complaints about the state of "colored" education. The Prime Minister had agreed to look into the questions they raised, agreed there was a backlog of needed improvements, and complained himself about the financial constraints he had always to consider.

Then, before concluding, the principal personalized his report slightly by quoting the Prime Minister directly.

"He said there were two things which must not happen with this boycott. 'I don't want UCT students involved whatsoever,' he said. 'This is not their affair. Secondly, I don't want foreigners involved. If foreigners become involved in this boycott,' he said, *'Hare sal vlieg, koppe sal val, en bloed sal vloei!'"*

The principal employed a booming *boere* voice to deliver this last line, after which he and most of the teachers in the staff room laughed —and everyone in the room seemed to turn to look at me.

"What was that?" I squawked.

Now the whole room roared with laughter. "Translation, please, Mr. Africa, for our American friend," the principal said.

" 'Hair will fly . . . heads will roll . . . and blood will flow,' " Africa said, with certain other teachers joining in gleefully.

"Great," I said.

The meeting ended on that note.

The controversy over the UTASA meeting with the Prime Minister was only beginning, however. There was, for a start, a great deal being written in the white press about a remark made by the Prime Minister at a press conference after the meeting: "My government and I are prepared to accept a programme whereby the goal of equal education for all population groups can be attained as soon as possible within South Africa's economic means." This, it was argued—"the goal of equal education"—signaled a major shift in government policy. UTASA appeared to buy that argument. As the *Cape Times* reported, "UTASA felt that the undertakings given by Mr. Botha should go a long way towards meeting the community's legitimate grievances in the field of education."

The first question was to what extent UTASA could claim to represent "the community." The *Argus* had *its* answer ready immediately after the meeting with the Prime Minister, when its editors wrote, "The delegates represent the deprived and the aggrieved . . . The coloured teachers and pupils have a strong case because it is a moral one. But besides this they have the backing of the entire coloured community." The Committee of 81 disagreed emphatically. It rejected the offices of the UTASA delegates. "We state categorically they are not the true leaders. Any decision or agreement entered into by such a delegation will be disregarded by the people they claim to represent. These persons do not represent the interests of the people but wish to project themselves as leaders of the community."

A second question concerned what the Prime Minister's pledge regarding "equal education" was actually worth, and again the boycotting students seemed to come up with a very different answer from that of UTASA or the white press. In a word, the students considered the pledge worthless. While a long way from the "Bantu Education" rhetoric of the Verwoerdian fifties, it made no mention of an end to apartheid in education, and bore a strong resemblance to a host of other unkept promises made by *verligte* officials in recent years. When I asked a member of the Grassy Park High SRC what the government *could* say that would be meaningful, he thought awhile, and finally said, "Nothing. Because they always lie."

There were teachers' organizations that were much closer than UTASA to the thinking of the boycott leaders, notably an ad hoc group called the Teachers' Action Committee (TAC), which had formed for the specific purpose of demonstrating solidarity with the students and had already held two mass meetings in Athlone. The non-racial TAC was working directly with the Committee of 81 and had denounced existing teachers' organizations as "reactionary" and "racist." TAC criticized the UTASA delegation to the Prime Minister for allowing itself to be politically manipulated by the government. This was what Chantal had meant when she called the principal a moron. Anti-UTASA sentiment was quite strong, I began to realize, on the Grassy Park faculty. Now I wished I had gone to the Athlone TAC meetings, rather than heeding the usual warnings about police surveillance and my job.

But anti-TAC feeling was also strong among the Grassy Park teachers. In fact, a large crack was beginning to reveal itself running down the middle of the spectrum of political attitudes on the faculty. To a great extent, this schism traced a generational fault line. Young teachers like Nelson, Matthew, Georgina, Alex, Soraya, and Chantal, along with a number of less assertive junior faculty like Conrad, Meryl, and Cornel, were on one side of the divide, along with one or two of the most liberal older teachers, like Liberty and a debonair, mild-mannered science teacher named Solly Marais. All the other senior teachers, and a few conservative young teachers like Da Silva and Khatieb, joined the principal on the opposite side. There was also a small faction of indeterminate allegiance, a group that included teachers in their late thirties like Pieterse, inveterate *jollers* like Grobbelaar and Dorian Nero, and a few people simply too timid to reveal their thoughts. The rough outlines of this split had been clear since the beginning of the boycott, but as the boycott approached the end of its first month, a new issue began to highlight the differences between the two camps. The question was simple, and it was finally becoming permissible for teachers to ask it out loud: Should the boycott continue, or should it be called off?

The obvious answer was that this was not up to the teachers, but up to the students. And that was exactly what Nelson told the principal when the principal eventually asked him—reaching straight across the growing political abyss at a tense staff meeting—if he would not use his influence with the students to persuade them to return to class. To be fair, this had also been the response of the president of UTASA when the press asked him after the big meeting with the Prime Minister whether *he* thought the boycott should be called off. Other "community leaders" had been less circumspect, however. Dr. R. E. van der Ross, the "colored" rector of the University of the Western Cape, had been ordering his students back to class since the second week of the boycott, and threatening dormitory residents with eviction. (And he had been publicly humiliated for his trouble by his students, who had refused to let him address them at a rally, and then protested vehemently when he tried to join them in singing "We Shall Overcome.") The Reverend Allan Hendrickse, leader of the "colored" Labour Party, had started calling for an end to the boycott immediately after the UTASA meeting with the Prime Minister, saying, "He deserves a chance to translate words into deeds."

The scorn that these "sellouts" came in for was often withering. "They never learn," a pro-TAC teacher at Grassy Park told me one day. "It's almost like they don't realize that we've heard it all a thousand times before. How can they say, 'He deserves a chance'? He's had ten thousand chances! Do you want to know the truth? These sellouts know exactly what they're doing. They simply prefer the status quo to a conscientized and mobilized people."

Yet the principal's pleas for an end to the boycott were not unaffecting. "The issue now, and it is becoming more serious every day, is the *education* of these children," the principal declared at one of the staff meetings which were now becoming almost daily events. "Will it continue, or will it be left off?"

The principal tended to make his points in long, passionate speeches which emphasized his own career. "I *believe* in education," he told the faculty. "I've spent nearly forty years working for improvements in the education of our people. I have no illusions that this government actually *cares* about the education of our people. We had to fight for everything we've got. We had to fight to make education compulsory. But we won that fight. And we shall continue to fight until our children are receiving the same quality of education white children receive. But the only way we can win is by getting all the education we can in the meantime. Without an education, these children will be lost."

I thought of the newsboys out on the trunk roads, most of whom were younger than our students, but none of whom had classes *to* boycott. This, of course, was just what the principal wanted me to think about. (The compulsory education he claimed had been "won" obviously did not apply to the newsboys. According to the law, compulsory education was slowly being phased in for "colored" children, but this law was not being enforced. Education was not even technically compulsory for African children. For whites, of course, education had long been compulsory for all children between the ages of seven and sixteen.) And then there was the commonplace about greater education leading inevitably to greater political awareness and ultimately to political power—and the sneaking suspicion that the most hardheaded white supremacists in South Africa quietly welcomed all shutdowns of black schools. . . .

When the principal sensed that he was not managing to enlist much new support for pressuring the students to return to class, he made his appeal to the TAC faction more direct. "I myself would not want it to be on my conscience that I did not do everything I could to see that these children received the best possible education," he said. "Do you really have no advice to offer these poor children, when they most need it? Or are some teachers simply afraid to offer it? There is nothing more to be gained by boycotting now, that is clear to all of us. The children have made their point. It's now time to return to our schoolwork, before the entire year is lost. But who will say so?"

While most of the younger teachers seemed to dismiss his arguments out of hand, I felt sympathetic to the principal's situation. He was dreadfully caught betwixt and between. There was obviously pressure being exerted on him by Coloured Affairs to curtail staff support for the boycott, and by extension the boycott itself at Grassy Park High. If he ignored this pressure, he might face censure and even firing. At the government commission of inquiry into the 1976 uprising, Van der Ross of UWC, who was now incurring the wrath of his students for his anti-boycott position—a wrath that would only increase in the weeks to come, achieving a truly daunting intensity after he called the riot police onto the UWC campus to crush a student

demonstration—Van der Ross had been accused by witnesses before
the commission of not having taken *sufficient* disciplinary action
against his students during the 1976 unrest.

Rectors and principals got it from both sides. In 1980, the government would soon begin demanding that principals expel boycotting
students. Meanwhile, the Committee of 81 had already declared that
principals or rectors "who carried out a threat to expel students or
teachers supporting the boycott would be considered 'enemies of the
people.' "

Our principal's position was made more poignant for me by his
occasional bitter observations that, if he had only not been such a
dedicated fighter of apartheid all his career, he would have been
promoted long ago to some higher post than mere high school principal—a contention more or less confirmed even by his detractors on the
Grassy Park faculty, who said it was true he had been passed over for
promotions to posts for which he was qualified. The posts had gone
instead, they said, to "more reliable quislings."

Teachers were also caught in the middle, of course, and having
their "reliability" tested by both sides—by their employers and by
their students. TAC proved to be a short-lived and rather ineffectual
organization. A much publicized resolution to "down tools" was abandoned after a few days in the face of its absurdity under the circumstances of the boycott, and the organization itself soon dissolved. It
had served its purpose, however, by demonstrating the support of
thousands of their teachers for the striking students. It had also, I
realized, served to mark its members. Did this mean that thousands
of bright young Cape Town teachers had just blighted their career
prospects? Or did it mean that they all expected a profound upheaval
in South Africa, nothing less than a change of government in their
time? Either way, I was impressed. At the same time, I was appalled
at the number of teachers at Grassy Park High who turned against
the boycott as soon as the principal gave the signal that it was becoming safe to do so—appalled not so much by their desire to protect their
jobs and to get on with their course work, as by the alacrity with
which some of them seemed to abandon all interest in the freedom
struggle which had been receiving their "total support" only the week
before. "Teachers are a fickle, untrustworthy caste" was Nelson's
inimitable analysis.

I was also appalled by some of the tactics adopted by the principal
in his effort to swing the faculty over to opposition to the boycott, once
he saw that a solid bloc of the younger teachers was definitely not

buying. He began to single out individual teachers who were vulnerable in one way or another. First he went after Jacob, whose base in Grassy Park was thin, and whose volatility and hard line put off even some of the pro-TAC teachers. The principal denounced Jacob as an "adventurer" in front of the entire faculty, and gave him no chance to defend himself. Next, the principal went after Alex, accusing him of "knowing nothing of the oppression we have suffered." But Alex refused to be race-baited into silence, and eloquently defended his rights as a faculty member to express his opinion.

The other side stooped to even less savory smear tactics, I thought, when Georgina began to tell people that Da Silva was a police informer. In the boycott atmosphere, this sort of rumor was enough to get someone killed. As far as I could determine, and I made an effort to get to the bottom of the story, there was no evidence to substantiate the charge. Unfortunately, it had credibility, partly because Da Silva was a conservative, but mostly because he was "white." Georgina, too, knew a vulnerable foe when she saw one.

All this faculty infighting and polarization over whether the boycott should continue was irrelevant to the *fact* of the students' boycott, of course. Debating the issue in endless meetings was simply many teachers' way of coping with the strains of the boycott. These meetings were also great opportunities for pose-striking and speech-making by those teachers who harbored their own political ambitions, particularly for those senior teachers whose sights were said to be set on posts in the Coloured Affairs bureaucracy. As opposition to the boycott grew, we were treated to interminable diatribes by the likes of Napoleon and Africa—Napoleon was beginning to move less cautiously around the campus, Africa had emerged from his office—each determined to publicize his own ideas about "equality through education."

What was my own position while my colleagues were all being flushed out of the political underbrush? I tried to lie low. I felt vulnerable, working illegally as I was, and I wanted to attract as little attention as possible. If there were indeed police informers among our students, as everyone claimed there were, and if they ever came to my awareness sessions, I was sunk. But I kept my mouth shut at staff meetings, and let myself be identified willy-nilly by the senior teachers with the fence-sitters on the faculty. Then the principal, after reviewing the list of awareness session subjects and remarking the absence of his own favorite chapter of political history from the courses offered, asked me to prepare a lecture about the civil rights movement in the United States—and I realized that I was about to be smoked out.

47

If the principal and the senior teachers at Grassy Park High had come to any of the awareness sessions I had conducted on the subject of foreign investment in South Africa, they might have been better prepared than they were for what I had to say about the American civil rights movement. I hadn't undertaken to expose American collusion with apartheid with any special zeal. (Indeed, I had once vowed never to curry favor abroad by engaging in America-bashing, and had wasted many hours in foreign lands defending my native superpower.) But neither had I tried to minimize the American role in the maintenance of apartheid. At Grassy Park High, where so many of our students were both uncritically adoring of the United States and desperately uninformed about South Africa's true international situation, this subject had simply seemed important, and impossible to present in any other way without discarding one's integrity as a teacher.

All the professional integrity in town did not ease my nervousness, though, when a hundred or so people crowded into the biggest classroom at Grassy Park High one morning in May to hear me discourse about the American civil rights movement. The principal and most of the faculty were there, along with a preponderance of the senior students. I knew what the principal wanted from me: an instructive, uplifting lecture about how equality was achieved for the black people in America. I went to work fast, talking without notes, as if to escape my misgivings by sheer momentum.

I sketched black American political history, using a blackboard. Slavery. Abolitionism. Dred Scott. Civil War. Emancipation. Reconstruction. Jim Crow. Plessy Ferguson. Going north. Ku Klux Klan. Jackie Robinson. *Brown* v. *Board of Education*. Rosa Parks. Dr. Martin Luther King. Little Rock and Selma and Oxford. Newark and Detroit and Watts. The Civil Rights Act. The Voting Rights Act. The Black Panthers and the FBI. Affirmative action and school busing and big-city black mayors.

Then came the hard part: the present situation, the prospects, and the relevance to South Africa of the black American experience. I took a deep breath and dove in. The civil rights movement in the

United States, I said, seemed to have come to a dead end, far from its envisioned goal of equality between black and white. Legislatively, there was really not much more to be done. In fact, affirmative action was now under attack and in retreat. School busing, while it had worked wonderfully in many places where it had been implemented, was very unpopular and was also being cut back. Educational segregation in America was actually getting *worse*. Profound inequality remained, and the causes were social and economic, and they were proving intractable. Centuries of oppression, and particularly the destruction of the black family, had created a huge urban underclass, a culture of poverty. Unemployment among young blacks was over 50 percent in many cities. Average black income was actually *shrinking* as a percentage of white income—it was now less than 60 percent. Many black urban neighborhoods, I said, were uninhabitable hells, worse in certain ways—such as in the prevalence of hard drugs—than the worst South African townships. Black anger and despair in America were, in sum, at least as intense today as they had been before the civil rights movement of the 1950s and 1960s. (Less than two weeks later, events in Miami would illustrate this rather vague point all too clearly, as three days of ferocious violence in the Liberty City area northwest of the city left 16 killed, 370 injured, and 787 arrested. These riots had been triggered, the news reports said, by the acquittal of four white former policemen on charges of beating a black man to death.)

The principal, I could see, was not pleased with my conclusion about his beloved civil rights movement. Yet I was not finished.

As for the relevance of the black American experience to the situation of black South Africans, I said that it seemed to me to be very slight. Both groups shared a history of conquest and/or slavery followed by second-class citizenship, but beyond that their situations differed fundamentally. In America, blacks were a minority; in South Africa, they were the majority. The historical stakes here were therefore infinitely higher, and the denial of black rights was far more systematic and remorseless—it was the law. In the United States, where today the laws at least were color blind, there was in theory some democratic redress against racial discrimination. But there would never *be* a *Brown* v. *Board of Education* in South Africa. The courts here did not have that independent power of review. Furthermore, a program of passive resistance and civil disobedience, such as that led by Dr. King in America, was not an option in South Africa. Its limits had already been demonstrated by the failure of the great

ANC Defiance Campaign of the 1950s to achieve any of its goals, and then the security legislation of the 1960s had removed the basic freedoms necessary to organize effective nonviolent resistance. Since the achievement of full black political rights in this country would inevitably mean the end to white-minority rule, and since the white government would apparently go to any lengths to prevent that from occurring, the resolution to the South African dilemma would clearly bear little or no resemblance to the American civil rights movement.

I did not go on to describe what course I thought things *would* take, both because it was not part of my topic and because my conclusion would have been the same painful one that most students of contemporary South African history seem to reach—that violent conflict between black and white will probably escalate until the whites surrender power. I didn't have to go on, though. I could see from the terribly serious expressions on the faces of the older students in the room, and from the terrible frowns on the senior teachers, that everyone had understood quite well my view of South Africa's prospects. As for the principal, he had walked out in disgust shortly before I finished speaking.

48

Nico and Shaun dropped by New Room 16 one morning in early May. They asked about Rachel, which they always did since the day they had visited us in Muizenberg. They asked how I liked living in Rondebosch. Then Shaun said, "Sir, do you think they will send us all the textbooks we need, and that will be the end of the boycott?" This was apparently one of the trio's prepared questions. The week before, the government had announced that boycotting schools should immediately submit new requisition forms for all needed textbooks, and they would be supplied. The deadline for requisitions had come only two school days after the announcement, and there had been a shortage of forms to boot, so there had ensued a huge scramble to determine what textbooks we had, in what condition, and so on—a process complicated by boycott conditions, and by the widespread bitterness and mirth about such inept, knee-jerk "administration."

"I doubt we'll ever see all those textbooks," I said. "And what about your other demands?"

"That's right. We want equal education. And we don't believe the Prime Minister when he says we're going to have it."

"Anyway, he only means that we should have the same the white children have," Nico said.

"I thought that was what you wanted."

"No, sir."

"No, sir. The same *standard,* yes, but not the same *ideas.*"

I was pleased to hear it. At that point, Wayne showed up. "Our class is just sitting, sir, doing nothing," he said. "Can't sir come and teach us something?"

6A6 was off performing one of their plays and I was free, so I set off with Nico, Wayne, and Shaun for the old building, where 7E1 was in its register classroom. "But not geography!" Shaun warned, and the four of us laughed. As we passed the domestic science room, we heard students singing along with a cassette of Pink Floyd's "The Wall," which was now banned in South Africa for both sale and possession: *"We don't need no education / We don't need no thought control."* The song had become one of the boycott's anthems.

The children were gathering in their normal classes more and more these days, rather than free-floating in small groups between meetings, sing-alongs, and awareness sessions. Some of my classes seemed to be getting more out of the boycott than others. 6A6 continued to show a cohesion they had not known before. Myron, their representative to the SRC, had gotten a little power drunk lately. In his reports from SRC meetings, he would stride back and forth in front of the class and harangue his mates about suspected "scabs" and "traitors" who were said to be secretly doing schoolwork at home at night. If any teacher tried to give them a normal lesson, Myron barked, he or she should be reported immediately to the SRC. A teacher at a neighboring school had attempted to do so, and she had been humiliated and forced to apologize publicly to the entire student body. I kept a close eye on Myron while he railed about "scabs," because he seemed to have noticed Wayan, who was obliviously reading a book. But 6A6 actually seemed to have the collective common sense now, I thought, to handle anything that arose themselves.

6A7, after a fast start, was growing aimless. Some of the more precocious children in the class—Terence, Mieta, Natalie, Angela—had hurled themselves into the boycott's *apertura* with great enthusiasm. I saw them at meetings, discussions, even history lectures, where there were no other Standard Sixes in sight. I thought these children regarded me with a new alertness, even a certain defiance, as if their "conscientization" had removed an almost physical veil of deference. Terence in particular spoke to me as if we were now suddenly equals, boasting to me about how he had begun resisting his father's demands that he go to church, and saying, "There are more important things to be doing, isn't it, Mr. Finnegan." But the class as a whole needed constant entertainment, needed to have its energy channeled, and 6A7's register teacher was Grobbelaar, who was a nonentity at school these days. 6A7 began to seem sour and frustrated as the boycott wore on. They played pop music on a radio all day long, and the girls danced together.

6A8 was as calm, as attentive, as well behaved as ever. The class participated in every available activity and occupied themselves when nothing was happening. Serious little Josef kept a group of boys spellbound with his skill at chess. Some of the girls who sang in a church group together turned boycott songs into four-part harmonies. One afternoon, when I looked in on 6A8 and asked what they were doing, Amy said, with a seriousness that made her classmates laugh, "We are waiting for the Committee of 81 to tell us what to do." Shireen added, "Perhaps sir would like to give us some vocabulary. 'Oppression means when they oppress us.' " The class laughed again. It struck me that 6A8 did have a rather passive, obedient attitude toward the boycott leadership. Dismayingly, though not surprisingly, Oscar had stopped coming to school after the first couple of weeks of the boycott.

7E2, my rowdy rebels, had virtually disintegrated as a class in the suddenly changed context of the larger rebellion that was the boycott. Being moody, self-destructive Misunderstood Youth simply had no cachet these days. Getting *die vier voorste* pulled out to enhance one's love life suddenly seemed more than a little beside the point. 7E2's case was not aided by the fact that their register teacher was the religion teacher who had parked herself and her sewing in the staff room for the duration of the boycott. The class seemed to have fragmented into six or seven separate entities, which attached themselves to other classes or haunted obscure corners of the school grounds in disconsolate clouds of tobacco smoke.

7E1, on the other hand, showed signs, like 6A6, of having been molded by the boycott into a more cohesive class. There were children who were obviously not comfortable in the volatile boycott atmosphere—notably, a chubby boy named Kamaloodien, who was delivered to school each morning along with his four brothers in an old blue Mercedes by their father, a Muslim who owned a number of corner shops. Kamaloodien normally had a sleepy, anteaterish look about him, but his eyes were wider now, as if he felt newly compelled to watch his flanks as he waddled around school. 7E1 seemed to take to the boycott intellectually. There were no especially fiery students, no rising young boycott leaders in the class—Nico was probably the fieriest—but there was clearly a consensus that it was time to revise their ideas about school, God, and country. A number of kids from 7E1 had suggested to me in different ways that the boycott was a vindication of the sort of geography I had been teaching them. "South Africa is quite wicked to some of these other people, isn't it, sir," said the same boy who had once protested my criticism of the migrant labor system. When I joined 7E1 on the day that Wayne had come to fetch me, they greeted me happily, and I gave them a lecture on the bantustan policy that was perilously close to being a lesson on South African geography, yet they did not object.

Relations during the boycott between the senior students at Grassy Park High and the hundreds of children in Standards Six and Seven were nominally democratic. But really the matrics were like some revolutionary vanguard party, with the younger children filling out the role of "the masses." Ambivalence, indifference, even outright dissension among the younger children were all drowned in the general roar of support for whatever the boycott leaders decided. There were also some matrics, however, who kept their distance from the protest hubbub. These included Kamaloodien's older brother, Ishmail, who hoped to study medicine at the University of Natal. He was among those about whom it was murmured that they were continuing to study at home. Warren, who hoped to become a Dutch Reformed minister, was another matric who seemed less than enthusiastic about the boycott. Whenever he came to New Room 16 to chat, Warren carefully kept the conversation on something other than politics. One day, he indicated a group of aimless-looking students in the field below my window and said, "It's no mystery why the children are starting to call it 'the borecott.'"

The high spirits of the first weeks of the boycott were definitely dissipating. Our program of activities had begun to wear thin, and fewer teachers seemed willing to teach improvised, unstructured lessons. Part of the problem, I realized, was that many of my colleagues were actually running out of things *to* teach. Cornel, Conrad, Andre, Chantal, Moegamat, Cecil—these teachers' own educations and experience had involved little beyond the high school syllabus and the Grassy Park community, with the result that they really did not know all that much more about things in general than their students did. Even some of the young, pro-boycott teachers were beginning to spend more and more time in the staff room, reading and socializing and only venturing out to attend, in giggling back-row cliques, the wildly popular sex education classes still being offered by the ever-obliging Meryl.

49

In the middle of May, the Committee of 81 decided to suspend the boycott in Cape Town for three weeks. The list of demands the Committee presented to the government—with the proviso that if they were not met within three weeks, the boycott would be resumed—was ambitious. It included an end to racial discrimination in teachers' salaries and the release of everyone detained in connection with the boycott (there were by now several dozen detainees). It seemed impossible that these demands would all be met. As it happened, on the day after the suspension of the boycott in Cape Town, the authorities closed indefinitely the University of Fort Hare, in the Eastern Cape —where the students had been boycotting classes for a fortnight—and the Committee of 81 promptly resumed the boycott in Cape Town in solidarity with the Fort Hare students.

A dynamic was developing which was paradigmatic in South Africa. While the government was trying to force the students to abandon their boycott, the only group that could make any decision about the course of the boycott, the Committee of 81, began finding it increasingly difficult to function. Security Police harassment escalated. Meetings were raided, routed, canceled. The Committee itself was being decimated by detentions. At Grassy Park High, we lost Elliot, our representative to the Committee of 81, in the first big wave of arrests. Like most of the others, Elliot was picked up by a squad of Security Police at 4 A.M. at home. He was taken to an unspecified prison and held incommunicado. The number of detainees held nationally soon soared into the hundreds.

The debate about the boycott which was dividing the faculty at Grassy Park High was now taking place throughout black South Africa. Most politically significant perhaps was the violent opposition to the boycott expressed by Chief Gatsha Buthelezi, leader of the KwaZulu bantustan. Buthelezi, though despised by many blacks for his role as a "homeland" politician, commanded a large following in the form of the militant Zulu "cultural organization," Inkatha, and Buthelezi seemed to take the boycotts personally. He denounced them as the work of "evil political forces who thought in their stupidity that they could attack Inkatha by mobilizing children." He accused unidentified white men of sneaking through the black townships near Durban at night and paying children ten rands a day to boycott. The boycott planners, said Buthelezi, were "political witches," and, he warned, "We are a people who know how to deal with witchcraft. We will destroy this evil among us." Buthelezi dramatically underscored these threats by leaving the stage at the rally where they were made, whereupon an Inkatha *impi* (tribal band) of two hundred men swarmed onstage and attacked a black minister who was believed to be a boycott supporter. The minister was felled with stick blows to the head and beaten senseless. His life was saved, said the news reports, only by the intervention of Dr. Oscar Dhlomo, the Inkatha secretary-general.

The anti-boycott faction on the Grassy Park faculty continued to tread somewhat more lightly than Inkatha. The time was clearly not yet right for opposing the boycott outright. Thus, when a rumor made the rounds at school that the Grassy Park SRC was considering taking a resolution to the Committee of 81 advocating a new suspension of the boycott, and the spoor of the rumor was traced somehow to the faculty, no one was in a hurry to own up as its source. A joint meeting of the faculty and the SRC was held, at which the possibilities for the rumor's origin were narrowed down to a handful of senior teachers. This meeting was an extremely emotional affair, with a number of students stepping forward to denounce the teacher who had betrayed their trust. I wasn't at all sure what was going on until somebody nudged me and indicated Pieterse, who was one of the four suspects. Pieterse was not his natural color. He was gazing rigidly at no one. The meeting was adjourned without a malefactor being named. A consensus had apparently been reached, however, about who it had been. Pieterse left school early that day. And in the weeks that followed, no matter how heated things became, he refused to be drawn into any aspect of the boycott debate. Pieterse became one of the staff room fixtures, his face buried in correspondence course textbooks from which he seemed to surface only to ask me about the nature symbolism in Virginia Woolf's *To the Lighthouse*. I never again saw Pieterse in the company of a senior student.

The students were supersensitive about attempts to divide them against one another. That was why they didn't like to vote in front of me. That was why they didn't like their deliberations leaked before they had reached a decision. As disquiet about the quality and direction of their boycott spread and as pressure from the government to call it off was increasingly augmented by pressure from more conservative black groups, the bulk of the students' attention seemed to be shifting from the issues at stake to their own rear guard. "We must keep our options open"—this tactician's motto was becoming the boycott's battle cry. Similar diversions, similar problems, and the same basic dispute had plagued all resistance campaigns in South Africa, according to Jacob. "We always have these same groups, the sellouts and the holdouts, at each other's throats, while the Boers throw them all in the shit together."

Jacob laughed. This was after school. We were driving through Grassy Park. Jacob had caught a lift with me, saying he was going to UCT. He seemed to be in his usual ebullient mood. "The Napoleons and Africas and Van den Heevers, they've been *ja-baas*ing the whites for three hundred years. They're the good boys. They'll always tell you they're working for change from the inside, but they're not interested in change. Their minds are colonized. They don't even realize what shit they're talking. They never even see that, without their collaboration, the system couldn't exist. They'll never admit it, but they actually believe that blacks deserve to be subjugated by whites. Because blacks are poor and uneducated, they don't deserve what the rich and educated have, that's how they see it. It's up to us to make it on the white man's terms, you know, never mind how the system makes that impossible for just about every black. And if you say, 'No, we want liberation *now,*' they say you must be crazy, you're a hothead, you're an adventurer. I tell you, Bill, what you're seeing here at little Grassy Park High has been happening all over this country for a very long time. It happened in the ANC in the 1940s, when the Youth League came along and told the old guard, 'Enough of this collaboration,' and the old guard said, 'Cool down. You're hotheads.' It happened in the fifties, with the PAC, and the sixties and the seventies, with BCM. There's always this struggle, between these Uncle Toms who have a little security, and those of us who want our freedom now. And then there are the intellectuals, like October." Jacob laughed. "They want to talk about Angola, or what Leon Trotsky had to say about the national question, but they don't want to fight *die boere.* Except *die boere* are the enemy, not anybody else."

I thought Jacob's openness with me was strange. He seemed to trust me before he knew anything about me. Not that I didn't appreciate that. Jacob was hyperactive, and as such slightly opaque, but I found his attitude refreshing. I gave him rides to UCT several times. Then, in late May, Jacob was detained. He had been warned beforehand, apparently, and was just leaving his house on a hasty trip to Johannesburg when the police vans arrived. Jacob, too, was taken to an unspecified prison and held incommunicado.

The atmosphere at school was really darkening now. There were angry rallies, at which the children railed impotently about freeing Elliot and Jacob. There were no more awareness sessions about rock-'n'-roll music. Attendance remained high, but few of the boycott leaders were to be seen around school. Clive dropped by my classroom one afternoon, looking haggard, and asked if I would mind if he turned up unannounced at our place some night needing somewhere to sleep. I said I wouldn't mind.

Clive did turn up unannounced at our flat in Rondebosch a few days later, though he did not mention needing a place to stay. It was a fine winter afternoon and he had with him a fresh-faced, stocky girl in a white sweater. Her name, he said, was Mattie. I wasn't quite sure why Clive *had* stopped by, unless it was to show off Mattie. That would have been understandable. She was black-eyed, olive-skinned, and very pretty, with a mop of short black curls and the sort of quick-but-calm quality that gifted athletes often have. Mattie was a matric at a school near Grassy Park High and very far from shy.

"Mr. Finnegan, can I call you Bill?" she asked when we were introduced. "Clive says you're the most informal teacher in the history of C.A.D."

Clive and Mattie joined a group of us in Alex's study, where another visitor—a rather hapless UCT student who had come by to sell us tickets to a Jimmy Cliff concert, or some dagga, or both, or, hey bra, just to have a cup of tea—was just finishing telling a long, shaggy-dog story about getting high with the workers in his father's brick factory. Mattie let him finish, then lit into him. "Why do you call women 'chicks'?" she wanted to know.

"Why not?"

"Because it's sexist."

And away they went, the black high school kid and the white university student, with the student getting the worst of it on every subject from female cardiopulmonary capacity to the political sociology of drug use in South Africa, until another round of tea, with its attendant fuss, interrupted them. The most nearly equal exchange between Mattie and the student took place on the subject of the upcoming Jimmy Cliff concert. "What's he doing here, anyway?" Mattie asked.

"He's a musician, he's come to play. In fact, the guy's a prophet. Have you heard what he's been saying about apartheid up in Joburg?"

"I've seen the pictures of him waving a Bible around, talking a lot of shit about how he's come here to save us. He makes me sick, frankly. Who needs his kind of prophet? He travels out here wearing fatigues and a beret trying to look like a revolutionary, when everybody knows that he's breaking the cultural boycott by coming to South Africa at all. He's here for the money, finish and *klaar*. And the government's cock-a-hoop he came."

The student shrugged, unpersuaded. "Well, I wouldn't miss this concert for anything. It's a once-in-a-lifetime thing in *this* country. They're holding it in Hartleyvale, anyway—the place will be packed out with blacks."

"So what?"

"So what do you want to do, tell people they can't go hear the best music going, just because they were born in South Africa? Isn't life hard enough, that they don't also have to just sit in the townships and never see the performers that the rest of the world gets to see?"

"That's their excuse for going to Hartleyvale. What's yours?"

"Pleasure," said the student, and gave a slow, stoned laugh. "Pure pleasure."

Mattie rolled her eyes, and grimaced at Clive, as if to say, "White students. Why do we waste our time?"

After tea arrived, Mattie began leafing through a stack of Alex's record albums. She grunted with approval, I noticed, over a Joni Mitchell album, and laughed quietly when she came to an extensive selection of reggae. Our student scalper departed without having made a sale—"Be very careful at Hartleyvale" was Mattie's parting advice to him—and conversation turned to the boycott. It was in a parlous condition now, it seemed to me—even the Committee of 81's *lawyer* had been jailed—but Clive and Mattie each contended that there was some leadership still intact. What seemed to concern Mattie was less the state of the protest in Cape Town than its health elsewhere around the country. Action was coordinated and militant in the Eastern Cape at the moment, and Natal seemed strong, despite Inkatha, but Soweto was disturbingly quiet. What was going on there? Mattie very deliberately solicited the opinions of the several people present, and listened closely to whatever anyone had to say.

After tea, some of us repaired to a north-facing porch to catch the last of the day's sun. There, Mattie asked me about how Americans saw South Africa.

"Most of the Americans who realize that South Africa exists see it pretty simply," I said. "And I think most of them just tend to wonder why the blacks here haven't gotten it together yet."

"And what will you tell them, when you go back?"

"I don't know. Maybe that there are a lot of forces at work here. Like black conservatism."

"What do you mean, 'black conservatism'?"

"You know what I mean. All the people you call 'sellouts.' All the old folks who think the boycott's wicked. All the black cops and home-land leaders. All the blacks who've got cars and houses and prefer the devil they know."

"Like your fellow teachers?"

"No comment."

Mattie gave a short laugh. "Spoken like a true teacher." She raised a fist. "Staff room solidarity!"

I expected Mattie to reject my emphasis on black collaboration, as Nelson and others had—the feeling seemed to be widespread that a white had no right to blame a black for any position taken under the devastating economic and psychological pressure of apartheid, even if that position provoked vehement rejection by his own people —but Mattie's response exceeded my expectations. As conversation swirled around us and the low sun gave everything on the porch a fine, golden glow, she began to speak, quickly but softly and carefully. "You know, you shouldn't mistake whatever it is you think you're seeing in Grassy Park for the whole picture. Black teachers have been a progressive force in this country for a long time. They've gone down quite a bit in the Cape under C.A.D., and since a few other professions have finally started to open up for the privileged few that can get the training—teaching and nursing used to be practically the only things an educated black could do. But look at what this so-called commission of inquiry said about Cape Town teachers in '76. And look at all the teachers who resigned in protest over conditions in '76, especially in Soweto.

"Also, you must remember, there is a political spectrum in any community. Here, those people who are most involved with the system, the cops and the C.A.D. stooges and so on, naturally have the most interest in keeping it going. They're going to provide the most drag on the politicization process. But that doesn't mean even they *accept* apartheid. Most black people are too busy just surviving to be politically active. A lot of others feel too vulnerable to get involved. If foreigners expect all black South Africans to have exactly the same political outlook, they're just being silly. And racist—they're not allowing us the diversity, the *humanity,* that I'm sure they allow for in their own countries. But if they think that because not all blacks are actively working for the revolution here, then all those blacks who aren't must accept South Africa as it is, they're also getting it completely wrong. *Conscientization* is the problem here, not conservatism."

Rachel, who had turned and started listening to Mattie, caught my eye and raised her brows in astonishment at such eloquence from a schoolgirl. I made a face back that seconded her surprise. I found myself wondering if Clive and Mattie were boyfriend and girlfriend. They were obviously cohorts, and they made a stunning pair—she even met the condition of going to a different school—yet Mattie was hard to picture as anybody's high school sweetheart. She was so fierce, so . . . "unfeminine." As the sun sank behind the mountain, Fiona suggested they stay for dinner, and Clive was clearly about to accept until Mattie deterred him with a few oblique words about an appointment she said they had in Wynberg.

"But it's been a pleasure, a *pure* pleasure," Mattie said, doing a good imitation of the poor departed UCT student, and grinning mischievously. "It's always nice to see how the other half lives. Thanks for the tea."

They set off, and we watched them from the porch, walking together along the railway line toward the Rondebosch station, Clive looking tall and frail, Mattie punctuating some point in their conversation with a gentle roundhouse right to the chest. Alex pointed to a white car parked up the street, with an oversized aerial and two men inside it. "What's the American expression?" he wondered. " 'The Shadow knows'?"

50

The second month of the schools boycott had a decidedly different cast from the first. In Cape Town, tens of thousands of students were still on strike, and many of the children were clearly getting tired of talking. I thought I saw a broad shift of mood signaled at the Jimmy Cliff concert. I didn't go, but the several UCT students I knew who did all got roughed up and robbed and returned to Rondebosch in shock, with tales of knives, lead pipes, and bottle necks freely employed on the few whites in the crowd. This was not the sort of thing that normally occurred in South Africa. After the concert, some revved-up fans on their way home even entered a whites-only car on a train, grabbed two young men from Pretoria, and threw them off between stations, seriously injuring one, a student at the University of Pretoria. These attacks bore no direct relation to the schools boycott, yet they seemed to me to reveal a critical new element of reckless confidence in the general, constant mass of black anger.

Then the boycotting students made a sudden move into the white areas in a dramatic, Peninsula-wide demonstration staged at half a dozen shopping centers on May 24, at the height of Saturday morning shopping. They invaded the supermarkets, disrupting business—pulling goods off the shelves, loading carts with groceries and refusing to pay once they had been rung up. They brought banking to a standstill by flocking to branches throughout the city to open savings accounts with minuscule deposits. The authorities were caught completely off guard by this mass action, although the planning for it had not been especially secret. Pamphlets had been circulated, and the day before at school, Shaun had boasted to me, "See how we get their attention when the whites get behind us in a queue tomorrow." And the shopping center protests did get the attention of the white public more effectively than all the weeks of boycotting had. The demonstrations got banner headlines in the white papers and provoked a deluge of editorial disapproval from every quarter.

Many of our students took part in the disruptions at the suburban shopping centers closest to Grassy Park, but the biggest demonstration occurred at the Golden Acre complex in downtown Cape Town. There, some three thousand pupils, after having brought shopping at the complex to a standstill, gathered in the central mall to sing freedom songs and refused a police order to disperse. In front of thousands of shoppers, they were attacked by riot police in camouflage, with truncheons and dogs. An unknown number were injured, seventy-six were arrested, and the broken glass and spilled blood were not, for a change, all on the Cape Flats.

The mood at school on the following Monday was furtively triumphant, but the slow degeneration of constructive boycott activities was not reversed. Those of us still offering awareness sessions were having more and more difficulty generating interest in lectures and discussions. Student-led activities were also retrogressing—marches turned into cricket tournaments, study groups became poker games. "This boycott is getting boring, sir," Elroy confided to me. "What can we do?" Inside this question, I heard echoing the principal's imprecation—"Do you really have no advice to offer these children?"—and I did have ideas, naturally, about how the students could most profitably spend their time at school. Yet the collective mood had not about-faced; teachers were still auxiliary to this children's crusade, even as it marked time.

Which is not to say that it was always easy to keep faith in the students' greater wisdom. One morning, I sat watching some Standard Six boys play cards in a corner of my classroom. Mock betting and snarling at each other in *skollie taal,* they were doing an uncanny imitation of middle-aged layabouts gambling on a stoep or in a shebeen somewhere, such that I could almost smell the cheap brandy and township cigars. I finally broke up their game, but not without awakening a type of sullen grumbling that I had not encountered before at Grassy Park High. None of the boys, I noticed, called me "sir," and they headed straight for another classroom where there was no teacher in attendance.

More teachers were emerging from their politic silences of April. The two women on the staff room couch now rose from their endless knitting to declare that they had known this boycott business to be wrongheaded all along, that in their considered opinion "the devil was afoot!" Yet the faculty as a whole continued to have little or no influence over the children, and many teachers now openly treated the boycott as a holiday. Faculty dress standards collapsed, as younger female teachers started wearing trousers to school and male teachers began turning up in pullovers and safari suits. (To the amusement of both students and colleagues, I stuck to coat and tie. Something about a bridgehead against cynicism.) Many teachers seemed to avoid the company of students. "Education for liberation" was coming to be regarded as something of a joke.

More significant than the erosion of teachers' support for the boycott was the erosion of parents' support. The shopping center protests, which had struck me as a risky but effective piece of civil disobedience theater, had apparently not struck the black community that way. There was widespread criticism by black parents of the students, whose seriousness and self-control, said the parents, had been called into question by the May 24 demonstrations. There were a number of parents' meetings in early June which produced resolutions calling on the students to return to classes. A sudden rise in student pregnancies was cited. Parents had a double influence over the students, since most of them retained not only their traditional authority at home, but also represented "the workers" whom students were increasingly convinced they had to follow, rather than lead, in the larger liberation struggle.

There was evidence that many students were heeding the calls of their parents to end the boycott. Pamphlets that were definitely not government-originated began to appear, pointing out, "The *boycott* is not the *struggle*. It is a weapon of struggle, one amongst many others. Since the continuation of the boycott threatens to split the students and the parents into those for continuation and those against, it must be altered." But the signals coming from the Committee of 81 were, by this stage, extremely confused. It was often suggested that the Committee had been commandeered by a clique of radical idealists who were out of touch with the wishes of students or the community and favored an indefinite boycott. In any case, events seemed to be gaining a terrible momentum of their own.

The government's reaction to the shopping center protests was one of spluttering fury. Louis Le Grange, Minister of Police, promised "very strong action" against any future demonstrations. "We are not going to play around with these people anymore."

What Le Grange meant was made brutally clear a few days later in Elsies River, a squalid "colored" township on the Cape Flats. The police first baton-charged a peaceful shopping-day crowd. Two hours later, at the same spot, an unmarked van, registered to the police, was stoned. From inside the van, men wearing T-shirts opened fire on the crowd with shotguns. Two youths were killed, six were wounded. One of the dead boys was fifteen years old. Witnesses said he had been simply walking past the scene.

The popular feeling about these killings found expression a few days later when the two youths were accorded a heroes' funeral. Twelve thousand mourners followed the funeral cortege in a procession two kilometers long. Student marshals from UWC helped to keep the demonstration peaceful. At the cemetery, the crowd was addressed by black religious and political leaders, all of whom blamed the government for the tragedy. I wasn't there. When I had asked people in Grassy Park whether they thought it would be all right if I went along, no one would give me a straight answer. Finally, somebody had mumbled something about "the community," and I had taken the hint.

On the first of June, a demonstration of an entirely different order took place in the Orange Free State. A series of spectacular explosions ripped through the huge government oil-from-coal plant known as

Sasol One, destroying a number of storage tanks and causing over seventy-five million dollars' worth of damage. A simultaneous but unsuccessful attempt was made on a second plant, Sasol Two, in the Transvaal, and the next day three more bombs were found at the offices of the Fluor Corporation, the American consortium that was building Sasols Two and Three. The ANC-in-exile claimed responsibility for the Sasol attacks, which were, in economic terms, the most successful guerrilla strike in South African history. The fierce, unspoken joy over the news was a palpable reality all that week at school.

Meanwhile, two more boycotts had been called in Cape Town. One was against local meat producers, in support of eight hundred workers who had been locked out in a dispute over recognition of workers' committees. Butchers all over the Cape Flats were refusing to sell red meat, and consumers elsewhere were being urged not to buy it. The second boycott was against the privately operated municipal bus service, after it announced fare hikes ranging from 30 to 100 percent. The boycotting students had been talking about the need to forge links between their action and the community at large—well, the bus boycott turned out to be ideally suited to the purpose. Students helped form street committees to arrange alternate transport for commuters. They convinced local taxis to lower their fares. And throughout the Cape Flats, the buses ran empty. Those buses that ran at all were stoned—over one hundred buses were damaged in the first three days of the boycott.

By this stage, stones flung by black youths were beginning to loom large in the fears of white Capetonians. White motorists driving to the northern suburbs via Elsies River were being stoned so frequently that traffic was rerouted. One day in Sea Point, I was stunned to see a city bus still plying its rounds past the nightclubs and delicatessens with all its windows broken out. The bus was full of elderly white women sitting grimly in the wind. That faraway nightmare, the Cape Flats, was starting to make itself felt even here on the antipodal Côte d'Azur. For some reason, our students called buses with broken windows "TVs."

Although some whites I spoke to couldn't believe it, I felt safe driving to and from school each day. My car and I were well-known along our route and in Grassy Park, where the main driving danger remained the distractions presented by the friends and pupils I was forever seeing along the road and turning to greet. A white stranger driving through Grassy Park might have had trouble, though I doubted even that.

Then, one overcast afternoon, Rachel and I took a drive out to Mitchell's Plain. Rachel had become interested in the place, and had already made a number of trips there, interviewing community leaders—including one who had been detained by the Security Police hours after she spoke with him. On that afternoon, we went out in search of photographs for an article she was writing for an American magazine. It was while driving from one vantage point to another, along one of the wide empty thoroughfares that characterize the place, with no one in sight, that we were stoned. There was a loud *bang* on the driver's door. A foot higher and it would have hit me in the side of the face.

My reaction was interesting. I pulled over and jumped out of the car, absolutely furious. This was not the recommended procedure, which was to roll up the windows, put one's head between one's shoulders, and step on it. But there was no angry crowd here. In fact, there was still no one in sight. I shouted for the cowardly stone thrower to come out of hiding. I wasn't sure what I would do if he or she obliged. Not upbraid them so much, I think, as justify myself. Demonstrate that I was *not* one of the oppressors and did *not* deserve to be stoned. It was silly, whatever I had in mind, and Rachel insisted I get back in the car and that we get out of there immediately. She would get her photos another day—with a black escort, if necessary.

Now, as the unrest spread, and the schools boycott neared the end of its second month, the government began to crack down in earnest. More and more activists were being jailed, and all gatherings of more than ten people were banned in terms of the Riotous Assemblies Act. The provisions of this law, which prohibited all outdoor gatherings except church services and sports events, had been renewed continually since 1976. Now, all indoor meetings were also prohibited. In its own words, the new law prohibited "any gatherings of a political nature at which any form of state or any principle or policy or action of a government of a state or of a political party or political group is propagated, defended, attacked, criticized or discussed, or at which any protest or boycott or strike is encouraged or discussed or which is held in protest against or in support of or in commemoration of anything." Professor John Dugard, a distinguished South African legal scholar, called this "definitely the widest proclamation of its kind in South Africa so far."

I didn't realize at first the exact import of the phrase "in commemoration of anything." But we were coming up now on June 16, which had become a sort of outlaw national holiday for black South Africans. Known as Heroes Day, it was the date on which the 1976 uprising started in Soweto, the day on which people honored the hundreds of children killed. This year, there was a call out for a two-day, nation-wide stayaway from schools and jobs. The authorities were trying to head it off. From where we were, in Grassy Park, it was clear that they did not stand much of a chance. The planned stayaway obviously had massive support. I never met a black who did not plan to observe it. Heroes Day also happened to coincide with the end of the second term of the school year; so a festive, school's-out atmosphere began to obtain at Grassy Park High as it approached. Our students, many of them bored and tired of boycotting, began to liven up. Increasingly, I noticed, they were talking about "action" with the same guilty relish that they had once said "boycott." When the sixteenth of June arrived, I found out what "action" meant. It meant war.

51

In the Western Cape, the first day of the stayaway was a huge success. Seventy percent of black employees did not turn up for work, and all major industry ground to a halt. The newspapers called it "the most powerful peaceful demonstration in the region since Sharpeville in 1960." The emphasis in that description was on "peaceful"—137 people had died in the Cape in the 1976 uprising, which had been nothing if not powerful—but the precedent was also ominous. "Sharpeville" referred, after all, to a massacre.

And June 16, 1980, was only relatively peaceful. Where people tried to hold commemoration services, the police, citing the ban on all gatherings, attacked with batons, tear gas, buckshot, and plastic bullets. In Soweto, many were injured and one person was killed outside the Regina Mundi Cathedral. In the nearby "colored" township of Noordgesig, seventeen youths were shot. Five more people were shot in Bloemfontein. On the Cape Flats, roads were barricaded, stones were thrown, and the police dispersed crowds with a "sneeze machine," which sprayed tear gas through a huge funnel mounted on the back of a truck. The main road into Grassy Park was closed by the police.

The second day of the stayaway was also a success, as over half the black workers in the Cape continued to stay home. But the random, hit-and-run skirmishes between black youths and the police escalated drastically on June 17, and the Cape Flats was turned into a giant battlefield. Barricades of burning car tires, bricks, oil drums, tree branches, ripped-out plumbing, mattresses, and even telephone poles blocked the major roads. Schools, shops, supermarkets, and rows of houses were set alight. Businesses were looted. Cars were torched and their burned-out shells began to litter the streets. In the midst of all this, the critical strategic weakness of Cape Town, from the government's point of view, was revealed, as every route to the city's international airport was cut. The airport itself became a hysterical scene, as cars, unable to reach the city, began returning with shattered windows and injured passengers. Eventually, the police had to start ferrying passengers to and from town in vans covered with protective wire mesh. The city's military airfield at Ysterplaat, located securely (and not accidentally) in a white area, with no black townships between it and the city center, was not imperiled—so that was where two planeloads of anti-insurgency riot police were flown in from Johannesburg.

As the police mobilized, rumbling into the townships in the armored trucks called Hippos, the tactical thinking behind the wide, straight streets on the Cape Flats came into play. In pitched battle, the open terrain greatly favored the police. It was sticks and stones against bullets, and there was no place for people on foot to hide. The police used shotguns, Uzi submachine guns, and high-powered rifles, and the rapidly mounting casualties were all on one side. *Skollie* gangs were being blamed by police spokesmen for the burning and looting, but no gang members were turning up at the hospitals and mortuaries. In fact, the number of women and children among the casualties seemed incommensurate with the kind of police action being described in official reports. The few reports coming from township residents charged that police were avoiding confrontations with gangs and simply shooting people indiscriminately—and the lengthening list of victims seemed to bear them out. A twenty-two-year-old mother of three shot to death. A forty-five-year-old woman shot to death, and her husband and son both shot when they went to look for her. A seventeen-month-old baby shot in the head in her crib, the police refusing to help transport the baby to the hospital, and the baby bleeding to death. A boy shot to death, and his mother prevented from going to his body by a policeman who shouted at her, *"Laat die donder vrek!"* ("Let the beast die!")

The worst carnage seemed to be occurring in and around Elsies River, but the news from Grassy Park and vicinity was also all bad. A fifteen-year-old Grassy Park boy shot to death—not, apparently, a student of ours. A fifteen-year-old Retreat boy, William Lewis, shot to death—he had been a Standard Six pupil at Lavender Hill High School. At the mortuary, they told his mother that he had been throwing stones. But, she said, he had been walking on a hill over two hundred yards from the road, on the way to the shops to buy milk for his puppy, when he was shot. In Lavender Hill, a fourteen-year-old girl shot to death. A policeman riding in an ambulance on the road into Grassy Park—at the place where it passed Jessie's Moslem Butchery and the Dandy Cash Store—had ordered the driver to stop when a stone or stones were thrown at the back of the ambulance. He got out and shot the girl, Shirley September, who witnesses said was far from the road and far from where the stone had been thrown. The bullet entered above her left eye and went out the back of her head. The policeman got back in the ambulance, which proceeded. A wounded boy in the back of the ambulance said he heard the policeman bragging about the shooting, and that they stopped several more times to allow the policeman to shoot into crowds. Shirley September, who had been a primary school pupil, lay dead for two hours before another ambulance arrived.

On and on it went. General Mike Geldenhuys, the Commissioner of Police, announced that the police would "shoot to kill" anyone seen burning or looting in the black townships. Minister of Police Le Grange vowed to have "no mercy" on rioters. "We will act relentlessly against them," he said. "They deserve what they will get." By now, however, the attention of the world media had been turned on the Cape Flats, and the "shoot to kill" announcement raised a storm of international protest—from, among other bodies, the United States government and the United Nations. The announcement was amended to read that the police "would maintain law and order at all costs." The subtle differences therein were undoubtedly lost on many of the victims of police gunfire—such as the twenty-seven-year-old man shot dead when police claimed they saw him trying to break into a petrol pump at Tudor Motors, Retreat.

It was impossible to get accurate casualty figures. The police had forbidden reporters to enter the townships, accusing "pressmen, especially those attached to foreign news media and television networks," of "openly inciting black youths . . . to stone-throwing and riotous behavior." The police had learned of this incitement, they said, from "certain members of the South African press." The Cape Town newspapers canvassed local hospitals and mortuaries and came up with a figure of at least forty-two dead and several hundred maimed and wounded. But the police would release no figures. And then Cape hospitals received "special instructions from Pretoria" not to release any information to the press.

All this time, I was in Rondebosch—listening to the radio, reading the papers, phoning friends in Grassy Park. "You probably know more than we do," Meryl Cupido said when I called her. "The cafes are all closed. We can't get a paper!" The paper boys, I noticed, were on the streets in the white areas in their usual ragged numbers. Did they even know about the stayaway? They all slept, someone had told me, in the sheds and vans and sidewalk stands of the newspaper distribution network—violating Group Areas and cut off from the township grapevine. Other than theirs, there were few black faces in sight in the shops and offices and restaurants. Although the "Non-White" side of the corner liquor store was open, it seemed to have no business. Yet the atmosphere in Rondebosch was really not far off normal. Some clucking and head shaking about "hooligans" and "unrest" in the bookstore. The maître d' helping out with the cooking at the Hard Rock Cafe, and the white waiters smirking. Maybe the executives in their office towers were having a hard time without their tea ladies—I couldn't tell. At the student bar up the road, I noticed the black wine steward who had once warned me about the beer they called Soweto working at twice his usual pace.

The next day—Wednesday, June 18—sporadic fighting continued on the Flats, if fighting is the word. But the factories in town were running, people were back to work. Alex and I, officially on vacation now, decided to climb the east face of Table Mountain. We ascended from Kirstenbosch, through the deep forests of stinkwood and yellow-wood, ferns and assegai. In the woods, we saw other hikers, a few spectral joggers, and a sturdy-legged girl with a tiny monkey on her shoulder. Eventually, we emerged onto the rocky heights, where there was no one else, and began working our way north along the ramparts.

Three thousand feet above the city, there was a cold wind flowing over the top of the mountain. We found a sunny, protected niche and split the beer and oranges we had brought. From there, we could see the entire Cape Flats—and, beyond them, the low green hills near Stellenbosch, the etched purple peaks of the Hottentots Holland, now dusted with snow, and the whole magnificent sweep of the False Bay coast. We could also see the townships burning. There wasn't much wind at sea level, and the smoke hung brown and ugly over much of the Flats. The few thick columns that rose straight up caught the jet stream blowing from the southeast at a certain height, where the smoke turned abruptly and bore northwest. The whole of Table Mountain, Alex said, apropos of nothing, was a White Group Area. On the mountainside below us, on more or less the route we planned to take down, we could hear baboons barking.

52

After all the bloodshed and destruction, a malaise seemed to settle over black Cape Town. The mood of popular rebellion, which had been gaining strength for two months as the schools boycott radiated its message of resistance into the community as a whole, seemed spent now. And the students were no longer discernibly in the forefront of anything. During the uprising itself, they had been overtaken by the tidal wave of general township rage. The fighting had yielded few clear images. Unlike Soweto in 1976, the Cape Flats in June 1980 could not be symbolized by a column of children marching under banners, with fists raised. The confrontation with the regime's guns, when it finally came, had been less focused than that. Like the Flats themselves, the battle had seemed scattered, brutal, chaotic. It was black South African tradition to give people killed by the police big public funerals. Indeed, these funerals often became battlegrounds themselves when the police tried to disperse them, sometimes resulting in yet more deaths, and another round of resistance funerals. Yet most of the dozens of dead in Cape Town were buried quietly, as if people at this stage lacked the heart for any more confrontation. Shirley September's funeral was attended by perhaps five hundred mourners. Her mother later told a reporter, "We thought we would never see a 1976 again but this time was worse for us here." The passivity in that remark spoke volumes. The communal pressure on Mrs. September to understand her daughter's death in political terms, as a casualty of the Struggle, seemed to be effectively nil.

I contrived a reason to go into Grassy Park as soon as the roads were open. At the point where I crossed the line, the scene was one of devastation. The road was charred and broken from the tire fires used to block it. Burnt logs and the remnants of barricades lay everywhere along the verge. The particolored glint of broken glass blanketed the streets and fields. Stop signs and stoplights had all been destroyed—lending new meaning to the idea of defensive driving. Smashed, blackened automobile carcasses were being loaded onto trucks.

But all this was on the outskirts of the community—in Lavender Hill, and in the open spaces between Grassy Park and the nearest white area. Grassy Park itself, as I drove around it, looked unscathed. And so, thank God, did Grassy Park High—except for some new graffiti. On the road beside the school, I saw three girls from 6A7, and we stopped to talk. They said they had all observed the stay-at-home literally, and had not set foot outside their houses from Monday night until Thursday. "It was dangerous here, sir!" No, they knew of none of our students who had been hurt. Someone had tried to set a fire at the school Tuesday night—people were saying it was the Vlei Monsters—but the fire had not caught. It was a miracle that none of the shops at Busy Corner had been torched. Had I been to Elsies River or Ravensmead? There, they had heard, all the schools and shops had been burnt to the ground. "It must be very terrible there, sir."

Talking with these girls—tut-tutting about the damage done to buildings, murmuring "Shame!" together about the people who had been shot, speculating whether the boycott would continue after the term break or not—I again had the eerie, dispiriting feeling that the essential connection between these past days and nights of fighting and the Struggle was somehow not being made, not even by these students. I returned to Rondebosch with a suffocating sense of wasted life and pointless suffering.

Militarily, the revolt on the Cape Flats had presented the government with some problems—notably, the inadvertent siege of the city's airport—yet it had never been more than the police could handle. As in 1976, no troops had been called out. The black townships had been easily sealed off, so that the unrest never reached any white areas. This was the first strategic priority of all urban planning in South Africa, the containment of township uprisings, and the Cape Town system had handily passed a serious test. Moreover, when it came to firepower, there had been no contest whatsoever. Dozens of blacks were dead, hundreds had been shot, while not a single policeman had been injured on the Cape Flats.

Exactly how many people had died became a matter of dispute. The police at first said nine. Then eleven. Then twenty-nine. Eventually, they said thirty-four. The opposition press stuck to its figure of at least forty-two. For some reason, the police refused to release the names of those who had been killed. It seemed the friends and families of those still missing were to be left in an agony of ignorance indefinitely. The police, in any case, had been indemnified en bloc by Parlia-

ment against any civil action being taken against them by their victims or, if they were dead, by their families.

The white press had deplored in unison the Cape Flats violence,
but beyond that the opposition papers and the government papers
differed sharply in their interpretations of events. The *Cape Times*
offered this trenchant, double-edged defense of the police: "The necessity from time to time to shoot people dead by the score is a conse-
quence of the system, not of defects of character or training on the
part of the men charged with maintaining law and order." The *Cape
Times* editors also took to task the many whites afflicted with "the
convenient thought that this is a mere law-and-order problem": "To
say, as the commissioner of police is reported, that the death and
violence in Cape Town last week was 'non-political' is another mile-
stone in the South African capacity for self-deception." (The white
South African capacity, they meant, of course.) *Die Burger,* meanwhile, also praised the police, yet discerned no indictment of apartheid in the uprising. The government paper issued pious calls for
"forgiveness, courage and faith from all communities," sternly told
the supporters of the schools boycott that they had been "warned from
the beginning that things could easily get out of hand," called the
work stayaway "abortive," and commended in classic *witbaas* fashion
those blacks who had not observed it: "The courageous workers who
did not take any notice of the agitators' call for 'solidarity' or their
threats deserve a pat on the back and the gratitude of their employers." In the capacity for self-deception department, I was perhaps
impressed most of all by *Die Burger*'s plea after the uprising had been
crushed: "Will brown leaders not come to the fore to lead their people
away from confrontation?" Did the government really not know that
it had already thrown virtually all the legitimate "brown" leaders in
jail?

At least 394 people had been detained since the boycotts began,
and at least 330 of them were still in jail, according to figures compiled
by the South African Institute of Race Relations. It was not even
known under which of the various security laws 90 percent of the
prisoners were being held. The *Argus* published a complete list of the
detainees, which I tore out and taped up on the kitchen wall of our
flat, among the Italian postcards, co-op notices, and opera schedules.
(No one mentioned this obtrusive addition to the decor, but I began
to wonder if it was not in fact a bit melodramatic, and after a couple
of weeks I took it down.) Once we knew where he was being held (in
a prison thirty miles from Cape Town), Alex and I discussed the

possibility of visiting our colleague, Jacob. But such a visit was always inappropriate, it seemed, for one reason or another, and eventually Jacob, Elliot, and fifty-five other detainees were reported to be on a hunger strike and refusing all "privileges," including visits, reading matter, and exercise, in protest against their detention.

You would never have known it was such a dull, depressed time from the letters I began getting from home. The mid-June violence had made headlines around the world, and it seemed everyone who knew I was in Cape Town suddenly wanted to know what was going on, and whether I was all right. It was at least good to hear that the world at large had heard about the uprising. According to the *Times* of London, events in Cape Town had "destroyed South Africa's carefully polished new image and exposed the reality behind the promises of reform." The *Observer* was more dramatic. "The drift to war has begun," that paper wrote. "When a normally peaceful community like the coloureds go on a violent rampage, as in Cape Town last week, it is time the world community woke up to the danger." Despite the restrictions on access to the townships, some film of the fighting had reached Europe, and its impact on public awareness had apparently been powerful.

In truth, the noises we were hearing from overseas seemed more than a little unreal. The drift to *war?* Bishop Desmond Tutu, then chairman of the South African Council of Churches, not yet the Nobel laureate, predicted in a speech in London that Nelson Mandela would be Prime Minister of South Africa before the 1980s were out. Britain, we read, had just joined forty-two other Commonwealth countries in a massive Release Mandela campaign. . . . It was as if everyone assumed that the government in South Africa was bloodied and reeling now. Which was not at all how it looked from inside the country. The Prime Minister went on television a few days after the Cape Flats uprising and calmly pointed out that the state had not yet used anything like its full might against rebellious blacks. However, he said, "if we are forced to do so, people will be hurt very much more."

The newspapers were full of ads for new, shatter-resistant window-laminates—"With the incidence of urban violence increasing daily, the average working and living environment is no longer safe." Home insurance policies were being rewritten to cover "political riot." And the property market in the Cape was reportedly slumping dramatically (our landlord in Muizenberg had sold just in time), as it had done after Sharpeville, and as it had done for a long while after Soweto. But even in Cape Town, the whites did not seem to me gripped

by any noticeable new apprehension during the weeks after the uprising on the Flats. The Minister of Finance reasserted his government's
commitment to "free enterprise," the date was set for the next yacht
race to South America, young couples got married at the usual rate,
and apartheid was enforced with the usual rigor. I heard what seemed
a common white view of "the unrest" one morning at the breakfast
table in a surfing companion's house. When his mother heard where
I worked, she delivered herself of a variety of opinions over porridge,
including, "Our girl tells us that nobody actually wanted to stay away.
It was just those schoolchildren, who are being led by communists,
forcing them. We let her stay the night here, never mind we don't
have a permit, just so she wouldn't have to stay away."

I was thinking of leaving South Africa. Not only did the country's
situation seem just overwhelmingly tragic and hopeless, but Rachel
had received the long-awaited news from home: her mother was very
ill; she would have to go to her. It was unclear if or when Rachel would
be able to return. We still had little money. It seemed our plans to
travel Cape-to-Cairo might be shelved indefinitely. I was deeply torn.
I felt an obligation to go with Rachel. I felt an obligation to stay with
my students. But would classes ever resume? Would I ever receive a
work permit? I did not look forward to the loneliness of Cape Town
without Rachel. Neither did I feel ready to return to the United
States. I still wanted to cross Africa overland.

In the end, Rachel flew home by herself. We didn't know if I would
be following her on the next plane, my application for a work permit
denied, or if I would be staying on for the five months of school that
remained, or what. Rachel and I had been together for nearly seven
years, and we had endured lengthy separations before. But this one
loomed unpleasantly ill-defined.

School inspectors, principals, spokesmen of every stripe had been
declaring the school year "a write-off" since the end of May. The
children's failure to write the normal mid-year examinations in June
had been the final blow, according to these experts. On July 9, when
the African schools in Cape Town were scheduled to resume classes
and the high schools remained completely deserted, it seemed the
academic year truly would be a washout. But then the Committee of
81 put out a call for students to continue to show up at school on school
days, as they had been doing throughout the boycott. And the next
week, when "colored" schools were reopened, attendance was nearly
as high as ever.

The first day back at school was chaotic, as no one seemed to know whether the boycott was still on. A Peninsula-wide referendum was held by the Committee of 81, although we teachers were barred from seeing the voting. Then, on the second day of the new term, the Committee of 81 made it official: the boycott was suspended. On the same day, Ronald Reagan was nominated as the Republican candidate for President of the United States. The day before, the fifty-seven local detainees who had been on a hunger strike had agreed to start eating again. And two days later I received my work permit.

PART III

"NORMALISATION"

53

It bordered on being a guilty pleasure, what the Committee of 81 called "the so-called normalisation of classes." Like almost everyone else, I had grown weary of the boycott in May and June, though I had not felt entitled to say so. It would be perverse to call the sensation *liberating,* but getting back to schoolwork at last, in the latter half of July, did relieve a great deal of generalized frustration among the Grassy Park faculty. As one teacher put it, "Sitting on your thumb is *exhausting,* hey?" At the very least, it was nice to feel employed again.

And the children, mindful of the amount of work they had missed, were suddenly intent upon their studies in a way I had not seen before. Their resumption of schoolwork was only conditional, according to the Committee of 81, yet judging by the number of after-school study groups the children had organized, it was also being conducted with an eye to the year-end examinations. The Committee of 81's authority was not what it had been, in any case. At the end of July, the Committee issued a call for another week of boycotting, to protest the continued detention of some of its members. The call was ignored.

"Staff-student relationships will never be the same again," one Cape Town educator had declared during the boycott. "The established ideas of education will have been altered irrevocably."

As the third term got under way, life at Grassy Park High did not seem to bear out these predictions.

Some things were different. Dress standards remained relaxed. The students still wore uniforms, but the hand-me-down pastiche of blazers, jerseys, skirts, shirts, pinafores, and trousers they presented was decidedly more casual than before. There were also fewer children in school. Though we had lost no students in the mid-June violence, we had lost a number of kids to the local factories and textile

mills. Either their parents had become exasperated with the boycott
and sent them to work, or they had succumbed themselves to the lure
of the wage—despite the fact that it was less than a dollar an hour.
Some Cape Flats schools had lost three hundred children. We had
suffered many fewer casualties than that at Grassy Park High, and
the silver lining on the dropout cloud was that we now had slightly
less crowded classes. (I lost two or three students in most of my classes;
six or seven in 7E2.)

But "staff-student relationships" were almost immediately, it
seemed to me, much the same as they had been before the boycott. In
fact, if anything, they appeared to have regressed. The matrics who
had been effectively running the school for the past three months and
who were now under the greatest pressure to catch up in their studies
—the matriculation exams they were scheduled to take in November
would be crucial to their futures—relinquished power *ipso facto* by
plunging into their schoolwork. The more dedicated teachers were
also suddenly working very hard, trying to make up for lost time, so
that progressive-minded refinements in classroom techniques were
soon getting more lip service than implementation. Who had time for
discussion and debate when there was so much course material to
cover?

Far more striking than these natural refluxes, however, was the
way the school's authoritarians—Napoleon, Africa, and others—seeing their opportunity, thrust themselves into the post-boycott leadership vacuum. These teachers now stalked the school grounds with
canes in hand, daring anyone to dispute their regained territory. It
was the mission school all over again, I thought, minus its earlier
charm. "People showed their true colors during the boycott," one
young colleague muttered to me. "So there's no point pretending
whose side they're on now."

The students as a group seemed dispirited. All the noise and
excitement, all the euphoria of power and new ideas, were gone now.
And what had the boycott got them, other than fewer classmates,
more broken windows, and two months of work to make up? Only
their most modest demands had been met. Many of their leaders were
still in jail. Feelings of defeat were unavoidable.

It seemed essential, therefore, to try to consolidate the boycott's
gains in terms of student awareness and organization. Over the objections of students who claimed they were sick of the whole subject, I
designed my lessons with that end in mind. (Since none of the classes
I taught "exam subjects" faced the government exams this year, there

was less panic and frantic studying among my students than among most others.)

In all my classes, we discussed the conduct of the boycott—where it had succeeded, where it had not. I urged the children to be self-critical. Had the boycott lasted too long? Few students were willing to say so, but I suggested that it had. Not because they had "made their point"—clearly, that needed to be done repeatedly until apartheid was destroyed—but because, if the boycott had been suspended while the students still possessed the unity and enthusiasm of its early weeks, then the possibility that they might resume boycotting at any time would have strengthened their bargaining position. As it was, the return to class had ultimately been more the result of boredom and parental pressure than of any dynamic decision, and the threat to resume boycotting was now seen to be empty. Both time and momentum had been lost. And what of the tactic that had separated their demands into categories of short-term and long-term—had that been well advised? Or had it just allowed the government to make some classroom repairs and provide some textbooks, and postpone addressing the larger issues, since those were framed as "long-term"? Again, few students seemed willing to second-guess their leaders. 7E2, which had scarcely survived the boycott as a class, was almost unnaturally quiet.

I asked my English classes to write letters to imaginary friends overseas describing the events of the last few months in South Africa. Some of the results were impressive, showing a solid comprehension of what the boycott had been about, and of where things stood now. "We were asking for our freedom, and the reply was in bullets," Shireen wrote. "Now we must prepare ourselves for more struggle." But many of the letters turned in were appalling. One girl was mainly concerned that people overseas not think the children here in South Africa were always so unruly. Another girl assured her reader that the students had been seeking "freedom, not communism as we find in Zimbabwe." This sort of thing, after all we had been through, was pretty discouraging.

At times it seemed impossible that these were the same children who had staged those clever, subversive little morality plays just a few weeks before, or had organized and run such an efficient, effective student government. Nowadays, the SRC, whose leadership had devolved into new hands when the matrics all left their posts to begin studying for their exams, concerned itself mainly with constabulary functions, like disciplining students caught smoking in the lavatories.

The new SRC's only memorable difference with the authorities came over the question of whether Muslim boys should be excused early on Friday afternoons so that they could go to mosque.

In my classes, I tried to counter student discouragement over the outcome of the boycott by pointing out some of its positive effects. World opinion had been strongly influenced, had it not? According to a June report from London, "Criticism of South Africa's policies in the Western European press has been increasing steadily since the start of the school boycott." More immediately and more importantly, black civic associations throughout South Africa had been galvanized into political action on a broad range of local issues.

But my efforts to maintain a positive, critical perspective in classroom discussions on the issues raised by the boycott continued to yield little. Was I particularly interested in what my students thought and felt about the mid-June uprising? Then they were particularly reluctant to talk about it. A few condemned the violence against black businesses, but most took the position that there was nothing to say. *Die boere* had all the guns. It was suicidal to attack them with stones. Yet people were so angry, they did so anyway. A government classroom was not the place to discuss such things, in any case.

Only the continued detention of Elliot and Jacob seemed to rouse the children's interest in the struggle these days; and even the detainees' plight seemed to be the source of more worry than anger. Prayer meetings were held, and a girl in 6A7 gave me a turn by writing in an essay that she "prayed every night to God to let the government release Elliot and the others soon." No one made any jokes about torture these days, I noticed. But neither were people lining up to denounce the cruelty and immorality of detention without charges. Perhaps the futility of such reproaches had been the boycott's most powerful lesson for our students.

While I was busy worrying about how to counter my students' discouragement, Clive came by my classroom one afternoon and said that he thought I was wasting my breath. His friend Mattie was with him, wearing the navy blue blazer of another school.

"It's not a bad thing, necessarily, if people think they've been defeated on an issue," Clive said. "When we lose a battle over bus fares or electricity rates or inferior education, the people learn something. They learn that these little issues are not the point. Power is the point."

Mattie demurred. "They aren't little issues. Bus fares are a big thing to most people. Talking about majority rule at this stage is for intellectuals, not for the masses. The people gain confidence from small victories, on specific issues. They begin to see the power they *have."*

As she spoke, Mattie was wandering around my classroom, inspecting the walls—the magazine pictures, the Careers Information poster, the tattered maps from my travels—and shooting me wry, inquiring glances as she went.

"But I don't think you need to worry about the students," Mattie continued, addressing me. "Their morale might seem low at the moment, but they've just been through a very big educational experience. They're more aware of their oppression now than ever before, more aware of the need for good political organization, and more aware of the role they will have to play. Seeing their friends and teachers detained, seeing the cops shooting down people in the streets, these are things no one will forget, don't you worry."

Clive and Mattie had come by, it turned out, to try to sell me a copy of a mimeographed pamphlet called "Inter-School Manual." On the cover was a drawing of a raised fist clutching a pencil. The price was ten cents. I took one.

The main article in "Inter-School Manual" was about the same thing we had been discussing: what was to be done in the aftermath of the boycott. Headlined by the international revolutionary slogan "The Struggle Continues" in four languages—English, Afrikaans, Xhosa, and Portuguese—the article cataloged what had been learned through both "victories" and "mistakes," and stressed the need for students to work for liberation during both "high points like the boycott" and low points, "periods of reaction," like the present.

"Inter-School Manual" also contained articles about the bus boycott, the meat strike ("Victory in Defeat"), corporal punishment in schools (including guidelines for "Group Confrontation of Reactionary Teachers"), and the need for SRCs. There was a synopsis of the Freedom Charter,* and a surprisingly good short history of the liberation struggle, beginning with the founding of the ANC, including a deft summary of the contributions of the Cape Town–based Unity Movement, and concluding with the hope "that this article will serve as a starting point for discussion amongst cadres." The tone of "Inter-

---

*A document produced in 1955 at the "Congress of the People," a historic meeting of the ANC and other groups, the Freedom Charter is still regarded by a broad spectrum of the resistance as the blueprint for a democratic South Africa.

School Manual" was nicely balanced—both hortatory and clear, critical yet not divisive. Its fourteen pages were decorated with drawings, diagrams, quotes (Brecht, Mandela), poems, and slogans. There was even a crossword puzzle, the answers for which included "profit," "amandla," "proletariat," and "PLO." "Capitalism" was identified as black South Africa's main problem at least as often as "apartheid" was, and "Azania" was the preferred name, not "South Africa."

My favorite article in "Inter-School Manual" was one titled "Teachers—The Stillborn Radicals." It scorned the "petty bourgeois attitudes" of teachers, and declared, "Our first, our second, our final impression of *teachers in general,* is that they are a misfit lot condemned to the Sewage Tanks of Athlone. Their sole concerns are their cheques, their bonds on houses, their cars and a host of other interests. As a body, they cannot be trusted." The article concluded with a typology of teachers—who had, it said, been "put under the microscope" by the boycott—listing five distinct types of teachers. Four of these were reactionary, although inclined to "spew out glib phrases as regards the struggle in the country." The fifth type "supported us in word *and* deeds" during the boycott and had not "reverted to the old dictatorial methods."

For my relations with my colleagues, the boycott had been a watershed. It had revealed and deepened the political differences among the faculty, and as far as some teachers were concerned, I had emerged as a member of a hostile party. No longer did the principal stop me in the courtyard to share with me his war stories. Africa and Napoleon seemed to have lost interest in my views on Charles Bronson's films. On the other hand, there were teachers who were more forthcoming with me now than they had ever been before.

A group of us had started gathering for lunch in the school library, rather than in the staff room. There were eight or ten regulars in this group, including Nelson, Alex, Meryl, Conrad, Solly Marais, and a shifting complement of senior students. Conversation among the library crowd was lively, literate, and in English. In fact, this group had exactly the sort of easy, witty camaraderie I had once hoped to find after work in the Grassy Park pub.

The library lunch group was amused by my surprise at finding "normalisation" so thoroughgoing and regressive. "What did you expect, the collectivization of marking?" Nelson asked. "Man, this is still a government school."

"The pupils have been boycotting classes, demanding changes, and returning to classes since *I* was in school," Solly said. "That was nearly fifteen years ago now!" That got a chuckle—it had been closer to forty years since Solly was in school. "It's true, though. There were often walkouts at the mission schools, especially in the Eastern Cape. Even before the war, and certainly all through the forties. School buildings were burnt down. The headmasters inevitably called in the cops. So-called ringleaders were expelled, and once they knew who you were, no other school would take you."

"This 'normalisation' is nothing, compared to that," Meryl said.

"Our unity is so much stronger now," a student said. "The government must be that much more careful—even while they're working to destroy us."

Yet I had heard and read stories about how, in Soweto, for at least a year after the 1976 rebellion, power had shifted dramatically from the nominal authorities to the students, so much so that nothing happened in the township that was not approved by the students. Why was this obviously not going to be the case on the Cape Flats in 1980?

"Nineteen seventy-six was far more traumatic," Nelson said. "Some people actually thought the revolution had come. Hundreds of teachers quit their jobs. The students were not well organized, but they seized the initiative to a degree nobody had ever seen before. This boycott was better controlled, but it had more limited objectives. The authorities didn't panic. They've become more resilient."

Conrad: *"Resilient?* Look what's happening at Crestway. That's not resilient, that's vindictive."

Crestway was a neighboring high school, where the principal was being harassed by a C.A.D. inspector whose edicts concerning student meetings he had ignored during the boycott. Before the year was out, the Crestway principal would resign.

"Resilient means to bounce back. So C.A.D. is bouncing back!"

"So watch out, they'll *pak* you next!"

Actually, no one seemed especially worried that they were about to be fired or disciplined for their actions during the boycott, but the fact that the forces of reaction now held sway did give conversation in the library a certain besieged air.

54

Throughout its tenure, the Committee of 81 had complained when the press described it as a body of "Coloured" students. All local African and Indian schools, it insisted, were also represented on the Committee. The preponderance of black students in Cape Town simply happened to be classified "Coloured."

But when the Committee of 81 decided to end the boycott, only "colored" and Indian children returned to classes. In the African townships of Cape Town, the boycott continued. Student spokesmen said the boycotters wanted to demonstrate their solidarity with the local meat workers who had been locked out. The boycott was also still in force in African schools in the Eastern Cape, in Kwa Mashu near Durban, and at the University of Fort Hare.

Leadership of the boycott in Cape Town was assumed by a student group known as the Regional Committee—but police harassment and the continued blanket ban on all meetings made it very difficult for this leadership to function. For the most part, schools were deserted. No awareness sessions were being conducted at those schools that did have students. The township streets were full of restless, idle youth. In the second week of August, when crowds gathered to commemorate the anniversary of the outbreak of the 1976 uprising in Cape Town, violence erupted. Vehicles were stoned near Crossroads (a huge squatter camp near Mitchell's Plain) and Nyanga, buildings were looted and burned, and five people were killed over several days.

The government showed little interest in getting the African children back in class. In Cape Town, the parents of boycotting students formed a Parents' Action Committee to meet with the authorities. This committee carried a mandate from the boycotting students, but the government insisted it would negotiate only with school committees and community councils—bodies long rejected by the students. The leaders of the Parents' Action Committee were soon detained, in any case. When student leaders attempted to meet in a Guguletu church, they were baton-charged where they sat by police. In the ensuing flare-up, one boy was killed and four people were wounded by police firing from inside a bus.

The anger of students in the African townships came to be directed increasingly at their teachers and principals. One night, the principal of Sizamile High School in Nyanga was watching television with his family in their eight-room house in Guguletu when a crowd of young people burst in the door and began silently pouring gasoline on the furniture. The family fled. The house was gutted, as was the principal's new car. On the same night, the principal of Fezeka High School in Guguletu was attacked in his house by children with stones and petrol bombs. He, too, had his house burned down and barely escaped with his life. A number of teachers' houses were attacked. And the students did not seem to be alone in their animosity toward those whom they considered "collaborators." One teacher sought refuge from angry children in a house near his school, only to be beaten up by the equally hostile parents inside the house.

Nervous jokes about events in Guguletu and Nyanga got to be a staple of conversation in the staff room at Grassy Park High.

The same sorts of things were happening in many parts of the country where the boycott continued. In the Ciskei bantustan, conservative rural parents were trying to drive children back to class with sticks. A student constable was killed in one clash with police, several children in another. The principal of a junior secondary school in the Alice district was stoned to death by students. After this incident, the Ciskei Chief Minister, Chief Lennox Sebe, declared, "People must now realise that we are no longer dealing with students but with terrorists who have no consideration for human life. . . . I am convinced these children will kill their own parents." Like the other bantustan leaders, Chief Kaiser Matanzima, the Chief Minister of the Transkei, blamed outside agitators for the school boycotts in his "homeland." Black education in South Africa had been destroyed by "Communists" who infiltrated among the people, according to Matanzima. His appeal to students to return to class had a certain pithy logic —"Where will you get education after you have been killed?" he asked.

The ongoing boycotts were occurring within a larger pattern of unrest. Every day the papers seemed to carry reports of police teargassing a crowd somewhere, baton-charging a school, shotgunning a child. In Grahamstown in July, a woman was shot dead in her yard by police while boycotting students marched nearby. At her funeral, a sixteen-year-old boy was shot dead, and a dozen people wounded by police gunfire. At *his* funeral, three more people were killed. In a township near Port Elizabeth, four children were killed and sixteen wounded by police during a Guy Fawkes Day celebration. In Guguletu, police killed two boys when they opened fire on a Saturday night crowd celebrating the victory of black American Mike Weaver over white South African Gerrie Coetzee in a heavyweight title fight.

On and on it went. Even from the "locations" near country towns, there seemed to be an unending stream of reports of children stoning vehicles, or stopping and looting bread vans, then distributing the loaves to the people. Finally, there was a great wave of industrial strikes—at the Volkswagen and Goodyear plants in the automobile manufacturing district near Port Elizabeth, at canneries and textile mills and factories in Natal and the Eastern Cape, at Sasol. Ten thousand black municipal workers struck in Johannesburg, as did the city's black bus drivers. Black workers continued to lose most battles with management, but some observers contended that this growing labor militancy was the most significant form of political resistance to flourish in the second half of 1980—even more significant than the boycotts of schools.

In September, the minister in charge of African education abruptly closed nearly eighty schools, including all eighteen African high schools and higher primary schools in Cape Town. Although most of the schools that were closed had been deserted for months, this act removed all hope of salvaging the year's work for nearly sixty thousand students. An indeterminate number of schools were closed in the bantustans, too, where hundreds of children were also reported detained for boycott activities. There had been little if any attempt by the government to address the demands made by the boycotting African students. Indeed, these demands were almost identical to those put forth in 1976, which never *had* been addressed.

As a result of the closings, dozens of African teachers were fired; many others were transferred to rural schools. In Cape Town, in September, African teachers suddenly had their pay withheld. "This is horrible," one teacher affected told the press. "We do not know what we have done." Again, this was the kind of thing that hit home among my colleagues at Grassy Park High, and the plight of these teachers was much discussed.

Why did African students continue to boycott after the "colored" children who had initiated the boycott were back in classes? The lack of any leadership capable of ending the boycott at African schools was often cited. A more basic reason was that conditions were simply that much worse at African schools, and in African townships. Certainly, the shattering impact of influx control on social, family, and economic life in many African townships contributed to a degree of systemic breakdown rarely seen in "colored" areas.

Did African boycotters feel abandoned by their "colored" comrades? Some undoubtedly did. In Cape Town, "coloreds" were accused of a "lack of sincerity," and one Fort Hare expellee declared, "Those who give recognition to the system by attending classes are traitors to the nation." This condemnation was meant to apply to the many African children who had returned to classes in Natal, as well as to "coloreds" in the Cape. "Colored" student leaders were more careful in their remarks about those who continued boycotting. They were uniformly supportive, even once it became obvious that the uncoordinated, unfocused nature of the continuing boycott was badly dividing black opinion and putting no effective pressure on the government.

Most of the schools in Langa, Nyanga, and Guguletu would not be reopened until March 1981, well into the next academic year—by which time the "social effects" of the boycott had been "devastating," even according to pro-boycott reports.

55

Among all the manifestations of black unrest in 1980—the disruption in the lives and education of hundreds of thousands of children, the dozens of dead and hundreds of wounded in the June uprising on the Cape Flats, the Sasol bombings, growing black labor militancy—none seemed to make nearly so great an impression on white Cape Town as the deaths of two men in the August violence near Nyanga and Crossroads. Both had been drivers of vehicles that were stoned and burned. One, George Beeton, a fifty-nine-year-old contract supervisor, had immigrated to South Africa from Zimbabwe with his family only six months before. The other, Frederick Jansen, was a forty-six-year-old father of five. Both men were white, which clearly had something to do with the deafening public outcry over their deaths. Outraged editorials filled the newspapers and were read on television, a fund to aid the families of unrest victims was belatedly begun, and there was talk of armed whites preparing to take revenge on black Capetonians.

Within a week, twenty-four people had been arrested in connection with the killings. One of those arrested, Oscar Mpetha, was a seventy-one-year-old trade unionist and highly respected civic leader who had told an enquiring reporter the day before he was arrested that he believed the police were responsible for the unrest in African townships. After four months in detention, Mpetha and seventeen others would be formally charged with one count of terrorism and two counts of murder each. How exactly the authorities had settled on these eighteen people as those responsible for the deaths of Beeton and Jansen, when the crowds at the scenes of the crimes were estimated at "several thousand," was never clear.

Undoubtedly responsible for some of the vehemence of white public reaction to the news of the deaths of Beeton and Jansen was a large, gruesome photograph published on the front page of the *Cape Times*. This photograph seemed to etch itself into the memory of everyone who saw it. It showed Jansen sitting on the ground waiting for an ambulance after his bakkie had been stoned and burned. Jansen was still alive when it was taken. Filthy, bloody, and burned, he was sitting in what looked like a puddle, with his briefcase beside him. One trouser leg had been torn off, and a thin, bent, pale leg filled the foreground of the photograph. Jansen's posture radiated trauma —his head hung down, his face was in dark shadow.

It was an arresting photograph by any standard, but its special fascination resided, of course, in the fact that Jansen was not simply another accident victim, but a prophetic symbol. Before one's eyes, this middle-aged Afrikaner was paying the historical debt. All the talk among whites was about the barbarity of people who could do such a thing. But I thought the subtext of this disgust was—besides simple fear that they or their loved ones might be next—an unspoken, even unconscious recognition that communal violence of this type was only retribution for the countless blacks killed and maimed by the forces of white rule over the years.

Somehow the worst part of the Jansen photograph was the way he had been left, half-immolated, like a sacrifice that would not burn properly, and was not worth any further trouble. The huge crowd standing nearby while the photograph was taken had been, according to the photographer, absolutely silent.

56

Compared to the violence and confrontation occurring a few miles away in Guguletu, these were quiet times in Grassy Park. Even so, the undeclared war between blacks and the government had a way of flaring up in one's face. One August morning, for instance, I was driving to school with Alex and Liz Channing-Brown. The commuter traffic going in the other direction was rush-hour heavy, but we were sailing along smoothly into the sun rising over the Flats. We had just crossed the line on Lansdowne Road when several white men armed with submachine guns stepped into the road ahead of us. The men were not in uniform, but I did not consider not stopping. These hijackers looked angry and ready to use their guns. As I pulled to the curb, Liz seemed to be going into near-paroxysms of panic. Her purse, I realized, was undoubtedly full of dagga and Mandrax.

We came to a stop and two of the gunmen approached, bent over and peering into the car. The one who came to my window was fiftyish, with a mustache and heavy sideburns and a beagle's face. He stared at the three of us, looked disgusted, then straightened.

"Go on now, get out of here," he said, motioning with his gun barrel. *"Voetsek."*

We proceeded. Pulling us over had been a case of mistaken identity, quickly corrected by a glance at our faces. The police—or traffic inspectors, or whatever they were—had been looking for unlicensed taxis carrying people to the townships. The bus boycott had increased the demand for such taxis a hundredfold, and Lansdowne Road was one of the major thoroughfares out to the Flats. There were roadblocks operating on the others, too, and all around the bus stations that people normally used. My old station wagon was just the sort of car blacks would use as a "pirate" taxi—that was why we had been pulled over.

Although Cape Town's bus system was privately owned, the crackdown on unlicensed taxis was just one of the ways the government was aiding the bus company in its efforts to break the boycott. Pamphlets had been issued over the imprint of a nonexistent Cape Town Taxi Drivers Association, urging an end to the boycott. Months later, the government admitted producing these pamphlets itself, just as it had produced the flyers denouncing the schools boycott signed "Concerned Cape Town Citizens." The Cape Town City Council eventually proposed a bulk-ticket scheme, through which employers could purchase at a discount a whole season's transport for their employees, and then figure this fringe benefit into wage calculations. That way, a worker would think twice about boycotting bus service, since the cost of bus tickets would be subtracted from his pay whether he took the bus or not.

Clive: "Do you see why we don't care too much for so-called free enterprise? The government joins up with private monopolies against the people and they call it free enterprise. We are not even permitted to choose our own transport from our ghettos to our menial jobs."

The 1980 bus boycott in Cape Town lasted, with slowly diminishing effect, for several months. While the boycott undoubtedly hurt the bus company's profits, it did not succeed in rolling back fares. If anything, according to company spokesmen, the boycott only hastened the next fare hike, by creating both a shortfall in revenues, and extra expenses for repairs to buses damaged by stone throwers.

57

It had been in remission during the boycott, for obvious reasons, but in the third term my little careers counseling program revived mightily. I held special classes for matrics on how to fill out applications for scholarships and bursaries. For those students interested in medicine, we organized a field trip to the big "Non-White" hospital in town, where they were addressed by black nurses and doctors and given a tour. Jillian and another girl who said she might like to study architecture, I sent to Fiona, who took them around an architect's office and answered their questions. For Michael, interviews with the local shipping firms that ran marine engineer apprenticeship programs were arranged. Warren stunned me by announcing that he had decided to go to UWC, after all; he was vague about his reasons, saying only that the boycott had given him the time to think about things.

My goal remained the admission of the maximum possible number of Grassy Park graduates to the University of Cape Town. There were application deadlines coming up at UCT, and for black applicants some advance planning was essential. The careers information service that I had been using put me in touch with an adviser at UCT who was willing to come to black schools to advise students about the best individual strategies for acquiring the necessary ministerial permit. She came to Grassy Park High and spent a long day counseling our matrics. Immediately thereafter, "Caggle" became the buzzword around school—short for "Comparative African Government and Law," a course offered at UCT but not at UWC. This was one of the ways for a black student to qualify for a permit: by seeking to study something offered only at a "white" university. Apparently, a number of black students had been granted permits recently after listing "Caggle" among the courses they wanted to take at UCT.

Meryl Cupido met with the adviser from UCT, I noticed. This pleased me no end. I had often pestered Meryl about her plans. When she had graduated from Grassy Park High the previous December, she had done so with no plans whatsoever, she said. And she had been *doing* nothing whatsoever when the opportunity to teach suddenly arose (Meryl started work the same week I did). Was she now thinking of applying to UCT, I wondered? "Perhaps, perhaps," Meryl laughed. I asked if I might consider her my first counseling triumph—a casualty of the precounseling era rescued and rehabilitated—and she invited me to jump in a vlei.

Meryl and I had become good friends. She lived with her parents just across the street from school, and we often did our marking together at the parlor table in their small, tidy house, while her mother and sisters banged around in the kitchen and brought us tea. Meryl had misled me when we first met, with a lush and subtle version of "playing the fool." Like me, she had been forced out into the open by the boycott, however, forced to reveal more of her thoughts than she would have done otherwise. And Meryl had turned out to be better informed, and more politically serious, than many of our senior teachers (whom she had always before been at pains not to threaten). Meryl was, in fact, a budding radical activist. One of the reasons she was so quiet about her politics, I realized, was the trouble they caused her at home. Not with her mother or her sisters, but with her father, who was a loading foreman on the Cape Town docks and, in Meryl's phrase, "a reactionary." I met her father only a couple of times. He was a small, sour, muscular man, who filled the front room of his house with so much copper bric-a-brac that there was nowhere to sit.

I got along well with Meryl's mother and sisters. One of her sisters was in my vocational guidance class; another, older, was in love with a Portuguese sailor and used to ask my advice, as a well-traveled man, about whether she could possibly be happy in Portugal, since they could not marry legally in South Africa, "due to a piece of *boere* work known as Mixed Marriages." When Meryl's father came home from work, our schmoozing would stop, and I would soon pack up and head for Rondebosch.

It was Meryl who first pointed out to me that not all of our matrics wanted to study beyond high school, and that I might be able to help some of those who wanted to go straight to work. As soon as I made an announcement to this effect, several students came forward—kids like James Booysen, who said his only ambition was to find the highest-paying job possible when he finished high school. It seemed that James had already succeeded beyond the greatest expectations of his parents, who were farm workers in the *platteland* who had sacrificed everything to lodge their son here in the city while he went to high school. I felt sheepish about having neglected kids in James's position, and began contacting on their behalf some of the more progressive employers in town—banks, international corporations, department stores. But I hedged my acceptance of these job-minded students' goals by also arranging presentations at school by recruiters from the local technical colleges, known as technikons.

Meanwhile, I had hit upon another possibility for escape from the closed circle of inferior education, this one for promising Standard Eight and Nine students: the American Field Service's high school student exchange program. It was a long shot—applications outnumbered places available by fifteen to one—but ten kids from Cape Town had been selected the previous year, and the Americans would undoubtedly see to it that the draw included a few black students each year. It was not easy to picture one of our Grassy Park students plunked down for a year in a small town in Kansas, but then that was the idea of AFS: cultural exchange. I talked with dozens of students about the program and compiled a short list of kids who seemed both qualified and interested. Then I contacted, through the local AFS office, a "colored" student who had recently returned from his year in the United States. His name was Roland and he readily agreed to come to Grassy Park to talk to my group of potential candidates about his experience.

Roland gave me a fancy slap-slide-twist-clench of a handshake when we met in the principal's office on the afternoon he came to talk. "How it is, my man," he said.

Roland was a tall, round-faced kid with rubbery features and a large, sculpted Afro. He was wearing bright blue sweat pants and a tight black T-shirt with the sleeves rolled up, and had a pair of rose-tinted sunglasses propped in his hair. He looked just like a black American college athlete—which was the idea, of course. Roland laughed and regarded me quizzically: "How the hell you come to be teaching in a place like Grassy Park?" His accent was an unsettling mix of Cape Flats and half-mastered black American.

Whatever concern I might have had about Roland's ability to convey his experience with AFS to a group of strangers was swiftly allayed. He was a practiced public speaker. He had spent his year, he said, in Richmond, California, just across the bay from San Francisco, where he said he had addressed American crowds many times.

"They give you three rules when you go over on AFS," he told the fifteen students who had assembled in a sewing room to meet him. "No drugs, no hitchhiking, and no political speeches." Here, Roland paused for effect, and smiled slyly. "But hey, I broke all three of those rules in one night!"

His listeners tittered nervously.

"But seriously," Roland said, "AFS is a great trip, if you can do it. It will open your mind right up. They have a rule that you have to come back here for two years after your AFS year is over, but I'm telling you, I was ready to break that rule, too. I didn't want to come back. When I had to leave all my American friends behind, I'm telling you, I *cried."*

I had a class to teach that period, so I had to leave. I stuck around long enough to hear about some of Roland's athletic exploits in America—how he had led his school's soccer team to the state championships; how he had broken his school's record in the 220, "but I was really cranked on speed, I admit"—and to confirm my first impression that his visit was turning into a disaster. Several of the prim, bright Muslim girls whom I left behind in the sewing room gave me terrified looks as I slipped out the door. I made signs to them to be calm, everything would be all right, I would be back.

When I did get back, the meeting had just ended. Roland was already gone, and the others were filing out of the room. I asked them how it went and several said, "It was very interesting." I finally cornered a precocious boy named Aaron and asked him what he had thought. He laughed heartily. "That guy was *weird,"* Aaron said. "He mostly just talked about athletics, and nightclubs, and all the white girls he took to bed. He made America sound like one big shebeen!"

"Did people ask questions?"

"Some people asked. The girls were too embarrassed, I think. They don't like to hear that kind of talk. All those *drugs.* And some of the rest of us, I'm sorry, but we just couldn't help laughing at him. He was so *Americanized."*

I tried to explain that Richmond, California, was not really a typical American town—which Aaron already understood. "But maybe you should explain that to some of these girls, who were a bit shocked."

Did he think people had been put off the idea of AFS by Roland? Had he been put off himself? "Not really. I can't speak for the others. But this guy was, you know, just what some people say you'll become if you go away to America to study. He was depoliticized. It's like he's too 'cool' now for the struggle. He can talk about it, but you can tell his heart's really in California. That's what struck me."

A number of girls, and several boys, *had* been put off AFS by

Roland's performance. In the end, there were only three or four serious applicants. Among them, Aaron had by far the best chance, I
thought. But then he withdrew his application. His family did not like
the idea of his going away for a year just now, he said. Among other
things, the family business was short-handed. Aaron's family owned
a garage, and Aaron himself already had a reputation as a Saturday
night terror with a tow truck—filling the family compound with
towed-away vehicles, which the owners then had to pay to retrieve.
I kept telling Aaron that, with his capitalistic instincts, he would do
marvelously in America. Which made him laugh his big, easy laugh.
But being in business here was depoliticizing enough, he said. He
didn't need equal opportunity to make it worse! In truth, Aaron was
not in dire need of widened horizons. And none of the other applicants
to AFS from Grassy Park High was accepted into the program.

Offering the starkest possible contrast to Roland's jazzed-up jock
manner, in the way of a Cape Flats high school student transformed
by a stint away from home, was Elliot's demeanor when he was finally
released from prison. He arrived at school one Monday afternoon in
the back of a bakkie. Classrooms immediately emptied as students
flocked to give him a returning hero's welcome. Elliot looked awful:
pale, dazed, frightened, and aged. But he stood up on the bed of the
bakkie and gave a short, moving speech in a clipped, militant language that he had not known when we last saw him. Detention had
not affected his commitment to the struggle, he said, except to
strengthen it. He had been kept alone in a cell, but had been able to
shout to other prisoners, including several resistance veterans who
had helped him keep his spirits up. He had celebrated his seventeenth
birthday in jail. Elliot gave a raised-fist salute, tears streaming down
his face.

"*Amandla,*" he called.

"*NGAWETHU!*" roared the students.

"*Amandla!*"

"*NGAWETHU!*"

A few weeks later, Elliot came to me for some counseling. He said
he was interested in going into computers. I had to ask him why.

"They seem interesting," he said. "And they're going to be using
them for nearly everything. There will be a need for people who
understand them."

This was true enough, of course, but I wondered if Elliot realized
how much of his time would be consumed by a full-time course in

computers at a university. He saw what I was getting at.

"I'll have the time," he said, looking at me steadily. "I just spent three months locked up. I was naive and inexperienced when I went in. Everybody knows I was interrogated. Some cadres come out working for the regime. It can take a long time to tell, after someone comes out, whether they still have their commitment. I understand that. The struggle must be protected."

Computers it would be, then, for Elliot, if he could possibly manage to catch up and pass his exams. "Jail is a good school," they say in the resistance. Talking to the new, post-detention Elliot, I could see what they meant.

58

It was wintertime now, the rainy season in the Cape, and the fishermen were out on the street corners in Grassy Park, selling long blue *snoek* from the backs of carts and trucks. In New Room 16, normalization proceeded apace. There were only so many ways to include the late great boycott in one's lesson plans, and it began to figure less and less in mine. In geography, we now addressed ourselves to neutral subjects like topography and the weather. I myself was particularly interested in learning more about how Cape Town weather worked—specifically, about when warm weather could be expected to return. There were mornings now when it was so cold that I could hardly concentrate to teach. On those mornings, my students tended to abandon their usual seating arrangements and all cram together into one corner of the room. They would laugh as I paced before them, stamping my feet, and they would laugh even harder when I finally gave up and squeezed myself into the relative warmth of their midst. Someone in 7E1 suggested that the belt of high pressure currently squatting somewhere over Angola was unjustly depriving us of heat and would apparently have to be forced to comply with the democratic wishes of the majority of the people.

I gave a series of pop-quizzes to check my geography students' retention of the material we had covered before the boycott. I was dismayed by the results, and I was further dismayed by the complaints of several students that the problem was the poor quality of their notes from earlier lessons. It seemed I had expected too much from them in the way of taking notes from lectures and discussions. Indeed, I was beginning to worry that my impatience generally—my unwillingness to go over simple material several times, slowly—was having ill effects on some children. While I enjoyed teaching, I began to wonder if I had the right personality for doing it well at this level.

In English, to the great distress of all those children who hadn't done theirs yet, we resumed our book reports. Reading was still a chore for most of them, as was public speaking. Neither had the boycott improved my students' taste in literature. I had been hoping for something a little livelier—I was pushing Jack London and Lewis Carroll—but the children were still intent on *Jock of the Bushveld* and Mills and Boone romances. Hester finally got to recount for us *The Book of Horse and Pony Stories.* Her elocution was good, but most of the children continued to mumble, mix up their tenses, and resort to Afrikaans in a pinch. I saw that all my worrying about stigmatizing my students' native speech was needless. My impact on their habits and self-perceptions was starting to seem more and more negligible.

I resumed assigning more homework than my students thought meet, more writing than prescribed to my English classes, and resumed keeping a close record of work done. The children began to avail themselves of the opportunity to review their records and were amazed to see how far ahead of the rest were a diligent few like Josef and Malcolm of 6A8. Charmaine was outraged to discover herself quite far behind most of her classmates. Her English was among the best in her class, she knew. But she had turned in very little work. I told her she could avoid failing by completing all future assignments, but not by simply passing her final exam, and she said, "Yes, sir." But she said it so slowly it was funny, and everyone listening laughed.

I found I had less energy now for trying to make my classes exciting. Just getting through the nine periods each day and keeping *something* happening in every class often seemed enough. I had less energy for outrage at the deficiencies of the system, too, although a siren going off at an inopportune moment, or failing to go off on schedule, could still incense me. One day in 6A8, the siren aborted a great lesson on Rudyard Kipling's *Rikki-Tikki-Tavi.* While the class clambered to its feet to await dismissal, I fumed. "You want to protest gutter education? *That*"—and I pointed in the direction of the siren —"is gutter education!" The children regarded me with concern and wonder. I wearily dismissed them. On their way out, Amy and Shireen stopped by my desk.

"It's true, sir," Shireen said earnestly. "They must keep to the schedule!"

"We can tell the SRC, and they can tell the principal," Amy said.

I loved those girls at that moment. Their faces were so serious, their empathy with my distress so spontaneous, I could have kissed them. Instead, I burst out laughing, and so did they.

I was worried about Wayan. I had taken to giving him lists of books to look for in the public library, concentrating on the adventure and fantasy fiction he loved most. He would sometimes stay after class, and we would talk about his reading. Wayan was still skittish and shy with me, but his enthusiasm for literature had the power to carry him away, over the barriers of his gawky reticence. "He has been living alone on the island for fifteen years, with only a parrot to talk with; then he finds a footprint in the beach sand!" I worried about how Wayan would cope with Robinson Crusoe the racist and slaver in the latter half of Defoe's tale, but I did not worry about his reading ability, which seemed to increase each week. Then Wayan suddenly stopped coming around to talk. When I asked him about what he was reading, he mumbled something about not having had the time to go to the library. Something was wrong, and a couple of days later I managed to pry out of Wayan what it was. There were a couple of boys —big boys—who were hassling him about being "teacher's favorite" and a bookworm. Wayan would not say who they were.

I told Wayan a story that seemed to startle him and cheer him up. When I was in high school, I told him, I had also been an insatiable reader, and my English teacher had taken an interest in me. One day, this teacher had come to see me at the gas station where I worked in the evenings, and we had stood around talking about some books of his I had borrowed. After he left, one of my fellow workers, a boy my age who had already dropped out of school, wanted to know who my visitor was. When I told him, the boy stared in disbelief, then muttered, "I never had a teacher who knew my name." After that, the boy became sullen and hostile toward me. Later that evening, he and I had some sharp words in the heat of a rush of customers, and he cold-cocked me. I was knocked off my feet. The pump I was holding flew out of my hand, gasoline went everywhere, I saw stars. The gas station manager saw the punch and fired the other boy on the spot. I never really blamed him for hitting me, though. I understood his resentment, I thought. "But that was wicked, to hit you when you were not looking," Wayan said, his expression astonished, outraged, and delighted all at once.

Wayan's troubles with his tormentors, whoever they were, seemed to pass in the weeks that followed. Yet I continued to worry about him, about his solitude among his peers.

Then, a great ray of sunshine. Aubrey September and I had resumed our tutoring sessions. The boycott had improved his English vocabulary somewhat, adding some new "political" words and subtracting some *kombuis*—notably, the word *baas*. He still seemed lonely, though—until the afternoon I looked out my classroom window and saw him standing talking in the field below with Wayan. They made a comical pair: tall, timid, literate, childish Wayan and sturdy little no-nonsense Aubrey. But besides their mutual isolation, there was a certain congruence to their characters. They were both quiet, sensitive kids, one delicate, the other salt-of-the-earth. Could they become friends? Could they ever. Aubrey and Wayan became absolutely inseparable. They came to class together, they sat together, and I saw them all over Grassy Park together, walking, conferring, with Wayan's hand always resting on Aubrey's shoulder. Aubrey's command of English continued to improve, for which I credited their friendship at least as much as my teaching, and before the year was out I even saw the two of them playing soccer with the other boys in 6A6 in the field below my classroom window.

Nelson and a number of his students dreamed up a singular antidote to post-boycott malaise. They called it the Grassy Park High Touring Club and embarked on an ambitious fund-raising program. Their plan was to raise enough money to rent a bus and driver for a two-week camping trip around South Africa during the Christmas holidays. Sixty children and a handful of teachers and parents would go. The Touring Club started sponsoring Saturday car washes, benefit concerts, raffles, parties, and dance marathons, and opened a bank account. Some of its fund-raising events were new ones on me, like the "stay awakes," in which students earned a certain amount of money, pledged by local businesses and well-wishers, for each hour they were able to stay awake over a long (a very long) weekend. Nelson hurled himself into the Touring Club project with astonishing energy. It was bizarre to see the man whom I thought of as a single-minded revolutionary dashing around in a sweatshirt washing cars, taking tickets at the door of the dance, and generally acting like the leader of a church youth social. When I told him so, Nelson the atheist laughed sharply. "The kids who are coming with us," he said, "are not the same ones you'll see in church."

Clive was a member of the Touring Club, as were several other matrics who had been boycott leaders. Among the teachers, whose assistance Nelson was constantly soliciting, Georgina and Meryl were prominent supporters. Meryl, I was beginning to realize, was a pro-tégé of Nelson's. She spent a lot of time at his house, avoiding her father and making use of Nelson's library, and the more openly Meryl talked with me, the more of Nelson's language and ideas I heard in her own.

59

My parents, whom I had not seen since leaving the United States, broke the long drought of contact by suddenly coming to Cape Town for a week in August. We had a lovely time together, catching up and seeing all the Cape sights. But the highlight of their trip, they said, was their visit to Grassy Park High. I was actually reluctant to take them there—it was unimaginable that any of my fellow teachers would bring *their* parents to school—but I was overruled by every-body else concerned, from my classes to the principal to my parents themselves. So we dropped by, one sunny afternoon. First we met with the principal in his office. Van loved having foreign visitors, especially Americans, and he regaled my parents with his version of the situa-tion in black education in South Africa, and with overblown praise for my work, especially my career counseling efforts. Then he insisted we take a tour of the school.

At that point, I had an inspiration. I hastily consulted a chart to find out where my various classes were during that period, and I directed our steps to those rooms. My apologies to the teachers whom we interrupted were brushed aside. As soon as we would enter a classroom, the entire class would leap to its feet, with all eyes fixed on our little party. This chance to see some of my family was obviously a bigger thrill for my students than I had realized it would be. In the first class we visited, I introduced my parents to the children, who chorused, *"Good afternoon, Mr. and Mrs. Finnegan,"* and then, after a second's pause, I decided to introduce each student individually. It turned out to be great fun, rattling off their names, watching each face blush or brighten as I ticked them off—Nico, Hester, Terence, Aubrey, Wayan, Elroy, Koos, Charmaine, Shireen—so I did it in each class we visited. The principal claimed to be astounded that I could remember all two hundred-and-some names. He said he had never seen such a thing before in forty years of teaching (and the event did apparently enter his collection of oft-told anecdotes). For me, too, introducing my classes to my parents was something special. It was a chance to show them in an unforced way both the density and charm of the world I was living in, and the depth of my involvement in it.

A group of senior girls, having heard my parents were coming, had prepared a little banquet for them. I had heard something about it, but I had not been consulted and I was stunned to see that it was really on—in my classroom, as soon as school was out. While we waited for the girls to complete their preparations, my parents chatted with a throng of students and teachers. My mother disconcerted everyone by casually sitting down on the landing outside my classroom. People scurried around, trying to convince her to take a chair, but she politely declined, and she was soon joined on the ground by several madly grinning students.

Seats at the banquet itself were limited and reserved for teachers, but we urged all the students still around to help us eat the vast pot of curry which was served as a main course. My parents were introduced to a whole range of Cape cuisine there in New Room 16—there were *bredie, samoosas, sosaties, frikkadels,* yellow rice with raisins and cinnamon, roast chicken, *bobotie,* and *buriyani.* My father was escorted through these strange and tasty dishes by Meryl. My mother, in conversation with Nelson, complimented him more than she knew when she said that, with his beard and beret, he reminded her of Che Guevara. Nelson later told me that he was astonished to find that an American of her generation knew who Che was.

My parents' visit to Grassy Park High did have some strange little repercussions, however. For a start, I felt funny about the raving over my mother's beauty and youthfulness that some people at school kept up for a while. It seemed impossible to them that a woman could both look like that and have a son my age. On the Cape Flats, of course, it was impossible. And there were some uncomfortable moments a few weeks later, too, when a Standard Six student showed me a letter she had received from my mother. It seemed this student, who was a rather slow and silly girl, had gotten my parents' address from them and had written my mother a letter. My mother, in replying, had made, I saw, a small but crucial mistake. Unfamiliar with the format for personal letters taught in South African schools, and unfamiliar with the local habit of giving houses names, my mother had obviously thought that the name of the girl's house was her correspondent's nickname. Thus, she had begun her letter, "Dear Victory . . ." I had to struggle to keep a straight face when I saw this, although little "Victory" clearly saw nothing funny about it. She just wanted to know why my mother had written to her house.

The more substantial fallout from my parents' visit to Cape Town was simply my own realization that I had received, in no uncertain terms, their blessing. Before their arrival, I had worried about what they would think of what I was doing with my life. Since my graduation from college, they had never been anything but supportive— never showing any undue alarm at, or offering unsolicited advice about, my long-term decisions and projects, unfathomable as I knew many of them must have been—but it had, after all, been years since I had seen them. This fretting proved unfounded, to say the least. Somehow, in all the months I had been teaching at Grassy Park High, it had never occurred to me that by working there I might be fulfilling one of my parents' fondest fantasies. This had been a willful ignorance on my part because, despite their conscientious restraint on the subject of what they thought I ought to be doing, I had long known that they did have their own ideas. These had changed with the times— the Peace Corps had given way to Nader's Raiders—but the theme was constant. It was: missionary work. Aiding the defenseless, for little or no pay. My mother, especially, had always been prone to rhapsodizing about young idealists who founded health clinics in Brazilian *favelas,* or lawyers who donated their services to the poor. Seeing me teaching at Grassy Park High had obviously elated both of them. In their minds, I realized, I had joined the long queue for sainthood. They were particularly pleased to hear about my career counseling work. I had become their son-who-had-dedicated-himself-to-helping-black-South-African-high-school-kids-get-into-college.

What was the problem? Did I or did I not seek my parents' approval? I did. The problem, and the painful irony, was that I was rapidly losing faith in both the specific goals of my career counseling work and in the idea that I was doing any good at all among the youth of Grassy Park.

60

A pamphlet that circulated among Cape Flats schools during the boycott declared: "Too many parents still believe that if we get certificates and 'good' results, our future will be brighter than their present condition. This is wrong. As long as there is racial division and exploitation, we can only reproduce our present system. We must convince our parents that the only way is to reject and replace this system."

While this attitude, which was widespread among "conscientized" students, seemed justified, I found it difficult to see how it could be put into practice by students. Could they found their own schools? Could they boycott existing schools indefinitely? If not, they would have to seize the government, or at least be able to compel it to "replace this system"—both very distant prospects at this stage. In the meantime, education and training had to be acquired, inadequate as the system for providing them might be. This seemed self-evident.

So I was irritated when it seemed that many of my colleagues, even some teachers whom I had come to think of as friends, were being almost pointedly slow in responding to my requests for help getting our matrics ready for life after graduation. Were people just being lazy? Certainly it could not be that they feared I was trying to make "another James Meredith here," for I had long since abandoned the idea that our students could go to any university they chose, anywhere in the country. My ambitions for our Grassy Park graduates had been scaled down and were, I thought, no longer unrealistic. And yet there was this diffidence, this unspoken reluctance to help. Was it simply timidity, like the initial reluctance of some matrics to pursue and nail down their real career opportunities? In teachers, that would seem unconscionable.

Slowly, over several months, these questions were answered and my righteous incomprehension was rectified.

"Bugger their labor shortage. It's not our problem," Nelson said. "They've been crying about so-called labor shortages ever since they got to the Cape and the Khoisan refused to be their slaves."

I was glad Nelson was willing to talk about the question of careers —too many teachers seemed determined to avoid it entirely—but I thought this objection to my figures about future demand for skilled labor irrelevant. "It's not 'their' problem if economic growth is checked," I said. "And the point is not to rescue anybody's corporation, it's to take advantage of the opportunities that arise. Blacks in this country must acquire more skills, it's as simple as that. Who's going to run things when majority rule *is* achieved? If blacks don't have the training—and it can't be gained overnight—things will go downhill here so fast—"

"Our liberation will not be achieved by supplying manpower to whichever sector the regime decides needs it," Nelson snapped.

This argument went around in circles.

Nelson eventually indicated a more specific reservation about my career counseling work when he casually asked me one day whether the careers information service I had been using was associated with something called "the Urban Foundation." I didn't know and said so. He nodded grimly and let it go. I began to make inquiries.

"The Urban Foundation? That's Oppenheimer's show, and Dr. Rupert's,"* Raphael told me. "They started it up in '76, to help get blacks into the system, particularly into big business. 'The adoption of free enterprise values by blacks,' that's what they say they're after. What they mean is they want to make sure a socialist revolution doesn't happen in South Africa."

The Urban Foundation was also, it seemed, vaguely government-associated in its origins. And the Urban Foundation was indeed the principal sponsor of the careers information service I had been using. This discovery shook me, even though I couldn't see how it changed my basic argument that opportunity was opportunity, whether the government was involved with providing it or not. Then I had a talk with Soraya, who *had* helped me to arrange various careers events, such as the hospital tour, but who was also extremely sensitive to community opinion.

"You have to be very careful whom you accept help from here," Soraya said. "There are so many front organizations that are out to use the unwary. That's why people are so suspicious and mistrustful. They don't want to be manipulated. They want to know everything about an organization before they become associated with it. If its roots are not truly in the community, they'll have nothing to do with it. Community-based initiatives, those are the only kind that have credibility here. And the Urban Foundation?" Soraya laughed at the thought. "No, it doesn't qualify. SACHED [the South African Council of Higher Education] is probably the best counseling service. At least it's seen as black."

The problem of credibility was, I had begun to see, a very real one. Why had I not thought to consult with more people in Grassy Park before I jumped in and started buffaloing my students?

Another aspect of my careers program that had been seriously underresearched was my insistence that students use the permit system. Gradually I had become aware that the permit system was not some new and exciting liberalization, that it was in fact well understood and deeply resented by blacks. The abolition of the permit sys-

---

*Harry Oppenheimer, the leading industrialist in South Africa and a primary backer of the Progressive Federal Party; Dr. Anton Rupert, another wealthy liberal industrialist.

tem had been one of the Committee of 81's first demands during the
boycott. My attitude, in the meantime, was that students should regard its restrictions as so much red tape to be cut through. "It's your
country, your university," I told them. "Your parents' taxes paid for
it; so let's use it." This approach, defeating apartheid by pretending
it didn't exist, had obvious attractions. What I didn't realize was that
there was a long-standing, countrywide boycott of the permit system,
that in the black community it was considered "collaboration" to
apply for a government permit. Community censure was heavier in
some areas than others, and relatively restrained when it came to
permits to attend "white" universities. Still, many students felt the
conflict as they considered my advice. And for months nobody told me
what the problem was—by which time dozens of students had already
applied for permits to go to UCT, citing reasons like their great desire
to study Comparative African Government and Law.

Clive's interest in going to UCT remained limited, and one day I
finally got him to elaborate on the reservations he had expressed from
the beginning. "I just don't want to get involved in minority politics,"
he said. "That's what happens to blacks at UCT. They're powerless.
They have no leverage. We're not the minority in this country. Why
should we put ourselves in that position? We're not interested in
'integration.' We're not interested in 'assimilation.' But that's what
blacks at UCT end up fighting for. They get sidetracked by being
there."

I was not persuaded that the anemia of black student politics at
UCT outweighed the great advantages of getting the best available
education, but Clive's scorn for the goals of "integration" and "assimilation" did give me pause. While I had never thought of these as goals
myself, I began to wonder if their assumptions did not underlie my
thinking. "Eurocentrism" had become a dirty word during the boycott, and one of the Committee of 81's long-term demands had been
for revision of the school curriculum to reflect black history, culture,
and achievements. Was I not hopelessly "Eurocentric" myself? Was
I not determined to usher as many of our students as possible out of
their poor Third World backwater into the mainstream of Western
culture, such as it flowed through the libraries and lecture halls of the
University of Cape Town? And what about the AFS exchange student
program I was pushing?

Then there was the emigration temptation. Clive, in a conversation about a classmate of his who was eager to study medicine, told
me, "Half of the blacks who qualify as doctors in this country turn

about and move to Canada or Australia." Clive's figures were undoubtedly high, but the phenomenon he described was apparently
real. As Clive put it, "Why would anyone stay in this hellhole who
wasn't forced to?"

I didn't have an answer for that, although I did have an answer
for the Standard Nine boy who blew up at me one day in the middle
of an interview, accusing me of misleading him and his classmates.
"We're not going to be scientists," he said. "We're going to be secretaries and clerks!" I gave him a spoonful of counselor patter: "Some of
you will be secretaries and clerks, but others of you, if you aim high
and work hard, both in your studies and for change in this country,
may become scientists." I meant every word of this. But I was actually
struggling myself now, much of the time, to maintain enthusiasm for
my career counseling.

I was getting into a real bind. I understood some of the objections
to my career counseling, and I was disposed to heed the revolutionary
injunction that tools should be provided only to break down the system, not to reinforce it. But I did not see how to implement that
injunction. By definition, I was incapable of generating "community-
based initiatives." While I could see the point of rejecting the system
at every turn, I could also see the great value, both to individuals and
to the freedom struggle, of higher education for the largest possible
number of blacks. Gaining skills meant gaining confidence. More
education meant higher expectations. Finally, while I could see the
psycho-political value of refusing to do the white boss's work—
of refusing, in Paulo Freire's phrase, to "be for another"—I was
too much the product of my own upbringing to be able to picture any
good coming from a widespread renunciation of individual achievement.

For better or worse, and despite all these second thoughts, my
little careers program had by this point gained its own momentum.
Grassy Park High matrics were writing letters, filling out applications, and going for interviews at a great rate now, and my role was
simply to give the best advice I could.

There was a larger context for my growing ambivalence about my
career counseling work, and that was the government's "total strategy." This was the white survival blueprint that had in many ways
superseded "grand apartheid." Total strategy was usually described
in military terms—terms that emphasized increased defense budgets,
the destabilization of potentially hostile neighbors, and ever-tighten-

ing internal security—but there was much more to it than military policy.

Grand apartheid had failed to address the economic and political realities of a modern industrial state. The skilled labor shortage was only one of many signs of the failure of grand apartheid. Total strategy, by contrast, faced certain facts—of black urbanization, of economic growth, of the inexorability of black advancement, even of the hopelessness of trying to channel all black political life into "homelands." The government had not abandoned the grand plan to use the bantustans as instruments for the denationalization of the majority of blacks. It had simply recognized that not *all* blacks could be denationalized, and that a futile effort to impose the original, fanatic-segregationist's vision would only hasten the day of a general uprising. Thus, slowly, and without any notable coordination, government policy over the past few years had been growing more realistic. Increasing numbers of blacks were being educated. Job reservation was being rolled back.

At the same time, P. W. Botha's government was working to tighten influx control. For the key to the success of total strategy would be to draw the sharpest possible line between black "insiders" and black "outsiders." In fact, the survival of white hegemony hinged, it was believed, on the development of a substantial black middle class. This was the unwitting irony of the "class analysis" our students favored—that it was shared by the Botha government, which sought nothing more earnestly than that class should become more important to urban blacks than race.

The government's political objective was co-option, of course. Give a certain number of blacks a certain amount of prosperity, enough to give them a material stake in the system. These relatively well-off blacks—"coloreds," Asians, urban Africans—could then serve internationally as evidence that apartheid was being reformed. More important, a black middle class would serve as a buffer between whites and the angry black masses. Numerically, the black middle class would always be dwarfed by the hordes still excluded from the groaning board of prosperity. Yet their presence "inside" the system, assuming they could be trusted to defend their own new privileges, would be immensely bolstering to the system. Traditionally, the tiny black middle class had provided the leadership of the resistance. Nelson Mandela himself had been a lawyer, as had Oliver Tambo; Robert Sobukhwe (founder of the PAC) had been a teacher; Steve Biko had been a medical student. If this class could be enlarged and its security assured, the absorption of its skills and sophistication into the status quo could be a killing blow to organized resistance.

The government's regular announcements that it would soon be repealing "petty apartheid"—removing all "unnecessarily hurtful discrimination"—were directed at the black middle class at least as much as they were at international opinion, for these restrictions, and not the profound oppression of influx control, were what most directly affected "coloreds," Indians, and Africans "legally" employed in the urban industrial heartland. The final lure to cooperation for black "insiders," now being dangled only in the far distance, was full South African citizenship. This might be offered, it was understood, only after the majority of blacks had been stripped of even their second-class citizenship by assignment to bantustans which had accepted "independence," and only after the black insiders had passed a succession of loyalty tests, undoubtedly including conscription.

Whether or not this scenario seemed farfetched, the government was already committed to the incorporation of large and increasing numbers of blacks into the First World economy, as the projections for future black high school graduates showed. The government was already committed, too, to a double-edged policy of slow reform and increased repression. Conditions were actually worsening in the bantustans as influx control was tightened and forced removals from "South Africa" to the bantustans continued. Opponents of the government were being banned, detained, harassed, imprisoned. At the same time, the government was working hard to entice black insiders to participate in the development of "a new dispensation." In 1980, this effort focused on an advisory commission called the President's Council, created to consider the constitutional question. A few Indians and "system coloreds," as they were called in Grassy Park, were included among its government-selected members, but no Africans. Even the white liberal opposition rejected the President's Council. More recently, the focus has been on the tri-cameral parliament.

This double-edged policy, this paradox, was and is the essential dynamic between the government and blacks. On the one hand, armed repression. On the other hand, a tireless if clumsy search for "reasonable" blacks "willing to negotiate." Many of the government's "reforms"—such as the tri-cameral parliament—had to be forced on incredulous blacks. And yet their reformist symbolism was important, both for its effect on international opinion and for the way it allowed whites to become accustomed to the idea of having a few "good" blacks inside the system with them. The government's attempts to co-opt insider blacks went on at every level, from the "toy telephone" community councils to the "multiracial" (as opposed to non-racial) sports clubs that offered superior facilities to those blacks willing to play integrated games—and to have their playing publicized for international consumption.

But this search, this drive to get at least some blacks to identify their interests publicly with the government's, produced many strange and pathetic episodes. In the latter part of 1980, for instance, the government was preparing to celebrate the twentieth anniversary of the founding of the Republic of South Africa.* In Pietermaritzburg, Natal, celebration organizers told "colored" residents that "money would be no question" if the residents would only agree to sponsor a stand at the local festival. School principals offered "colored" children "free tracksuits, sweets and cakes" in exchange for their participation. The government's offers were rejected. They hadn't decided to form a republic, community leaders said, the whites had. For blacks, Republic Day was a day of mourning. This kind of episode was becoming increasingly common in South Africa—the government entreating blacks for their "cooperation." It was obscene, somehow, for it was only the system's bottomless contempt for black people dressed up as goodwill.

What did all this have to do with my career counseling work? Simply that, as I came to understand the general outlines of total strategy, I began to see that, by encouraging our students to go on to college, by emphasizing individual achievement and individual career goals, I was helping to provide candidates for the government's envisioned buffer class.

61

In the second half of August, I made arrangements with my classes, told the principal that I would be taking my allotted absences for "personal business" all in a block the following week, and drove five hundred miles up the Indian Ocean coast to Cape St. Francis.

"The perfect wave" was the myth. The reality was a sandy, windblown, fifteen-mile-long cape the eastern shore of which contained a series of sweeping points and bays that formed the heavy winter

---

*South Africa left the British Commonwealth after attacks on the country's racial policies at a conference of Commonwealth prime ministers in 1961.

swells from Antarctic storms into long, clean lines of surf of variable quality. The spot made famous by *Endless Summer* was a rocky bit of coast near the tip of the cape where the waves could actually be surfed only a few days a year, when conditions were ideal. A far more consistent break was located at Jeffreys Bay, near the eastern base of the cape. There was a modest Afrikaans beach resort there, with a couple of small hotels and a scattering of stucco summer houses strewn across the dunes. In the winter, the town's population seemed to consist mainly of visiting surfers—Australians, Americans, Brazilians, French. I took a room at a boardinghouse on the beach, where I could see the waves from my bed.

The weather was sunny and cold and the surf that week was up. Each day, I would rise before dawn, make a cup of tea in the boardinghouse kitchen, struggle into my clammy, frigid wetsuit, and be in the water before sunrise. Some days the waves were good; some days they were magnificent. The prevailing wind blew offshore, sculpting the waves into rough-grained, ruler-edged cylinders that roared down the coast for hundreds of yards without a significant flaw. The rides were long, fast, and ferociously intense. I spent many exhausting hours in the water. At night I slept profoundly. After a few days, my surfing began to regain the sharp edge it had lost since I moved to Rondebosch. I began to feel, in fact, that my life was suddenly back on the track it had been on before I came to South Africa—the old world surfing odyssey.

Grassy Park seemed to exist in another reality entirely. (I never saw a black person on the beach or in the water at Jeffreys Bay.)

That most of the people I met at Jeffreys were foreigners only added to the sense that I had somehow departed South Africa. The other guests at the boardinghouse were all surfers. None of them knew, or wanted to know, anything about the country. They were there for the waves.

Of course, South African reality was always flickering in the frame of even this otherworldly scene. Jeffreys Bay had a "location," the boardinghouse had a black staff—even visiting surfers couldn't help but notice what only a few knew was called apartheid. "It's a bloody rugged system, I reckon," one young Australian said one shining evening, while a number of us were sitting drinking beer after dinner. "But they say it works."

"Fair dinkum it works," one of his mates said. "These people have got a bloody good life, especially when you consider that this is Africa. People are starving to the north of here."

"It works if you're white," a lean, quiet Tasmanian said.

"These wogs don't have it so bad. They've got bloody good schools, and they don't even pay taxes."

"Where did you hear that?" I wondered.

"Eric. He reckons this is the most misunderstood country in the world."

Eric was the owner of the boardinghouse, a tall, curly-haired Englishman in his fifties who had come out to southern Africa twenty years before. Eric wore baggy khaki bush shorts, had a strange, bouncy, slightly fey walk, and liked to buttonhole his young boarders on his spacious, glassed-in, ocean-view stoep. From him they received an endless free supply of misinformation about southern Africa, such as the canard about blacks' paying no taxes in South Africa. (The truth was that blacks' taxable income was always a higher proportion of total earnings than whites'. Whites, moreover, received rebates for getting married and for each child, which blacks did not. This was meant to encourage white population growth, of course, while discouraging black population growth.) I avoided Eric, though I couldn't help overhearing some of his monologues. He had a deep, chain-smoker's voice, and his spiels actually held for me a certain morbid fascination.

Eric had first lived in Northern Rhodesia, where he had been an apprentice electrician "until it started going black." His life since then had been a long, slow, comfortable march southward before the tide of black liberation—over the course of which Eric had acquired an Afrikaner farmer's daughter as a wife, two daughters of his own, a hatful of opinions about World Communism and the African Mind, and a degree of wealth and leisure beyond the dreams of most working-class Lancashiremen of his generation.

"Best move I ever made was to leave England," Eric said, often. "I'd have ended my days in jail if I'd stayed."

Relaxing in his favorite chair on his luxurious stoep, pecking at an endless series of gin-and-tonics supplied by a maid in a checkered doek, Eric liked to reminisce about all the Africans he had "taken down from the tree" and turned into laborers. He himself was not a racialist, he said. That had been proved when he befriended some black American diplomats in Swaziland. But black Americans, according to Eric, were no more like Africans than the Chinese were. The African, he contended, was "only two steps removed from a bloody animal." African political aspirations were a Communist fabrication, he believed. "The African would rather be fed and in chains than hungry and free"—this was one of Eric's favorite sayings. Moreover, the only whites an African respected were the Afrikaners. "Because with the Boer he knows exactly where he stands."

Eric's wife and her parents—who were all living at the boardinghouse—were good demonstrations of the second part of this otherwise faulty piece of reasoning, I thought. They were Afrikaners, and there was a sort of dynastic placidity about them that contrasted sharply with Eric's high-volume, aggressive/defensive English racism. The three of them, plain middle-aged daughter and stout bespectacled parents, would sit in their living room in the evenings watching television beneath a framed set of portraits of Boer leaders dating back to the Great Trek, sipping coffee from pink and white cups, and clearly not feeling much compulsion to justify themselves to passing surfers. One afternoon, I heard a kid from California tell the old man that a window in his room wouldn't shut. "Tell the boy," the old man said, indicating a middle-aged black man who was working nearby. When the American hesitated, the old Boer called to the black man himself. He called him "kaffir" and ordered him to assist the *"baasie"* in a firm, nonchalant tone that I could not imagine his *soutpiel* son-in-law ever quite mastering.

The only person in Jeffreys Bay whom I told about my job back in Cape Town was a black woman named Julia who worked at the boardinghouse. She was about my age, Xhosa-speaking, with three children and a husband who worked at the Goodyear factory sixty miles away in Port Elizabeth. Julia had a bantering, flirtatious manner with the surfers at the boardinghouse, which changed abruptly with me when I told her I was a teacher at Grassy Park High. She became reserved and serious. I asked her if any of the children in the Jeffreys Bay location went to high school. A few did, she said, although the nearest "colored" high school was many miles away. Had there been boycotts there? "Only a few naughty children made trouble, and they were expelled," Julia said, and hurried off with a load of laundry.

I tried to ease Julia's new awe and mistrust of me over the days that followed by saying nothing else alarming, and by sharing little jokes with her in *kombuis* that the other boarders could not understand. Slowly, she seemed to decide that it was a nice change after all to have a guest who knew something about South Africa. And when it came time for me to leave, she surprised me by pressing on me a bag full of pastries, and by telling me I was "a good Christian." It was not my fault, she said with ill-suppressed mirth, that I was "born *wit.*"

The journey back to Cape Town went quickly. I picked up a hitch-hiker, who turned out to be a lawyer from San Francisco who had come to South Africa overland from Cairo. I was very interested to hear about his trip, which had taken him almost a year, and he was eager to hear about South Africa—all he had heard since he got here from the exclusively white motorists who gave him lifts were, he said, "kaffir stories." Somehow he had managed to cross all of Africa without realizing that blacks could not see in three dimensions, judge distances, or think rationally, and without truly appreciating the import of the idea that before white conquest blacks had not employed the wheel or written language. He had labored in this intellectual darkness, that is, until white South Africans had seen fit to point out these things to him *ad nauseam.* (After a week at Eric's, I knew too well what he meant.) I tried to satisfy my rider's curiosity about South Africa. In fact, I was embarrassingly voluble, especially on the subject of Grassy Park High. I realized that I missed my students, and couldn't wait to get back to my classroom.

62

While it was still fairly opaque and inexpressive, my students' writing had changed. There were now odd glints of boycott jargon, the occasional tweak of a teacher's nose, and glimpses of real life under apartheid that would never have surfaced in compositions during the first part of the year. "The people" appeared as often as ever, but for some children they had become a political entity: the People of the boycott guerrilla theater. Here was Malcolm of 6A8 writing about the view from the cable car station on top of Table Mountain:

> We saw Cape Town, Lion's Head, the sea and Robben Island. We could not see Grassy Park. It is only so-called White Areas by Table Mountain, because it is beautiful there. Robben Island is where they keep the leaders of the people in prison.

Terence, telling a story of hardship overcome:

> A boy named Gil was living in a land named France. He was a member of the oppressed in France, not the ruling class. He liked to play sport, especially tennis, but he was forbidden to play at the same tennis courts where his daddy played when he was a boy. Gil played tennis in the roads. Then the people grew angry and marched to the places where the ruling class lived and drove them away. Some were

killed. This was called the French Revolution. When it was finished, Gil went to play tennis at the courts in Green Point [a once-integrated area in Cape Town] with his friends and nobody stopped him.

Elroy, in an essay about life at Grassy Park High:

It's a good school, but it could be better. There are some nice teachers. Miss Cupido gives us science. She is nice. So is Mr. Finnegan. He has green eyes and brown hair. Sometimes he is angry with the children, but he will never beat them. I hope he is never angry with me. He tells us many stories. He buys his clothes at the Real American Discount Man's Shop in Athlone. They must improve this school.

My students never directly criticized their other teachers in their essays. They seemed to know I would discourage their doing so. (With me, they apparently felt more free. I did *not* buy my clothes at the Real American Discount Man's Shop in Athlone.) But the frequent sidelong comments and backhanded compliments they handed out were indications that they were still looking critically at their education and didn't mind if their teachers knew it. I was pleased to see this, for the most part, although it led now and then to small confrontations with students who seemed to have absorbed the overall idea of defying authority more than they had its progressive intent. There was Myron, in 6A6, who insisted on taking class time to make reports back to his classmates from SRC meetings, dragging out his reports with great officiousness even when he clearly had nothing to say. There was Ralph, in 6A7, who tried to insist that I send a noisy classmate to Napoleon for caning since he, Ralph, had been caned the day before for making less noise in another class. I reminded Ralph that he had carried a placard during the boycott that read "Abolish Corporal Punishment." He admitted he had, but did not seem to see its relevance, and then was mortified when his classmates hissed to him in Afrikaans the meaning of the placard's message, and began to laugh. Other challenges to my authority in the classroom were better advised. Zainul and Jasmine, in 6A8, demanded to know why I made them sit apart when they studied just as well in one another's arms, and I realized they were right. Koos complained that my marking on essays was too complicated and subjective, and I simplified my system. In general, my students were still unwilling to argue with me, and I was not always pleased when they did. But we did seem to have moved some small distance toward a healthier balance of obedience and independence.

In other Cape Flats schools, from what I could tell, the post-

boycott atmosphere was a similar mix of nonsense and new seriousness. At one school, there was a stayaway on the day of the British
royal wedding. When the surprised principal went to the head of the
school's SRC, he was told that this was a protest against Afrikaner
domination. "Because the Afrikaner is giving us such a rotten deal,
we're going to show our loyalty to the Queen." At another Cape
school, Macassar High, continued student protest focused, far more
sensibly, on the racism contained in an Afrikaans school dictionary.
In this dictionary, the definition given for *baas* was "the name of a
white man." For *meit* (maid), it was "the name of a black or coloured
woman." Derogatory racial terms were included with no suggestion
that they were objectionable—thus, *swartgoed* (black thing) was
defined as "black labourer." The Macassar students tore up, threw
away, and burned copies of the dictionary, and when a C.A.D. inspector came to their school, they pelted his car with copies.

63

At the end of August, the long dormant objections of some of my
fellow teachers to my deviations from the government syllabuses
were revived when a dreaded event was suddenly scheduled for the
following week. The inspector's annual visit! Napoleon and Pieterse
each called a meeting of all the teachers in their respective departments, at which they went over what the inspector liked to see in the
way of documentation of a teacher's progress on the syllabus. They
each asked me what I planned to do. I admitted I had no plan—a
response that seemed to cause some of our more cowed colleagues
literally to shudder. Of course, my insouciance was easily come by,
since my job meant almost none of the same things to me that my
colleagues' jobs meant to them. And my unconcern about the approaching inspection only increased when I happened to see the name
of the inspector written down somewhere. It was the same fine fellow
who had helped me get my job in the first place.

On the appointed morning, he established himself in the vice-
principal's office, where he started interviewing trembling teachers at
a brisk rate. I was one of the first called.

"*Ag*, I can't believe it," the inspector said, when I walked in. "I
thought I knew the name. So you've lasted all this time, right through
our boycott and all our troubles. And you've been teaching guidance,
too, I see. Well, you must tell me all your impressions."

My interview with the inspector lasted at least an hour, and was altogether convivial. I told him about my career counseling work. He talked about the new aptitude tests he wanted to start administering to matrics. We never did get around to discussing where exactly my English and geography classes were with the syllabus. The inspector simply said, "And how are your other classes?" And I replied, "Fine."

When I emerged at last from the vice-principal's office, there were four or five teachers waiting outside, their own interviews having been delayed by the excessive length of mine. They eyed me with alarm, sympathy and, in at least one case, hopeful gloating. I laughed and gave them the thumbs-up sign.

But Nelson did not smile when I told him about my little triumph with the inspector.

"That guy, with all his worthless so-called intelligence tests? When he came to talk to us at Harold Cressy when I was in matric, we walked out on him. We refused to listen to him."

"Why?"

"Because of what he is. Because of what he does, and what he stands for. He's a paternalistic liberal, who thinks he's helping us by enforcing the system in a friendly way."

I was shocked. I liked the inspector, and I imagined that his feelings must have been terribly hurt by the deliberate rudeness Nelson described. Nelson was probably right, the inspector probably was a paternalistic liberal. Yet snubbing him so pointedly and scornfully did not seem necessary to me.

But then Nelson and I rarely agreed about ostracism. Nelson believed in it. He would join in energetically whenever people were gossiping about someone who had broken some boycott or other. He even urged people to organize themselves "to get rid of that fascist," Da Silva. I found such group behavior thoroughly distasteful.

"But that's because you're a cowboy at heart, a true American individualist," Nelson told me one day. "You think renegades should be allowed to go their own way. You think of them as 'nonconformists.' But we have *group* objectives we must accomplish. And we understand reactionaries to be the enemy."

Nelson's special affection for ostracism as a political weapon stemmed partly, I decided, from his work with the movement for non-racial sport, a movement in which opprobrium seemed to be a major instrument. I saw this instrument at work on Philip, the talented cricketer in 6A7, whose predicament typified the double bind that many young black athletes faced, between "collaboration" and community ostracism on the one hand, and virtual inactivity on the other. Philip was a fast bowler with long, lithe arms that fairly cannoned the ball down the pitch. He was also a very quiet, polite boy, whose English compositions revealed an unusual sensitivity to the several sides most problems have. This kind of awareness could not have helped him much as he struggled to decide where and whether to play cricket.

The local cricket team for boys Philip's age had been riddled with dismissals of players and managers who had violated the SACOS "double standards resolution." This resolution was intended to punish players, administrators, and even spectators who associated themselves with "racial" organizations by barring them from all SACOS-sponsored activities. All the dismissals meant that Philip's cricket team, which played in a SACOS-administered league, was effectively defunct. Philip desperately wanted to play cricket, but the only team feasible for him to join now was a local "multiracial" squad.

Multiracialism (or "multinationalism") had been the government's response to its banishment from international sports. Multiracialism involved the partial integration of certain amenable clubs and leagues. Racial distinctions still abounded in the multiracial setup. The government's objective was clearly not the abolition of apartheid in sports so much as it was the pacification of international opinion. SACOS sought to discredit multiracialism overseas as a cosmetic, and its efforts had been largely successful. SACOS was the only South African sports federation recognized by the Supreme Council of Sport in Africa—that was what gave SACOS its effective veto over the readmission of South Africa to the Olympic Games.

But this great international leverage was not always matched by the stature of SACOS inside South Africa. Relentlessly harassed by the government, SACOS had great trouble organizing in townships where the threat of banishment to a bantustan hung over anyone who dared to support SACOS—with the result that it was not particularly strong in many townships, including Soweto, and was in fact viewed by many Africans as a predominantly "colored" and Indian organization. Even in the communities where SACOS was powerful, its efforts to implement its policies were a constant struggle, undermined on one side by the inducements offered to black athletes by well-funded multiracial clubs, on another by outright government suppression, and on still another by community resentment of its methods of enforcement. In Grassy Park, people complained that SACOS was rigid and failed to take into account all the pressures operating on black athletes, especially those applied to workers by their employers, and that most people didn't really understand SACOS policy in any case. Philip didn't understand SACOS policy, he told me one day. Still, SACOS had strong support throughout the community, and at Grassy Park High. Philip had no idea what to do.

His father was urging him to join the multiracial club. The club that wanted him, which was still all white, had magnificent facilities, Philip said—like nothing he had ever played on before. And the coaching was supposed to be top-notch. Moreover, the chances for advancement for a black player over the next few years would probably be tremendous. SACOS could certainly offer nothing comparable in the foreseeable future. This was his great chance to make something of himself, Philip's father was telling him—to compete with whites on a more or less equal footing for once, to advance on merit. Philip himself seemed mostly interested in simply playing cricket against real competition, but his father's arguments were obviously affecting him, too.

The often garbled signal from SACOS, meanwhile, was that this generation of black athletes would simply have to sacrifice their own dreams for the sake of future generations. SACOS shunned on principle all international sporting contacts, and it would continue to do so until a non-racial society had been achieved in South Africa. Indeed, this was yet another way to get banned by SACOS: having anything to do with tours into or out of the country, or even inviting overseas experts to South Africa as guest coaches. If Philip decided to play for the multiracial cricket club, he would be immediately banned from all SACOS-sponsored activities—which, in Philip's case, meant that he would be kicked off his rugby team, which was in a healthy SACOS league and commanded nearly as much of Philip's devotion during the winter as cricket did in the summer. And then there would be the ostracism, the social rejection and personal abuse he would suffer at the hands of his classmates and neighbors—and the likes of Nelson.

I thought of the shining, if narrow, avenue out of the ghetto that excellence in sports represented in the United States. How straightforward it seemed. I wondered if Philip was actually moved very much by the great SACOS tenet: "No normal sport in an abnormal society." This was the only society Philip had known. He was fourteen years old and he loved to play cricket. From talking to him, I gathered that he did understand, almost instinctively, the terrible difficulties an organization like SACOS faced at every turn, trying to behave "non-

racially" in a country where virtually every institution, every aspect
of life, had been rendered "racial." But the most powerful element in
Philip's deliberations, from what I could tell, remained—I had to
hand it to Nelson—the awful specter of community ostracism. When
cricket season began, Philip did not play.

64

It was only after we got there that we realized Da Silva had invited
only the other white teachers to his wife's birthday party. "I suppose
Miss Channing-Brown couldn't make it," Da Silva fussed as he ushered Alex, Fiona, and me inside. He and his wife lived in a little row
house in Observatory, an old working-class neighborhood on the railway line between Rondebosch and downtown. The streets of Observatory were narrow; the houses were one-story bungalows with big dark
porches and small grubby yards. Before Group Areas, Observatory
had been "mixed." It was now zoned "white," though a few "colored"
families still hung on in some places. "Play whites" tended to try their
luck in Observatory, and white railway workers lived there in numbers.

It was a strange scene inside the party. All the usual furniture
had been removed from the living room and the walls had been lined
with straight-backed chairs. About a dozen people occupied these,
including several old people, some small children, and several very fat
young women. They all sipped punch from paper cups, were absolutely silent, and did not look at us as we passed through the room.
From the bedroom, disco music blasted. I stuck my head in there and
saw another room rendered furnitureless, except for a large portable
sound system, which was being manned by a flashy-looking black guy.
Otherwise, the room was deserted. Otherwise, too, the party was
whites-only. The bedroom was evidently the dancing room, and the
black guy was evidently the evening's DJ. I headed for the kitchen,
where a few more people milled and the alcohol could be found.

The birthday girl was Afrikaans, which explained some of the odd
mix of extended-family-get-together and modern rock-'n'-roll party.
But who were all these huge young women? I struck up a conversation
with a very pretty, normal-sized, vaguely familiar young woman
wearing a rugby shirt, and I was promptly enlightened. "Most of the
girls here are secretaries at Coloured Affairs, who knew Alison when
she worked there. I'm there as well. Aren't you one of our teachers?"

Now I knew where I knew this woman from. She worked in Loubser's office. She had always been curious about who this American was, she said. We began to talk.

Her name was Marina and, like the Da Silvas' infant son, she was half Portuguese, half Afrikaans. Her mother's family had come to the Cape from Angola when her mother was young—Marina did not know why. Her father was a detective with the Special Branch. Marina mentioned her father's occupation so matter-of-factly, I thought at first she was kidding. But she wasn't. Her boyfriend, she said studiedly, was an "appie" (apprentice) who was at present "on the border."

We talked for quite a while, Marina and I. I was amazed to hear that she had only been out of Cape Town three times in her life—twice to a nearby beach resort and once to Pretoria, for a week. When she spoke of Pretoria, Marina grew animated. The discos there! And the streets were so clean! After her boyfriend came back from the army, and had completed his apprenticeship as a boilermaker, and they were married, she hoped they might move to Pretoria. "I'd also like to see Hollywood," she said. "I thought I might like being a film actress. But I've heard that's actually quite difficult to organize."

At some point, Da Silva hurried by with his flushed, rather miserable-looking wife, to whom I heard him hiss, "Shouldn't we start the dancing, honey?"

At another point, after the old folks and small children had left and the dancing had definitely started in the back room, but there seemed to be even more vast, dour young women silently occupying the chairs around the edge of the living room, I asked Marina if these new arrivals could possibly all be secretaries at C.A.D., and she said, "No. Those twins you see there, they work at Bantu Affairs. And I think some of the others are also at Bantu Affairs."

It was a weird feeling, standing drinking in that placid crowd of apartheid bureaucrats. I found myself wondering how many of the pimply young men traveling back and forth between the refrigerator, the "disco," and the bathroom were policemen. Were these really Da Silva's friends? More likely, they were his wife's, while the half dozen Portuguese-looking people who had just arrived, including one in a heavy gold necklace talking very loudly about how much he enjoyed taking business trips to New York, were his. Still, it was now clear to me what a gamut of assumptions, all bad, people at school would instantly make about the connections and allegiances of a guy like Da Silva. They would be able to picture this whole scene, and many others, all too clearly after two minutes of conversation with him. No wonder everybody at school was so ready to believe he was a police informer. Yet Da Silva in this crowd struck me as something of a beacon of enlightened humanism. There was a bookshelf in the passage on which I had noticed *Bleak House, Faust,* and *Cry, the Beloved Country.*

Marina and I were several beers along now, and she was beginning to get a little reckless. "Mario says you get on well with the coloreds at your school," she said, inadvertently revealing that she knew quite well who I was. "I don't mind the coloreds," Marina went on. "I might not mind mixing with them socially, even. Many of them are quite nice. But the Bantu, they are why we need apartheid here. They must just stay in their own places. I myself can't bear to have them around me. I don't like the way they *smell.*"

I tried distracting myself from these remarks by recalling Orwell's notion that the most profound difference between the working class and the middle class in England was olfactory, that if one group didn't like the way another group smelled, there was truly no hope for amity between them. But Marina recaptured my attention by asking me sharply, with her black eyes flashing, "So what do you think of South Africa?"

I was feeling reckless enough myself by now to reply, "I think it would be a great country if only it weren't for people like you."

Marina took this badly, and while I watched her face fall, I also tried to watch a beefy blond boy standing near her, who had been edging closer to our conversation for some time. I had decided that he was a representative of Marina's absent boyfriend, making sure nothing untoward passed between us. I thought he might wheel on me for my rudeness. But he didn't. And Marina just turned away without a word.

I wished I could take my harsh words back, but knew there was no use explaining. I went and found Alex and Fiona, who had been ready to leave the party since the moment we arrived, and we left.

65

The police released Jacob without notice one sunny Friday in late September, and for reasons we could never quite fathom, he came straight to our place in Rondebosch. When I answered the door, Jacob cackled at my reaction to seeing him standing there on the step. "Boo!" he said, and he did look a bit ghostly. After four months in jail,

Jacob's black skin had gone gray. Otherwise, however, he seemed exactly the same. Same high, crazed laugh, same high-speed chatter. "They don't mind waiting outside," he said, indicating a white sedan parked across the street, and darted past me up the stairs. Inside the sedan, two Security Police were making no effort to hide their interest in me or in the license plates of nearby parked cars.

"It was a *lekker* holiday," Jacob said as he munched the hamburger I made him and took small sips of beer. "The accommodations were good. The company was excellent. Nothing to do all day but relax and read the Bible. Victor Five Star, we called it." Jacob laughed at his own joke—the prison where he had been held was called Victor Verster. "But the view was rather poor. And the food was terrible! Somebody must teach those Boers how to cook!"

Alex and I had been desperately trying to think of what to offer a man who had just spent four months in a jail cell, but Jacob didn't seem interested in any ritual observances. He had turned down an offer to take him out for the best meal in the city; he seemed indifferent to the beer. All he wanted to do was tell jokes on his captors.

"Those warders, I'm telling you, they're so thick. They're so easy to confuse. We've just been driving them mad. Singing in the middle of the night, shouting back and forth. I'm telling you, that's why they let me out, I was giving them all nervous breakdowns!"

Every few minutes, Jacob would jump up, cross to the pantry window, peer out, and laugh or shout something to the policemen parked outside. "Still there! They never give up, those guys."

While Jacob told his jail stories, imitating the crude Afrikaans of the guards at Victor Verster with great gusto, and while the afternoon shadows falling through our fake-stained-glass kitchen window slowly lengthened through several rounds of tea, I found myself less fascinated by the antics and insults and petty punishments being described, than by the closeness, the Laocoön-like intimacy Jacob seemed to feel with his tormentors. He didn't say much about the interrogation he had endured while detained this time, and nothing about being tortured, if indeed he had been, and we didn't ask. Yet I felt as though I was looking upon an essential mystery as he spoke, a relationship so fierce and deep, that between black and Boer, that an outsider like me, or for that matter Alex, had no chance of ever understanding it. All the talk, all the theory, all the cases and analyses and close observations we interested parties could offer, counted for nothing really in that primal struggle between the aging *baas* and the rebelling slave.

Jacob asked us almost nothing about events at school in his absence. When we told him that C.A.D. had continued to pay him, that the principal had been keeping his checks for him, and that no one had been hired in his place, he just nodded and said that in that case he would see us on Monday. He left about sundown, declining a lift, or even company as far as the station platform. "Hell, I brought my own escorts," he said, and laughed.

After he left, we were left with the question of why Jacob had come to see us immediately upon his release. The best possibility was that he had simply wanted some time to collect his thoughts in a safe place—safe not only for himself but for the struggle. A more convoluted possibility was that Jacob had meant to draw a red herring across his path, to start the Security Police thinking that we were among his comrades. The Security Police were famous for insisting on believing that whites were behind every black political movement, and their operatives were forever trying to unearth the connections between the subversives (blacks) they knew and their "masters" (white), whom they wanted to know.

In our deliberations about Jacob's motives for coming to see us as he had, we never entertained the possibility that he had simply come to see us because we were friends. Certainly, we had been on friendly terms before his detention. But things just weren't that ingenuous between blacks and whites in South Africa in 1980, at least not between whites and politically active blacks. The Security Police were far behind the times in this regard. The era when sympathetic whites had been widely trusted and accepted as allies by the black liberation movement had passed at least a generation before.

There were many explanations for why this should be so. The apartheid laws themselves worked to keep blacks and whites physically and politically apart, of course. And the impact of these laws was, despite the recent gestures toward reform, still growing. This ever-deepening segregation was especially vivid in Cape Town. For example, the railway line to Mitchell's Plain had just opened that winter. Like the railway line from Johannesburg to Soweto, it had no provision for carrying white passengers. Even the Cape Town city councillor for housing had been prevented by the railway police from traveling by train to Mitchell's Plain. The urban planning assumption was that no whites would ever have legitimate reasons—social, commercial, or cultural—for wanting to travel to a black suburb. The gulf between even the few non-racist whites and the few highly educated, cosmopolitan blacks was widening constantly. Dr. Nthato Motlana, the chairman of the Soweto Committee of Ten and an internationally known spokesman, had recently told an interviewer, "I spent six years at Witwatersrand University Medical School, and I still have no white friends."

The heyday of black and white political cooperation had been the 1950s, when radical (mostly communist) whites and progressive blacks had worked together in the Congress Movement, and been indicted together in the epic Treason Trial of 1956–61. By the late 1960s, though, especially once Black Consciousness had begun to flower, the commitment of anti-apartheid whites to genuine change, which had long been questioned by blacks, was being broadly rejected. There were exceptions to this rule: a handful of whites whose help might still be accepted by black revolutionaries; various moderate black organizations that still welcomed certain kinds of white participation. And the resistance was due for a rebirth of black-white alliances in the 1980s.* But the issue remained a deeply divisive one: the ANC and its affiliates accepted white members; the PAC and most Black Consciousness organizations did not. And the bare fact was that a man like Jacob did not have white comrades.

It had taken me some months to figure this out for myself, and I had resisted its implications every step of the way. While I had never expected that the black militants of my acquaintance would reveal their political agendas to me, I had not yet accepted a corollary social exclusion. I still thought of Grassy Park as the center of my life in Cape Town. During a shaky period after Rachel left, I had even taken to squandering my Saturday nights in Grassy Park honky-tonks— drinking and dancing and refusing to think about the finer moral issues raised when a white crossed the line where a black could not. These Saturday nights had let me in for some merciless Monday mornings, as my students seemed to derive endless pleasure from officiously announcing, "Sir *enjoyed himself* at the weekend." The obvious uneasiness of some of my friends at school—Meryl, Conrad, Nelson, Soraya—when they would hear that I had been seen *jolling* at places like the Jolly Carp (an old roadhouse near the vlei) or Traffique Lights (the new disco at Busy Corner) also contributed to my decision to abandon this frantic merrymaking.

Yet I continued to go to Grassy Park whenever I had the slightest

---

*Notably in the United Democratic Front, a broad-based coalition founded in 1983. See Epilogue.

excuse to do so, and there were several late-winter Sunday afternoons there that were near-epiphanic for me. I might find myself walking down the road, somewhere near school. The sun, riding low over the dark wall of the Constantiaberg, would be soaking everything in a rich, buttery light. Kids from my classes would be passing on bicycles, or walking along with linked arms, or playing soccer in a sandy side street. Shouted greetings, jokes, laughter. People puttering about in their yards, old people smoking on their stoeps, a quiet group picnicking on the field behind the school. I might be on my way from seeing a student who had been ill. I might be on my way to Meryl's house for tea and some of her mother's delicious coconut tarts. A feeling would come over me, both calming and poignant: I was home. I knew so many people here, so many knew me. I had such warm feelings about the place. I knew, of course, that it was really everyone else's home, not mine—that was where the poignancy arose. But it had been so long since I had stayed anywhere long enough to become widely known, and to get to know a lot of people well, that I would just let the sense of being home flood me. It was exquisite. And I was in no rush to repudiate this connection I felt in Grassy Park merely because such connections had been "discredited" for people who were classified "white."

Alex and Fiona slowly became for me the representatives of a more resigned attitude toward the color line. At a staff braai near the beginning of the year, Fiona had been verbally abused by a drunken ex-teacher, and she had since declined to attend any more staff functions. When some teachers started talking about going camping up the coast somewhere for a weekend, Alex quickly begged off. He told me that he and Fiona had gone on a similar outing the year before. Everyone had been drunk the entire time, he said, and someone had squirted toothpaste in Fiona's hair while she slept—"not exactly our idea of fun." As it turned out, the camping weekend did not happen in 1980, but Alex's suggestion about "our" versus "their" ideas of fun stuck in my mind.

Alex and Fiona had been in Cape Town only two years and did not know many people. But their social world was solidly centered in Rondebosch and oriented almost exclusively toward other whites. They had more experience and fewer illusions than I, and their stoic acceptance of their appointed place in the South African scheme of things often made me feel foolish as I rushed off to some gathering or other in Grassy Park.

66

Social life in the student ghetto of Rondebosch did have its interracial facets. A few blacks would appear at parties. There were some well-known black drug dealers. A couple of miles up the road toward the city center, in Woodstock—a crumbling old district between Observatory and what was left of District Six—there were several nightclubs with "mixed" clienteles. These clubs led a tenuous existence on the far side of the race stipulations in the liquor laws, but were quite popular in the meantime among white students eager to dance and romance with the blacks who came there for the same purpose. There were also said to be a number of brothels in Woodstock where the Immorality Act was ignored in deference to the democratic lusts of white students. One of our neighbors in Rondebosch, a music student named Roger, was in the habit of patrolling the main road through Woodstock in his car in search of black girls adrift on the night, and these beneficiaries of his hospitality could often be seen straggling off to the railway station in the mornings as we left for school. Then Roger discovered one day that a number of his possessions had departed along with his most recent guest, which put him in a quandary over how to report the loss to the police so as to collect on his insurance without having his life destroyed by charges brought under the Immorality Act.

UCT students were denied a sense of full membership in the international youth culture by apartheid. For example, there was a rock festival held on a farm about fifty miles from Cape Town. All the top local bands were scheduled to appear. People planned to sleep out under the stars. The music would play night and day. It would be just like *the* Woodstock, or the Isle of Wight, in miniature. Except that the laws forbidding "mixed" camping prohibited black people from attending. It was unlikely that many blacks were dying *to* go to a sixties-style rock festival, yet the feeling of absurdity that overhung that meadow full of ostentatiously "free" white youth in the middle of an overwhelmingly black country pretty well spoiled the festival's charm for many participants, I was told. The same problem seemed to me to obtain around the local punk rock scene. There were a couple of punk clubs in Cape Town, and a number of bands with names like the Rude Dementals. I sometimes went to these clubs and thought it was great stuff—the ragged, aggressive, no-stage wildness. And yet I would find myself falling out of the whole *jol* every time I remembered that this was all happening in South Africa. It was as if these high-style punkers were cavorting on a platform magically suspended in midair, prevented from crashing to earth only by their collective fantasy that they were in Soho or Chelsea or West Hollywood. The fantasy involved forgetting not only that the earth below was African, but that the opportunity for this scene to exist was being provided by a police-state machinery of massive exploitation, repression, and what much of the world was calling genocide.

A very stoned student once enunciated for me some of the hapless bewilderment he and his friends felt. "It's like science fiction," he said. "The Earth has been captured by this race of evil aliens. The Rock Spiders. They're completely crazy, and they're very stupid, but they're tough, hey, and they can be quite cunning. They've enslaved all the black-skinned earthlings, and they've given the white-skinned earthlings a choice. That's their real cunning: The Choice. You can be with them, and enjoy the fruits of rulership, or you can resist, and *die*. You can't possibly understand this situation here. In America, almost everyone's an earthling. Not so here in South Africa. We've been invaded and conquered by the Rock Spiders From Outer Space."

Talk about "rocks" and "rock spiders" and "hairybacks" was actually much less common in Rondebosch than it was among, say, the English-speaking surfers I had met in Muizenberg. Blaming Afrikaners for apartheid seemed to be widely understood among students as an obvious and even racist cop-out. Many male students had already been confronted with the Choice in its most concrete form: conscription. Some of those who had "done their service" spoke bitterly of the abuse they had received from Afrikaner officers and fellow soldiers, but others talked about their time in the army as having been an opportunity to get over some of their anti-Afrikaans prejudices. A few even raved about the class-leveling aspect of military service. "I would never have associated with guys like that otherwise, poor whites and real *platteland boere;* I was raised to believe they were inferior."

For nearly every student who had been in the army—and many of them had already seen combat—the experience had clearly been, if nothing else, sobering. There was far less undergraduate silliness among these boys than among their not-yet-drafted classmates. Their youthful romanticism seemed to have been taken out and shot somewhere in the deserts of northern Namibia or southern Angola. They had few illusions about either their true position in southern Africa or the ultimate differences between themselves and Afrikaners.

Along with the student radicals—whose ranks were periodically thinned by detentions without trial—the ex-soldiers among the students in Rondebosch gave the political atmosphere a certain seriousness, a heaviness that belied the lighter-than-air impression one might otherwise gather from the downtown punk clubs or the country rock festivals. The two things went together somehow: the palpable irrelevance of English-speaking whites to the real national struggle for power, and a suffocating sense of moral and historical urgency. White South Africans—at least those afflicted with a form of social conscience that I recognized—lived with a generalized psychological pressure of crushing intensity. They were forced to justify themselves every day at a level that few people—certainly very few Americans or Europeans—ever had to acknowledge. Their vast privileges, their endless opportunities, the terrible crimes being committed every moment in their names and for their benefit . . .

Where most South Africans, black and white, seemed to dismiss with contempt white student radicalism, I acquired while living in Rondebosch a substantial respect for the student radicals I came to know there. Some were silly; many were infatuated with the revolutionary clichés. There were always gross contradictions in their situations. Once I phoned a young woman whose politics resembled those of the Red Brigades, and ended up speaking with the family maid, who was happy to take a message for "Miss Janice." There was a poster I saw up in several student households that declared, beneath a woodcut showing insurgent blacks armed with rifles and hammers, "Their Struggle Is Ours"—one hesitated even to ask who was trying to convince whom here. Still, the seriousness of most white student activists, the thoughtfulness of their positions, their knowledge of radical political and economic theory, were in general far greater than anything I had ever seen among, say, leftist American students. Their situation was simply so much more serious. The repression in South Africa was world-class. The inequity to be remedied was absolutely immense. And the liberation that these students so fervently envisioned would involve profound and unspecified sacrifices by all whites—the end of their way of life, as it were—a prospect that other whites never tired of throwing in the faces of these few renegades. Many white student radicals would no doubt dilute and slowly lose their "commitment" with time. But their efforts to reconcile their situations with their consciences while still in the cocoon of white university life seemed to me admirable, even if doomed.

* * *

There *were* black people living in Rondebosch—mainly caretakers, gardeners, maids, and "meths drinkers." The latter were an especially miserable species of alcoholic, addicted to methylated spirits (wood alcohol). There were untold thousands of meths drinkers living in Cape Town, most of them homeless—one saw them sleeping in parks, fields, ditches, alleys, and doorways. Some of them lived in caves on Table Mountain.

A more or less stable company of meths drinkers lived in the ditch beside the railway across from our flat in Rondebosch. One of them, an ageless little man named Wendl, had attached himself to Alex, whom he called "my master" and whose car he often washed—Wendl called the car "my beauty." I got to know several of our meths-drinking neighbors. All of them claimed to be casualties of Group Areas. They had grown up in Mowbray or Newlands or District Six, they said, but now their families were scattered all over the Flats, in Bonteheuwel and Vrygrond and Elsies River and they didn't know where. The police were forever arresting them, beating them up, and telling them to stay out of white areas. But, they said, they had nowhere else to go. Their physical stamina was amazing—they slept on the cold ground, they seemed to eat almost nothing, they destroyed themselves daily with meths, and yet they kept on going. In fact, getting hit by cars seemed to be the main cause of death among them. Staggering meths drinkers were a major motoring hazard all over the Cape. I had several near accidents while swerving to avoid some wretch who had lurched into the road.

These battered specters filled the edges of one's existence, and it was never easy to know how to react to them. One day, I was panhandled by a local meths drinker outside our flat while I stood talking with Nelson, who surprised me by glaring at the beggar and then stonily ignoring his pleas. After I had given the fellow something and he had staggered off, Nelson said, "I can't bear those people. They have no pride, no purpose. They don't even have any brains left." Then he added pointedly, "They live off do-gooders."

But that was how it was, I thought, living in a place like Rondebosch. A person was driven to do-gooderism. There were always black people with terrible problems around—women at the door asking if we needed any housecleaning done; teenage mothers asking for food for their babies. All our black neighbors seemed to live in perpetual insecurity, and to know them was to get involved. When the caretaker of our block of flats was fired, he came to me. We had become friendly when I borrowed some of his tools to work on my car.

After that, I had occasionally sat with him and his wife in their windowless garage apartment sharing tea and biscuits and small talk. Couldn't I help him now? He and his family would be sent to the Transkei if he lost his job.

Fiona and I went down to the offices of the company that owned our block of flats. We talked to a series of managers, who basically told us to mind our own business. The next day I got a call from the owner of the company, who called me a "terrorist" and said he would have me arrested for trespassing if I hadn't moved out by the following morning—my name wasn't even on the lease! I didn't leave, and I was never thrown out, but the caretaker did lose his job. The reason he was given for his dismissal was that the place did not look spruce enough—which was absurd. The place looked great; the caretaker had worked on it seven days a week, from morning to night. The real reason he was being fired, the caretaker told me, was that a man who coveted his job had accused him to the owner of having run his old bakkie as an illegal taxi during the bus boycott. He hadn't done it, the caretaker said, but his accuser had been hired in his place.

Fiona and Alex were far more used to this sort of thing than I. At one point, Fiona suggested that we hire a maid. She had recently taken a job and was too tired in the evenings to do her share of the housecleaning, she said. Besides, there were so many women who needed the work. I demurred. I had always cooked and cleaned for myself, and I had no desire to start acting like a white South African now.

"This isn't America, you know," Fiona said. "Acting like a middle-class American here won't help anyone or solve anything. If white people all stopped employing servants, all it would do is throw a few million more black people out of work."

She was right, but I wouldn't budge. What would we do, pay the standard starvation wage? Fiona, upset, said she believed a maid deserved more pay than an architect did, since the work was dirtier, but she didn't know how to put that principle into practice. Alex, for his part, stayed neutral. Fiona wasn't thinking of a live-in maid—just someone to do some cleaning. And this was far from an extraordinary idea. Most of the white students who lived near us had black domestic help and I knew of at least one "commune" that had a live-in maid *and* cook. But, in the end, we hired no one.

The job Fiona had taken was her first "in her field." She was now working as an architect for the Cape Town City Council. Her first assignment: helping to design the houses for the next phase of Mitchell's Plain. Fiona hated the work with a fine passion. It was easily the highest salary she had ever earned, but she meant it when she said she didn't deserve it. For Fiona, spending her days planning the details of the drab little boxes that black people were forced to live in, trying to ameliorate their cheapness and sterility on a limited government budget, was like a worst nightmare come to life. It was everything that was most horrid about being a white South African. She kept at it for a number of months, steeling herself with the usual rationalizations about doing as humanely and creatively as possible the nasty work that would be done anyway. But she suffered, despising herself, and eventually she began calling in sick more and more often, and spending her days at home huddled under the huge Chinese umbrella that covered the ceiling in her and Alex's room, making airy drawings of imaginary cities, or losing herself in the book Alex had given her for her birthday: Douglas Hofstadter's *Godel, Escher, Bach: An Eternal Golden Braid.*

Fiona reminded me of a Nadine Gordimer character. Raised in Johannesburg by apolitical, English-speaking parents—her father was a mining engineer—Fiona was a victim of too much consciousness. She had been an anti-apartheid activist at Wits. In 1976, she and Alex had both been been beaten up by white vigilantes in a march to demonstrate solidarity with the students of Soweto. Her politics were still about as radical as nonviolent politics came. Fiona seemed to me to look forward genuinely to the day when a black government would rule South Africa, not because the country would necessarily become a haven of justice and freedom then, but because she would finally be able to breathe freely, to stop feeling that she was living at someone else's expense.

In the meantime, however, Fiona was paralyzed. She did not have the nerves for underground activity or the stomach for the endless compromises of "legitimate" liberal politics. All the existing career options were either pathetic or objectionable. She was too bright and self-critical ever to let herself forget who she was and where she was. Or the killer: *what she must look like to black people.* At some level, I came to believe, Fiona respected that black perspective on her life above all others. It had, after all, a truly massive moral authority, accumulated over the centuries of oppression. And Fiona refused to pretend that it was any less hostile, any less rightfully scornful of her every little white gesture, than it was. Fiona was too sensitive to survive in South Africa. Yet I found that I choked on my attempts to suggest that she might be happier anywhere else.

67

I was going through my own fits of self-loathing these days—mainly having to do with my job. The basic problem was that I was a foreigner, and thus unappraised of much local lore. But this didn't just mean that I didn't know SACHED from the Urban Foundation, or the history of the permit system, or even that I brought "Eurocentric" assumptions to an African situation, and had to learn to see "total strategy" as a context within which we all worked. It also meant failures and bumbling that could not be so simply remedied. It meant, I had decided, a terrible lack of communication with my students.

There were all those jokes I didn't get—and jokes were so much of my students' self-expression. A group of matrics and I are talking about what courses the University of the Western Cape will offer next year. A boy in the back starts singing, *"Daar kom die Plato,"* and breaks up his classmates. I request an explanation. Through her laughter, Shahieda tells me that PLATO is the hobbyhorse of Richard van der Ross, rector of UWC. It's some sort of computer education system that Van der Ross is installing at "Bush" and touting at every opportunity as the wave of the future. "Daar Kom die Alibama" is a famous folk song. It was composed, Shahieda thinks, when a Confederate raider called the *Alabama* put into Cape Town during the American Civil War—on this point, there is some discussion. Yes, that's it. Probably. Anyway, that song has become a kind of "Cape colored" anthem and is sung on all sorts of occasions. I am about to ask what sorts of occasions when it occurs to me that all the laughing has long stopped, and the mood among the group has quite changed, as we labor through this explanation. This kind of thing, I think, happens far too often.

It happens in another form when I counsel students. I just don't know which buttons to push. A Standard Nine boy has decided to drop out of school to start working full-time as a box boy at a supermarket. He claims he lost too much ground during the boycott ever to be ready for his final exams. I go to the supermarket where he works to remonstrate with him. I try every argument I can think of, including reciting the latest statistics on the relative incomes of high school graduates and high school dropouts. He seems more embarrassed than anything else. I realize that I have to reach him on some more emotional level. I have an almost physical sense of the images—the names, jobs, ideas, symbols—I should be invoking to get his attention and to have any real chance of persuading him. But I simply don't know them. A local teacher would, but I don't, and we part after the boy tries to cheer me up by saying that maybe he'll try Standard Nine again next year.

It happens in still another form when my ignorance of local conditions causes me to steer students wrong. Two girls want to get jobs as bank tellers. Until recently, I am told, there were no black bank tellers. I've seen them all over town, though. I call around and set up interviews for the girls with the personnel department of a leading bank. On the day of the interviews, I get a call from the bank. It seems that neither of the girls has turned up for her appointment. I seek out the girls, who are sullen and ashamed, and I demand an explanation. Eventually, one of them blurts out that the bank I set them up with is Afrikaans and does *not* employ black tellers. They were hoping for jobs with one of the big *English* banks—Barclays or Standard. Those are the only ones that have black tellers. These *boere* banks obviously didn't realize they were black when I made the interview appointments. When I hear all this, I apologize. I didn't realize; I didn't mean to embarrass them. We can set up interviews with Barclays and Standard. The girls are now wary. Finally, I talk them into trying again. As with my initial misconceptions about certain "white" universities, this is the sort of ignorance that can be remedied, piecemeal. But the damage to my credibility done by each of my little counseling mistakes, the diminution of my ability to get students to trust me, is lasting, at least with this year's matrics. And how many more years' matrics do I really plan to counsel?

My inability to communicate flowingly with my students undermines, finally, the quality of our classroom repartee, the workaday back-and-forth that does so much to establish the liveliness of a class or a lesson. Part of the problem is just language, my not speaking Afrikaans. It's also culture, the fact that I don't know in any detail what happens at home to these children, don't know their parents, couldn't *be* their parent the way most of my colleagues could—and in that sense it's also "race."

The worst part of all was the effect that I continued to worry I was having on some of my students—not on those who avoided or mistrusted me, but on those who listened and looked up to me. What kind of role model for these kids was I, anyway, skating through their world, cut loose from family and place of origin, completely free of the crushing responsibility to their people that bore down upon the best of them?

Clive was the student who crystallized these anxieties for me. He came by our place fairly often now. The slow death of the high hopes of the early days of the boycott had disappointed Clive more than most, and he seemed to be growing cynical. "This country, the whole thing, is so *befok,*" he would say, shaking his head. He and I would argue about his future. Clive now claimed not to be interested in going to either of the two universities in Cape Town. "A club for the rich or a bush college, both a waste of time." He didn't even want to talk about it. Instead, Clive liked to ply me with questions about my life and travels. He often mentioned his brother in Europe and wondered what he might be doing now. Then one day Clive announced that he had made up his mind. After graduation, he would just go to work, save some money, and then take off overseas. All he wanted to do was travel and write. It seemed Clive's dreams about the world beyond Grassy Park had become an individualist's, like mine.

68

There was a short break between the third and fourth terms. Alex and I decided to take a camping trip into a mountain range called the Cedarberg, about a hundred miles north of Cape Town. We invited Nelson to join us and he said he would.

But on the morning we were scheduled to leave, Nelson suddenly said he wouldn't be able to go. "I knew he would do this," Alex said. "It's always something. They always do this."

I didn't need to ask who "they" were.

We decided to force the issue and went to Nelson's house. He answered the door looking sleepy and suspicious and surprised to see us. He did not invite us in. We offered to help him with whatever he had to do. Nelson just studied us, standing there on his porch. Finally, he laughed. He said he had to go by his brother's place and drop off some things, but if we didn't mind waiting awhile . . .

Within an hour, we were on the road north. By way of explanation of his near absence, Nelson simply said, "Most of my friends refuse to have anything to do with whites. They'll probably criticize me for going on this trip."

We drove through the rolling hills and wide plains of the western Boland, past the farm towns of Malmesbury and Moorreesburg. Then we turned northeast, climbed up a steep pass through rocky hills, and crossed into the valley of the Olifants River. Suddenly, the high, dark, wild-looking wall of the Cedarberg stood up against the sky to the east. The highway angled down to the valley floor, which was patch-worked with orange groves. We stopped at a fruit stand, where the boy selling sacks of oranges might have been one of our students except that he kept shuffling and scraping and *baas*ing us to a degree that shocked me. "We're in the *platteland* now," Nelson said. "I bet that *klonkie* has never seen the inside of a classroom." And if this boy's parents were offered a chance, I thought, to send him to town to get an education in exchange for some housework? This was the region where some Capetonians were said to recruit their "slaves."

That we had left cosmopolitan Cape Town became even more apparent when we stopped for gas outside the town of Citrusdal. Several bad advertisements for country living were lounging around the lube bay at the gas station, and our arrival became the occasion for much heavy staring and comment passing. It seemed Citrusdal whites had some strong convictions about seating arrangements in automobiles, and to their way of thinking, we had it all wrong. Nelson should not have been in the front seat, much less looking at them and smirking in that way. *"Gaan kak in die mielies,"* Nelson muttered, just slightly too quietly for our glaring audience to hear. ("Go shit in the corn.")

We took the old road north from Citrusdal, following the east bank of the Olifants. Physically, the valley began to remind me of Morocco—the dark green fruit trees, the bone-dry mountains. At the same time, the fishermen we saw, waist-deep in rubber waders in the rushing river, kept reminding me of the western United States. Half-way between Citrusdal and Clanwilliam, we turned onto a dirt road and headed up into the Cedarberg. The mountains soon surrounded us, steep walls of rock rising endlessly, while we followed a clear, twisting stream a few miles up to a campground.

We parked, and I began to get nervous. The campground was a peaceful, sprawling place, shaded by eucalyptus and ironwood, with stables, barbecue pits, a small sloping meadow, a big ablutions block, and a ranger's office. It was very quiet in the midday heat. The prob-lem was that I had been in South Africa long enough by now to know at a glance that this was whites-only territory. *This,* I realized, as much as any political convictions about non-association, was what had given Nelson second thoughts about coming along with us. With-out a word, we piled out of the car and shouldered our backpacks. We had a map already. We hit the trail, marching double time.

In the first half mile we tramped, we saw many small parties—

picnickers, fishermen, families, couples—all white. We didn't stop to chat with any of them, nor did we speak to each other. I was mortified by the amount of dread I felt about the prospect of trouble. The trail zigzagged steeply up the mountainside, and the people soon thinned out, but we kept up a brutal pace for a good two hours, and it was only exhaustion that finally crowded the dread from my thoughts.

We rested when we reached the ridge. The air was cooler and the land was greener on the summit, and the view was magnificent. Great piles of boulders, gray-white and sculpted into weird shapes by the wind, rose everywhere to the east, while the vista to the west seemed to stretch all the way to the Atlantic, some forty miles away. Long dune grass grew between the rocks on the ridge, and here and there we could see lone survivors of the cedar forests from which these mountains drew their name. They were huge, heavily gnarled, beautiful trees. It was hard to conceive how nineteenth-century loggers had managed to haul countless thousands of them down to the coast from here. ("With oxen and slaves, that's how," Nelson said.) It was now late afternoon. We set off again, across the plateau, and presently came to an old stone hut in a meadow, where we decided to make our first night's camp. There was no one around. The silence and grandeur up here were primeval.

The trail we followed the next day wound all through the high country of the Cedarberg, skirting deep gorges, traversing broad plateaus where hares darted through the protea. The landscape was fantastic—an ocean of boulders heaped up like thunderheads—and we didn't see anyone else all day. In a sheltered spot near a spring, we found the ruins of an old sheepherder's house. Built of whitewashed adobe, with a cedar hitching post still standing out front, it looked to me like somewhere Butch Cassidy and his men might have holed up. But then we were confronted, in the next valley, by a large troop of baboons, who disputed with hysterical barking our right to proceed. We slowly made our way past the apes, who noisily retreated. African wilderness, I decided, had an antic, otherworldly quality that was inimical to the suave saddlebag outlawry of the frontier myths I had been raised on.

In the late afternoon we emerged onto the eastern ramparts of the Cedarberg. Here the expanse in the distance was the Great Karroo— a vast semidesert—rather than the sea. Far below us, among the rolling brown hills in the nearer distance, a dirt road ribboned its way down the valleys to a hamlet of whitewashed buildings, rendered discrete and toylike by our altitude. That, Nelson said, was Wuppertal. While we rested, chewing on biltong, the jerked meat the Boer pioneers ate, Nelson waxed lyrical about Wuppertal.

"Life down there is so peaceful and healthy. There's no apartheid. No inequality. Look at how isolated it is. Pretoria just leaves it alone. Why? Because there are no whites there, of course! Maybe a German missionary or two, now and again. You see that big building there? That's the mission. And that big shed on the hillside? That's the factory. They make *veldskoens* [traditional shoes]. Wuppertal is the last place that makes them properly." Nelson paused, then shook his head. "People from Wuppertal can't believe it when they must travel in to town somewhere, and they see what a balls-up this country is." We were all quiet for a while. Finally, Nelson said, "Wuppertal's a test case for non-racial socialism in South Africa. One day, it will be a national monument. The plaque will say, 'People lived sanely here even under apartheid.' "

Nelson chuckled, but his tone was so brooding and earnest that I thought better of pointing out that Wuppertal was really more a relic of the past than a portent of the future, that as an intact Moravian mission station it might more easily symbolize that stage of colonial penetration when the missionaries first organized the indigenes into Christianized communities, ready for exploitation by the traders, settlers, and capitalists to follow.

The wind was blowing northwest now, weatherwise a bad sign. Alex had his map out. He indicated it and said, "If we don't find this hut fairly soon, we might do well to start for Wuppertal ourselves. It is not going to be a nice night."

We set off in search of the hut, and found it high on an open, west-facing mountainside. It was empty. There was another hour of sunlight left, so Alex went off with his camera to photograph cedar trees while Nelson and I cooked supper.

Since leaving Cape Town, the three of us had observed an unspoken moratorium on talking about school. Getting away from the workaday grind was, after all, one of the best things about going camping. The long day of trudging through the mountains had cleared my head in unexpected ways, though, such that I found myself taking a longer, calmer view than usual of many things. In particular, my worries about teaching, about the effect I was having on my students, had organized themselves for the first time into a concise form in my mind. While we simmered rice and watched the sun sink into the cloud bank that was building in the west, I quietly, almost confessionally, described my misgivings to Nelson.

When I had finished, he shrugged. "That's inevitable," he said. "If you come into a situation like ours from a background like yours, it takes time for you to understand things. As for your influence on the students—I don't think you're seen as somebody who's pushing a particular political line. A liberal, collaborationist line, for instance. So it's not a matter of students being led astray like that. You might represent some things that certain students find . . . glamorous." Nelson laughed. "But everyone realizes you come from a different world. If I were you, I wouldn't worry. I don't see that you've done any damage to any student's development. Maybe you've even taught something to one or two!"

This was a reassuring perspective, to say the least. But there was something else I suddenly wanted to know. I asked Nelson: "If you had grown up somewhere else, in the West, do you think you would have become a Marxist?"

Nelson took a long time to answer. Then he simply said, "No."

It was what I had wanted to hear.

Alex returned with a story about a leopard spoor he had seen, and antelope grazing higher up the mountain.

We sat and ate with our backs against the hut while the western sky turned into a conflagration streaked with long purple clouds. With the silence on the subject of school broken, conversation turned to our students. I told a story about a girl in 6A8 who had asked me during a class discussion whether I believed in God. I had declined to answer. She had persisted. I finally said that it wasn't fair for a teacher to have to declare himself on such a personal matter to his students, to which she replied, "Mr. October tells us!"

Nelson roared with laughter. "I don't even teach that class! I only spoke with them once or twice during the boycott."

"Well, I was curious to know what you had told them, so I asked. And she said, 'Mr. October *doesn't* believe in God. Shame!' "

"Of course that's what I told them."

Alex turned to Nelson. "But where do you draw the line in class when it comes to politics?"

"Politics doesn't come up so often in physics," Nelson said.

"Then how is it that at least half the matrics seem to get at least half their political ideas from you?" Alex asked.

"Not in class," Nelson said. He paused for a minute, then went on. "Most of the matrics I see, I've taught for three years. When I first get a class, in Standard Eight, I try to categorize all the students in terms of their potential for political development. There are a few you have to write off—the totally untrustworthy characters, the children of policemen, and so on. But most of them I try to work with in one way or another.

"Those with a limited amount of potential, I steer toward certain organizations—sports clubs, community groups, and so on. I also try to see that they get certain books to read in Standard Eight, certain others in Standard Nine, and certain others in matric, according to what I think they're ready for. Those students with somewhat more potential, I steer toward different groups, and give more difficult reading. Those with a great deal of potential, I treat differently still. We have study groups, we work on certain projects, and we stay in close touch after they leave school.

"I've had three classes now that I taught for the full three years. Many of my ex-students are very active, in various organizations. So it's possible to have a sort of spreading impact as a teacher. That girl who asked you whether you believed in God, she's the youngest sister of a girl I taught who's quite active at Bush now. In fact, she's a member of a study group that might interest you, Bill. I'd be interested to hear what you think of our reading program, anyway. I've already picked Alex's brain for suggestions. Everything that interests us is banned, of course. But we've managed to develop a very strong analysis, I think."

Dusk was deepening. We sat quietly sipping coffee spiked with brandy. I found Nelson's description of his systematic cultivation of Grassy Park students astonishing, and I was very surprised he had told us about it. At the same time, I felt honored by his confidence.

"Someone's coming."

Alex pointed to the north, where a flashlight bobbed in the dusk. We watched it approach. The outline of a hiker slowly took shape behind the light, moving across the mountainside. When it was fifty yards away, a jaunty "Hello!" was thrown in our direction.

It was a tall, tanned young Englishman with short dark hair and a huge blue rucksack. He wore Swiss-style knickerbockers and heavy climbing boots, and said his name was Louis. We invited him to share the hut with us that night; he accepted. We watched him prepare his supper, all silently marveling at the abundance of high-tech mountaineer's gear he kept pulling out of his rucksack. Louis told us that he was an art student in London. He occasionally came to South Africa on family business, he said, and he always tried to get away for a few days' "climbing" while he was here. The Cedarberg was one of his favorite ranges in Africa, he said, although he did most of his climbing in the Alps and the Himalayas. I was watching Nelson for his reaction to Louis, but it was hard to gauge the exact meaning of his occasional chuckles in the darkness that soon enveloped us.

The weather did change overnight, and the sky in the morning was threatening. We had planned to climb one of the peaks in the southern part of the range that day, but all the higher country was shrouded in clouds. We hiked in that direction, anyway, accompanied by Louis. After a couple of hours, it began to rain. We found a shallow, low-ceilinged cave in a cliff face and made ourselves comfortable there. Louis began producing more marvels from his luggage, and we were soon feasting on arcane energy bars from his brother's mountain-outfitting shop in Oxford. We contributed the last of our brandy. Though very solemn and an art student, Louis was all right, we decided. He wanted to hear all about Grassy Park High, and we three tried to oblige. What amused me most in the course of this impromptu party was when Nelson, drinking spiked tea from a tin cup, began to muse out loud about how this cave, these mountains, put him in mind of the Sierra Maestra in Cuba, the mountain fastness from which Fidel and Che had launched their revolution. Nelson's eyes shone as he spoke, and lying there in his dirty coat and battered hat and week-old beard, he did look rather like a South African *guerrillero,* I thought. More so than he did a schoolteacher, anyway.

Perhaps it was the talk of the tropical wilds. More likely it was having gotten wet and cold on the trail. In any case, I began to shiver uncontrollably as we huddled there in the cave, and then I began to sweat. I knew the symptoms; it was a relapse of the malaria I had contracted in Indonesia a year and a half before. I climbed in my sleeping bag, and began to get a bit delirious. I said that, as soon as the rain stopped, we should make our attempt on the peak we wanted to climb. But the others knew better. When the rain did stop, we set off downhill, making straight for the nearest road. It was only a few miles, but I was so weak that it took several hours, and when we finally got to the road I immediately got in my sleeping bag again. Alex stayed with me. The last thing I saw before I fell asleep, and it made me laugh, was Louis and Nelson striding off—or, rather, Louis striding, and Nelson having to trot alongside to keep up with Louis's giant, solemn steps. They were headed for the campground, which was ten miles up the road.

They returned with the car just after dark. By then, my fever and chills had passed, leaving me rather blissfully exhausted. I insisted that we not try to drive all the way to Cape Town that night, but sleep at the Cedarberg campground instead. We did so, and it was only when we were all stretched out in sleeping bags in the meadow there, having cooked our dinner in one of the barbecue pits and washed off some of the trail dust at the ablutions block, that I recalled how nervous I had been when we first passed through this campground. Our chances of being hassled were far greater now that we were actually staying here, I realized. But the whole business simply didn't interest me now. The idea of being a "mixed" party seemed too absurd even to think about. The stars looked like tiny diamonds sprinkled on a black velvet cushion, and apartheid was another country.

The day after we got back to Cape Town, Louis phoned. He wanted to take us out to dinner at his hotel. Alex and I accepted, and Fiona came along, but Nelson sent his regrets. He had a meeting, he said. This time, I noticed, we didn't even discuss forcing the issue. The dinner was lovely, and Alex and Louis made arrangements to meet in London in a few months' time, when Alex planned to be traveling in Europe. Louis's hotel was one of Cape Town's best, and thus probably had "international status," although looking around the big, candlelit restaurant, I could see nothing but white faces, so it was hard to be sure.

69

Back at school for the final term, I found myself looking at my classes through the lens of Nelson's revelations about his system for the political cultivation of students. I tried to imagine this farm system for the revolution, recruiting and promoting players not for their strong right arms but for certain qualities of mind and character. What qualities? Intelligence, obviously. But the movement could hardly restrict itself to recruiting only the brightest children. Mass mobilization was the ultimate object, after all, and much of the work to be done—the pamphleteering, the legwork—required no great intellectual ability. The brightest children were also most subject to the lure of the few opportunities for self-advancement, to the great temptation to make for oneself a separate peace. Integrity, then—idealism, discretion—and courage. Yet integrity was hard to measure. As with courage, it was most likely to emerge or fail under pressure, when a "cadre" was already in a position to damage the cause.

I had often contemplated the Grassy Park High faculty with these questions in mind, trying to see what factors determined which few teachers were openly "political," while the rest hung back in their various sloughs of apathy, cynicism, preoccupation, cowardice, ambition, or outright conservatism. Age was a factor, but scarcely definitive. Neither was personal integrity the sole determinant. There were mean-spirited sneaks like Georgina associated with the struggle, while stolid straight shooters like Cecil Abrahams and Moegamat seemed to avoid as if by instinct the endless ambiguities of politics.

With my students, things seemed even less clear. My classes were young; that was part of it. Nelson said he began culling children in Standard Eight. Half of my students would never reach Standard Eight. But what would Nelson make of some of my students? What kind of "potential" would he see in a Wayan, a Hester, a Terence, a Shireen? And Shaun, Nico, and Wayne? What would Nelson make of a class like 7E2? I guessed that there wasn't a single student in 7E2 whom he would try to recruit. Their silliness seemed, at least to me, unanimous and irremediable. Then again, I could be missing something. All kinds of factors hidden to me, having to do with the political complexion of families, churches, out-of-school lives, and organizational discipline, would undoubtedly be taken into account.

The boycott had been a mass action, at least as far as students were concerned. Nelson's farm system—particularly his postgraduate "study group"—sought to produce leaders for the coordination of mass action. The young people whom Nelson "conscientized" became activists in a great range of organizations—trade unions, community associations, sports federations, student councils, ad hoc committees, professional bodies. This I gathered as I began to meet some of the others in his study group. They were teachers, clerks, nurses, university students. They met irregularly, in each other's houses and rented rooms, yet they seemed to keep up a great flow of books, pamphlets, and ideas among them. Nelson ran down some of their main texts for me. The list was heavy with the works of Marx, Engels, Lenin, Trotsky, Fanon, Cabral, Genovese, Debray, Castro, Guevara, Giap, Cesaire. When he asked for suggestions, I tried to leaven the list a bit with Orwell, Antonio Gramsci, Rosa Luxemburg, John Reed, Paul Goodman, James Baldwin, and E. P. Thompson, and to counterweight it with Solzhenitsyn and Koestler—the latter suggestions were coolly received. What I could really offer to Nelson's study group, I discovered, was a connection to some American documentary film distributors. There were several recent films about the struggle in South Africa, which had been banned in South Africa, that we now undertook to import through a well-placed employee in the Cape Provincial library—right under the government's nose, as it were.

How strong or weak was "the analysis" developed by Nelson's group I really couldn't say. It placed a lot of emphasis on the revolutionary models provided by Cuba, Vietnam, Zimbabwe, Mozambique, and Angola. The world anti-apartheid movement was seen as an ally, but apartheid per se was not seen as the ultimate problem in South Africa. The disinvestment movement in the West was welcomed, but not only because withdrawal would isolate and weaken the Botha government. Nelson's group rejected international capitalism itself, regardless of who ruled South Africa. They seemed to value some of the insights of the Black Consciousness movement, but generally regarded the movement as naive. "BC was too easily hijacked by reformists in many communities," Nelson said. He and his associates advocated total noncollaboration with the authorities, wherever possible, and in that regard were in the old Unity Movement tradition. They were completely uninterested in compromise, in politics as the art of the possible. They anticipated total victory over the enemy in the end.

I had my doubts about much of this. Not because I still thought Black Consciousness was the most promising liberation ideology available to black South Africans. On that score, I now shared Nelson and company's reservations, and realized, too, that some of the movement's original appeal to me had had to do with my being American. That is, a doctrine of black pride and black self-reliance had struck me as essential partly because I came from a country where blacks were an oppressed minority group, suffering all the onslaughts on their self-image which that status can bring. In South Africa, though, blacks were not a beleaguered minority, and whites were not the dominant culture in the same way they were in the United States. The problem here was not how to survive as blacks in a white society, but how to create majority rule. My doubts about Nelson's group's analysis mostly concerned its practical implications.

To begin with, I had to wonder just how much contact these urban intellectuals had with "the masses." Several of them, including Nelson, were learning to speak Xhosa, but all of them were "colored" and none of them seemed to have any extensive connections with Africans. I also had to wonder what their organizational affiliations were. Did they work with the outlawed liberation movements? If so, I did not want to know about it—here, the underground ethic of need-to-know definitely applied—but if not, how *were* they connected to any broad-based movement? All their reading seemed intended to enhance their ability to judge the ripeness or unripeness of the revolutionary situation in South Africa, but it wasn't at all clear to me how they intended to create or control that situation. Black anger was the molten material with which these would-be popular leaders had to work, yet I somehow doubted that their endless discussions of class warfare and dialectical materialism were really in tune with that anger. I wondered, finally, about their air of purism, of absolutism. They scorned "bridge building"—alliances with more moderate groups—yet it was very hard to picture how apartheid would ever be brought down other than by a broad coalition of its opponents. Patience was esteemed an overriding revolutionary virtue by Nelson and friends. "The long march" was the metaphor of choice for the revolution's historical schedule. But could sectarianism not postpone liberation indefinitely? And then there was the melodramatic but fundamental question: Just how many of these bright, serious young students and clerks were actually prepared to risk their lives for their beliefs? Because without that final commitment by many, many black South Africans, the continued failure of their struggle, given white might and determination, seemed inevitable.

I mention these reservations about Nelson's group, but the fact was that I admired the few members I met immensely, and never doubted the ultimate importance of consciousness-raising groups like theirs to the freedom struggle as a whole. Some of these questions only occurred to me later, while looking back, when I could no longer ask them of Nelson or his friends. At the time, I mostly felt honored to be trusted as much as I was, given the suspicion-fraught atmosphere in the South African resistance.

70

The end of the year was approaching, and my classes were no longer what they had been. 6A6 now took responsibility for itself. Disputes between classmates were settled by subtle, even subconscious, group action. It was no longer necessary to break up 6A6 into small bunches to get anything done. With the emergence of a solid whole-class identity, 6A6's attention span had lengthened markedly. They were still a big, less than brilliant group, but they could now cope with digressions and distractions in a way they could never have done at the beginning of the year. All in all, 6A6 was something of a collective success story.

6A7 had also changed. They remained a hip, aggressive group, but their sense of style as a class had shifted—from that adapted black American jive routine, "rappin'," to a more international mystique: reggae, the Third World, and generic liberation struggles. Among the rock bands, soccer stars, and elephant families on the walls of New Room 16, a new image had been tacked up: a dashing young Zimbabwean guerrilla, complete with cold battlefield stare and AK-47 Soviet assault rifle. I figured someone in 6A7 had brought in the picture; certainly, they seemed more excited about it than my other classes did. And they were nearly beside themselves when their classmate Terence came to school one day with a camouflage-patterned beret. He wasn't actually wearing it, but the other children kept urging me to ask him what he had in his bag, and when I finally obliged them, he pulled it out with a great grin and clapped it on his head at precisely the right revolutionary angle. *"A luta continua,"* Terence said, and the class sighed wildly. The subculture of revolution, that which had been all the rage during the boycott, seemed to have caught on in 6A7. 6A7 liked its flair.

There was less style but perhaps more substance to whatever "conscientization" 6A8 had undergone over the course of the year. We continued to have the best open-format discussions I had with any of my classes, partly because a number of children in 6A8 had begun reading the daily papers. I considered this a breakthrough, and it had a clear multiplier effect, inciting more kids to start reading the news every time some of their classmates showed they were conversant with the big world of current events. 6A8 retained their great feeling for each other's welfare, even after a classmate had dropped out— Koos often brought me greetings from Oscar, along with reports on Oscar's campaign to get his father to let him try Standard Six again next year.

Although 7E2 remained unbowed, the class had become noticeably more subdued over the course of the year, especially since the boycott. They were also somewhat divided now. Some of the boys continued to clown compulsively, but the idea of losers-as-heroes had been so discredited during the boycott that a number of children, including Mareldia, had managed to break with their class's regnant ethos and establish a beachhead of quiet industry and good marks. Since most of the rowdies would no doubt fail, this development gave one hope that those kids who managed to pass might find themselves next year in a more inspiring group.

7E1 was riven by a series of lurid episodes near the end of the year. A clean-cut, green-eyed class leader named Brian, who had been the individual standout for Grassy Park High at the intermural track meet back in March, allegedly punched Mario Da Silva in class. This led to his suspension from school, and then to some more alleged fisticuffs between Brian's *mother* and Da Silva. A top student named Janet abruptly dropped out amid a hail of rumors that she was pregnant. Another boy got into trouble with the police for stealing. All this was surprising in a class I still considered to be composed mostly of goody-goodies. But the most upsetting twist of events for me in 7E1 was the sudden, unexplained coldness of Shaun. I had obviously done something to offend him; I did not know what. Shaun would not look me in the eye; he would barely answer when I called on him in class. Wayne and Nico were still friendly to me, but they, too, stopped hanging around after class to chat, and when I asked them what was wrong with Shaun, they looked miserable and said they didn't know. I decided I would let Shaun come to me about it when he was ready. With over two hundred students, I felt spread too thin to be chasing after one who was pouting, especially one about whom, if the truth were told, I had always had mixed feelings.

71

As many of our Grassy Park High matrics would soon be doing themselves, I was starting to run into some hard home truths about their futures. I had by now more or less resolved my consternation about my careers counseling work. Recognizing my own irrelevance to the political development of our students had helped a lot. Nelson had convinced me that our kids were being recruited and prepared for roles in the freedom struggle by friends, teachers, neighbors, and relatives in ways I couldn't perceive, much less participate in. This knowledge let me off the hook. If people thought I was leading some student down the primrose path to stoogedom by helping him or her apply for a ministerial permit or financial aid to go to college, they could speak to the student themselves—and, I now realized, they *would.*

I also felt stronger in the face of the simplistic revolutionary view that individual achievement by blacks constituted "reform" and was thus at base counterrevolutionary. This was the idea Nelson suggested when he scorned the "so-called opportunities" provided by the skilled labor shortage, and that the great black psychiatrist Frantz

Fanon expressed in its fundamental form when he wrote, "The native's laziness is the conscious sabotage of the colonial machine . . . Under the colonial regime, what is true for the Arab and the Negro is that they should not lift their little fingers nor in the slightest degree help the oppressor to sink his claws deeper into his prey." This view made the most sense, I decided, when the task at hand was that of forcing colonists to return to their homeland. But this was not the task at hand in South Africa—not unless "Drive the whites into the sea!" was one's rallying cry and program. I liked Elliot's attitude, his self-discipline and high seriousness about gaining a technical education.

But the "laziness" issue was important. I never brought it up, but it was so much a part of the white racist stereotype of blacks that it redoubled the challenge to our matrics to do more than was expected of them. Political reservations about individual achievement, combined with fear of the community censure of "sellouts," could too easily feed the universal predilection for indolence, I thought. Certainly, I believed, "success" as such should not be shunned. There had never been enough of it to go around in black South Africa; there had definitely never been enough of it in the freedom struggle.

But this tentative renewal of my enthusiasm for helping our matrics prepare for life after graduation was always running into new waves of discouragement. Looking around Rondebosch, I would find myself overwhelmed with awareness of what a *white* place it was. How could I encourage our students to go to UCT? The hub of student social life in Rondebosch was a sprawling pub called the Pig and Whistle. I never saw a black inside the Pig who was not in a wine steward's uniform. Nor inside any of the other bars, cafés, restaurants, and pizzerias of liberal little Rondebosch. Soaring above the Rondebosch main road, casting a long psychological shadow, were two eighteen-story student dormitories. There were no blacks living in them, of course, just as there were no blacks living in any of the countless student flats and "communes" in Rondebosch and nearby suburbs. Black UCT students were commuters, outsiders, invisible. They were not, it was safe to say, having a well-rounded university experience.

A more specific discouragement involved my slow realization that Grassy Park High was not in the first rank of "colored" schools in Cape Town. Many of my colleagues had gone to more highly regarded schools—Nelson and Soraya, for instance, had both graduated from Harold Cressy High, which was considered the best—and some of them made obvious their disdain for the comparatively poor schooling at Grassy Park High. Grassy Park was probably in the upper one-fourth of "colored" high schools in the Cape academically, but I began to see that, for my purposes, that was not good enough—a preponderance of the black students at UCT had graduated from the handful of top "colored" schools at which English was the predominant first language, a handful that did not include Grassy Park High. Solly Marais had three daughters in medical school. When I asked him how he had contributed to this incredible achievement, he mentioned the second job he had held for years, as a liquor store clerk, and his penchant for living with "women who think they can do anything, no matter what I say," but he also cited, in all seriousness, having managed to get each of his daughters into Harold Cressy.

What really set me back on my heels, though, was when I finally looked up the results of the previous year's matriculation examinations at Grassy Park High. Barely half of last year's matrics had passed, it seemed, and less than half of those had achieved the minimum scores for what was called "exemption." *Exemption was an entrance requirement at UCT.* I went to see Meryl, who was one of those who had earned exemption in her class, according to the list. Could this pass rate possibly be correct? Meryl said it was. Had her class done unusually badly? They had not. Could this year's matrics expect to fare better? On the contrary, Meryl said. I couldn't believe what I was hearing. So only a small minority would earn exemption, probably? "I'm afraid that's true, Bull. It's very unfair."

I had to struggle to accept what this news meant. It meant that of the dozens of matrics whom I had encouraged and helped to apply to UCT, the majority would be academically ineligible to go there, permit or no permit. Did our students not realize this? "Of course they realize it," Meryl said. So they were all just hoping against hope. But what else could they do? They didn't know who among them would pass, who among them might earn exemption. Except they did, to a great extent, according to Meryl. "I think I could tell you right now who's going to pass from these matrics, and which ones are likely to get exemption," Meryl said. "There are usually very few surprises."

I was almost afraid to ask Meryl for her predictions. I mentioned a couple of names—Hector, Glynnis. Meryl said, "I will be very surprised if those two even pass. They both had trouble passing Standard Nine." I was devastated. These were kids with whom I had been trying for months to decide exactly what courses they should take at UCT, which professors they might like, and so on. I asked Meryl who she thought might earn exemption. She mentioned two students whom I had never counseled. Both had seemed to avoid me all year long. Did Meryl know anything about their plans? "I understand they've both applied to UCT," Meryl said. "So perhaps they'll go there." The awful pattern was now becoming clear. Seeing my dismay, Meryl said, "I suppose it's not very nice to feel that some of these matrics have been wasting your time with their applications for bursaries and such, when they're not even likely to pass."

I assured Meryl it wasn't that.

"Well, I think you've done something quite nice myself, by giving certain matrics hope that they might succeed, after all."

That was exactly it. That was the pattern. The students who had been relying on my help all year, many of them, were the very students who had little or no chance of even passing their exams, much less of getting into UCT. I was a vehicle for their fantasies, a source of hope to keep them going. Meanwhile, those few students who really did have a chance of getting into UCT had not needed me. They already had, from somewhere, whatever information they needed. A system, however informal, for channeling the top students toward the few available opportunities *did* exist. I just hadn't been able to see it.

"And then there's myself," Meryl said. "I've also applied."

This was great news, and I was very happy to hear it. But I was no longer inclined to consider Meryl's interest in UCT a counseling triumph of mine. She would undoubtedly have done exactly what she had done, I now thought, whether or not I had ever come to Grassy Park High—just as it seemed every other Grassy Park graduate or would-be graduate would also do.

Sitting in the library, contemplating the shambles that my career counseling project had become (at least in my head), I found myself staring bleakly at the shelf for careers information that we had created with the armloads of brochures and prospectuses that had come in the mail. For months, I had struggled to keep all the literature intact and in order. The collection was hugely popular, even with the younger children, so there were always bits and pieces scattered around the library, and around the school. Lately, I had given up trying to keep track of it all, and the careers shelf was rapidly disintegrating as a result. It was not easy to watch it happen, but I kept asking myself: What about next year? Who besides the instigator of this project cares enough about it to try to keep it together? That was the point—not that "these people" didn't take good care of things, or that my efforts would all go for naught, but that the project repre-

sented by the careers shelf was mine. It wasn't a goddamned community-based initiative. It was missionary work.

The matrics rented a disco in Athlone for their annual dance.
There were some notable no-shows—Clive and Nelson among them—
but the great majority of matrics and teachers attended. I went, and
was glad I did. The dance had a flowing, joyful quality that took me
back to my first, infatuated feelings about Grassy Park High. Everyone was in fancy dress, the boys in dinner jackets and ruffled shirt
fronts, the girls in long ball gowns and elaborate hairdos. The disco,
known as Galaxy, was a soft-edged universe of colored lights, driving
music, and happy laughter. Even the principal could not spoil the
party; the speech he made was short and surprisingly sweet. What
was different from eight months earlier, of course, was that I now
knew all the players in the pageant, knew their faults and foibles as
well as their warmth and charm. But the matrics' dance was a holiday
from real life. I even let Napoleon spirit me out to the parking lot for
a nip at the bar he was running from the trunk of a car.

Over the course of the evening, I must have danced with every girl
in matric. The girls were taking the initiative and asking teachers to
dance, which, considering how stunning they looked, made the night
seem altogether too good to be true. I danced with girls I knew well.
I also danced with some I barely knew—including Jean, one of the
students who Meryl thought might get in to UCT. As we left the dance
floor, Jean pleased me more than she knew by asking, very tentatively, if I would ever have the time to talk to her about university
bursaries. Glynnis who wanted to be a veterinarian, Desiree who
wanted to be a doctor, Miriam who planned to major in accounting at
UCT—with each of whom I had spent hours helping them plan their
futures, none of whom I now expected even to graduate—all asked me
to dance. And I realized that I wasn't even vaguely irritated with any
of them.

The evening passed in a long, slow swirl of illegal ("mixed" dancing) fun. And on Monday my nasty-minded little Standard Sixes had
their fun, cackling about how "sir *enjoyed* himself" at the matrics'
dance.

72

A sort of mass hysteria about the approaching final examinations began to prevail at school, and it seemed to intensify with each passing week. Absenteeism among matrics and Standard Eight students —the grade levels that faced government examinations—became chronic. The students in those classes who did come to school were pasty-faced, hollow-eyed wrecks. With the self-conscious swagger of prizefighters chatting to an awestruck public between rounds, they turned up with tales of all-night study marathons, of classmates who were cracking under the strain.

In my classes, it was business as usual, though. This seemed to make some of my students slightly panicky, especially those who had not been doing their work all year. They had gambled that I was bluffing, that in the end I *would* weight their final exam scores as 80 or 90 percent of their grades. As I continued to insist that my exams would not be a great grueling ordeal and would only count for 10 percent of their final grades, their uneasiness mounted. What were we doing still reading topographic maps? What were we doing still writing *compositions?* Why weren't we memorizing animal gender terms and collective nouns—a pod of whales, a leap of leopards, a warren of rabbits—the way other English classes were doing? I was sympathetic. But I had no choice. I pushed on with my program, only lessening the load of homework because of the sudden upsurge in studying the children were having to do for their other classes.

On the subject of final exams, Napoleon gave me a scare. He called a meeting of the Standard Seven geography teachers and announced that the senior teacher among us, a gentle, chalky, rather slow-witted man named Fourie, would be preparing the final exam that we all would use. This was unthinkable, as far as I was concerned, and I told Napoleon so in private. His eyes glittered.

"Why? You've been teaching from the same syllabus. I don't see what the problem could be."

"The boycott disrupted everyone's lesson plans," I said, playing lamely to Napoleon's feelings about the boycott. "I know what I was able to cover with my classes, and what I wasn't. You can check over my exam, if you like. But I really think I should set the exams for my classes."

If I was not mistaken, Napoleon was enjoying this. He said we could just wait and see what sort of exam Fourie prepared, and if there was any problem, we could do some editing.

Now I knew very well that Fourie, left to his own devices, would not have his exam ready until the morning it had to be administered. So I started hounding Fourie to prepare his exam as soon as possible, even offering to take his classes during my free periods so as to give him more time to work. Fortunately, Fourie, though clearly astonished by my browbeating, responded and got his exam ready well in advance of its due date. Equally fortunately, it was awful. There were unanswerable questions, unsolvable problems, and much misleading and even wrong information. I immediately pointed all this out to Napoleon, and he did seem shocked—whether by Fourie's incompetence, or by my unwillingness to let it pass, I wasn't sure. He had to consent, in any case, to my preparing another exam for my own classes.

I was much relieved and decided I wouldn't show my exam to Napoleon until the last possible minute. Even if I did not plan to weight the final exam heavily in my students' year-end marks, I wanted it to reflect the work we had covered, including the politically sensitive material that would probably horrify Napoleon.

But I found all this fuss and fever about exams to be a terrible bore. And it was making me panicky, too. It was coming too soon. I was not ready for this reckoning that seemed to be suddenly upon us. (What had been learned, what had been accomplished, over the last nine months?) The school year *wasn't* over; I had more work planned. But my classes were being distracted from their lessons. And the anxiety of those students who were beginning to realize that they were very likely going to fail was a further distraction for the rest. My classes were slipping away from me before I was ready to let them go.

73

The best-funded department at Grassy Park High was the woodworking department. Some said it was nearly as well equipped as its counterparts in white schools. This was due to an old Cape tradition of "colored" artisanry, I was told, one that dated back to slave days. "Hewers of wood, drawers of water," Solly Marais said. "Next they'll be giving us a water drawing department."

The head of the woodworking department was a strange young guy named Steenkamp. He wore pin-striped suits and very shiny needle-nosed shoes, and drove a souped-up Toyota bakkie. Short and slight, with a high, lacquered pompadour, Steenkamp gave off an impression of almost cartoonish *narrowness*. He had narrow eyes, a narrow mustache, a narrow mouth, and an incredibly narrow head. And Steenkamp's narrowness was not just physical. His main interest in life seemed to be his Toyota. His English was poor, so he and I had never talked much. But he had once asked me, while we were driving somewhere in his bakkie, what other parts of South Africa I had seen. I described the tour that Rachel and I had taken when we first arrived in the country. He was shocked to hear that we had slept in our car. That was unwise, he said. "The people here is *dangelous*." Then he recalled hearing that the people in America were actually even worse. "They don't care about each other. They just do whatever they want. They're not all together like here."

During the boycott Steenkamp had kept a singularly low profile. Never eager to leave his woodworking domain in the first place, he had become the Grassy Park faculty's invisible man. When his presence at a staff meeting had been absolutely, unavoidably required, Steenkamp had hovered grudgingly in the background, chain-smoking and not saying a word. (He had a distinctive way of holding cigarettes in his tiny hands—like drooping, faintly obscene white darts.) As a first line of defense against having to commit himself, Steenkamp wore a perpetual smirk on his nonexistent lips.

Thus I had, over the course of the year, come to believe that Steenkamp's obsequious anonymity outside his woodwork shop was a permanent arrangement.

But that was before the Woodwork Exhibition.

The Woodwork Exhibition was an annual event, a sort of final examination *cum* crafts fair. For several evenings before the start of finals, the doors of the woodwork shop were thrown open to the public. On display was the best student woodwork of that year. I had noticed flyers tacked up around school and at Busy Corner announcing the exhibition, but it only really caught my attention after it had opened, when Steenkamp suddenly underwent some startling changes. Overnight, the impeccable carpenter began showing up in the staff room in what was for him complete disarray—tie undone, hair all windblown and flopping down his forehead, stiletto shoes exchanged for sensible brogans. Weirder still, the new Steenkamp was almost gregarious—making jokes in Afrikaans, favoring people with shy little smiles. I asked Meryl what could have gotten into him. She said he was just unwinding now that the Woodwork Exhibition was set up and successful. "The exhibition is the big event of his whole year, you know," she said, laughing. "So he's very relieved that it's going well. And he comes out of his shell a bit, to enjoy the spotlight. He does it every year."

This, I decided, I wanted to see. That same evening, I returned to Grassy Park to tour the exhibit.

It was a far more elaborate affair than I had imagined. In fact, the Woodwork Exhibition turned out to be a full-blown community happening. Although it had been going on for several nights already, there were scores of people outside the woodwork shop and dozens of cars parked in the courtyard. Most of the crowd seemed to be young adults, though I also saw a number of our students and their families. I was struck by how well dressed everyone was. Pop music spilled from the door to the woodwork shop as I made my way through the chatting, perfumed throng.

The Woodwork Exhibition was organized like a model home. One wandered from "room" to "room." The furniture was all student woodwork—a fact not obvious from its quality, though, which looked to me quite professional. Imbuia wardrobes, mahogany headboards, stinkwood coffee tables, all gleamed impressively in their respective settings. The dominant style was slightly glossy and showy for my taste. On the other hand, I preferred all this polished, inlaid wood to most of the newer furniture I had seen in real Grassy Park homes— the five-piece "Cologne" and "Pasadena" lounge suites bought on hire-purchase from downtown department stores. Some of the work —the accessories, the knickknacks—I recognized from the projects that my Standard Six and Seven boys had been carrying around with them all year: the shoeshine kits and plant racks and cutting boards. Indeed, it was the details that struck me most as I strolled through the exhibition.

For it was clearly in the details that the great drawing power of this little show resided. Or rather, it was in the "total environment" that Steenkamp and company had worked to create, and which the details worked to complete. There were ashtrays and packs of cigarettes on the night table next to the (fully made-up) bed. There were plants in the plant racks, magazines in the magazine racks, a telephone and telephone book and even an address book on the teak telephone table. Clothes (all new and natty) hung in the wardrobe, lamps and lampshades hung on the lampstands, there were flowers, there were ferns. The study looked eminently ready for its master to enter at any moment and address himself to his oak desk, right down to a brace of sharpened pencils. The dining room table was set with somebody's silver and somebody's china and somebody's best wine glasses. The kitchen was arranged to suggest an elaborate meal just about to be cooked.

That this whole idyll was being evoked inside a high school woodwork shop had been ingeniously disguised. A pleated yellow stage curtain hid one brick wall; the kitchen had been improvised around the shop sink, with a frilly little orange curtain covering the adjacent window, which was otherwise covered with industrial-strength steel mesh. Dim and meticulous lighting aided in the creation of the illusion, and also served to emphasize the separate character of each "room"—the living room was bathed in hot red light, green and yellow were the study and bedroom, and the dining room was illuminated by a soft blue that gave the silver on the table a dull, magic glow. The music complemented the "environment"—it was Little Anthony and the Imperials during my tour. The DJ, I noticed, grooving in the shadows next to the stereo, was Moegamat, the dapper junior woodwork teacher who had also played DJ at our party in Muizenberg.

And the feeling of the Woodwork Exhibition *was* almost that of a party—a long, slow, mellow Grassy Park party. Some of the people touring along with me were half dancing through the rooms. But this was far more than a party, just as it was far more than a high school Open House. This exhibition was really more on the order of a shrine. It was a "model home" in the fullest sense of the term. These "rooms" represented a community fantasy, a local Platonic ideal of domestic luxury and serenity which its visitors could both enjoy and aspire to own. The student artisanry on display was being admired, no doubt, but the real significance of the exhibition was in its totality, as a concrete apotheosis of a collective dream. This modest, conservative, even kitschy dream was the other face, I thought, of the same community that staged angry general strikes and battled the regime's police in the streets to protest its oppression.

I found Steenkamp in the shadows of the unused portion of the shop as I completed my tour. He left the group he had been standing with to receive my congratulations on the exhibition. For some reason, Steenkamp was wearing a red velvet smoking jacket—as if he were about to take possession of the study. At first glance, the jacket looked ridiculous, especially as it seemed to be several sizes too large for him. On second glance, though, I decided that the jacket did a great deal to soften Steenkamp's usual narrowness—as did the Woodwork Exhibition, in some larger sense. Steenkamp was still a strange little guy to me, yet I could now see that he had a role in Grassy Park that went beyond simply making a living teaching wood shop. Steenkamp was also custodian of a specific and passionate popular fantasy. No wonder he thought people here were "all together."

Back outside, I started talking to a Standard Nine boy I knew. I asked how his studying was going, and he said that he was taking the evening off. "It's my turn to sleep here tonight," he said, and nodded at the woodwork shop. It seemed that, each night it was up, Steenkamp and some of his students slept inside the Woodwork Exhibition, guarding its fragile grandeur against the depredations of those who didn't share in the fantasy.

74

A strange thing happened to Liz Channing-Brown just before finals started. She showed up at school one day and was told that she had been given a medical leave of absence for the rest of the year for "nerves." It was strange because Liz's nerves had been ragged and visibly drug-stitched all year long, but just lately had been much improved. Also, there was virtually no work left to do this year except "invigilation" (exam monitoring) and exam marking. But her replacement had already been hired; Liz was presented with a fait accompli by the principal. She didn't even get a chance to say goodbye to her classes. I thought I detected a certain amount of grim satisfaction in the staff room as Liz packed her things and left. I watched her straggle off down the road, wanly hitchhiking, with her arms full of composition books that she had defiantly announced she still planned to mark.

I asked Soraya why the principal had forced Liz out *now*. Soraya shrugged. "The girl who is taking her classes is the daughter of a friend of the principal's," she said. "She needs two months' experience to qualify for a full-time position."

The principal apparently had no trouble pulling such strings, just as he had had no trouble protecting me from Coloured Affairs in the days before I had a work permit. I sometimes wondered why he had continued to protect me after I had let him down during the boycott. Soraya said, "You were probably just a pawn in a power game he was playing with the Boers. You were his American. They wanted to get rid of you. Van was probably just showing off his strength by keeping you around."

When finals started at last, and our schedule of classes turned into absolute chaos, the principal provided us all with some entertainment by going on a rampage. Students were wandering all over school, confused and taking advantage of the general confusion by not being where they were supposed to be. Suddenly, the principal came barreling out of his office, scattering students like bowling pins, roaring and waving a piece of yellow chalk. He charged into classrooms, where he started turning over all the unoccupied desks. This was hard work for a man in his sixties, even a big man like the principal, since the desks were heavy and unwieldy. But the principal was possessed. On the bottom of each overturned desk, he slashed a large "X" with his yellow chalk, and commanded the teacher in attendance that the desk not be turned back over this year. The student who should have been in it would not be examined; he or she would automatically fail! By the time he reached New Room 16, the principal appeared to be flagging. But he still managed to overturn a dozen desks.

"He's mad," chortled the few students who had been in their places in my room at the time of the principal's passage. But his performance, I noticed, did seem to shake up the school as a whole just enough to make people finally settle down to the great five-week business of final exams.

Invigilation gave me a lot of time to think. Sitting there with my silent classes, watching them scratch away on their various exams, I felt vaguely obliged to try to sum things up, to try to evaluate what had happened over the course of the year in New Room 16. Less than I had hoped, I felt sure. We had largely succeeded in avoiding the government "schemes" for English and geography, but had we managed to replace "gutter education" with anything more worthwhile? Were my students more "critical, articulate, informed" now than when I had met them? Were they better writers? My big plans of March now returned to mock me in November. It was so difficult to know what, if anything, had been achieved. The boycott had disrupted the year's schoolwork so thoroughly. Of course, the boycott itself had been the year's signal event, dwarfing anything that had happened inside my classroom. But had it really been the "very big educational experience" for our students that Mattie claimed? Watching them struggle with their exams, and imagining that at least some of those exams were as careless and irrelevant as Fourie's geography exam, yet not hearing a word of protest through all the weeks of finals about any aspect of the whole examination ritual, one had to wonder.

I had changed, anyway. Now, when I glanced out through my

classroom window and saw a police bakkie parked across the field with its load of pass-law prisoners and the cops calling out to the schoolgirls, my pulse did not quicken with outrage, nor did my throat constrict with sympathy for the people locked inside the steel cage. No, my responses had been dulled by too many months in this country. The bakkie was part of the landscape; I noted it ruefully and forgot it.

75

A telegram came from home. Rachel's mother had died. I had spoken to her on the phone a few weeks before and felt we had said goodbye, but the news of her death still shook me.

For the second or third time since Rachel's departure, I thought about getting on a plane to California. I could afford to buy a ticket now. And there was little left to do at school—just exams, and holding firm on my exams and my marks. But Rachel herself wrote that I should stay. She had been offered a visiting lectureship at the University of Zimbabwe starting in February. I could meet her there. We might make it Cape to Cairo yet. With mixed emotions, I applied for an extension of my visitor's visa, so as to be able to stay in South Africa beyond the end of the year.

This mix of emotions was becoming complex. I was homesick, I was lonely, and South Africa was driving me crazy. What bugged me the most, I decided, what really disoriented me, was simply the government's lack of accountability. The millions of people being brutalized daily by apartheid had absolutely no legal, peaceful recourse. This self-evident fact ate its way into one's soul in South Africa.

But the real conflict in my feelings about staying on in South Africa came to the fore when I thought about going back to the United States, because I was both homesick—and slightly sick at the thought of home. Running into other Americans in South Africa was part of it. My name and number had evidently landed on some informal but well-circulated list of "contacts" for certain kinds of visitors to Cape Town—journalists, academics, friends of friends—and a number of them had looked me up. Their voices, their clothes, everything about them conjured up for me a world: the America I missed. And yet I felt out of phase with it all, felt it receding even as I savored it. I had been repeatedly put off by the callowness of the individuals who brought with them this symphony of home-and-hearth associations. The film-

set designer from Los Angeles interested only in buying the maximum
allowable amount of Africana; the junior congressional aide impressed by Mitchell's Plain; the college literature teacher bound for
a job at the University of the Transkei, unaware even that blacks
resented the sham independence of the bantustans; the free-lance
journalist seeking an introduction to a "student spokesman" (I knew
the type he wanted: the angry young township radical breathing fire
about "the oppressor." I had long wondered if these "student spokesmen," who appeared regularly in articles about South Africa in foreign newspapers and magazines, were real people. My doubts on that
score deepened when I tried to picture putting this American together
with kids like Mattie, Elliot, or Clive, because I knew very well that
none of the politically committed kids I knew would talk to him. They
would consider it a security risk with no possible gain, an ego trip,
"adventurism." But no sooner had I thought the words *ego trip* than
I knew I had the student spokesman for the job. Roland! He of Richmond, California, track and soccer and bedroom fame. I phoned Roland—hey, he was agreeable. He and the journalist made a date, and
the thank-you note the American later sent me claimed that their
interview had been "very moving"); the California surfers at Jeffreys
Bay—they all seemed so naive, so ill-informed, as if understanding a
place like South Africa on its own terms involved an intellectual effort
that either was beyond them or they simply didn't consider worth the
trouble. They seemed, I suppose, only like what they were: citizens of
a superpower, visiting a distant colony. But my irritation with their
insularity distressed me doubly. Would I be able to fit in back home
at all?

    Tina Turner didn't help matters. Along with Ray Charles, Jimmy
Cliff, Betty Wright, and Blood, Sweat and Tears, she broke the United
Nations cultural boycott by touring South Africa in 1980. Turner
compounded her sins, however, by being a singer I liked, and by going
far beyond the limp excuses offered by most performers when questioned about their reasons for coming to South Africa. She had arrived, she told local reporters, "under the impression that South
Africa was one big safari scene—people running around in the trees,
etcetera," and she had been pleasantly surprised. Turner was not
much impressed by apartheid. "Look at the buses; both blacks and
whites are permitted to ride together," she said in Cape Town (the
only place in the country where the buses were integrated). "This
would have been unheard of years ago. Significant changes are coming around." In any event, Turner announced, she herself was a Bud-

dhist, and so took the long view. "I am not angered by the plight of blacks here: it is through such suffering that they will become enlightened." Turner did not, thank Buddha, go as far as Cashears, a black American nightclub entertainer and Turner's opening act, did, when he announced to the Cape Town press that he thought P. W. Botha deserved the Nobel Peace Prize for his efforts in office. But I still had a hell of a time trying to explain to my classes, after Turner's remarks appeared in the local papers, how black Americans could think this way. The truth was, I didn't know.

And then there were Rachel's letters, which, along with letters from other old friends, were painting a picture of American life that sounded less than inviting. It was the year of the hostages in Iran, which was not doing much for the national mood. A "period of reaction," my students might have called it. Rachel was teaching two courses at the University of California, and was appalled by her students. "They're like Martians to me," she wrote. "So cynical. So conservative. So materialistic." For people who had gone to college a few years before, the sharp rightward shift in student politics felt a bit like instant middle age; yet it extended to many of our peers as well. Half of the people I knew seemed to be going to law school; half of the rest seemed to be going to business school.

My closest friend, with whom I had traveled and surfed in the Pacific and Asia, had preceded Rachel back to the U.S. by a year, and had written us long, ecstatic letters about how wonderful it was to be there. But his feelings had changed. Now he wrote, "Returning was like walking through the biggest amusement park in the world—now, well, it's still the same amusement park, but it is dark, and I've ridden every ride, and I have no money and I've lost my car keys. Adjustment —jesus, have I traded my sanity for three years in the South Seas? . . . I just hope things are easier when you return." This friend was now struggling to make a living writing for magazines that he said all seemed filled with "the same cool snippets of modern-life nonsense." Both he and Rachel described feeling overwhelmed by the sheer size of the country. Rachel hoped life in Zimbabwe would be on a more manageable scale.

Even from the letters of friends who seemed happy, I got a sense of cheerful farce that unnerved me. Perhaps I had lost that taste for the stylishly absurd that sustained one in late-twentieth-century America. Perhaps I had lost my edge that way from living too long in less absolutely commercialized cultures. What I found myself wondering now was whether I really wanted to return to a society so shapeless and vast. Because life in South Africa, for all its horrors, at least didn't lack for issues you could sink your teeth into.

Despite all the restrictions on public discourse in South Africa, a nonstop debate raged here that was as serious, as profound, as they came. The question was: how to create a political framework that would be regarded as legitimate by a majority of South Africans. It was argued constantly, in every corner of the country—even, despite appearances, among the government and its supporters, who spent their time concocting reasons why the debate was unnecessary. It made history and ideas important in a way that they could never be in a more settled society. I had heard the meaning of events a hundred and fifty years old hotly contested among functional illiterates in a shebeen—it *mattered* whether blacks had gone along willingly on the Great Trek or not. And words like "freedom" and "justice" and "democracy" rang out in South Africa with a resonance, a power, that one simply did not expect them to contain any longer in the great, dyspeptic, democratic West.

My absentee ballot for the 1980 presidential election only found me on the American election day, far too late to send it back. So I took it in to school that day, thinking someone might want to look at it. As it turned out, *everyone* wanted to look at it. Teachers and students pored over the packet of pamphlets and forms, marveling. Look at all these "propositions," and all these pages and pages of arguments! What's this, Spanish? And *Chinese?* Here's Jimmy Carter, Ronald Reagan, John Anderson—but who are all these other names?

Actually, my more militant friends at school—Clive, Jacob, Meryl, Aaron, Nelson—refused to get excited about my ballot, and I didn't blame them. They were not admirers of a political system they considered to be a creature of corporate capitalism. Were American elections not invariably an occasion for the local white opposition press to lament that no similar national whoop-de-do was taking place here in South Africa? And I was, in fact, ashamed, watching people paw over my absentee ballot. Not ashamed of the American political system, but of my own blasé attitude toward it. Reagan was a menace, I believed, and I hoped Carter would win. But the *idea* of voting failed to move me, while it clearly moved many of my students and colleagues deeply. This, I thought, was the difference between life in America and life in South Africa.

76

The yellow X's were fading on the rerighted desks as exams wore on.

I finally gave Napoleon my geography exam on the afternoon before it was scheduled to be administered. The next morning, he and I met in the staff room. There were some problems with my exam, Napoleon said stonily. Some questions were poorly organized. And there were a large number of questions that did not pertain to syllabus material. Why were they on the exam?

"We spent class time discussing them."

"You spent class time discussing why Cape Town was twinned with this, this—city in Taiwan?"

I admitted we had, and tried to explain that the subject had been a takeoff point for lessons on Taiwan, China, South Africa's foreign relations, and relations between Pretoria and Cape Town (where the "twinning" had been unsuccessfully opposed on the City Council). "China is not part of the Standard Seven syllabus," Napoleon said. "And geography is not civics. I suggest you delete this question."

There was more, much more, that Napoleon objected to in my exam. He had never heard the term "economic colonialism" before, and he did not consider it a concept that Standard Seven students were ready for in any case. He was shocked to find a whole section of my exam devoted to the geographic implications of the Group Areas Act. "And nothing here about urban geography, which you should have covered *before* the boycott." The Group Areas material actually *was* our urban geography work. But rather than argue, I tried to direct attention to the noncontroversial parts of my exam that Napoleon claimed were poorly organized. Here, I had to endure disparaging comparisons of my work with Fourie's, which stung, but at least I could concede point after point without feeling like I was selling my students down the river.

In the end, I managed to beg off from any more "editing" with the excuse that it was time to draw up a final draft and mimeograph it. Napoleon scanned my exam, his eyes narrowing at all the SWAPO, FRELIMO, and apartheid that remained among the questions. Finally, he handed it back to me, shaking his head. "I just hope no inspector ever sees *this*," he said.

I gave the exam, which I was still quite pleased with, to my students. And many of them responded with surprisingly high marks. Had they simply memorized the material, or had they actually absorbed some of the ideas in it? I invigilated while 7E1 took their exam, and I had a strange moment when Nico glanced up, caught my eye, and gave me a quick, inscrutable, Black Power raised fist. On his exam, Nico described FRELIMO as "the FREEDOM FIGHTERS that liberated Mozambique and changed the name to Maputo." Had I given my students the idea that they could get good marks by producing revolutionary rhetoric? It was a disturbing thought. Certainly, those who got high marks on their final exams got them for having their facts straight, not for agreeing with me. But had that been true all year long?

When it came to final grades, I stuck to my announced policies regarding the relative weights of assignments and exams. In 7E1, the pattern of late-season catastrophe continued, as several good students, including Shaun, did badly on the final. They all passed the course, though, on their accumulated records. In 7E2, nearly half the class failed geography, which was actually not as bad as I had expected them to do. The insurgency of newly diligent students—Mareldia and company—blitzed their final exams with what I took to be angry excellence. Some of their most reprobate classmates made desperate efforts, the first real work I had seen them do all year, and then laughed hollowly about the prospects of a third or fourth try at Standard Seven.

In English, 6A8 finished stronger than ever. Not a student who was still coming to school failed—Marius Le Roux's aunt could rest easy—and Malcolm and Josef piled up truly prodigious final marks. 6A7's colors were less flying, and several students came up short. I had to fail them, although I expected to hear from at least one of them: Terence, he of the camouflage-patterned beret and the winning smile, who had passed his final easily, but had simply turned in too few compositions over the course of the year. In 6A6, where the general level of performance had risen steadily since the boycott, there was the same problem, however: three kids who had passed their final exam but failed the class. Myron was among them. So was Charmaine, who had earned one of the highest marks on the final. The good news was all the children who had managed to pass—including Aubrey! I was elated to find Aubrey's aggregate mark working out to exactly the official pass percentage. His faithful completion of all his assignments had just carried him over the top.

I braced myself for blasts from Charmaine, Myron, and the others as I handed in my marks to my department chairmen. But there were other blasts awaiting me first.

"You must be joking, Bill," Pieterse said. "A pass rate of ninety percent? Where do you expect us to put all these children next year?"

Somehow, no one had ever told me that there existed, besides the official passing percentage, an unofficial passing curve. Only so many students could be promoted each year—and that figure was closer to 50 percent than to 90. It had been sheer blindness, willful ignorance, on my part not to have seen it all along. Each grade level at Grassy Park High had close to twice the number of students that the next higher grade level had. There were no teachers, no facilities, no funds available to handle any more. What had I been thinking? This was the funnel of black education at work, spilling most of its contents onto the ground.

My students, I realized, knew the score. They knew how many of them would not pass. Nevertheless, I found it heartbreaking to go back through my class lists, looking for students to fail. Elroy? But he had missed three weeks with pneumonia! Joanna? But she had painstakingly rewritten every composition, correcting all her mistakes, for no extra credit. Aubrey? But he had worked so hard! I wanted to protest, I wanted to shout at Napoleon and Pieterse—this just wasn't *fair.* But they knew it, and what could they do? Did my students deserve to pass any more than the students of other teachers did? There were only so many spaces in each standard. That was the system.

So the blasts I had expected from the students I was failing never came. In fact, the year was ending and my students were drifting away with a most unsatisfactory whimper. As the examination schedule staggered slowly toward completion, children wandered into New Room 16 when I was not invigilating to chat or to say goodbye. Would sir be back next year, a few asked idly, plainly aware that I would not. A group of girls—Hester, Amy, Shireen, Mieta—offered to help me take down the pictures, posters, and miscellany on my classroom walls "before the *skollies* steal everything." They took the things they liked; I kept my maps. I gave Wayan a copy of Tolkien's *Lord of the Rings,* and Hester a copy of *Black Beauty.* Shaun never came to see me. Nico and Wayne did—we made vague plans to go surfing over the summer. A number of matrics took my phone number—Hector, Michael, Ishmail, Shahieda, Warren—so they could let me know how they had fared with their exams and various applications. There was no graduation ceremony, it seemed, no end-of-year ritual. There were no yearbooks to inscribe, no class photographs. Summer vacation simply crept over the school, as some kids finished their exams a week or more before others. Laughing groups in shorts and T-shirts now waited outside examination room doors for their friends to emerge. Tennis racquets were waggled in windows—when I hissed *"Voetsek!"* at one, a roomful of Standard Nine students taking an Afrikaans exam laughed.

The faculty was unwinding, too, as invigilation duties lightened and exam marking was completed. In one case, this relaxation seemed to involve a wholesale personality transformation. It was the next-to-last day of school. I was walking past Da Silva's classroom when I heard a guitar and someone singing. I stopped and looked in the window, and there beheld Da Silva himself, performing for forty rapt students. He was singing Peter Sarstedt's nasal folk ballad "Where do you go to, my lovely?" in a rich, booming voice. And I was spellbound, too, standing there listening to DaSilva sing about a woman who talked like Marlene Dietrich, danced like Zigi Jeanmaire, and wore clothes made by Balmain, with diamonds and pearls in her hair. "Extraordinary," Solly Marais murmured in my ear. He had joined me at the window. We tiptoed away together.

The last lunch of the year in the library with the good group that gathered there was the usual jollity under a lowering cloud. Nelson's Touring Club was in desperate straits—there were only three days left until they had to come up with the final payment for the bus they wanted to rent, and they didn't have the money. If they didn't make the payment, they would lose their deposit and the tour would have to be canceled. Each of the people on hand seemed to have a funnier and less practical suggestion for an emergency fund raiser than the last. The principal featured in several ideas that were surefire money-makers if only he would consent to being bombed by cream pies or water balloons or spending a few hours in a ducking chair. Africa and Napoleon also had potential in this area. Meryl thought Grobbelaar might draw a paying crowd with some of his dirty folk songs, until she was reminded that young Ivan had recently become a devout Muslim and forsaken all forms of vice. I had a small speech of gratitude and farewell in my throat during much of this session, but it never seemed quite appropriate, and I figured I would be seeing everyone there again, anyway.

77

On the last day of school, we had the first staff braai since before the boycott. While the end of the year for our students might have been a vague, uncommemorated, anticlimactic affair, we teachers received a double paycheck on that last day, and we knew how to mark the occasion. The braai started early and drew dozens of teachers—nearly the entire faculty. It was held not at one of the vleis near Grassy Park, but at a picnic ground in a pine forest in Tokai, on the lower slopes of the Constantiaberg.

It was a gorgeous day—cloudless and warm, with the dizzy pure freshness of early summer. New grass, extravagantly green after the spring rains, carpeted the clearing in the forest where we gathered. The very blue skies, the light south breeze, the pine scent mixed with the smell of *boerewors* on the braai, all carried me back to my first days in the Cape, when the wind called the Cape Doctor was blowing and I decided to stay. That time now seemed like it had happened in some other life. But this was a day for glimpsing larger designs—a sad, heady day.

Stevie Wonder was blasting—*Everyone's feeling pretty / It's hotter than July / Though the world's full of problems / They couldn't touch us even if they tried*—from the stereo in Dorian Nero's car, which was parked in the middle of everything with the doors thrown open. I was sitting on a fallen tree with half a dozen other teachers, eating and drinking, when Meryl turned to me. Gnawing on a rib and watching me closely, she said, "I got my letter from UCT yesterday."

I held my breath. "Go on."

"I've been admitted."

Meryl could not control a huge, messy smile. Neither could I. We clinked my plastic cup of beer against her can of Coke. "I'll kiss you after you find a tissue."

"You will not. This is still South Africa."

We sat there grinning like fools. Happily, nobody asked us why. Anywhere else, I thought, news like this would merit general congratulations and celebration. But achievement inside the system was such an ambiguous business in black South Africa—especially when a government permit was involved—that any public display on this little occasion would have been inappropriate. Recently, while reading letters from friends overseas, each describing their own latest triumphs and disappointments, I had realized that I had even come to regard less schizoid societies—where people clambered up the ladder of success as best they could without overwhelming qualms—as strange. Severe alienation, the perpetual tension of life in a moral minefield, now seemed like normal existence to me. Anything else sounded catatonic, vicious, or both. Still and all, I was deeply glad for Meryl.

People had started dancing. Meryl and I joined them. The music now was Donna Summer. Arms were waved, hips were shaken, dust was raised. The forest boomed with libidinal bass. I danced with Soraya. I danced with Chantal. Then I pleaded thirst and retreated to a group of male colleagues who were standing around the braai pit working on a bottle of Mainstay Pure Cane Spirit.

"To Oscar Mpetha," I said, taking a swig.

There were grunts, both noncommittal and seconding, a couple of nervous laughs, and some blank looks. *"Amandla ngawethu,"* Pieterse said sarcastically.

Conversation paused, then resumed.

"So what will you be doing for Christmas, Bill?" Ralph Pereira wanted to know.

I hadn't really thought about it.

"We'll be seeing you on the beaches, I hope," Solly Marais said, and everybody laughed. Beach segregation was a burning issue in the Cape at the moment—as it had been every holiday season for the past few years, according to the newspapers. Controversy was already raging over which beaches, if any, would be "open" during the upcoming season.

"That's another good thing about scuba," Cecil Abrahams said, and people laughed again. "The Boers haven't got around to marking the reefs!"

"Not yet!"

"Can't you just see one of them popping up from behind a rock?" Malooi imitated a policeman trying to talk through a respirator. *"Waar's jou pass?* [Where's your pass?] These fishes here is for Europeans Only!"

Trevor Pieterse, who was drinking steadily, turned to me. "We'll be seeing you at the Coon Carnival, too, I trust," he said.

It was a strange, surly remark. A couple of people laughed derisively. "No," I said. "I don't go to Riotous Assemblies." More people laughed. This year's Coon Carnival, which was scheduled to take place shortly after New Year's, promised to be the most pathetic "Cape Mardi Gras" yet, for it had been restricted to two remote venues so as not to conflict with those provisions of the Riotous Assemblies Act that were still in effect. "Will you be there?" I asked Pieterse.

"Of course," he said officiously, then threw back his head and began singing "Daar Kom die Alibama." Everybody laughed, and I slipped away.

The braai was turning into a rowdy party. It was, after all, the office Christmas party and the first day of summer vacation rolled into one. With their big holiday-bonus paychecks in their pockets, most of the faculty seemed to be feeling almost frantically happy. The long hard school year was over, all its conflicts and pressures survived. Colleagues to whom I had hardly spoken in months were suddenly eager to talk—young Erasmus, eyeing me glassily and wanting to know what I *really* thought of "our South African women"; old Fourie politely inquiring about my geography students' final marks. Unfortunately, I was feeling estranged from the prevailing festive spirit. I, too, was relieved that school was over, and probably as pleased as anyone to have made it through to the end. Yet I didn't feel much like celebrating. And I really didn't feel like drinking. I found myself wandering off, away from the braai.

Entering the forest, I hiked vaguely uphill across a springy floor of fallen pine needles. The disco noise from the clearing soon faded. Toasting Oscar Mpetha—that had been a strange thing to do. Earlier that same day, at Pollsmoor Prison—which was only a couple of miles from these piny woods—eighteen men and youths had been charged under the Terrorism Act with one count of terrorism and two counts of murder each in the deaths of George Beeton and Frederick Jansen, the white motorists killed on the Cape Flats in August. All of the accused lived in Guguletu, Nyanga, or Crossroads. Mpetha was the seventy-one-year-old community leader who had been arrested after suggesting to a reporter that the police bore some responsibility for the violence. He and the seventeen others had spent the last four months in prison. Mpetha's wife had been too ill to visit him and his daughter had been refused permission to do so. That morning, as he and the others were being led into the prison courtroom, each had raised a clenched fist to the crowd of supporters gathered there, and when the brief charging procedure was over, the courtroom audience had risen and started singing "Nkosi Sikelel' iAfrika" while guards hustled the accused from the courtroom.

There were other local detainees I might have toasted, including two still being held without charges in connection with the school boycott. One of them was a teacher in Mitchell's Plain; they had both

been in for eight months now. There were also six schoolgirls—two of
them fourteen years old, three of them fifteen, one of them seventeen
—who had been jailed without charges for the past four months. Their
families had also been refused permission to visit them. But Oscar
Mpetha was the best-known Cape Town detainee at the moment, and
everybody present knew I meant every political prisoner in South
Africa, anyway.

My bringing up such a subject in the middle of a party had not
been appreciated, I knew. But I was feeling perverse. Taking this walk
in the woods had been partly to avoid doing anything more offensive.
How could I, a white foreigner, take it upon myself to remind black
South Africans of their failure to effect their own liberation from an
oppression that I not only did not suffer, but that I had been directly
benefiting from in many different ways since the day I arrived in their
country? I couldn't justify it. Perhaps I had, over the course of the
year, simply come to share Nelson's scorn for certain kinds of "socializing." Perhaps, if I were to continue teaching at Grassy Park High,
I might not attend another staff braai. Would I then be off with Nelson
or Jacob, doing whatever it was they were doing today instead? Probably not, and not only because I was not black. For I also felt mired in
an increasing hopelessness about things in South Africa, a sort of
low-grade despair that was no doubt what made me want to be perverse.

Everything just seemed so deadlocked. For all the confrontation
and bloodshed this year, had the cause of black emancipation been
significantly advanced? I couldn't see that it had. But perhaps I had
no perspective, no imagination. Nadine Gordimer's then forthcoming
novel, *July's People,* would be set in the future, during the final throes
of the South African revolution, and she would trace the genesis of the
climactic uprising to this year's events. "It began prosaically weirdly.
The strikes of 1980 had dragged on, one inspired or brought about by
solidarity with another, until the walkout and the shut-down were
lived with as contiguous and continuous phenomena. . . ." The inscrip-
tion for *July's People* would be taken from Antonio Gramsci's *Prison
Notebooks:* "The old is dying and the new cannot be born; in this
interregnum there arises a great diversity of morbid symptoms." I
could certainly see the interregnum, and a goodly diversity of morbid
symptoms. But I could not see around me any of the signs of mobilization for black victory. Not now, not in Cape Town.

It hit me, suddenly, what I would do for Christmas. I would get
the hell out of town. Alex had invited me to spend the holidays with

his family in Johannesburg. I could make that a destination. I would hitchhike there, across the Great Karroo. Sleep outdoors. Wake up in strange surrounds. Throw open the soul's windows, let the wind blow through! The past ten months had been the longest period for which I had ever held a normal Monday-to-Friday job. I had not realized until now how restless with the workaday routine I had become. I was not feeling exhausted, or vacation-lazy—on the contrary, the very thought of my time being my own again filled me with energy.

I was walking along a level, wooded ridge now. As I came to a break in the trees, the sound of taped music reached me on the light south breeze. Half a mile below, I could see the staff braai in the clearing. Dorian Nero's baby blue car looked like some ugly modern sylvan shrine. Its worshipers milled around it in the sinking sun. If I squinted, I could identify individuals, but the scene was already so far away that the dancers did not seem to be moving.

PART IV

TRAVELS with MATTIE

78

It was a few days before Christmas. Alex had already flown to Johannesburg. I was at my desk, dashing off notes letting people know that my address would not be changing for a few more weeks or months, after all—my visa extension had come through. My backpack was out of the closet, leaning against the bed—battered survivor of a thousand passages, redolent for me of the Road, and now half-packed with clothes, books, maps, mess kit, and Christmas presents. There was a knock at the door downstairs; I shouted that it was unlocked. Footsteps came up the stairs, accompanied by murmurs and a short, hoarse laugh. Clive appeared in my doorway, with his friend Mattie peeking around him and rapping smartly on the jamb.

"Knock, knock," she said.

"Who's there?"

"Starsky and Hutch. Hands up."

Clive had a Christmas-rush job as a stock boy in a men's clothing store downtown, and he had taken to stopping by our place on his way home from work—this was the third time I had seen him in the week or so since the end of school.

"You going to Joburg?" Clive nodded at my backpack. He and Mattie had made themselves comfortable on my bed.

"First thing tomorrow morning."

"See you there," Clive said.

"You're kidding."

Clive grinned. "They've hired the bus. We have about four more fund raisers in the next four days, but we're leaving on Boxing Day, it's settled."

"That's *great.*"

Clive shrugged.

"I might see you there as well," Mattie said.

Clive laughed sharply, and he and Mattie looked at each other, then at me.

"You're going on the tour, too?" I asked.

"No. But I may be going on my own."

"Man, she wants to go right away," Clive said. "You should let her go with you."

"With *me?*"

"You're hitchhiking, isn't it?" Clive said. "She doesn't have the money for the train."

They had caught me by surprise. And I was doubly surprised to hear Clive talking for Mattie.

"Why do you want to go to Johannesburg suddenly?" I asked Mattie.

"I need a holiday," she said, and she and Clive laughed.

"Do your parents know you're thinking of going?"

"It's fine by them."

"Your hitchhiking a thousand miles across the country is fine by them?"

Mattie shrugged.

Clive said, "She's eighteen, man. You said you were sixteen when you went traveling all over America and Europe. This is just a two-day trip."

"This is different."

"What's different?"

"She's female, for a start."

"She'll be with you."

I was getting more cautious in my old age, obviously. Clive was right about my big jaunts as a teenager, which had included bumming around Europe with my girlfriend, sleeping in forests and fields without giving personal safety, hers or mine, a thought. What really *was* different about this idea, though, was not only that I was older now, but that this was South Africa and I was white and Mattie was black. Clive and Mattie were undoubtedly more conversant than I was with exactly what kinds of problems *that* could cause. But I was not eager to discover them the hard way. Neither, however, did I feel like raising this particular objection while they were both sitting on the edge of my bed watching me closely.

"Why do you want to go, again?"

Mattie waited a long beat. "I just want to," she said. "It's not a hundred percent certain that I need to go—"

"Now it's *need* to go—"

"That's right. But I'd like to know if the option's open."

"Oh, boy."

I couldn't tell whether or not Mattie was in trouble, whether my immediate assumption—that the Security Police were after her—was correct. And she was clearly not going to tell me herself. She didn't *seem* to be pleading for help. But then, that would not have been her style. The fact was, I couldn't really see how to deny her. "Well," I finally said. "If you're sure it's okay with your parents . . ."

I had arranged a lift out to the highway for early the next morning. I told Mattie to be back by first light if she decided she wanted to go.

"Smart," she said, and she and Clive left.

The next day, I rose before dawn. I was getting ready to leave, feeling increasingly confident that I would not be seeing Mattie, when I heard a car pull up outside. I went to the window. It was misty out, and not yet fully light. But I could see, in the road below, Mattie saying goodbye to her father. She was wearing a heavy peacoat and carrying an old khaki rucksack with a sleeping bag lashed beneath it.

79

An architect friend, a colleague of Fiona's, drove us out to the highway. I studied him as we chatted, trying to tell if he thought we were crazy. He betrayed no such opinion, although he did take us farther than I thought necessary, finally dropping us off near Paarl, about twenty miles out of Cape Town. He wished us luck in a perfectly ordinary way, made a U-turn, and disappeared into the stream of commuter traffic headed back to the city.

There were few cars going our way. We were in flat, green countryside, with the great dark wall of the Hottentots Holland looming in the mist a few miles up the road. A police car went by, its driver turning to study us.

"Are we doing anything illegal?"

"I don't think so," Mattie said. "Not that that ever stops them."

"Maybe if a cop questions us, you should let me do the talking," I said. "Maybe I'll say we're both tourists—you're from Brazil or someplace."

Mattie gave me a sidelong look. "I never had any bus-catching problems," she said.

I had to laugh. In Grassy Park, light-skinned people were sometimes said to have had problems catching buses. Drivers of whites-only buses, seeing them standing alone at a stop, would make a snap judgment that they were black and drive past, while drivers of "non-white" buses would decide at a glance they were white and also drive past. I had to laugh at Mattie's remark because it was true that I had been hoping that she, with her olive skin, might attract less attention on the trip ahead than a darker-skinned woman would, traveling with somebody of my hue. It was no doubt a vain hope.

We soon got our first ride: with a beefy, soft-spoken Afrikaner in his late thirties, driving a brand-new Audi. We sailed up into the mountains, over the high, rocky pass at Du Toits Kloof, through a wall of clouds, and into bright morning sunshine. "Over the garden wall," I called back to Mattie, who was in the back seat with our bags. She chuckled. The architect, while driving us out to the highway, had offered his view that it was "good" that we were getting out of Cape Town. "A favorite professor of mine used to tell us, 'The Cape is a garden. You mustn't just settle in here and never leave. Look over the garden wall!' " Mattie had snorted when he said this, and when I caught her eye, she had gestured with her chin toward a ragged little shantytown sprawling over the dunes of the Cape Flats. Some garden, her expression had said.

Sheer mountains soared all around us now, cliffs and canyons and peaks-in-clouds in spectacular profusion. I was twisting and turning in my seat, marveling at the various views, while our driver nodded proprietarily, beaming at each of my exclamations. "Yes, yes," he kept saying. "And over there?" Mattie was also gaping at the sights, although her only comment, much repeated, was a hushed "Smart!" We emerged from the mountains, then quickly descended into the valley wine country of the Boland.

Our driver was an inspector of dried fruit, he told us. He lived in Paarl, but had to come over the mountains nearly every day. His dream was to introduce almonds as a major cash crop to the Boland; they were now being grown experimentally by the government. He himself came from the Boland. In fact, he had a little time—would we like to see his family's wine farm? We turned onto a secondary road, and sped down winding country lanes that our driver obviously knew cold. He would inherit this farm from his father in another ten years, he told us, and he and his wife and children would then move back to this area permanently. We pulled into a circular driveway and parked in front of a large, freshly whitewashed, eighteenth-century Cape Dutch farmhouse. A red-faced woman in an apron came to the front door as we climbed out of the car. "My mother," our driver said. The woman in the doorway called happily to her son and gestured for me to come inside. Mattie, I noticed, stayed in the back seat.

"Aren't you coming?"

Mattie looked embarrassed. "You must be joking."

I hesitated, shocked.

"Go on," Mattie said. "I'm all right. Just don't stay all morning."

I went inside the house. Our driver's mother shook my hand warmly and offered me coffee. I declined, hoping that would help to shorten our stay. She bore her son off to the kitchen, leaving me in a high-ceilinged, luxurious room, full of antique furniture, glass display cases, and a grand piano. There were oil paintings on the walls: dark, Flemish-looking portraits in ornate frames. This was obviously the manor house of some very old Cape gentry—descendants of the burghers who had not trekked, whose sons all went to Stellenbosch University, sometimes even studied overseas, and now filled most of the top jobs in the government. More cosmopolitan, less *verkrampte,* generally, than their upcountry compatriots, these were the sort of Afrikaners who could usually be counted on to harbor relatively liberal racial attitudes. Thus, no objection would be raised to the fact that Mattie was traveling with me, yet Mattie, I realized, would not have been welcome in this front room. I was about to go back outside and join her in the car when our driver returned. His mother pressed a bag of cakes on me, shook my hand again, kissed her son, and stood beaming and waving in her doorway as we wheeled out of the driveway.

The fruit inspector dropped us outside the Boland town of Worcester. There were a number of other hitchhikers standing along the highway there, so we walked awhile, then caught a short ride in a farm bakkie out to a rather desolate intersection in the Hex River Valley.

Traffic was steadier now, and most of it looked long-distance. Whole caravans of Mercedes-Benzes with Transvaal plates were streaming past bound for their beach holidays at the Cape, while station wagons piled high with luggage went by in our direction. But all the cars seemed to be driving terribly fast through here, and nobody stopped.

We decided to make a sign. I found a scrap of cardboard and began laboriously stenciling "JHB" on it with a ball-point pen. Mattie took it from me and rapidly produced on the other side of the cardboard a strikingly good-looking sign with a soft pencil from her rucksack.

"My father's a sign painter," she said. "I've been working for him since I was a lighty."

We got on to the subject of families and passed the next couple of hours taking turns sketching the characters and narrating the histories of our respective clans. Mattie seemed to have a vast family, with branches all over the Western Cape, a small offshoot in Germany, and roots deeply tangled with the origins of Cape Town itself. Mattie had not been the first member of her immediate family to finish high school, she said, though she would be the first to attend a university. Two of her brothers had gone into sign painting with their father; her older sisters were all housewives. In general, the family got along well together—but for one brother-in-law, whom Mattie despised. It was the same rift over politics that seemed to divide so many black families: the brother-in-law was "reactionary," "opportunist," "cynical," according to Mattie. He believed, in other words, that working to overthrow white rule was hopeless, and he liked to mock Mattie for her political activism.

Mattie, for her part, seemed mainly interested in my family's political experiences and associations—my father's brushes with the film industry blacklist during the McCarthy era, his brother the mountain-climbing FBI agent, my brother's student radicalism, my sister's feminism, my own experiences in the student anti-war movement. Mattie seemed fascinated by my descriptions of a couple of Black Panthers I had known circa 1970. "They were a suicidal clique, it seems to us here," she said. "Waving guns, practically asking the police to wipe them out. They had some very good ideas, but we can't understand what their strategy was meant to be."

It seemed a propitious time to ask again why she was going to Johannesburg. Mattie shrugged, sighed, looked down the highway, stared at me. Finally, she said, "Do you know COSAS?"

I did, vaguely. The Council of South African Students was a new national organization of black high school students, headquartered in Soweto. Its leaders had been detained shortly after its formation, and it had not been active during the schools boycott, so COSAS had not been much in the news this year. I had never heard the organization's name mentioned in Grassy Park.

"Well," Mattie said, "COSAS is trying to coordinate certain struggles in the Transvaal with others in the Cape. And communication is a problem. The telephone's insecure, the post's no good. So people end up having to travel back and forth. This isn't the first time this year I've gone to Joburg."

"Didn't COSAS call for a stayaway from all black schools that had any white teachers?"

Mattie smiled ruefully. "Together with AZAPO [the Azanian People's Organization—a small, radical, aboveground black political group], at the beginning of this past year. It was a flop."

"Why?"

"Partly because the government preempted it by withdrawing all the soldier-teachers from Soweto this year."

"But shouldn't the soldier-teachers have been the focus of the protest to start with, rather than all white teachers?"

Mattie shrugged. "I don't see why. Plenty of white civilian teachers are spies for the government. And even those who aren't can do an incredible amount of damage. No offense meant."

"What sort of damage?"

"Co-option, confusion. At my school, for instance, we had this white geography teacher, this 'liberal' who was very friendly to his students, invited them to his house, and so on. Some of us quite respected him. He had all these books he used to lend us, and these ideas about history. He seemed quite interesting. But then slowly we discovered his real political agenda. He wanted to turn us all into so-called *reasonable* blacks. Finally, someone saw him coming out of a PFP office in Pinelands. He lost all credibility after that, and he had quite a hard time of it this year. I'm sure he won't be back. But a lot of students were confused and misled by him."

"Did anyone bother to find out *why* he was at the PFP office?"

Mattie snorted. "Why? It was obvious already who he was working for."

It was my turn to snort, I thought, but I decided to let it pass.

Motorists were continuing to flash past us at a breakneck rate, with scarcely a glance in our direction. It was now early afternoon—and hot, windy, dusty, and very dry. We had been eating the fruit inspector's mother's cakes, and desperately needed something to wash them down. Across scrubby fields, beside railroad tracks, we could see a general store of some sort.

What sort of store it was became obvious to me only when we had nearly reached it—it was the whites-only sort, with a window on the side of the building through which blacks were served. I stopped in confusion when I saw the arrangement, but Mattie just laughed tightly and headed for the outside trading window, around which a number of farm and railway laborers were gathered. Someone was shouting inside the shop. I couldn't see what else to do, so I went in the front door.

Once my eyes had adjusted to the gloom, I saw that the yelling was being done by a very fat white woman behind the counter. She was producing a steady stream of crude abuse in Afrikaans—half of it directed at a young black shop assistant who was scrambling up and down a ladder plucking items from shelves, half of it at the customers pushing arms, heads, and whatever else they could manage through the trading window. I was the only customer in the "white" section of the shop, and the shopkeeper didn't see me at first. Her black customers, I noticed, tittered quietly at some of her remarks, which seemed to egg her on. When the woman finally noticed me, she gasped. Her mouth clapped shut and she hurried, blushing, to the counter, calling me *"meneer"* and asking in very poor English what she could do for me. I bought a Coke and drank it outside, in the shade of a railway warehouse.

As we walked back to the highway, Mattie said, "Do you see why we think whites are stupid? It's because the very stupidest whites are always given positions of direct, petty power over blacks. And we just have to sit and endure them, and watch them create and perform. You should have heard what those workers were saying about that rubbish woman in the shop." Mattie snickered. "It was so dirty, there are no words for it in English."

We resumed our post at the side of the highway. After a few minutes of silence, Mattie suddenly said, "When blacks get anywhere in this country, you know that they are very, very clever. A black who gets a master's degree is probably a genius. But a white with a master's degree? It doesn't take anything special at all. An average person can manage it."

A Mercedes sedan slowed down and looked us over. A black man was driving, with another black man in the passenger seat. The passenger gave us a raised fist salute and laughed as they sped away. We cursed them both at the tops of our voices. "See you in Azania, brother," Mattie bellowed.

Some minutes later, I said, "You know, Azania is a terrible name for this country. If you look at its etymology, you'll see that it comes from an Arab word for *East* Africa, and that it originally had something to do with slave trading. You probably couldn't come up with a *worse* liberation name if—"

Mattie cut me off with a murderous look. "Now you want to tell us what we can call our own country? I just can't believe white people sometimes. Do you have any idea what 'Azania' means to the oppressed in this country? Maybe we don't *care* what you think of the word, or where you think it comes from. It isn't being used to please you."

"All right, all right."

This was beginning to look like it was going to be a long trip.

80

We finally got a ride out of the Hex River Valley in a truck pulling two semitrailers. Leafy vineyards and rocky mountains gave way to sheep ranches as the landscape widened out into the brown plains of the Little Karroo. Our driver was a small, dark man in a cowboy shirt who said his name was Charles. We introduced ourselves across an expanse of engine cover. Charles said he lived in the Cape Town suburb of Plumstead, and I found myself wondering whether he would be classified "White" or "Coloured"—there was a Plumstead (Lower) and a Plumstead (Upper). His accent was strong—English was not his first language—but inconclusive to my ears. Most truck drivers were black, although I had been told that until very recently they were all white. As Mattie and I were crammed into a seat designed for one person (thin), and the truck's cab was noisy, and Charles was a good ten feet away, I asked Mattie what she thought. She shook her head. "You've been in this country too long," she said.

"Or not long enough."

"White," she said. "So-called poor white."

We had been traveling with Charles for perhaps an hour when I noticed, out of the corner of my eye, something moving in the crawl space behind the truck's cab. I twisted in my seat. To my astonishment, there was a middle-aged African man lying there, three feet from my shoulder. The man smiled at me and nodded. I nodded back. Charles noticed and said, "Don't mind him. He's dead as a stone."

I introduced myself to the man in back nevertheless, and he smiled again, though more tentatively. Charles stared at me across the cab. Finally, he said, "That's Wellington."

"I'm Mattie," Mattie called out to Wellington. *"Molo."** *

"Molo," Wellington murmured.

Charles stared at Mattie, but said nothing.

---

*Xhosa greeting.

At sunset, we stopped at a hamburger stand in Laingsburg, a small, American-looking highway town on the Groot River. Wellington stayed in the truck while the three of us went to eat.

A peculiar thing happened while Charles and I were standing near the takeaway window, trying to decide whether to go inside or get our burgers to go: a tall, pimply white boy of about fifteen leaned through the takeaway window and said, indicating the restaurant with an air of terrible, self-conscious magnanimity, "It's okay. It's all races." Mattie was nowhere in sight—she had gone straight from the truck to a gas station rest room—so it was obvious that the kid thought Charles was black. Charles looked furious and I felt embarrassed for him.

We went inside and sat. Though avoiding my eyes, Charles surprised me by muttering, through clenched teeth, "I've been chucked out of pubs because they wouldn't believe I'm white. It's a bastard. I have to carry my Book of Life [an identity document] with me everywhere."

Mattie joined us. Charles asked me to remind him "to get a sandwich and cool drink for the boy," as he called Wellington. While we ate, Charles told us a long story about how his boss had forced him to take this trip after the regular driver fell sick. He was not a truck driver at all, he stressed. He was a mechanic. He didn't like coming way out here in the *bundu* where he didn't know anyone, and no one knew him.

By the time we got back on the road, it was dark. We rumbled out of Laingsburg and up the low bluffs across the Groot River. A rising full moon suddenly filled the windshield as we emerged onto the immense plateau of the Karroo. Mattie gasped, and murmured, *"Smart."* The highway leveled off and the truck slowly ascended through the roaring scales of its multitude of gears, finally arriving at the deep, soothing timbre of its cruising ratio.

A great sense of well-being began to steal over me, a sense less aesthetic—although the silver-blue countryside streaming by, the sisal and thorn bushes against the moon, were beautiful, and the evening air pouring through the truck's open windows was intensely fresh and sweet—than existential. *Hitching a ride:* some combination of passage, shelter, and irresponsibility that I had always treasured. It had to do with feeling lucky: feeling safe and snug in the eye of a storm of uncontrollable circumstance. And with feeling unfettered: what joy to be bombing through strange and wide-open country, with one's needs pared down to a few—full belly, a good view, forward motion. Most of all, it had to do with hiatus: adventurous respite, the stolen caesura, the suspension of answerability. It was the innocence and luxury of uninvolved observation, and perhaps the single thing I loved most about travel. It had been a long time since I had felt it in such pure form.

"This is great," I sighed.

"What is?" Mattie wanted to know.

"This," I said, indicating our surroundings in general.

"What a romantic you are," Mattie said, not unkindly.

"Not as romantic as you."

"*What?* I'm not a romantic. Not a chance! What is it you imagine I'm romantic about?"

"Revolution."

Mattie was outraged. She shoved me against the truck's engine cover and punched me in the ribs. "You're mad," she declared. "I'm not romantic about revolution."

"Yes you are. I'm not saying there's anything wrong with that."

"But there is a great deal wrong with it. We don't need romantics in the struggle. They're hysterical."

"You're not hysterical. Not that often, anyway."

"*Yussus,*"* Mattie said.

"You're also a Puritan."

Another shove, another punch or two. "What do you mean by *that?* A Puritan is someone who goes about disapproving of everything and can't enjoy themselves, isn't it?"

"That's the idea."

"And you think I'm like that?"

"I think you believe that there is no point in doing anything that doesn't serve the struggle. Doing anything for pleasure, for self-advancement, or just for the hell of it, is out. It's a waste of time, it's immoral, it's reactionary. There's survival and there's the struggle, and the rest is meaningless."

Mattie was silent for a minute. Then she said, "That's true. That is what I believe. So I'm a Puritan. And you, what are you, a hedonist?"

"I wish." A passenger train was streaming across the veld in the distance, a toylike column of lighted boxes. I imagined I saw people standing in a saloon car. "But I wouldn't mind a beer right now," I said.

---

*A mild Afrikaans profanity.

"Oh, that's what you are, a drunkard," Mattie said. "We can't have drunkards in the struggle either."

"So I've heard."

A few minutes later, Mattie muttered, "I think those students in Tehran have the right idea about how to cope with Americans. If you give me any more uphill, I'm going to take you hostage."

With that, Mattie fell asleep against my shoulder.

It was after midnight when Charles finally dropped us off, outside a tiny railway village called Leeu-Gamka. Mattie and I stood sleepily beside the highway for half an hour without seeing a vehicle pass in either direction. Then we tramped off into the veld a couple of hundred yards and unrolled our sleeping bags. The moonlit land around us seemed absolutely empty.

"We're well and truly in the Karroo now," Mattie said. "Do you know what they call this bush?" She indicated a low shrub that she was tramping down as a mattress. "Hottentot bedding," she said, and she laughed. The shrub had a lovely, herblike aroma. "Did you know there's not a single hotel for blacks between Cape Town and Kimberley?"

I had heard.

We climbed into our bags and lay looking at the moon. I was deliciously tired from the long day of travel.

"The Cape is not a garden," Mattie's voice, disembodied, said. "What shit they must talk at UCT!"

A little while later, Mattie's voice again: "But the Cape is really a *peninsula,* you know, politically as well as physically. It's easy to get isolated there from what's going on in the rest of the country."

I lay thinking about South Africa, the whole vast, variegated sprawl of the place. Although the grade was rarely noticeable, we would be climbing steadily all the way from Cape Town to Johannesburg—nearly six thousand feet in all. We were going from the coastal shelf up onto the great African escarpment, as we would have said in geography class. From a Mediterranean region, through a semidesert, to the highveld.

But we had only covered one-fifth of the Cape Town–Johannesburg journey today—and Christmas was just three days away. "Do you have any plans for Christmas?" I asked.

"No."

"Your family doesn't mind your being away at Christmas?"

"My mother probably does."

"But you don't?"

"Christmas means nothing to me. I'm not a Christian."

I laughed.

"What's funny?"

"Nothing."

A while later, Mattie asked me what my plans were after this trip. To stay in Cape Town awhile and write, I said, and then to head north across Africa. Beyond that, I didn't know. I asked Mattie what her plans were.

"Go to university," she said, without enthusiasm.

"UCT?"

"Of course not. I'll go to Bush."

"What do you mean, 'of course not'?"

"Why should I go there? To listen to the shit they talk?"

"It's a better university than UWC. You'd get a far better education there."

"That's not my first priority."

"Realizing your own potential is not your first priority?"

"No. I'm not interested in finding out what I can do. I'm interested in finding out what the people can do, what the masses can do."

"Give me a break."

"What does that mean?"

"It means that sounds hopelessly romantic."

"Too bad."

"You're not going to find out what 'the masses' can do at UWC any more than you would at UCT."

"I know they talk a lot of shit at Bush, too. Even the politically committed students. They talk a lot of theory, a lot of jargon, and they get bogged down in an academic approach to struggle. They use words that ordinary working people don't understand. Workers relate to action, not words. But at UCT, *ag,* it's much worse. Black UCT students have very little credibility in the black community. People who go there lose their gut connection to oppression. I don't want that to happen to me."

This was more or less the same argument I had had many times with Clive. Still, I could not accept the idea that someone like Mattie should waste her brains at a place like UWC. It went against my grain at a level deeper than politics. I had a strong suspicion that Mattie had served on the Committee of 81, where I had heard that the UWC representatives had effectively dominated the other delegates, behaving with particular arrogance toward their comrades from UCT. I was about to suggest that her motives for wanting to go to UWC had as

much to do with more-oppressed-than-thou one-upmanship in the
world of black student politics as they did with anything else—when
I realized that Mattie's breathing had lengthened into the long sighs
of sleep.

Lying there, looking up at the moon and the southern stars, listening to Mattie breathe, I found that my appetite for argument had fled
and been replaced by an overwhelming sympathy for my young companion. "These poor children"—a phrase that I had come to hate in
the mouths of conservative teachers and administrators—suddenly
felt richly descriptive. Here she was, this spunky kid, too poor to take
a train or a bus, hitchhiking a thousand miles with a bedroll to talk
to a bunch of other teenagers about how to overthrow the government. And look what they were up against: a neo-Nazi police state
with a huge, highly trained army—which now had, according to many
reports, nuclear weapons. For Mattie, her own country was enemy
territory—her phone was bugged, her mail was opened, the secret
police were everywhere. And all this grief simply because of the color
of her skin?

What kind of experiences had shaped Mattie's thinking, I wondered. How and when had she been "conscientized"? Had 1976 been
her introduction to the struggle? She had been in Standard Seven
then. Would her dedication to the cause deepen with time, or would
it become proportionally less of her life? If it deepened, would she be
driven underground? Would she take up arms? The struggle was like
the church. You felt a vocation, you had the faith, so you gave your
life over to poverty, obedience, and the greater good. Mattie was like
some foul-mouthed mystic nun. As I drifted off to sleep there in the
veld, the last thoughts I had that I could later recall involved images
of the Struggle as some gigantic wave, or whirlwind, or juggernaut,
to which tiny, trembling figures were being drawn from every direction. It was a primitive religious cartoon, like the drawings of the
Apocalypse in the tracts given away by Christian fundamentalists,
and I felt before it some of the lost soul's dread and awe.

81

The sun rose early, and when I peeked out the top of my sleeping bag
—the mild summer night had turned chilly in the hours before dawn
—I woke up fast. Our little campsite in the veld, which had seemed
a faraway, moonlit world of its own the night before, was plainly

visible both from the highway and from a collection of shacks on a small rise a few hundred yards to the west. I scrambled out of my sleeping bag, quickly made two cups of tea, and woke Mattie. She sat up grumpily, stared at the tea I offered her and at my little gas cooker, mumbled something about "Boy Scouts," took the tea, and turned her back on me and on the blinding sun. I could now see people moving around in the little shantytown on the rise. I pointed them out to Mattie and suggested that we break camp immediately.

Mattie looked at the squatters' camp for a minute, then said, "They won't bother us."

I accepted her judgment. Mattie continued to study the squatters' camp. "Those people have some of the hardest lives you can imagine," she said quietly. "They wander from place to place all over the Karroo, working for white farmers. They get paid almost nothing. Their children don't go to school. The kids are constantly ill, in fact, and a lot of them die. And most of the adults are illiterate. They don't know anything except how to survive from one day to the next."

"Are those Africans or so-called coloreds?"

"Both. They're not too strict about Group Areas in that kind of a place. A lot of the Xhosa people out here are Afrikaans-speaking. There used to be a lot of intermarriage, before Mixed Marriages. Do you see those women?"

A group of women in *doeks* was setting off from the squatters' camp, heading north across the veld. "They're going for firewood," Mattie said. "They probably have to walk for miles. All the wood from around here will be gone, and most of these little Karroo *dorps* [country towns] have laws against wood gathering around the so-called location. They'll probably have to buy a 'draggie' someplace, and carry it back." Mattie shook her head. "It's not capitalism these people suffer from. It's feudalism."

We sat in silence, finishing our tea. Mattie stretched and yawned. "Do you know what they call this early morning sun out here?" she asked, her voice suddenly full of its usual vigor. " *'Armemasebaadjie!'* The poor man's coat!"

We packed up our things and headed for the highway.

Leeu-Gamka consisted of a railway station, a hotel, a gas station, and a few houses. At the gas station stood a queue of about twenty-five cars waiting for the pumps to open. This was why there had been no traffic late the night before: all gas stations in South Africa were closed by law from 6 P.M. till 7 A.M. during the week (and from 1 P.M. on Saturday till 7 A.M. on Monday). The gas station was just opening up as we arrived, so I began working the cars in the queue immediately, while Mattie went around back to the "Non-White" rest rooms to wash up. A middle-aged white couple in a white Mercedes cheerfully agreed to give me and my friend-who-was-in-the-rest-room a lift. We put my backpack in the trunk of their car. But when Mattie appeared, the couple had a change of heart. Muttering something about needing the back seat for their ice chest, they put me out. I avoided looking at Mattie and decided to use a little hitchhiker's Mau-Mau.

I went to the head of the queue, where a young white couple in an old Ford were filling up. I rather breathlessly asked them for a lift for me and my friend-who-was-in-the-rest-room. Obviously embarrassed, the couple hesitated, then agreed. I waited until they were ready to leave and the long queue behind them was growing impatient, however, before I called to Mattie. She hurried over and jumped in the car and we were on the road before the couple got a good look at her. When they did, they looked startled. I didn't mind that, so long as they got us to a less desolate place than Leeu-Gamka, but Mattie seemed to feel differently. She sat through some awkward, mumbled introductions, glared fiercely at me, and then took the damp white washcloth she had just been using for her morning ablutions and hung it over her face.

It was a strange ride. I talked a bit with the couple, who had a three-month-old baby on the seat between them, while Mattie sat like some kind of faceless sphinx beside me. The couple was from Potchefstroom, they said, in the Transvaal. He was a clerk in a government office. They had been married just a year. They were Afrikaans. They were very polite, and reminded me of nothing so much as the photographs I had seen of my parents and their friends from the early 1950s, when they had all been newly married, owned shabby-genteel cars much like this Ford, and had new babies, and the men all had little-boy haircuts like our driver's. The young woman's frequent little panic-stricken, helpless-fawn looks at her husband struck me as excessive, but otherwise they seemed to me like ordinary, inoffensive folk. Our conversation deteriorated drastically, though, after the young man asked me what I thought of the life here in South Africa and I replied, "It looks comfortable if you're white." Mattie snickered from beneath her washcloth—the only sound she made for over sixty miles—and our driver finally filled the loaded silence that followed by pushing a country western tape into the cassette deck.

On the outskirts of Beaufort West, a sprawling Karroo town,

population twenty thousand, we got pulled over. Our driver was given a ticket for speeding. The cop was "colored" and the tension inside our little Ford throughout the episode was incredible. Our driver's wife seemed to be nearing a nervous breakdown. After the cop let us go, we proceeded at a snail's pace into the center of Beaufort West, where our driver pulled to the curb and gestured to us that the lift was over. I nudged Mattie and we disembarked.

"Look at them," I said, as we walked away from the Ford, which remained parked where we had left it. Our driver and his wife were embracing where they sat, and including the baby in the embrace in a desperate-looking huddle. "It's instinctual," I said. "In a time of trouble, they automatically form a *laager.*"*

"I don't want to look at them," Mattie spat.

"Oh, come on. They're just a poor little family. They've just got a speeding ticket. They're trying to comfort each other. I feel sorry for them."

"Sorry for them," Mattie exploded. "They're sick! And they're going to make that baby sick! Did you see what they did when they saw me in their car?"

"They didn't do much."

"You're blind, in that case, as well as mad. Their skin was crawling. They were in a complete panic. *They* make *me* sick."

Mattie and I argued our way through the dusty streets of Beaufort West. At one point, she said, "You know what your problem is? You're not a racist." I took that as a compliment, but Mattie did not mean it as one. She elaborated: "In this country, you have to stereotype. If you meet some Boer, and they don't differ radically from the typical Boer, you just assume they're racists and fascists and leave it at that. You can't go about giving every individual the benefit of the doubt. That's naive. And naiveté is a luxury we can't afford. A government clerk and his little *boeremaisie* from bloody Potchefstroom are not innocent until proven guilty. They're guilty, full stop. Because of who they are and what their sick culture does and what it stands for."

We stopped at a Greek grocery and bought rolls and juice and ate our breakfast in the shade of a blue gum tree, but we did not stop arguing. I said something about how "relations between groups" were a problem everywhere, and Mattie blew up again. " 'Relations between groups' is not the problem in South Africa! What a white liberal delusion that is! *White people are the problem.*"

---

*A defensive formation of circled ox wagons favored by the Boer pioneers.

Later, as we were approaching the highway roundabout where we would be able to start hitchhiking again, I got fed up myself and shouted, "What do you want, anyway? Do you want all the whites in this country just to pack their things and leave?"

Mattie laughed. "Oh, that would be far too much to hope for," she said.

82

A police car cruised slowly past us, with both of the cops in it turning to stare at Mattie and me. A few minutes later, the same car came around the roundabout again. Another long, hard look from the S.A.P. of Beaufort West. We discussed abandoning the shade of the pepper tree we were standing beneath for some spot farther out of town.

"I just hope you're not carrying any Urban Foundation literature in there," Mattie said, pointing at my pack.

I laughed. So Mattie knew about my career counseling follies. She was referring, at the same time, to a recent news story in which a distinguished visitor from Canada, the wife of a former Quebec cabinet minister, touring South Africa as part of a study group, had been stopped and searched by police in the Johannesburg airport after a flight from Cape Town. It seemed that one of her fellow passengers had informed the police that the Canadian woman had been reading "communistic literature" on the flight. The literature in question had turned out to be the annual report of the Urban Foundation, which the police confiscated. The incident had gotten into the press and embarrassed the government.

"I just wish you hadn't got so much sun yesterday," I said. "You could use some of that Karoo Freckle Cream."

Mattie glared. "I take back what I said about your not being a racist!" It was true, though: we were both sunburned from the long day of sitting at the side of the road—which only added to our disinclination to start walking down the blindingly bright and treeless highway beyond the roundabout.

I had already picked up a number of Afrikaans swear words from Mattie, curses that I now began to hurl at the backs of the vehicles that passed us. I was still unclear on the exact meanings of most of these expressions, but my use of them seemed to slay Mattie. She laughed until the tears stood in her eyes. "If you only knew what you were saying!" My accent in Afrikaans, she said, was "quite exotic. You sound like a bloody German or something."

Mattie and I were getting more comfortable with each other. We both enjoyed arguing, and we could make each other laugh. Mattie, moreover, had already become quite unreserved with me, physically. Not only was she constantly shoving, punching, and pinching me, but while sitting there under the pepper tree at the roundabout, she would lean against me, with her forearm on my knee, to read our road map, and remain like that for several minutes, with an absolutely natural air. Such physical ease did not come to me quite so naturally, although I was well acquainted with its roots after a year in Grassy Park, and had always found it wonderful, and knew better than to imagine that Mattie meant anything more by it than an expression of acceptance and trust. It was affectionate, and at some level it was probably exciting, but it was blithe, not romantic, and decidedly not sexual. Still, I found myself wondering whether the Beaufort West police would see it that way when I saw them entering the roundabout yet again. They cruised past us once more without stopping.

A few minutes later, we got a ride at last, in the back of a pickup truck. The driver was a young, bearded white guy who said he was going to Britstown. His black companion rode in the cab beside him —an unusually humane arrangement. We jumped into the truck's bed and dug ourselves in among the tools, pipes, and machinery piled there. It was nice to be moving again—we had been in Beaufort West for five long hours—but the sun and wind were punishing, and Mattie and I were both soon swaddled like Bedouins.

Seen from the depths of a makeshift burnoose—towel hood, sweater muffler, sunglasses, long-billed baseball cap—the land we drove through took on an almost unreal harshness. Burnt red rock and scrubby veld stretched away to a horizon broken only by the stark mesas called *kopjes*. Dry, savage-looking gullies *(dongas)* testified to the flash floods that tore through this part of the Karroo after summer rainstorms. We passed some desolate-looking dry lakebeds and some nearly-as-desolate-looking farms, the weathered buildings huddled around windmills above the precious boreholes. Karroo farmers were legendarily tough characters; seeing this country, I could easily understand why. The road signs were for places called Renosterkop (Rhinoceros Head), Wagenaarskraal (Wagoneer's Corral), and Sodium.

By the time we reached Britstown, it was late afternoon. We were dropped at an intersection about two miles beyond the town, back in open country. It was a bleak spot. Off to the west, eighty miles across the veld, was, according to the highway signs, some place called Prieska—to the east was De Aar. The graffiti scratched into the sign-posts was angry, ominous stuff, cursing the local farmers and claiming that its authors had spent four hours—nine hours—two days!—stranded here. Many of the names written on the signs bore military designations—ranks and regiments and squadron nicknames—and I wondered if there was some kind of base nearby. That question seemed answered when the first car we saw dropped off a young soldier before turning around and returning toward Britstown.

The "troopie" ignored us, although he stood barely twenty yards away. He was blond, sunburned, crew-cut, in uniform, with his cap tucked smartly through a loop on his shoulder. He was, I guessed, not much older than Mattie. It was strange to think that he and she were enemies and might one day fix each other in their respective rifle sights. When a car came along, the soldier did not put out his thumb, but the car stopped anyway, as patriotic motorists were urged by road signs to do whenever they saw a serviceman standing by the road. Over the next hour, two more soldiers came and went in similar fashion, with virtually no traffic passing other than the cars that dropped them and picked them up. None of the soldiers spoke to us. It was a bit eerie, as well as irritating. Then things became distinctly more menacing as one pickup truck, carrying three young white males, passed us twice, slowing down for a long look on the second pass. I recalled reading about an incident that had occurred a few weeks before—was it near here?—in which four young soldiers from Pretoria had stopped their car on the highway and simply begun shooting black children, killing one boy of nine. We had to get out of here. It would be dark in a couple of hours.

A car appeared in the distance, going our way. It occurred to me that, with her baggy pea coat, shapeless trousers, and short hair, Mattie could easily be mistaken for a boy. Only half-seriously, and expecting nothing but abuse for my trouble, I said, "Show them you're a girl." Mattie surprised me—and the oncoming car—by doing a swishy little dance into the road and lifting one pant leg to reveal a girlish knee. It got us a ride.

A gloriously long ride—all the way to Kimberley. In a new station wagon, with a friendly, nearsighted Afrikaans woman in her late twenties named Estelle. Estelle who said she had stopped only because Mattie's little jig had made her see that she was female, which she would not have noticed otherwise. "*Got* to get you some high heels and a miniskirt," I said to Mattie, who slugged me happily. Kimberley was less than three hundred miles from Johannesburg. I dozed as we sped through the long summer dusk, and only awoke as we were entering Kimberley and the light was fading from the western sky.

Estelle was looking forward to a cold beer and "Dallas" in her motel room, she said. My sun-weakened brain swam at the mention of cold beer. But there was little chance of rendezvousing with such a thing, I knew, while traveling with Mattie. Estelle asked if there was anywhere in Kimberley she could drop us. She was going on to Johannesburg tomorrow, she said, and would be happy to take us there, if we could manage to meet her in the morning. At that moment, I spotted a sign for a caravan park. "Right here," I said.

83

It was a sprawling, unkempt, half-deserted, whites-only caravan park. We climbed over a small fence, stayed well away from the caretaker's cottage, and availed ourselves of the park's showers. An old man came in the rest room while I was shaving, but Mattie said she had seen no one on the women's side when we reconvened. We stashed our bags underneath a hedge and went in search of supper. About a mile down the highway, we found a hamburger stand. After getting the nod from a black waitress, we went inside and ate heartily, finishing up with big slices of homemade apple pie and several cups of coffee. Then we strolled back toward the caravan park. On a long, curving bridge where the highway vaulted over a railway yard, we stopped to watch the trainmen working below. I started explaining the various shunting moves being made, showing Mattie the American versions of the lantern signals being used. Soon I was regaling her with stories of peril and courage on the high iron and descriptions of some of the great California railroaders I had worked with. Mattie, to my surprise, seemed fascinated. Then two young white guys walking by carrying duffel bags interrupted us.

"Aren't you two people hitching to Joeys?" one demanded, in an Afrikaans accent. He sounded drunk.

I admitted we were. I remembered this pair from the crowd outside Worcester the day before.

The same one spoke again: "What, aren't you going any further tonight? Do you have a place to stay here?"

"We can't stay here, man," his companion, who sounded equally drunk, said. "We must get there tonight."

"Right. Well, if you see us by the side of the road, and you're passing by, tell the people you're with they must stop. Say we're your cousins or something."

Mattie, who had been hanging back from this conversation, burst out laughing. The two sodden wayfarers chuckled, too, but not as if they got the joke. It was dark on the bridge, and it seemed they had not got a good look at Mattie.

We resumed our trek back to the caravan park. I observed that the next day was Christmas Eve, and that if Estelle came back for us, and probably even if she didn't, it looked like we would be in Johannesburg for Christmas. Mattie replied in an icy voice that she couldn't care less about Christmas.

"So you say," I said, feeling stung and snapping back. "But you're in a small and toffee-nosed minority. 'The masses' care about Christmas. It's a holiday, a time for people to have fun. In fact, 'the masses' are mostly devout Christians."

"What do you know about it?" Mattie erupted. "Were you here in '76? That was a so-called Black Christmas, when celebrations were banned in the townships by the students. No holiday decorations, no drinking, just gatherings to mourn the dead."

"And people were burying their booze in their backyards, and the students were digging it up and smashing the bottles," I said. "And students were accosting people in the streets if they thought they'd been drinking, and forcing them to drink water, then shoving feathers down their throats to make them throw up. No, I wasn't there, but I've heard the stories. And I know that the students didn't 'conscientize' many people that Christmas."

"How do you know what conscientizes people? Do you live in the black community? Some of us thought this year should have been a Black Christmas. And we know better than you do what were the aftereffects of '76. Christmas and alcohol have been issues in the townships for years. So don't you bother lecturing me about them."

"Fine."

This was not one of our bantering, enjoyable arguments, but a bitter, bruising quarrel that seemed to me to have come out of nowhere. When we arrived back at the caravan park, I dug a book out of my pack and went and sat under a streetlight to read. Mattie spread out her sleeping bag and lay down without a word on a patch of grass in the dark some distance away. My concentration on my reading was imperfect, for I was upset, and the light pulsed and flickered because of a cloud of moths. But I kept at it for an hour or so, by which time I assumed Mattie was asleep. Then the nasal howl of a muezzin, emanating from a mosque down the street, split the air, giving me a start, and when the prayer was over, Mattie piped up from the dark. "You forgot to mention all the devout Muslims."

"That's next lecture."

Mattie laughed, and a little while later she joined me under the streetlight with a book of her own. She was reading John Reed's *Ten Days That Shook the World*—a *lekker* book, she informed me. (I was reading Edward Roux's *Time Longer Than Rope: A History of the Black Man's Struggle for Freedom in South Africa,* a volume of which Mattie also approved, although I was finding its lengthy discussion of the early days of the South African Communist Party heavy going.) We started talking about journalism and history, and I ended up writing out a reading list for her. Then Mattie surprised me by suddenly saying, "I'm just not used to this. That's why I was so stroppy."

"Not used to what?"

Mattie looked off in the direction of the mosque and replied very carefully. "I have never spent so much time with just one person before."

"Never?"

"No. Maybe a day or something, but never just continuously, one day after the other like this. There have always been lots of people around me. My family, my friends, my schoolmates. So this is weird for me. And confusing."

"You, confused? I don't believe it."

Mattie laughed, then grew serious again. "Such as when you were telling me about the railway workers in California, how it was dangerous and some of them got hurt—I couldn't handle that. Because we don't think about America that way. We think of it as this rich, capitalist, imperialist exploiter that sends the CIA out to fuck up progressive movements in the Third World. So when you start telling me about your friends, making them sound like normal working people with normal worries, it fucks me up. It confuses me. It's not your fault, but that's why I get so touchy sometimes."

I took this as an apology and muttered something about how I probably deserved whatever I got. Although Mattie's explanation had shed light on gulfs of cultural difference between us—a life so thoroughly *peopled* was to me almost unimaginable—I felt closer to her in the wake of her confession. So when she asked me a while later, as we were lying in our sleeping bags, about what sort of writing I wanted to do, and whether I just planned to travel around forever, I tried to answer her less superficially than I had the night before.

I had recently sold my first feature article to an American national magazine, a long essay about living in a village in Sri Lanka. But I was feeling queasy about the whole business. What was I really doing, I wondered, describing Third World politics and daily life, and all the permutations of my First World reactions thereto, for the leisuretime amusement of those few Americans whose education and class inclined them to read such things? Was I doing anything, that is, beyond satisfying some of the idle curiosity of the wealthy about how the rest of the world lived, beyond irritating and then massaging the thousand loose-waving nerves of liberal guilt? What right did I have to fix real people's lives inside my American frame? And now I was getting inquiries from editors about whether I was planning to write anything about South Africa. No, I was not planning to write a word about South Africa!

"Why not?"

Because it wouldn't do any good. Because I suspected that many of my fellow Americans got a secret kick out of reading about "apartheid," and I didn't want to be the one to give it to them. If I wrote any more magazine articles at all, I announced, I would restrict myself to the lightest subjects—surfing, vacations—for only the breeziest publications.

This announcement drew catcalls from Mattie. She thought the idea stunk. I asked what she thought one could usefully write about South Africa for American readers. She promised to come up with suggestions—but not tonight. Then she fell asleep.

I lay awake feeling conflicted, confused, homesick, and old. Mattie had asked me whether I "just planned to travel around forever," and that had triggered my raving as much as any thoughts about what to write had. I was tired of traveling, tired of being an expatriate, and in some deep sense I wanted to go home. Wandering the world's back roads and byways had begun to seem like a hopelessly self-indulgent thing to be doing. And yet I was no longer sure where home was. How I envied Mattie's clarity, her certainty, her sure sense of connection to even this tortured country. I didn't believe it when she said that her life would be meaningless without her political commitment, but she believed it, and that was what mattered.

I liked traveling with Mattie. She was good company, and she could tell me things about what I saw. Traveling with her also gave things a certain adrenaline edge of outlawry that I liked. But we saw different countries, Mattie and I. Everywhere she looked, she saw things to be done. She saw outrage, injustice, the tabula racista on which she and her comrades would one day write a whole new message. She saw a world to be unmade, and a brave new world to be made. While I saw something infinitely more static and fixed—a place to be contemplated, understood, and described. This difference, between the South Africa Mattie saw and the one I saw, was what made me feel old.

I turned and watched her sleep. I wondered what she thought of me. The uppermost thing in her mind, no doubt, was her mission. In terms of that, I probably figured as some offbeat kind of cover. And otherwise? Mattie wore her scorn for sappy sentiment on her sleeve. And the rigor of her manner discouraged melting thoughts. Besides that, romance would be "bad security," as they said in the struggle. Did she regard me as a teacher, still? I doubted it. In fact, I rather regarded her as one.

84

Estelle returned for us in the morning. Joyously, we tossed our "JHB" sign in a bin. Estelle wanted to visit the Big Hole, she said, before we left Kimberley. This was the town's main tourist attraction: a vast excavation, said to be the world's largest, out of which three tons of diamonds had been mined since the 1880s. We spent an hour there, wandering around a museum gawking at replicas of famous diamonds, walking the streets of a Disneyland-type reconstruction of frontier Kimberley, and gazing into the Big Hole itself. A mile around and half a mile deep, the old mine looked, I thought, like a high mountain lake, a deep blue gem of catchment in some sheer glacial cirque. Mining continued from an ungainly-looking and silent barge. I smiled to recall the description of the Big Hole on the Grassy Park High Touring Club's itinerary: "We will visit the so-called Big Hole, where South Africa's first industrial capitalists, led by the arch-imperialist Cecil Rhodes, began to exploit the country's mineral wealth and enrich themselves with our undistributed wages."

As we left Kimberley, we saw two ragged-looking figures on the side of the road ahead, gesturing angrily at the passing traffic. It was the pair of Afrikaners we had met on the bridge the night before. Mattie thrust her head out the passenger window, threw her arms wide, and cried "Cousins!" to the startled hitchhikers. Estelle didn't get it, but Mattie and I laughed all the way into the Transvaal.

We had left the Karroo the previous afternoon. Now we were in the highveld. The land was green from early summer rains, with rolling grassy plains, small farms, rivers—all very soothing to the Karroo-seared eyes. Although we had left the Cape only two days before, it seemed like longer. Mattie and I were both deeply sunburned; our lips were swollen and cracked; my tongue felt swollen. We traded our stick of "lip ice" back and forth, rolling it on in thick minty layers.

Estelle was in a talkative mood. She told us about the toy manufacturing business she had started, which was booming. With her profits, she said, she had recently bought a "piece of ground" outside Johannesburg, on which she was soon going to build a house. She planned to do everything on the house herself, from the architecture to the laying of the bricks. She would hire a man only for some of the heavy lifting. Her family thought she was mad, Estelle said with a laugh. To be nearly thirty and not even worried about being unmarried! She was becoming "the black sheep," she said. Although she wasn't interested in politics, her relatives accused her of being a *kaffirboetie* (nigger lover)—Estelle looked ruefully at Mattie when she said this, and I wondered if she had managed to prove herself an "innocent" Afrikaner in Mattie's eyes.

Around midday, we stopped in a small Transvaal town for Estelle to make some phone calls. After she left the car, Mattie also climbed out, saying she would try to find us some snacks. I drowsed in the sun —so that I was caught by surprise when a few minutes later a brown arm, reaching through the car window, silently set a quart bottle of ice-cold Lion Lager in my lap. The bottle had a ribbon tied around the neck. "Happy Christmas," Mattie said.

That beer ranked with the best I have tasted. Mattie laughed in disbelief at my groans of appreciation as I drank, and told me to be quiet, lest I draw unwelcome attention from "the local *tannies*"— Afrikaner "aunties" known for their devotion to public decency. My puritanical young friend refused to taste a drop herself, although she admitted that her tongue, too, felt swollen. "Not enough Bushman blood on my side of the family," she said.

On we drove to Johannesburg. Billboards multiplied, traffic increased, highways converged, factories and mine dumps appeared on the land, and smog began to rouge the horizon. On the way into the city, we skirted Soweto. At last I got a look, albeit a quick one, at the famous township, which looked exactly like the older townships on the Cape Flats, only bigger. We passed Baragwanath Hospital, where so many dead, dying, and wounded schoolchildren had been taken in 1976. Then we caught our first glimpse of the knot of downtown skyscrapers. Estelle had offered to take us to the address I had, so we turned left and headed for the northern suburbs. Soon we were cruising wide, shady streets lined with huge homes. Uniformed gardeners watered the lawns in the sultry late afternoon heat. The area looked like Beverly Hills—only bigger. The mansions seemed to go on for miles. Finally, we found the address we sought. Mattie and I dragged ourselves and our bags out of Estelle's car and thanked her inadequately for her kindness. She drove away and we stood staring at what we could see of a long, low, brown stucco house, flanked by very high walls that ran for fifty yards down the street in each direction.

"You didn't mention you were going to prison," Mattie said. That was exactly what the house looked like: some kind of modern jail. The only windows we could see were barred. There was no sign of life.

It took a long time to get any answer at the front door. A black maid in uniform eventually appeared. She regarded the two of us very suspiciously and seemed about to shut the door. Then I mentioned my name, and she relaxed. I was expected. We were ushered into the entranceway. Alex appeared, looking pleased to see me safe and sound, but more than a little taken aback to see Mattie. We were escorted farther into what looked to be a vast house.

"What *is* this place?"

Alex laughed. "My sister is house-sitting for some friends of hers. I couldn't believe it, either. Your room is about the fifth one along that passage over there, on the right."

I had arrived just in time for the big Christmas Eve dinner, it seemed, which was due to be served in a couple of hours. Everyone was off getting ready for it now. I just had time to clean up, change, and —and do whatever else I needed to do. Which, I realized, meant "do something with *her.*" I took Mattie aside and asked her what she wanted to do. She said she wanted to get out of there as soon as possible. She, too, had friends who were expecting her. I went back to Alex, who agreed to let me use one of the house's fleet of cars.

With Mattie navigating, we headed south and west in an aged Morris Mini (the children's Shetland pony, apparently, to all the German and Italian thoroughbreds we had glimpsed gleaming in a long garage). We left the rolling hills and jacaranda-canopied promenades of the northern suburbs, followed a railway line through a warehouse district, then clattered into a maze of bleak brick houses and concrete tenements. Mattie had been here before and kept seeing beer halls and street corners she recognized, but she could not find her friend's house. The streets were full of people, many of whom bent over to peer through the windows of our car, yet stopping to ask directions seemed unwise. "I guess they don't see many whiteys around here," Mattie said, in reference to the shouts that erupted repeatedly in our wake. I was just glad we had not borrowed a Mercedes or a vintage Alfa for this trip. Finally, we saw a woman in an otherwise empty road. We stopped. Mattie mentioned the name of her friend. And the woman directed us to his house without hesitation.

I dropped Mattie off outside the back unit in a shabby old duplex built against a hill. A girl of about sixteen came out and hugged her, followed by an old woman who remained in the doorway and several little kids who ran around excitedly. Mattie and I stood there, searching for something to say. "Perhaps you'd like to meet Mohamed," she said, gesturing toward the duplex. But her friend said, "He's sleeping." Mattie shrugged and said, "Anyway, he's banned. So who could introduce you?" She laughed her hacking, ironic laugh. "Joke," she said to me. "He can only be in the same room with one other person who's not in his family."

"I got it," I said.

"Well, okay. Then see you around."

"See you around. Merry Christmas."

85

Rising early and making tea or coffee for any tea- or coffee-drinking companions who seemed to be stirring was my usual way of starting the day. In Rondebosch, this habit seemed to amuse Alex and Fiona, who would make remarks about my livery ("Really must get the boy new khakis") and my political correctness ("And the intellectuals shall wait upon the workers!"), but in Johannesburg, staying in that vast house in the northern suburbs, I never managed to indulge it. Every morning, my first waking impression was of a uniformed figure gliding from the child's bedroom where I slept. On a tray on the table beside my bed would be a small pot of hot coffee, a silver urn of hot milk, and a china cup and saucer. This was how most white South Africans started the day, I knew, but it must have been three, possibly even four days before I got used to it.

The house itself I never did get used to. It contained at least twenty rooms, which jutted off, fell away, and turned back on each other at such a variety of angles that it was entirely possible to get lost in transit between wings. Over the week that I stayed there, I repeatedly ended up, while trying to find the kitchen, in a small, crowded study of some kind, without ever understanding how I got there. Neither did I understand the architect's intentions with respect to the domes, alcoves, split levels, skylights, and oddly curved walls that seemed to litter the house at random. It was as though each room had been designed by a different person and each designer made to work with a different set of gimmicks. One unifying feature of the house was its lack of windows, and the fact that none of the few windows could be opened. This gave the house a certain uniform airlessness.

There were plenty of sliding glass doors, opening out onto the terraces, swimming pool, and wide sloping lawns of the backyard. The problem was that the six or seven Great Danes that patrolled the backyard would instantly surge into the house through any door opened onto their domain. Outdoors, these dogs were menace enough —huge, filthy, evil-smelling beasts, covered with flies, slobbering and affection-starved. Indoors, they were simply out of the question, bounding hysterically down the halls, skidding on slick floors, knocking over vases and tables and people. So the sliding doors had to remain shut at all times. As a result, the house tended to heat up unbearably over the course of a day. There was supposedly some kind of air conditioning, but none of us could figure out how to turn it on.

In residence, besides Alex and three or four servants and me, were Alex's sister, her husband, and their two-year-old son, who normally lived together in a flat in another part of Johannesburg, and Alex's mother, who was "out from England" on a holiday. The owners of the house were skiing in Europe somewhere, so calling them for advice about how their house worked was out, although the lack of air conditioning was only one of many similar problems. The house was loaded with technology that only the servants, and they only sometimes, knew how to use. Again and again, while groping my way through some dim passage or antechamber, I would come upon fellow guests punching away hopelessly at light-switch panels the size of drafting tables. Heating up some water on the stove required a degree in electrical engineering. Without the servants, I became convinced, the rest of us would have all starved to death in the dark, since none of us ever mastered the multitiered security system that controlled the one door that led to the outside world.

Although the house was kept dusted and polished by the several maids, it also gave an impression of profound neglect. The little items with which any house is stocked all seemed to be missing—there were no clothes hangers, no razor blades, no pens that worked. Much of the house's gadgetry was simply broken: the intercom system, the trash compactor, the garbage disposal. The swimming pool's custom-designed self-cleaner was acting up and poisoning rather than purifying the water. Even the basic appliances like the washing machine were on the blink. Going out to buy the little things the house needed turned out to be a major enterprise, since it was miles to the nearest shops. And then there was the security system, inhibiting casual outings with its arsenal of sirens, buzzers, floodlights, and automatic armed response.

So the house as a metaphor for white South Africa was inescapable, so to speak. The airless luxury, the helplessness of the masters without their servants, the sense of being trapped inside an over-heated, incomprehensible labyrinth—it was all so like being white under apartheid.

The most alarming part was the way that staying there began to affect me. The house got on my nerves like a rash, until I felt like screaming highly un-guestlike questions at the ceiling. *Why* can't we go in the swimming pool today? *Why* are there no more Ping-Pong balls? *Why* must the backyard be a sea of dog waste? Although the servants were the obvious people to ask these questions of, and although I began to suspect that the gardener deliberately left rafts of dog waste outside each sliding glass door so as to increase the privacy of his little cottage at the bottom of the backyard, I did not ask them. I was ashamed enough just to be thinking them.

In this state of mind, fighting this rising tide of self-disgust and rage over Ping-Pong balls, I was somehow especially ill prepared for what I found in the stack of mail Fiona brought when she flew up from Cape Town on Christmas Day: a copy, the first I had seen, of the American magazine that contained my essay about living in a village in Sri Lanka. I took one look at the magazine and thrust it to the bottom of my backpack. The next morning, I tried to feed the magazine to the trash compactor in the kitchen. "That machine do not work," a maid named Sunny said, having come up behind me silently. She took the magazine from me, studied it, and took it with her back to her living quarters. I hadn't bothered to think through my reaction to the sight of that essay in that magazine, but I knew that my mortification, my sense of unworthiness, had everything to do with the Sunnys of the world, and with my having somehow appropriated their misery for my own dubious purposes—for the entertainment of the sort of people who owned this house, in fact. So I could appreciate the poetic justice of her rescuing the magazine from the shredder—she was scarcely literate, so what she planned to do with it was a mystery to me—and I returned to my child's bedroom and my little pot of coffee without further tantrum. Also in the stack of mail from Cape Town was a telegram from Rachel saying that there had been some kind of foul-up in Zimbabwe and that she might not have a job at the university there after all.

I had a pretty dismal Christmas, all things considered. The dinner on Christmas Eve was lavish, but I knew only a handful of the twenty-odd guests, and I was too tired from Karroo-crossing to enjoy it. There were gifts on Christmas itself, and a certain amount of family holiday feeling, but it was not my family, and I did not feel close to anyone in it.

Alex's sister was a speech therapist; her husband was a management consultant. Both of them were thrilled with their luxury house-sit and conducted regular guided tours around the house for friends and acquaintances, each time pronouncing the Pierneef landscapes (the house contained a number of canvases by the eminent South African painter Pierneef) "vital" and the little waterfall by the swimming pool "clever." Their son was painfully spoiled, and kept up a near-continual screeching while parents and servants scurried around trying to pacify him with sweets and toys.

Alex himself was listless and withdrawn. From what I saw of his and his sister's interaction, his decision to hide his head in books in distant corners of the house whenever possible, and to nod agreeably and do as he was instructed the rest of the time, seemed understandable. His sister was older and obviously felt some profound compulsion to dominate and criticize him.

Their mother made some attempts to referee and, under the circumstances, I got along best with her. She was a charming woman, with a wealth of stories about her years as the young wife of a game warden in what is now Zambia. These tales—of marauding elephants and man-eating lions a hundred miles up the Zambezi River from the nearest road—I discovered in the course of several long conversations held in an alcove overlooking the poisoned little swimming pool. Sometimes Alex's mother would sigh and compare her present life in England, where she and her husband were the caretakers of a barrister's country house and garden, and hunted rabbits rather than rhinos—and could not afford the air fare for both of them to visit their children—with those adventurous days gone by. But she remained a breath of jolly fresh air in that vast, claustrophobic house.

For my part, I made myself scarce after a day or so, spending virtually all my waking hours wandering around Johannesburg.

86

I had things to do in the city, which entailed visits to bookstores, offices (of organizations offering bursaries for which Grassy Park High students had applied), and the library at Witwatersrand University. These errands took only a fraction of the time I had at my disposal, though; I filled many more hours simply wandering at random around the city. I walked, hitchhiked, and rode municipal buses—the Morris Mini was not loaned again. And I saw a different Johannesburg from the one I had seen eleven months before.

It was no less wealthy or Western, but its pizzerias and supermarkets no longer knocked me out, its whites-only gun shops no longer gave me pause. Seeing the hotel where we had spent our first night in the country, passing the deli where my eyes had filled over a bite of real cheese, I got the sort of fond jolt that usually comes with a memory many years old. Not that I didn't find the downtown streets exciting now. The Africans in central Johannesburg had far more flash and sparkle than the blacks in downtown Cape Town did, I thought. Or maybe it was just that I had grown used to the English, Afrikaans, and Xhosa one heard on Cape Town streets, and found the din of Zulu, Tswana, and Sotho that filled the thin and hectic air of Johannesburg—Egoli, the Africans called it, the city of gold—exotic. But the people, the blacks, seemed more confident, more raucous, too, both more "modern" and more "tribal." I listened to a man whose face bore a network of ritual scars play electric guitar on a street corner in the financial district. He had a small amplifier, and the chords he played, which were both bluesy and unmistakably southern African, bounced off the steel and glass walls of the skyscrapers with a poignancy and plaintive beauty not quite like anything I had heard before.

My sense of Johannesburg as a whole was much expanded since my earlier visit. It is essentially a gold-rush town that has not stopped booming since it was a clump of dirty tents less than a hundred years ago, and I now strolled its parks and malls always aware of the tremendous warren of tunnels underneath my feet—and of the myriad "compounds" outside the city where migrant workers from every corner of southern Africa lived without their families between long, dark, dangerous shifts in the mines. Those miners and the arbitrary value of the yellow metal they spent their lives extracting from the earth were the spring from which all of Johannesburg's wealth flowed. They were the only reason the city was built. Indeed, South Africa as we know it would never have existed without the Witwatersrand gold. It was easy to forget that bizarre yet basic fact while living in the Cape, but in Johannesburg one felt close to the harsh, thudding heart of the country.

I fell in with an assortment of people in the course of my roaming. An Indian businessman who picked me up hitchhiking took me to lunch. An African clerk with whom I played chess in Joubert Park invited me to visit him and his family in Orlando West, Soweto. I went into a downtown cafeteria for lunch one day and found myself surrounded by a group of curious municipal workers who first wanted to know why I was eating there—no apartheid signs were posted, but mine was the only white face in the large and crowded room—and then, discovering I was American, wanted to know all I could tell them about Mike Weaver. That same evening, by way of the broadest possible contrast, I spent in a gently lit café in fashionable Hillbrow, having run into two young women in a bookstore whom I knew slightly from Rondebosch—they were UCT students, home for the holidays—who insisted on taking me to hear their friend play sixties-style folk music while we sipped wine and ate impala steaks.

The strangest crew I fell in with consisted of four young Afrikaners on motorcycles from the white working-class suburb of Vrededorp. One of them, Mickey, had picked me up hitchhiking and invited me to his friend Kiewit's house. Kiewit's parents were away visiting relatives, Mickey said, so they were going to have a *jol.* Kiewit's parents' house turned out to be a small, white-brick affair somewhere deep in a maze of blocks of identical houses. Three late-model touring bikes stood in the driveway, and Kiewit and his friends, Hennie and Dirk, were busy fussing over them when we arrived.

They were a colorless bunch to look at, all quite pale, with longish dirty brown hair. "This *ou*'s from America, *kêrels* [gents]," Mickey announced, and they each wiped their hands and shook mine eagerly. After that, however, they couldn't seem to find much to say to me— their English was minimal, I began to suspect—and they soon returned to their bikes. Mickey, saddled with talking to me, nodded toward the house, from which a barrage of anonymous rock music poured, and asked me how I liked Boston.

I said that I had never spent more than a week or two there, but that I liked it fine.

Mickey looked disturbed and began oiling his bike, too.

Later, Kiewit took me into the house. He and the others had been taking turns running in and out, and now Kiewit showed me why. There was a half-empty bottle of brandy standing just inside the front door. I pleased Kiewit by taking a belt. Glancing around the front room, I realized what had happened with Mickey a few minutes before. The record on the stereo had been made by an American band called Boston.

While communication with my newfound friends continued to be bedeviled by such missed cultural connections, the brandy eventually took some of the edges off our conversation. I discovered that all four of them worked at the post office and that all four of them still lived at home with their parents. Their English was indeed poor—worse than that of my worst students at Grassy Park High. So we talked in a crude pidgin that relied heavily on the few Afrikaans curse words I knew—which seemed to be the heart and soul of my companions' vocabulary, too. None of them had finished high school, and none of them seemed to know anything much about the world beyond Vrededorp—except what they had seen in the army. (Hennie asked me if California was a bigger city than Joburg, and no one blinked.)

The army had obviously made a huge impression on all of them. With increasing frequency as the brandy disappeared, Kiewit began breaking into drill chants and marching songs, insisting that his friends roar their parts of the call-and-response routines and looking aggrieved when I declined to learn any lines. Mickey had apparently disgraced himself in the army somehow, and his friends taunted him about the incident. All I could gather was that he had become separated from his squadron while on patrol "on the border," and had been helped back to camp by a local woman. Mickey clearly hated being reminded of this misadventure. He kept threatening to *donder* anyone who mentioned it. But his friends only laughed harder when he glared and teased him more gleefully.

As the sun went down, talk turned increasingly to "the club." This was a *lekker* night spot, I was told. I would love it. The women were beautiful, plentiful, and amorous. Kiewit favored us with several repetitions of a scarcely credible tale about his success the night before with "this English chickie" whom he had met at the club. His friends finally diverted him from this anecdote by asking Kiewit if he was sure he wasn't thinking of "the coon girl"—they indicated the servants' quarters behind his parents' house—whom he might have confused in his extreme drunkenness with the English beauty of his dreams. This suggestion infuriated Kiewit and, like Mickey's little Waterloo in Namibia, immediately became a theme for the evening.

I was happy to be leaving Kiewit's house for the club, since I was lost and did not fancy trying to walk from the depths of Vrededorp to somewhere else, but I was not properly attired for the club, Mickey said. He insisted that I put on a pair of his "stoves"—narrow-ankled white Levi's. He and the others were all wearing them, and there was no reason I should be left out. Although they were several inches too short for me, and I thought they looked ridiculous on the others even when they fit, I put on the pants and we set off for the club, which turned out to be in downtown Johannesburg.

The manager of the Club Europa shared my opinion of "stoves," it seemed. After a long argument at the door, he finally agreed to let us into the place, but only if we sat at a table off in the shadows and did not go on the dance floor. Another problem then arose: a cash-flow problem concerning the cover charge. I had loaned my companions several rands before I realized the true state of our party's financial affairs—which was that they had little or no money among them and were expecting me to pick up the tab for the evening. I bought the first round of drinks and resolved to nurse mine.

Looking around the room, it was easy to see why the manager had been concerned about our group's appearance. While we sported T-shirts, jeans, and motorcycle boots, the other men in the club all wore coats and ties or their best safari suits. The women were also dressed to the teeth. My companions obviously fancied themselves a sort of biker outlaw faction at the Club Europa, and I noticed that they had each adopted rebellious sneers as soon as we entered. If this act was meant to attract adventurous women, I had serious doubts about its efficacy, especially as Kiewit and friends began to turn the air above our table blue with some of their raunchiest talk yet.

Meanwhile, everyone else seemed to be having a wonderful time. There were probably two hundred people in the club, most of them in their twenties, but a good proportion of them middle-aged. Virtually everyone seemed to be Afrikaans. The scene reminded me of a bar somewhere in the American West more than it did a big-city discotheque. The older men all looked like Idaho truck drivers: potbellied, ruddy, muscular, with brilliantined hair and a fondness for polyester. The women wore unfashionable pantsuits, and the icy expressions behind their makeup could be seen melting into unpretentious grins whenever somebody spoke to them. I saw lone males shaking hands and forming teams, and I overheard boys urging tables full of strangers to go over and ask their sisters to dance.

Nobody asked the post office clerks *cum* hoodlums at our table to dance with their sisters. And their company became steadily less charming as everyone else in the club ignored them. Conversation began turning back compulsively to Kiewit's chances of getting some "coon *poes*" when he got home that night. Finally, after Mickey ordered a second round for the table, I couldn't take any more. I went to the men's room and changed back into my own pants. I rolled up Mickey's "stoves" and gave them to a club employee standing near the street door. As I pointed out the table to which I wished he would deliver the parcel, I noticed a barmaid standing beside my erstwhile companions waiting to be paid. I made my exit, and I jogged all the way through the dark and silent Johannesburg financial district to the depot for buses to the northern suburbs.

"Real rock spiders!" was the delighted pronouncement of the breakfast table the next morning when I described Mickey, Kiewit, Hennie, and Dirk.

"You've actually met some! They're not easy to meet!"

"I've never even been to Vrededorp, though I've been riding past it all my life!"

"Now you can see why this country's politics are such a cock-up! It's because such people have the vote!"

Over the next few days, I was asked to recount my escapade with "the Vrededorp *jaapies*" again and again for friends and visitors— until I feared I might become part of the guided tour, after the Pierneefs and the waterfall. But I quickly lost interest in the story myself. I didn't share the wealthy liberal's notion that poor, ignorant Afrikaners were the cause of all of South Africa's problems, and I didn't like to feed that conceit. If anything, I felt more sympathetic to the fears of the uneducated white supremacist than to the disdain of the wealthy sophisticate. It was the former's unskilled job that was threatened by the prospect of black advancement, not the latter's investments. It wasn't that "such people" had the vote, but that so many others did not.

At the same time, I had been pretty well horrified by the mentality of the boys from Vrededorp, such as I had glimpsed it. We hadn't talked politics, we hadn't discussed "race"—we hadn't needed to. Mattie was right when she said that you didn't have to talk at length with every white you met to know where he or she stood. And Clive had been right, really, with his blanket damnations of the white working class while we sat on the station platform at Muizenberg. Mickey and his friends were descendants of the *bywoners,* the Boers who had lost their farms during the first decades of the century and moved to the cities. They had scrambled out of poverty with the help of the government and at the expense of blacks. Upper-class Afrikaners like the people on that Boland wine farm ran the government, but post office clerks were the backbone of the National Party.

I disliked sweeping generalizations and ironclad pigeonholes and preferred to look at people first as individuals, but I was beginning to have to admit the shortcomings of this approach in a situation like South Africa's. I was also beginning to tire of a longtime traveling habit of mine: the uncontrolled digression; the side trip without a point; experience for its own sake.

87

Mattie was not an easy person to reach while we were in Johannesburg. I had a phone number for her, but the people who answered there never acknowledged that they knew her; they simply offered to take messages. Mattie returned my calls, but she had to use a pay phone, she said, and functioning pay phones were scarce where she was staying. She was also extremely busy, she said, running all over the Rand. I was surprised, therefore, when, a few days after Christmas, she suddenly announced that she had arranged for me to meet someone who could give me better advice than she could about what was worth writing about South Africa: Zwelakhe Sisulu, news editor of the *Sunday Post* and president of the Media Writers Association of South Africa, a national union of black journalists. I had mentioned Sisulu a couple of times in conversation with Mattie but had never considered that she might have access to him. She had made the appointment of her own accord, and I was touched as well as grateful.

Sisulu had caught my attention a couple of months before with his address to his union's national congress in Cape Town, which read in part: "In our situation, the question is not whether one is a propagandist or not, but whether one is a collaborationist propagandist or a revolutionary propagandist. Because we have expressed a desire for radical change in the scheme of things, we must be propagandists for change. It has been said that there are no politics of neutrality in this country and conversely there cannot be a journalism of neutrality. We accept that the press has to be responsible, but responsibility of the press in this context merely means co-option—that the press must not interrupt social coherence at the expense of political fulfillment."

I began to prepare some questions about the uses and abuses of a "journalism of neutrality," and to wonder whether or not I should ask Sisulu anything about his parents. His father, Walter Sisulu, was serving a life sentence on Robben Island. A former secretary-general of the ANC and still a hero throughout black South Africa, he had been jailed for sabotage since 1963. His wife, Albertina—Zwelakhe's mother—had been banned continually since 1964.

On the day before we were scheduled to meet, however, Zwelakhe Sisulu was himself banned for three years. By order of the Minister of Justice, he was forbidden to leave his house between 7 P.M. and 6 A.M. on weekdays and was under blanket house arrest over weekends and public holidays. He was forbidden to receive visitors other than his parents, his in-laws, or a medical doctor. He was forbidden to enter any newspaper office, industrial complex, or educational institution. He was forbidden to attend any social or political gatherings. He was forbidden to enter any black residential area other than the part of Soweto in which he lived, and he was confined under all circumstances to the Johannesburg magisterial district. As with all banned persons, it became a criminal offense to quote him or to publish his photograph. As with all banned persons, no reasons for the banning order were given. Sisulu's career as a journalist and trade unionist was simply terminated that day, for a minimum of three years. He was removed from society. Another vital figure erased.

The next time I spoke to Mattie, I told her I still wanted to go to Soweto, if only just to see the place. She said she would try to arrange something, and we met the next day outside a black cinema in west Johannesburg. An Indian friend of hers would drive us to Soweto in his car, Mattie said. There were people expecting us there, some of whom I might find interesting. We set off on foot for our driver's house —there were no "white" buses plying the route. It was a couple of miles' walk, which gave us time to talk.

Mattie was curious about my luxury billet, and she howled with laughter at my descriptions of life inside the "prison" in the northern suburbs. Then she admitted that she had been feeling nonplussed and impatient herself during much of the past few days. Her main business in Johannesburg had been accomplished during a couple of meet-

ings of "the executive." She would be ready to return to the Cape as
soon as a few last questions had been settled. In the meantime, her
time was her own, and she had been using it to check out as many
local political groups as possible. "But some of these people up here,
I just don't know about them," she said, and she shook her head. The
night before, Mattie said, she had gone to a meeting in Lenasia, an
Indian township near Soweto, of the Unity Movement's local chapter.
"I'm telling you, Bill, it was *pathetic.* Just a talking shop, nothing
more. They all think we're still in the 1950s or something." A visit she
had paid to the home of Zenani Mandela had been much more inspiring, it seemed.

I pointed out a piece of graffiti on a bus shelter we were passing.
"ANC," it read, in big, hurried letters.

"Ja," Mattie said quietly. "You don't see *that* in Cape Town."

"The lines seem more sharply drawn up here," I said.

"For so-called coloreds, they definitely are. The system oppresses
all blacks more equally here. These Transvaal Boers don't hate you
less if you're classified colored, like some of the Cape Boers do. In fact,
they hate you *more.* Your existence proves that their *oupa* slept with
African women."

"I didn't mean color lines. I meant battle lines."

Mattie shrugged. "Same thing in South Africa," she said.

We had been following a dusty, truck-filled thoroughfare. Now we
turned off, hiked up an embankment, and entered a treeless suburb
of low-roofed, pastel-colored houses. I followed Mattie to the door of
a yellow stucco house. An older woman let us in, but Mattie's friend
was not there. We waited in the front room, sitting on hard-backed
chairs set against the walls, drinking tea and nibbling on spicy pastries called *samoosas.* The house smelled of Indian cooking and incense. Finally, the phone rang. It was Mattie's friend. Something had
come up. He couldn't go to Soweto today. Mattie was embarrassed. I
was disappointed. She said she might be able to arrange something for
the following afternoon, and I walked back to white Johannesburg by
myself.

The next morning, Mattie dumbfounded me by turning up at the
front door where I was staying with three Ping-Pong balls in her
hand. Mattie seemed to get a kick out of my expression. "You said
there was a table but no balls," she said, pushing past me. "Are you
prepared to be beaten?"

I gave Mattie a quick tour of the house. She found the Pierneefs
"smart," but virtually everything else "disgusting." Then we raided

the kitchen, turned up the radio, and got down to Ping-Pong. The maids muttered darkly, but everyone else was out, fortunately. Mattie would not say how she had managed to find the house again or how she had gotten there. "My secret, your serve," she barked, slashing at the air with her paddle. We were evenly matched at Ping-Pong, and we had some good games. But then the house began to heat up. We decided to make another run at Soweto.

Mattie did not have transport arranged this time. So we hitchhiked downtown and made our way to the main Johannesburg railway station. Mattie bought two tickets for Soweto and we headed for the platform. But trains for Soweto, it turned out, ran from what was virtually a separate station—the "Non-White" station—and I felt hopelessly conspicuous as we hurried through a grimy entrance hall toward the gates to the train. A black ticket checker stepped into my path. He ignored the ticket I thrust toward him. Watching me closely, he just kept saying, "I'm sorry, sir. I'm sorry, sir."

We retreated and reviewed our options. Buses were out for the same reason as trains. Share-taxis would never take me, either—they had enough problems with the law already. We couldn't afford a private taxi, even if we could convince a driver to break the law by taking me to Soweto without a permit. I certainly couldn't afford to rent a car. We might be able to hitch a ride in the direction of Soweto, although it was unlikely that anyone going into the township would be willing to take me in. Going in without any way to leave again was foolish and presumptuous, in any case. And simply walking into Soweto, over hill and dale, was, for a white, according to Mattie, an even more foolish plan.

While we weighed and rejected these possibilities, we were walking in the general direction of Soweto, and hitchhiking cursorily. We got a couple of short rides, and found ourselves trudging through a sparsely built industrial area. It was here that I noticed a road sign for "Crown Mines." Alex and Fiona had often mentioned Crown Mines. They had lived there while they were Wits students. I even had an address in Crown Mines, where some friends in Rondebosch had said I would be welcome to stay. At my suggestion, we turned and followed the road indicated by the sign.

The road went under a railway line—through a narrow, timber-framed underpass—and seemed to emerge in another country. Crown Mines was an old mining village. Rich-hued and sleepy in the summer heat, with abundant hedges and blooming hydrangeas tumbling over ramshackle fences, the little community sat at the center of a ring of grassy hills, like a fascicle of flowers floating in a bowl. Mattie and I walked up and down the three or four short, unkempt streets quietly, as if we had wandered into someone else's dream. There was an old wooden church shaded by weeping willows. A stereo played country blues behind a screen door. Two little boys—one black, one white— pedaled by on tricycles. Then a young white guy in overalls crawled out from under a Volkswagen and gave us directions to the address I showed him. We found the house. It was a pleasant-looking old place with a screened-in porch and a rusting metal roof.

Nobody answered my knock at the front door, but we could hear a radio playing inside. I tried the door and found it unlocked, and we went in. The house was cool and cluttered and airy. We went through to the kitchen and found a young African man sitting at the kitchen table sewing a patch on a jacket. Our appearance startled him. He turned down his radio. I explained whom we were looking for.

"She is not here," he said. "She's gone to Cape Town. No one is here. They're all gone on holiday. I'm looking after the place."

We introduced ourselves. His name, he said, was Abraham. He put the kettle on for tea and said that if we needed a place, we were welcome to stay in the house. Mattie and I looked at one another. What an idea! Mattie had been complaining about the place where she was staying—indeed, I had decided that the reason she had come over so unexpectedly that morning had been to escape from all the wrangling there. For my part—who wouldn't prefer the lovely, elegiac atmosphere of Crown Mines to my situation in the northern suburbs? When our tea was made, Abraham returned to his sewing, and Mattie and I took our cups and wandered through the house. There was a living room and three bedrooms, all full of plants and books and posters. We sat in a fuchsia-bordered bay window that looked out on the street, sipped our tea, and decided to come back the next day with our things. It really was like some charmed otherworld, Crown Mines. Both Soweto and white Johannesburg seemed very far away.

We told Abraham we would see him the next day and walked back out through the looking glass/railway underpass. It was too late now to go to Soweto today, Mattie said. She had things to do, anyway. A bus came by, with its destination marquee showing the name of the township Mattie was staying in. She flagged it down, squeezed my arm, and was gone.

I continued along, past marshy fields littered with the shells of stripped cars. I could see Soweto in the distance, its endless rows of metal roofs shining in the sun. Why did I want to go there? If it was simply to see the place, the government ran sightseeing tours five days a week. These approached the city as if it were a game park, whisking white tourists out from downtown in air-conditioned buses, with scheduled stops at a folklore park and a model kindergarten, and a chance to take photos on "Millionaires' Row." No; I hadn't even brought my camera from Cape Town. And I knew what a black township looked like.

But Soweto had, particularly since 1976, a special status among black South African communities. It was not only the largest township in the country; it had also come to be seen as the heart, soul, and leading edge of the freedom struggle. Whether or not this reputation was justified—and it could certainly be argued that the workers in the Eastern Cape were more organized and militant, that the townships around Durban harbored more armed guerrillas, that the people in Sharpeville and the other townships south of Johannesburg were more brutally oppressed and angrily explosive, that the students on the Cape Flats had marched far ahead of their brothers and sisters in Soweto in 1980, and that depoliticized, American-style *joller* consumerism was more advanced as a culture in Soweto than anywhere else in black South Africa—it was still this mythic stature that made me want to visit Soweto. I had nothing special to do there. I didn't particularly care whom I spoke to, so long as I had a reputable guide, which I assumed Mattie to be. In fact, I realized, I was no different in this respect from those foreign journalists whom I had come to disdain for their skin-deep approach to black South Africa. Soweto was an established locale and bit player in the world media, so I wanted to talk to a Sowetan. Any Sowetan would do.

There was more to it than that, though. There was the feeling, the frustration, that had nagged at me all year in Cape Town: a sense of not being at the center. As Mattie said, the Cape was a peninsula; it was not representative of the country as a whole. And "coloreds" were a special case. And urban blacks were generally less oppressed than the millions who lived on the land. Where exactly the center of things, the true nexus of oppression and rebellion in black South Africa *was*, nobody seemed to know. It just always seemed to be somewhere else. Of course, "the rural areas" were a hard place to think about coherently, for they were by definition spread all over. And many of them were also, in their own ways, special cases. I sometimes wondered if the key, the nerve center of the liberation movement, was even *in* South Africa. Was it not, perhaps, in exile, at ANC headquarters in London or Lusaka or Dar es Salaam? This idea I had often heard scorned by activists—the belief that salvation would come from afar had been a fatal weakness of the freedom struggle for many years. Still, I continued to imagine that the essence of black South Africa, the blood and marrow of that unfledged nation which was preparing to rise, somehow ran in channels I had not yet seen. And Soweto *was* widely thought of as the center—that was why I wanted to go there.

The more I thought about it, though, the less important a quick visit seemed. I appreciated Mattie's efforts to get me there, but I decided I would survive if I did not make it to Soweto this trip. Soweto was the center of many things, certainly. But Cape Town was the center of others. Durban, Port Elizabeth, Pretoria were also key cities. Even Dar es Salaam had, as they say, a role to play. Grassy Park was only a detail, one panel in a very large tapestry. But I had not come to South Africa to take a poll, or to map the country from end to end. I had blundered in and would blunder through, seeing what I could see.

As things turned out, I never did make it to Soweto that week. Neither did Mattie and I move to Crown Mines. She had too many things to do the next day, she said. I was also busy. Then she said that she was nearly ready to leave Johannesburg and couldn't be bothered moving across the city for just a couple of nights. And I, too, gave up the idea—although I suspected that Mattie's real reasons for not moving to Crown Mines had less to do with logistics than with second thoughts about leaving a difficult situation in a black township for an idyllic, "non-racial" haven in a white area. Also, before I left Johannesburg, a woman whom I met at a New Year's party in the northern suburbs, a friend of Alex's and Fiona's who lived in Crown Mines, disabused me of my fond notions about life in her neighborhood. It only *looked* as if the place was inhabited entirely by white students, hippies, radicals, and their black friends, she said. In truth, most Crown Mines residents were white miners and their families, who had lived there for generations and who hated the gentle newcomers. These simple working folk were forever calling the police, she said, claiming to have glimpsed violations of the Immorality Act taking place inside the houses of the *kaffirboeties*. Every time you walked down the road, she said, you could see the curtains in their windows twitch, pulled aside by baleful observers. Last year, she said, there had even been full-scale street fighting, after a mob of longtime residents attacked an afternoon braai at which blacks and whites were dancing together in her front yard.

* * *

Mattie and I did get together again a couple of days later, at a shopping mall called Oriental Plaza. It was a crowded, noisy, yet strangely sterile place—a government creation, it had been built to accommodate some of the Indian merchants forced out of the central business district by Group Areas, and by white businessmen covetous of their downtown locations—with hundreds of stalls and shops selling Asian trinkets and discount clothes. We ate *samoosas* and wandered around. I got into an animated conversation with a young white couple about Sri Lanka, where they had vacationed. When I said something afterward about what a friendly pair they had been, Mattie said, "Whites are so cold. Blacks speak together like that all the time, even if they're complete strangers."

"You know, you should go to work for the government," I said. "You've always got a racial generalization ready to hand."

"And you should watch yourself, before somebody takes you hostage."

I bought a baseball cap at an outdoor stall. The cap it was meant to replace was ready for retirement—I had been wearing it for nearly two years, since Indonesia—but Mattie took the old cap from me and put it on. With her curls springing out from under it, she looked like a short, prettier Luis Tiant. With my permission, she said, she would wear the cap back to Cape Town.

We had never discussed our return travel plans, Mattie and I. I had avoided assuming that we would even make the trip together. But now Mattie said that she would be ready to leave Johannesburg the next morning. I said I would be, too.

"For Durban," she added.

"For *Durban?*"

Yes, she had people to see in Durban. Besides, she had never been there before. And how far out of the way was it, really?

"Eight hundred kilometers!"

Mattie shrugged and pulled my cap down low over her eyes. "They've got surfing in Durban," she said.

We strolled awhile in silence—out of Oriental Plaza, along a hot quiet street of crumbling warehouses. I finally said I reckoned that anything was better than crossing the Karroo again.

88

Alex's brother-in-law had offered to give Mattie and me a lift across Johannesburg to the highway to Durban. Mattie had said she would be at the house by nine that morning. While we were still eating breakfast, the telephone rang. A servant announced that the call was for Alex. It was someone named Nelson, she said. Alex and I each rushed for phones in different rooms.

Nelson's voice was faraway but energetic. "The tour is going fantastically," he said. "We've been all over the show already. We're in Kimberley now. And we're coming to Joburg today. But we've been having trouble getting in touch with this church group who were meant to tell us where we can stay. So listen, Alex, man, haven't you got a place there where we could kip for a night or two?"

"You don't mean the whole touring club?" Alex's voice was incredulous.

"Yes, of course. Just a place to park this bus, you know. We can sleep on the bus."

I put down the phone and ran into the kitchen, where Alex was talking. He looked distraught. He said, "Hold on, Nelson," and covered the mouthpiece. "What shall I say? They can't come here."

"Why not? There's plenty of room in the backyard. The bus could park down there by the garage. The wall's so high, the neighbors would never see it. They could use the bathroom out by the pool."

Alex's expression was so shocked that I stopped speaking, although the idea of the Grassy Park High Touring Club camping in the backyard had already fixed itself vividly in my mind as both feasible and wonderful, and a number of other points in recommendation of the plan were on the tip of my tongue. Alex turned away.

"Listen, Nelson," he said. "I'm sorry, but there's really no place here. I'm staying with friends myself—"

I left the kitchen. Back at the breakfast table, the others were curious about who was on the phone. I was vague in reply. While I was wondering if we should perhaps postpone leaving for Durban and try to rendezvous with the Touring Club somehow, Mattie arrived at the front door with her rucksack. My companions at breakfast made a fuss over her and insisted that she join us for fresh fruit and coffee. I found that I had lost my appetite, but I sat with the others while they chatted and ate, and I eventually decided that there was no point in suggesting to Mattie that we stick around. Alex's mother politely questioned the safety of our hitchhiking across the country; Alex's brother-in-law said heartily that he had done it all the time when he was a student. Then he announced that it was time to leave.

Alex finally returned from the kitchen as we were saying our farewells. I tried to signal silently to him that I understood his reluctance to ask his sister's permission for the Touring Club to stay in the yard and that I was sorry I had mentioned the idea, but he would not look at me.

We had an easy trip down to Durban. We caught a ride with a white salesman in a swift little car who took a looping, secondary route, passing through the country towns of Volksrust, Newcastle, and Greytown. It was not the same road that Rachel and I had driven a year before, but the countryside and the season were the same, and it took me back. Upon leaving the Transvaal, we descended the escarpment, from the highveld plateau down to the tropical coastal hills of Natal. We crossed a huge coalfield near Newcastle, where long grimy coal trains snaked through green hills. In the distance to the west, we caught glimpses of the sheer purple eastern wall of the Drakensberg. Then we entered KwaZulu, and started seeing African villages scattered across the hillsides, little groups of mud-walled rondavels with thatched roofs and abstract patterns in black and white and ocher painted around their cavelike doors.

Mattie and I talked little, and our driver did not talk at all. He was a big man, English-speaking, with a mustache and sunglasses and skin like rare roast beef. He made a number of brief calls on customers at car dealerships and garages. At most of these stops, black children in rags came around the car to beg. I asked Mattie if she had seen this sort of thing before. "Not quite like this," she said. Her voice was low and troubled. She gave a few cents to each child who approached until she had no more change. A black gas station attendant chased a group of children away from the car at one place, then grinned ingratiatingly at us. I asked Mattie if she understood Zulu. *"Sakubona,"** she said quietly. "And *amandla ngawethu.* That's about it."

The sections of KwaZulu we passed through were arid but heavily populated. Women walked along the road with earthen jugs balanced on their heads. Barefoot boys herded cattle. Men smoking pipes stood under trees with knobkerries under their arms. Mattie had her nose pressed to the window, her eyes glued to the passing scene. This tour

---

*Zulu greeting.

of ours, I thought, would probably prove at least as educational for her as it would for me—even if I was the only one taking notes. Mattie gave a grunt of approval as we passed a sign indicating the road to a monument at Isandhlwana. Isandhlwana was where the Zulu army had defeated a British imperial regiment in 1879, killing eight hundred Englishmen. I glanced over my shoulder. Mattie grinned and gave me a raised-fist salute.

We arrived in Durban in the early evening. It was overcast and muggy, and the streets were deserted where the salesman dropped us. We walked down rows of shuttered Indian clothing shops, past a park full of British colonial statuary. The skyline of the city's waterfront —a row of tall, heavy, undistinguished buildings—rose up in the east. At an Indian café, Mattie made phone calls while I sipped tea and watched night descend on a Muslim cemetery across the street. Durban, I had read, was the largest Indian city in the world outside India —there were more Indians living here than whites, than "coloreds," than Africans. Mattie was unable to reach her main contacts, but said she had spoken to one guy who had offered us a place to stay. "That's quite an exclusive area," the proprietor said when we told him the address. It had begun to rain, so we let him call us a cab.

The cab took us to a sprawling, split-level house perched on a hillside. The door was answered by a little girl, who took one look at us and screamed, "Pat!" Pat appeared. He was a tall, overweight Indian medical student. He and Mattie had obviously met before. He shook my hand and brought us inside. The house rose up from the entrance hall, then fanned out to either side. Except for the painting of Krishna at the top of the stairs, the house could have been anywhere in the hills outside Los Angeles where I grew up. We met Pat's mother and grandmother, both of whom wore saris. They sat us down and fed us curry, sambol, and yellow rice, with chapati on the side. I noticed Pat's grandmother lecturing his little sister in the kitchen in Hindi, and heard the little girl answering in English.

After dinner, Pat and Mattie and I repaired to a small, windowless lounge. Mattie surprised me by shaking her head when I began to pull out my notebook. Pat, who did not strike me as the paranoid political activist type, politely ignored the exchange. I put the notebook away, and he began to bring Mattie up to date on recent developments at his university. Names I did not know soon filled the air, and he and Mattie became embroiled in a complicated doctrinal debate about "the BC line" being taken by a student organization Pat apparently headed. To amuse myself, I began to count the acronyms they used—those I knew, and those I didn't. There were twenty-one of the former, somewhat fewer of the latter. But I began to sense that my presence was becoming a constraint. So I retired to the guest room that Pat's mother had indicated was mine for the night.

As I lay in bed, I could still hear, through the wall, Mattie and Pat talking. Then the doorbell rang, and at least two more voices joined theirs in the rise and fall of intent conversation. Perhaps these others were the people whom Mattie needed to see in Durban. All these kids, I thought, trying to forge a viable resistance out of the bottomless grievance and scattered forces of the black majority. What a long, dark, difficult road it seemed, from the splintered resistance of that historical moment to a full-fledged national liberation movement. There were the ANC and the PAC, of course, but they were in exile. There were the new black trade unions, which were still struggling to get off the ground. There were the tiny aboveground political organ- izations—AZAPO, the Unity Movement—and all the student, civic, professional, ad hoc, and single-issue organizations. But could these many disparate groups ever come together beneath one banner and *act?* How would the crucial links be forged, and when? Could the ANC lead the way? How large, how powerful, could the underground be- come in this computerized police state?

89

"I suppose you want to go surfing straightaway," Mattie said in the morning. We were drinking coffee in Pat's dining room, while the rest of the household bustled around us, getting ready for work and school. Mattie looked as though she had hardly slept.

I said I had surfed in Durban before. In fact, I had agreed to travel this way only because Mattie wanted to—I was not interested in mediocre waves swarming with aggressive adolescents. I asked Mattie what her plans for the day were.

"I have nothing more to do in Durban," she said. "I'm actually ready to leave whenever you are."

"In that case—Transkei, here we come."

We caught a ride down to the highway with Pat's father, a sleek businessman driving a brand-new Mercedes sedan.

"Is it any wonder that Pat talks such shit sometimes?" Mattie asked me, pointing with her chin at Pat's father's car as it glided away from us, headed downtown. We stood in the red mud beside a freeway on-ramp. "Naturally he's going to prefer a racial perspective on the struggle. Because he and his family are rich! They're capitalists. No wonder he rejects a class analysis! They want to keep their money and be seen as liberationists both!"

"But aren't a lot of Indians in that position?"

"No. Only a few are. They get all the publicity, but most so-called Indians are poor and oppressed. In fact, they've probably suffered from Group Areas more than any other 'group.' Look." Mattie pointed to a nearby hillside covered with makeshift hovels. "Those are so-called Indians living in those pondoks there."

It was a sparkling, hot, rain-washed morning, and we received a quick series of short rides south, all of them with Indian drivers. We passed through a heavy industrial area behind the Durban port, then wide fields of sugarcane. From the back of a carpenter's Japanese pickup, we watched a series of "white" resorts roll by, each with one or more high-rise hotels or apartment houses set on the bluff above it—"like Monopoly properties," I said, and Mattie snickered.

At Umzinto, we turned inland, and the rides immediately got scarcer. There was very little traffic, and all of it was local: mud-spattered cars and farm trucks, each ride carrying us a few miles farther up into lush, tangled hills where canefields alternated with forests. The sky clouded over, and a rain wind began to blow.

We sheltered from a short, violent downpour under the eaves of a small grocery store attached to a mechanic's shop. There was local produce set out in cardboard boxes underneath the eaves, but it all seemed to be hard green mangoes and nearly black bananas. We bought soft drinks and a roll of biscuits inside the store, where the proprietress was a young black woman with glasses in rhinestone-studded frames. A heavyset white mechanic with long red sideburns emerged from the garage next door to stare at us suspiciously. When I looked back at him, he grunted and disappeared.

The rain stopped, and we returned to the roadside. A flatbed truck came rumbling out of a farm road across the way. I managed to persuade its driver with frantic gestures to let us join the ten or twelve laborers already riding in back, and we clambered aboard. Our companions on the truck seemed astonished to find us in their midst, but we had soon shaken hands all around, and become involved in separate conversations—Mattie with a young guy in sunglasses, I with an older man in a straw hat who said his name was Stephen.

Stephen told me that he had worked in the mines near Johannesburg for fifteen years. "But I never liked the bachelor life," he said.

Agricultural work paid very poorly, but going away for eleven months a year was just not worth it to him anymore. He had five children. One of his sons was studying to become a Methodist minister—Stephen said this with obvious pride.

One of the men who was listening to our conversation said something to Stephen in Xhosa. "This man seeks to know what place you are from."

I told them, and the news went around the group.

Stephen received more instructions in Xhosa. "They seek to know how you find South Africa," he said carefully.

I said I found it a rich and beautiful country, but that the wealth and the power did not seem to me fairly distributed, because the whites had most of it.

Stephen translated, and there was a round of whistles, chuckles, moans, and implosive clicks which I could not interpret. Then Stephen said, "These fellows believe the same, too. It is not a right thing. We have too little money, and too little land, and not enough school for our children." The truck suddenly flew over a rise, tossing us all a foot in the air. Somebody shouted something at Stephen, and everyone in the truck roared with laughter. I asked Stephen for a translation. He said, "He say we must be careful what we speak."

Mattie and I left the truck on the outskirts of the country town of Ixopo. I asked her what the young guy in sunglasses had been saying. *"Ag,* he was talking a load of shit about Inkatha," she said. "That group really brainwashes these poor *ous."*

It was midafternoon now, and much cooler than down on the coast. The hills had opened out, and lifted around us in great green swells, with dark groves of eucalyptus filling the draws. "Listen for the titihoya bird," I said. "This is *Cry, the Beloved Country* country."

"Is it?"

"Ixopo. Yes."

"Alan Paton was a sellout," Mattie said.

"What?"

"That's right. He wrote about the Alexandra bus boycott of '44, right? People all over the world read his book and thought, 'Hey, here's this great white guy, he's really on the side of the oppressed in South Africa.' But when the Alexandra bus boycott of '57 came, Paton, who was a famous author by then, went and got involved, supposedly on the side of the people. But he was really working for the Johannesburg Chamber of Commerce. He made secret deals to try to end the boycott. He completely sold out the people."

"Where did you hear this?"

"Everybody knows it. He discredited himself completely."

An old Ford came wheeling off the highway onto the shoulder at that moment, spraying gravel and putting an end to this conversation. (I later checked Mattie's story and found that, while there were many versions of Alan Paton's role in the 1957 Alexandra bus boycott, one of them believed by many people, and possessed of a solid body of evidence, did have him working to end the boycott by compromises worked out with the Johannesburg Chamber of Commerce when he had no popular mandate to negotiate on behalf of the fifty thousand black workers who were then walking twenty miles back and forth to their jobs rather than pay increased bus fares. The episode had certainly destroyed Paton's political *bona fides* among many black South Africans.) The old Ford's driver was a boisterous middle-aged African in a porkpie hat. He had with him a lanky young "colored" guy with sharp yellow eyes. They were headed for Mount Ayliff, in the Transkei, they said. It didn't take us long to see that they were both fairly drunk, as we tore through the hills toward the border station at Umzimkulu. They asked us loud questions about our itinerary, declared that we would spend that night at the driver's house near Mount Ayliff, and passed a bottle of brandy back and forth between them. They also passed a number of rapid, chortling comments in Xhosa back and forth, the sound of which I did not like.

The Umzimkulu border station was a bustling modern facility—"a sick joke," Mattie pronounced the operation, as we were issued five-day visitor's cards, to be surrendered when we left the Transkei. "These people running these bantustans are also playing Monopoly." The atmosphere inside the border station, where uniformed officials laughed and chatted and jauntily stamped documents, really was more like an office party than an international frontier. Our driver and his sidekick, who were already in a festive mood themselves, decided to have a drink in a large, noisy bar attached to the border station, and told us to wait for them in the car. Mattie and I quickly cadged a ride with a young white couple coming out of the border station, and left Umzimkulu without saying good-bye to our friends inside the bar.

The road curved back and forth over the border between the Transkei and Natal several times in the next fifty miles, though there were no more border stations. The couple dropped us at Brooks Nek, at the summit of a long, steep climb up from the town of Kokstad. From there, the next two hundred miles south would be entirely

Transkei, and the change in the landscape at that point was dramatic. Looking to the north and to the east—back into Natal—one gazed upon a Western land of fences, farmhouses, barns, eucalyptus windbreaks in rows, and rectangular fields. Looking south and west, one saw Africa—vast, treeless hills with round white huts scattered almost randomly across them, a myriad of footpaths weaving red lines across the green earth, with small herds of cattle and goats, small plots of corn and vegetables, and human figures dwarfed by the scale of the land. There was a dirt road running off to the southeast at Brooks Nek, with a sign for Port St. Johns, a town—the only town—on the Transkei coast. "I've heard nice things about Port St. Johns," I said. Mattie laughed, then said, "Why not? We've got five days." A bus came by, turning onto the dirt road. We flagged it down. Port St. Johns, the sign said, was 145 kilometers away.

It was a South African Railways bus, coming from Natal, with a NON-WHITES ONLY sign still stuck in the window. The fact that it picked me up was a reminder that petty apartheid would not be applied in the Transkei. The bus was dusty and crowded, and Mattie and I took seats in the back. Many of the people around us had luggage, I noticed. "Contract workers coming home," Mattie whispered. The other passengers began singing a hymn of some kind. "That's a song of homecoming," Mattie guessed.

Whatever it was, it was beautiful, and the singing seemed to carry us along on a wave of Xhosa voices as the bus rumbled over the hills. It was late afternoon; the sun streamed through the streaked, dusty windows. The bus stopped often, to pick up and discharge passengers; people shouted greetings to bicyclists and pedestrians who stood beside the road waiting for us to pass. I moved to a window seat when one became available, as much for the fresh air as for the view—there was a powerful stench of unwashed bodies inside the bus. "Showers to the people," I muttered to Mattie, who frowned, then laughed, widening her eyes in agreement.

"Port St. Johns!" the driver yelled as we stopped at a fork in the road. He was talking to us and pointing down the road he was not taking. Mattie and I grabbed our bags and disembarked.

After the bus had roared away, the immensity of the land seemed to amplify around us. We started walking along a broad-backed ridge. We were now in the midst of the African landscape that we had seen earlier from a distance, and its loveliness was absolutely stunning. The sun was going down, drenching the hills in golden light and deep, glowing shadows. People were cooking and chatting outside their huts, weeding in their corn plots, driving cattle along the spindly trails, calling to one another, greeting us with shy, curious smiles. We could see a game of soccer in progress on a field on the next ridge west, and we could hear the laughing shouts of the players. The feeling, looking out across the land, was one of seamless community. There seemed to be no villages—just a loose carpet of family *kraals*. There was a sense of harmony and near-perfect proportion. This land was fully inhabited, fully humanized, yet it did not seem overcrowded or overbuilt. The whole scene bore a strong resemblance to my idea of an earthly paradise.

Which is not to say that the people we saw appeared to be leading a life of leisure. Most of them were working—if not cooking or herding or weeding, then grinding corn, hoeing the earth, or carrying water, firewood, or roof-thatching. They just looked great doing whatever they were doing. The children who ran behind us looked healthy and happy. The place was more than picturesque; it seemed to radiate tranquillity.

"So this is a brutally oppressed and impoverished bantustan," I said.

Mattie harumphed. After a while, she replied, without much conviction, "This is underdevelopment."

"You think they should build an oil refinery on that hill over there?"

Mattie sighed and said nothing. She, too, seemed to be under the countryside's spell, and I told myself to stop baiting her. I really knew better than to equate bucolic charm with the good life. In the case of the Transkei, I had seen the figures—it was one of the poorest states in the world. On a map of South Africa showing zones of economic activity, all the bantustans looked like uninhabited territories. One only had to note the scarcity of ablebodied men in the scene around us to recall the real function of a region like this one in the larger society. And the people here were certainly aware of their exploitation. This area, known as eastern Pondoland, had been the scene of the most significant peasant uprising in recent South African history. It had occurred in 1960, when thousands of tribesmen rebelled against the government-appointed chiefs, established an alternative administration, and even sent a representative, a local tinsmith, to the United Nations, protesting Bantu Education, the pass laws, and the lack of black political representation, as well as local conditions. The Pondoland revolt lasted nine months before it was crushed by the government, which declared a state of emergency and imprisoned nearly five thousand people.

Another bus came along, and carried us as far as Flagstaff, a

crumbling old colonial outpost with a single muddy street and a ram-
bling, low-roofed, arcaded hotel. It was now getting dark, and we were
told there would be no more buses to Port St. Johns till morning. So
we checked into the hotel. A sleepy clerk showed us to a moldy-
smelling room with two beds and a cement floor and a barred window
that opened directly onto the street. We left our bags there and went
to eat. The only restaurant in town was the hotel dining room, the
hotel clerk said. It was a dimly lit, cement-floored, impressively barren place, with half a dozen empty tables. It reminded me of a hundred other decrepit frontier dining rooms I had seen in a dozen other
ex-colonies. There was no menu. We were served—by the clerk once
again, who for all we knew was also the chef—slabs of tough beef and
some slimy, unidentified vegetables.

After dinner, we took a walk up and down Flagstaff's one street.
It was Saturday night, and there seemed to be a lot of people out, but
the street was extremely dark, so strolling was difficult, and we soon
returned to the lighted area under the hotel's arcades. A number of
young men joined us there, all of them frightfully drunk. They wanted
to know our names, to shake our hands, to buy us drinks, to ask us
questions that their English and our Xhosa were not up to. The hotel's
all-purpose employee came out and chased them away, and Mattie
and I retreated to our room. More drunks soon joined us, by way of
our street window. After some more unsuccessful conversation, we
yawned theatrically, and closed a pair of heavy wooden shutters that
the hotel had thoughtfully provided for the window.

"This is worse than Retreat on Saturday night!" Mattie said.

Over the next hour, while we sat reading, the occasional drunken
shouts, howls, and roars in the street grew more frequent. Then the
lights went out. It was pitch-black inside the room, and the sound of
the hotel's generator grinding to a decisive halt outside suggested that
it was going to stay that way till morning. We took our cue and
retired.

But falling asleep was impossible while the racket in the street
persisted—especially after a tape deck arrived outside our window,
playing Boney M's disco version of "Rivers of Babylon" over and over
and over.

Then somebody began pounding on the shutters and shouting. I
got up and pounded and shouted back.

"It sounds like a lunatic asylum out there," Mattie said, her voice
slightly tremulous in the darkness.

Voices and footsteps started echoing in the hotel corridor. I groped my way to the door and checked the lock. A moment later, somebody started pounding on the door. The pounding on the shutters resumed. The effect was unsettling, to say the least. There were now angry, drunken male voices at both door and window. The pounding seemed to reverberate and build inside the small room, like the wake-up scene in a nightmare. This time, I did not pound back. Instead, Mattie and I sat on the edge of one of the beds, holding hands tightly, and agreed to say nothing. The men trying to get in obviously knew we were in there, but the sound of our voices—especially Mattie's—would only make them crazier, we reasoned. The screaming and roaring up and down the street seemed to be reaching some kind of climax. Bottles were being smashed against the wall just outside our window. I even thought I heard gunshots.

After a couple of minutes, the pounding on the door stopped. The pounding on the shutters stopped soon after that. And the pandemonium in the street slowly died down. But Boney M jangled on, more and more slowly as the tape deck's batteries ran down, and it was hours before I managed to sleep.

90

The hotel's ubiquitous factotum banged on the door first thing in the morning. He had brought us coffee—instant coffee in tin mugs on a beer tray, to be sure, but still a welcome holdover from more decorous days. We asked about the previous night's riot. He clucked his tongue disapprovingly, and said, "Every Saturday night, these people are drinking and troublemaking. And you will never see them in church!" I asked about the chances of getting a bath, and he said there would be hot water soon.

The bathtub was in an ablutions block behind the hotel proper. I wandered out there to watch the hotel man fire up the ancient, coal-burning water heater. It belched brown smoke, which drifted away across the misty, bright green fields. Behind the hotel was a scatter of tin-roofed huts. An old man wrapped in a Basuto blanket came out of one, pissed in the grass, inspected the corn in his vegetable plot, then went to fetch a donkey tethered to a fence post. The old man led the donkey past the spot where I stood, greeting me quietly, and I saw that his blanket was festooned with blue airplanes flying across a red and yellow sky. Behind me, the hotel man hacked bananas from a raft that hung from the eaves outside the kitchen. The scene took me back to Asia, to the South Pacific—and ahead to "Black Africa." This was the low-rent, arcane travel milieu I had left behind when I came to South Africa. I felt it beckon: the lethean life that allowed me to avoid for weeks at a time thinking too much about what I was and was not doing. When the tank of water was hot, the hotel man took an old steel bucket and began filling the bathtub by hand. Had I said I was tired of traveling? The tub was full of rust and the water quickly cooled, but I couldn't remember the last bath I enjoyed more.

There was, we were told, only one bus from Flagstaff to Port St. Johns on a Sunday morning: Grim Boy. Apparently, the local buses were named, like ships. Mattie and I walked over to a market square where the buses were parked. Flagstaff did not look any the worse for its night of revelry, although it did strike me now, in its physical layout, as a sort of African Dodge City. Two men on their way to church in stiff, black, museum-piece suits helped furnish this conceit. We found buses called Broadway and My Mother's Love before we came upon the one with "Grim Boy" painted in fancy lettering on its flanks. We bought two ears of roasted corn for the ride and were pleased when the bus left only an hour behind schedule.

On the way to Port St. Johns, I suggested to Mattie that we had been vouchsafed a glimpse of the origins of the Afrikaner's obsession with *swartgevaar* (black peril) the night before. "They may not experience it directly now, in their whites-only suburbs, but it's still their most basic cultural memory—being surrounded by strange, hostile, black people. Think of all the thousands of nights they spent huddled in their homesteads, wondering if the 'natives' would attack that night or not. Think of all that fear, generation after generation of it. I think it makes their paranoia, their racism, their determination to have their own 'group areas,' more understandable."

While she had never admitted to being frightened, the assault on our hotel room the night before had obviously made an impression on Mattie. Her face was drawn and serious. Still, she refused to concede my point. "The Boer's big fear is not of black 'barbarity,' " she said. "It's of black competition. That's what Group Areas and influx control are all about: unfair advantage, privilege, exploitation, not the frontier wars that ended a hundred years ago, and that they won, anyway."

Grim Boy dropped us on the bank of a wide, green river—the Umzimvubu—just short of Port St. Johns. There was a car ferry there, and the first white people we had seen since Natal, and the ocean's salt smell was in the air. We rode the ferry across and got a ride into town, catching glimpses of the sea in the distance.

Port St. Johns was a pretty place, old and solidly built. It reminded me of a New England fishing village, transferred to the tropics. There were lots of white tourists, their Land Cruisers and station wagons bedecked with canoes and beach chairs. There was even a sign saying SURFING BEACH, with an arrow pointing west across the dunes.

We spent the next couple of days in and around Port St. Johns. The "surfing beach" was a wide, sandy cove with an outdoor restaurant under a grove of spreading shade trees. The waves were small and shapeless, but the sea was warm, so I borrowed a surfboard and talked Mattie into the water. She cursed nonstop, clutching the rails of the board, as I pushed her out through the gently slapping lines of white water, then turned her around and shoved her into a wave. She rode it all the way to the beach, lying down, steering between the bathers scattering out of her path, and when she jumped up on the sand and looked back out, I saw that her face was lit with a great, childlike grin. Soon, she was insisting that I let her paddle out herself and catch her own waves, and that I show her how to get to her feet. She was agile and strong, and learned quickly, though she continued to swear continually under her breath.

We stayed in a holiday camp about a mile east of Port St. Johns, on the other side of the Umzimvubu. The shoreline was steep and rocky there—the Transkeian coast is known to sailors as the Wild Coast, and the wind and waves crashing against the headlands made it obvious why. Mattie and I spent our time reading or walking along the cliffs—postponing our return to the highway and Cape Town for as long as we dared.

One conversation we had, while sitting on a sunny point watching Xhosa fishermen pull in *galjoen* with bamboo poles, is worth noting. Mattie had said that she would tell me what she thought I should try to write about South Africa. Now she admitted that she didn't know. "If people in America *want* to know what is happening here in South Africa, they can easily find out already. So much has been written. Most of it is banned here, but just from looking at the lists of banned publications, we can see how much is available overseas. The horrors of apartheid are very well documented. Anyway, you haven't spent your time here in the resettlement camps, or the jails. You've been in Grassy Park, at Grassy Park High, where the people aren't hungry or subjected to influx control. You've seen people, particularly the students, engaged in struggle. But will that sort of thing interest Americans?"

I doubted it. But I was interested in what black South Africans would like to see written about them by Americans.

Mattie pursed her lips. "Frankly, I doubt there is anything you could write that could help us here," she said. "We need international solidarity and material aid, but nobody really expects that to come from America. In fact, we expect America to try to prop up the regime when it begins to fall, just as it is supporting the system now with all its investments here. But you must write for Americans, isn't it? You said you don't like to think of writing just for the ruling-class liberals in America who are the only ones who read. But who else would you write for? I think you must go back there and see for yourself what things are like. You can't run away from it forever. Also, I think you mustn't just give up and write only about surfing. And I say that as one surfer to another!"

On the morning we left Port St. Johns, we stopped for breakfast at an old hotel in the center of town. At a nearby table sat an extremely fat, pink-cheeked priest with a snow-white beard. He stared at us while we ordered, then introduced himself in a loud voice, without getting up, as the proprietor of the place, and started asking us questions. "Where do you people come from?" "How long have you been in the Transkei?" I found his questions rude, the manner of his interrogation outrageous, and the man himself repulsive, and I began to ignore him. But he had already zeroed in on Mattie. When she said she had just finished high school in Cape Town, he demanded to know, "What do you colored children think you're doing, boycotting your classes? Who put you up to that nonsense?"

"Apartheid put us up to it."

"What does disobeying your teachers have to do with apartheid?"

"We were trying to make a connection between the two."

I was amazed that Mattie was willing to keep talking to the man, and that she was able to answer him so levelly. I couldn't even look at him, for as he spoke he was busy stuffing his vast face with fried eggs, ham, and a huge stack of toast, and snapping greasily in Afrikaans at a scared young serving girl.

Now the old priest was claiming not to be a racist. "I live in the Transkei, don't I, where the government of the country itself is black. But there's simply no point in pretending, you know, that Africans can advance from tribalism to modern life in one generation, or even in several generations! It took us whites thousands of years to achieve this level of civilization."

"First of all, the Transkei is not a country," Mattie said, still as calm as could be. "It's an apartheid labor reserve. And the government isn't a government. It's a lot of hired warders. And the question isn't whether blacks are prepared to act like whites. It is, 'What gives the white minority the right to rule over the black majority?' And the answer is, 'Nothing.' "

No, I thought, the answer is "force of arms." But I didn't say so.

Mattie and the priest went on in this vein until we had finished our meal. Mattie never raised her voice or lost her temper, though the priest continued to produce self-satisfied drivel on every subject they touched. She didn't even react, beyond making a certain, surprised sound in her nose, when the priest declared, "I know how the colored people think. I worked with them for years."

When we got out on the street, I demanded to know how and why Mattie had been able to put up with all the old priest's rubbish, when she blasted me for every remark she considered overly "white." Mattie laughed delightedly and said, "From each according to his capacity, to each according to his need. There's no use getting angry with someone like that. They won't listen anyway. But you, you're not so old. There's still hope for you. You're worth shouting at."

We got a ride from Port St. Johns back to the main Durban–to–Cape Town highway in a BMW with two young Indians from Durban. They were in the Transkei on business, they said—selling appliances. I asked them what it was like doing business in a bantustan, and one of them said, "Very frankly, terrible. The level of graft is appalling. These officials want so much baksheesh that we can't make a profit."

We made a pit stop at a gas station where I stood watching some country women prepare for the hike back to their villages—and suddenly recalled how Rachel and I had been thrilled by the Transkei a year before. How remote, and how benighted, that earlier enthusiasm now seemed. South Africa had relieved me of a virginity I had not known I owned. While Pondoland could still put me in mind of an earthly paradise, and "Black Africa" could still fill the immediate future with a promise of sweet, colorful oblivion, I now looked upon that old passion—to journey to the heart of faraway and tribal places, to lose the white middle-class American self in every form of Third World funkiness—with considerable skepticism. What interested me now, I realized, about the Transkei was not its homemade beer, its native music, or the white bracelets the witch doctor wore. Indeed, these were some of the same exotica the South African government tried to peddle as evidence that Africans could not be included in a modern political dispensation. What interested me now was the more mundane matter of the region's political life. The newspapers banned, the journalists jailed, the hundreds of political prisoners, the dozens of organizations suppressed by the Matanzima regime, the risk that Reagan would try to make the United States the first country in the world to recognize Transkeian "independence" (he had declared his interest in doing so), the true feelings of most Transkeians about their pseudo-citizenship, the dead-end economics of the Transkei's particular form of—yes, Mattie—underdevelopment, the grim figures for health care, malnutrition, infant mortality, life expectancy, literacy —these were the things that seemed important to me now. If these Xhosa villagers, with their bare feet and cascading bracelets, their long-stemmed pipes and ineffable African grace, had some primitive wisdom to impart, then it seemed I might miss it. The past year in South Africa had made history seem too urgent for such recondite absorptions.

91

The Great Kei River bridge looked more like an international border than Umzimkulu had, although the Transkei authorities scarcely glanced at our visitor's cards when we tried to hand them in. The land had been getting steadily drier since southern Natal, and now, as we entered the Eastern Cape, it was impressively harsh—white boulders, chalky earth, and cactus. We were traveling in a noisy lime-green Volkswagen with a chubby, thirtyish, flaxen-haired lecturer in history at Rhodes University in Grahamstown. When we passed through King William's Town, which was where Steve Biko had spent the last years of his life under a banning order, our driver shouted over the roar of his engine that he had gone to Biko's funeral. He called it either "a very heavy experience" or "a fairly iffy experience"—Mattie and I later disagreed about which it had been.

Grahamstown is an odd little English-looking college town with a particularly miserable and violent "location." Mattie knew people there, but they had no phone, and as it was dark by the time we got to Grahamstown, going on foot to look for them was out of the question. It was the middle of the university's summer vacation, so the city center was deserted. We hiked through silent, leafy, street-lit white residential neighborhoods, eating takeaway curry-and-rice and stepping into the shadows when police cars passed. We slept in a eucalyptus grove at the bottom of a ravine somewhere east of the city.

In the morning, we caught a ride to the coast and Port Elizabeth with a handsome, high-strung young African named Jimmy in a canary-yellow Plymouth Duster. It wasn't clear how Jimmy came by such a car, particularly not after it broke down in a township outside Port Elizabeth where we had been delivering his sister to work, and I had to loan Jimmy the ten rands to get it fixed. Jimmy worked as an assistant at a hardware store, where a ten-rand advance to repay me turned out to be beyond his credit. I gave Jimmy my address in Cape Town, so that he could just send the money when he got it, but his distress over the situation would not be allayed. He paced back and forth in the parking lot next to the hardware store, talking and making tight, anguished gestures with both hands to illustrate.

"And now this boss, my boss, he says I must just stay here and work. Because I am late, you see, because of the car. So I may not take you to New Brighton to look for your friend as I said I would. I am very sorry about this. And why won't he give me advance on my pay? I am a good employee for him. I don't like this job. But I must have it. If only I had finished my Standard Nine. If only we were allowed to write our exams in '76. Then I would have my matric, and my training, and some better job."

Jimmy reminded me of my old squash partner, Patrick, except that his life wasn't working as well. Mattie and I tried to calm him down, but when his boss called him in to work, Jimmy's last words to me were a miserable, vehement, "I will post you the money, Bill!" (Which he did, in a money order that almost beat me to Cape Town.)

Jimmy's hardware store was in a white suburb many miles from the black township of New Brighton, where Mattie had someone she wanted to see. We started walking in the direction of New Brighton, trudging along a bright empty thoroughfare past houses with yards full of flowers. After an hour, we came to a freeway. It was the road to Cape Town. We abandoned the New Brighton plan and clambered down the ice plant embankment to the freeway. A truck pulling two tank semitrailers stopped. The ride that followed was a bit unearthly. The truck and trailers were painted white, the white-haired Afrikaner driver wore white overalls, and the tanks he was pulling were, he told us, full of milk. But the driver was a jolly old soul, I thought. He and Mattie talked the entire sixty miles to Humansdorp, all in

Afrikaans, while I tried to see across the dunes whether there was surf at Jeffreys Bay. As soon as the milk truck had dropped us off, however, Mattie exclaimed, "My God! Couldn't you understand what that old *toppie* was *saying?*"

I admitted I couldn't.

"He wanted us to come stay with him in Humansdorp. Rather, he wanted *me* to come. And he kept telling me about how he would come to see me tonight, once his wife was asleep. I couldn't believe my ears!"

"Was that what all that jolly chuckling was about?"

"Yes! He was going into great detail!"

Our next ride took us as far as the Storm River Bridge, at the east end of a scenic coastal strip known as the Garden Route. There were a gas station and a cafeteria beside the bridge, which is a tourist attraction for the deep, intricately tiered gorge it spans. Traffic thinned out noticeably while we waited there, though, and the gas station and restaurant closed. Things began to look a little desperate. We were standing in a dense, ferny forest, probably forty miles from the nearest town. There were vervet monkeys scampering around in the bosky gloom, darting forward to raid a roadside trash can. The sun was going down; it would soon be dark. When an old truck pulling a battered stock trailer screeched and wheezed to a halt a couple of hundred yards beyond us, we did not ask questions, but sprinted after it and clambered in.

My hitchhiker's early warning system went on red alert immediately. There were four black men in the cab—two "colored," two Xhosa—and two Xhosa teenage girls. The girls were huddled behind the passenger's seat. They looked battered and terrified. They said nothing and did not acknowledge us. Mattie and I were on the engine cover, wedged against a bunk that was full of machinery, with two men on either side of us. The driver was silent and sober, but the other three men were boisterous and reeked of homemade beer. They talked loudly to Mattie in *skollie taal* Afrikaans as we roared along into the night. To my relief, Mattie talked just as loudly back, in Afrikaans just as crude, and she frequently managed to make them laugh. I could not follow the conversation, beyond recognizing that it was not being kind to *die baas*. I did understand the reply, however, when Mattie asked how far the men were planning to travel tonight. There was a hesitation, and then their spokesman said, with a poor attempt at offhandedness, that they were tired and would soon be pulling over to have a rest. At that point, we were descending into Bloukrans Gorge, a vast wilderness canyon, and we had not seen another vehicle for at least fifteen minutes. It was an utterly black night.

Suddenly, we were in a traffic jam. That is, we came upon a line of cars stopped bumper to bumper on a steep, narrow curve. The truck's cab resounded with outraged swearing. More cars soon arrived behind us, and the queue did not budge. We could not see what the obstruction was. I picked my moment, then started climbing over the men on my left, gesturing that I wanted to relieve myself. They tried to stop me, indicating that traffic was about to move, but when I pushed, they let go. I jumped to the ground, turned, and shouted for them to throw down our backpacks. There wasn't much else they could do. I was standing in the road, in the headlights of all the cars behind us. The backpacks came flying out, and then Mattie appeared and jumped down.

We hiked along the line of cars until we came to the cause of it all. It was a truck that had hit the mountain and jackknifed across both lanes. Emergency vehicles—police cars, fire trucks, road department trucks, ambulances—stretched away in a line of whirling lights beyond the accident. Mattie and I watched as a road crew tried to pull the truck away from the mountain. There was a tow truck hauling on a cable, but most of the work was being done, astonishingly, by hand. Thirty or forty black men were engaged in lifting the front half of the truck, carrying it onto the road, and preventing it from running away, while at least a dozen white supervisors shouted at them. It was a harrowing operation, as the blacks struggled desperately to keep the truck from rolling over on top of them, and the whites worked themselves into a frenzy. Mattie, who had been so cool and resourceful throughout the ride in the stock truck, now began to lose it. "Look at those *ous*," she hissed, backing away. She meant the white supervisors. In the whirling red lights, they did look demonic, screaming at the tops of their voices. Some had guns on their hips, some had *sjamboks* in their hands. "Those are the people that join the Wit Kommando,"* Mattie said, her voice thin and distorted with fear.

As we retreated from the scene of the accident, I stopped to petition a tall young white guy with a black mustache who was standing beside his BMW smoking a cigarette. He agreed to take us to George —another eighty miles west—as soon as the road was cleared.

That took hours, as it turned out. Once we got started, though, the trip was swift and painless. Our driver was a doctor in the army, he told us, on leave from his post at Ondangwa, Namibia, up near the

---

*The Wit Kommando (White Commando)—a right-wing terrorist group.

Angolan border. I asked him what it was like living there. It was bleak
and dangerous, he said, but worth it. He and his wife, who was also
a doctor, were making a fortune in hazard pay, and would soon be able
to buy their own office building in George.

I thought our being rescued by this dashing soldier-doctor from a
gang of *skollie* truckers was pretty ironic, but when I turned in my
seat to see what Mattie thought about it, I saw that she was fast
asleep. Her violent reaction to the spectacle of the white supervisors
at the accident in Bloukrans Gorge had surprised me at the time. But
when I thought more about it, it made more sense. Mattie was a city
girl. She didn't often see black-white relations in their rawest form—
the way one would, for instance, on a farm. Whites ruled and blacks
served everywhere in South Africa. But one rarely *saw* the *sjambok*
in town. Mattie and her comrades spent their time trying to decide
how to fight white racist rule, but they probably came face to face with
their enemy only in the tumult of township uprisings or when they
were detained by the police. The road crew supervisors were no doubt
just typical whites from some nearby small town. No wonder the sight
shook Mattie.

We reached George sometime after midnight. Hitchhiking was
hopeless at that hour, so we lay down to sleep in the first vacant lot
we found. It immediately began to rain, big, cold drops, driving us
down the road in a frantic search for cover. We took refuge in a bus
shelter, where we tried to doze sitting up. The rain quit, but dawn
seemed to take an eternity to arrive. When it finally did, and we got
back on the road, we were both stiff, cranky, and exhausted. I got out
my trusty cooker. There was a sharp little wind off the sea, which
made it difficult to boil water. Two cups of coffee were produced eventually, though, which took the edge off the chill we had both caught,
and made the day more bearable generally. "Boy Scouts to the rescue
again," Mattie murmured.

A Volkswagen bus, driven by a clean-cut young Afrikaans couple,
stopped. They were bound, they said, for Cape Town. We climbed in,
silently rejoicing, stretched out in back, and slept for most of the day.

It was midafternoon when we awoke. We were crossing the plateau east of the Hottentots Holland, less than thirty miles from Cape
Town. As we rolled over the summit of Sir Lowry's Pass, the whole
Cape Peninsula sprang into view: the Cape Flats shining in the sun
in the foreground, with the entire length of the *berg*, from Table
Mountain to the Cape of Good Hope, etched like a great blue sleeping
lion across the western horizon. In my enthusiasm for the sight, I
yelled out, *"Jou moer!"*

Mattie stared at me in horror. I was aware of the couple in front seeming to freeze in their seats, and of their falling sharply silent. I asked Mattie what the matter was, but she just kept shaking her head in disbelief. Finally, she whispered, "What made you *say* that?"

I actually hadn't thought about it. *"Jou moer"* was an expression that Mattie often used, and I liked. If I did think about it, I knew that it was highly obscene, and meant, roughly, "Your mother's womb." But because I didn't speak Afrikaans, the words were to me more sound than meaning. "It just came out," I said. Mattie seemed to have trouble accepting that explanation and kept glancing at the couple in front, who had tentatively resumed their conversation. "We're lucky they didn't stop and chuck us out on the road right there," Mattie muttered.

Disgraced but unejected, we proceeded down the mountain to the broad plain of the Cape Flats, and headed for town. I was elated to get back, and I said so to Mattie. "I can't believe we actually made it," I said.

"Why not?"

I remembered how reluctant I had been to travel with Mattie when she and Clive first presented me with the idea, and I laughed to myself. Mattie had been the best part of the trip! My misgivings, it occurred to me now, were probably not unlike the way Alex had felt at the prospect of the Grassy Park High Touring Club descending on him in Johannesburg. The difference was that I had only myself to worry about, while Alex had his family. That was the difference between me and South Africans in general. I was a free agent here. I wondered what had happened to the Touring Club in Johannesburg, and where they were now. I also wondered why Mattie did not seem to be as pleased as I was that we were getting back to Cape Town.

I asked her about it.

"I am pleased. And my mother will be more pleased still. But we don't see these things like you do, Bill. You think it's great fun to go out and take risks and survive and come home. But we're not interested in having adventures. We can't afford to be romantic about these things like you can."

"Jou moer," I said quietly.

"Sies, jou vark." (Shame, you pig.)

"You little Puritan, you'll never forgive me for calling you a romantic, will you?"

"No, man, I never will." Mattie laughed, and pointed to a pondok in the dunes. "Hey, it's nice to be back in the so-called garden."

The young couple who had brought us from George, whose names we had never learned, delivered us to the train station at Observatory, deep in the afternoon shadow of Table Mountain. Mattie went to the "Non-White" window and bought a third-class ticket to Retreat. I went to the "Whites Only" window and bought a first-class ticket to Rondebosch. Then we stood together on the platform, arm in arm, while the commuters around us stared, and waited for the train.

EPILOGUE

It was nearly a year after the events described here before I managed to leave southern Africa. I saw more of South Africa, including, at last, Soweto, although my involvement with the country felt relatively superficial once I was no longer teaching. Rachel did get a job in Zimbabwe, and settled there. We did not make it Cape to Cairo. I traveled overland as far north as the Serengeti Plain in Tanzania before running out of money, screwing up my courage, and returning, via Europe, to the United States.

Coming home was less harrowing than anticipated. I was soon making a living by writing. My reservations about American magazines faded, and I was too busy to attend to all the tremors of the long culture shock of returning. South Africa stayed with me, though. The South Africans I knew, their humor, their intelligence, their heroism, their country's uncompleted tragedy—my own view of the world had been enriched, and darkened, I realized, by all this. I decided to try to write about South Africa, after all, for Americans, proceeding from my own experience. The result is this book.

Many things have changed in South Africa since 1981. After a period of comparative political quiet, thirteen thousand people from throughout the country gathered at Mitchell's Plain in August 1983 to found a new multiracial anti-apartheid coalition called the United Democratic Front. Opposition to the following year's elections for the tricameral parliament was the rallying point for the formation of the UDF, but the organization's political roots went much deeper than that. The UDF endorsed the Freedom Charter, and the list of its patrons included Nelson Mandela, Walter Sisulu, and other ANC leaders. Albertina Sisulu and Oscar Mpetha were founding presidents. Essentially an umbrella organization, the UDF within months contained over six hundred youth and community groups with a membership estimated at 1.5 million, making it the largest formally organized national resistance seen in South Africa since the Congress Alliance of the 1950s.

COSAS, the student organization that Mattie worked with, became a major voice of dissent for young blacks and a key UDF affiliate. A number of independent black trade unions also joined UDF, and started working toward the creation of a national labor federation capable of challenging the government directly. UDF-organized consumer boycotts, work stayaways, and protests against Bantu Education, the pass laws, and other injustices became more and more frequent and well coordinated. The successful boycott of the elections for the tricameral parliament dealt the government's "reform" program a crippling blow.

After the August 1984 elections, a wave of violent protest began to sweep black townships throughout South Africa. By early 1986, over a thousand people had been killed, including twenty-one gunned down by police near Port Elizabeth while on their way to a funeral on the twenty-fifth anniversary of the Sharpeville massacre. Black anger often focused on black collaborators with the government, resulting in attacks on black policemen, local authorities, and the new Indian and "colored" members of Parliament. School boycotts became semipermanent in many townships—by early 1986 some schools had been deserted for nearly two years. Troops were called out with increasing frequency to help the police crush protests, but the still unequal confrontations with security forces, the furious destruction of the outposts of apartheid in the townships, were no longer confined to urban areas like the Cape Flats and Soweto, as hundreds of obscure "locations" began to rise up in every corner of the country.

In July 1985, the government declared an official "state of emergency" for the first time since Sharpeville, granting security forces sweeping new powers to act against dissent. Thousands of activists were jailed without charges. In September, COSAS was outlawed. At the time of writing, the UDF had not been banned, although a number of its leaders had been charged with treason (for allegedly conspiring with the ANC to create a revolutionary climate). Despite martial law, the death toll continued to mount. Latin America–style death squads, widely suspected of connections with the security forces, began to operate in South Africa, kidnapping and murdering teachers, lawyers, and other community leaders.

Inkatha, the Zulu nationalist organization led by Chief Gatsha Buthelezi, predictably resented the rise of the UDF. Inkatha *impis* took to breaking up UDF meetings and rallies, then proceeded to attacking UDF funerals. Several brutal murders of UDF members were generally attributed to Inkatha. There was also friction between UDF and AZAPO. AZAPO remained a small but highly vocal group, claiming for itself the mantle of the Black Consciousness movement, continuing to exclude whites from its membership, and attacking UDF for its "popular front" approach to the liberation struggle. Local clashes between UDF and AZAPO supporters were sometimes violent, particularly after the state of emergency was imposed, making it impossible for groups to meet to iron out their differences.

A severe economic downturn, the worst in South Africa since the Great Depression, began in 1983, sending black unemployment soaring and reducing opportunities for black school-leavers. The projections made in the boom year of 1980 for the skilled labor shortage had to be scaled down. Even white workers began feeling the economic pinch, and those whites who blamed the government's "reforms" for their deteriorating position continued to defect to the far-right political parties, which by 1986 held eighteen seats in Parliament. Foreign investment in South Africa declined, because of depressed local conditions, the likelihood of increased unrest, and pressure from the international anti-apartheid movement.

That pressure, and particularly the tremendous upsurge of anti-apartheid feeling in the United States, seemed to belie Mattie's pessimism about America's potential role in the South African struggle. International economic sanctions have long been a centerpiece of resistance strategy, but few foresaw the impact of the August 1985 decision by American banks—under pressure from the disinvestment movement—not to roll over their short-term loans to the South African government. The South African economy went into a profound crisis, the rand plummeted, and the government was forced to suspend repayment of its $14-billion foreign debt. The debate in the West over disinvestment had already swung dramatically in favor of the disinvestment movement, as polls began to show that a large majority of black South Africans supported disinvestment, even if they believed it would hurt them personally in the short-term. (Many blacks were already making sacrifices, of course, in the campaign to undermine the apartheid economy—through strikes, stayaways, sabotage, and some remarkably successful consumer boycotts.) Anti-Americanism among blacks grew by angry leaps and bounds during the Reagan years, but has reportedly been accompanied by a growing awareness that many Americans in fact support their freedom struggle.

The Botha government, after a period of improved relations with the West—largely attributable to the "constructive engagement" policy of the Reagan administration—seemed to remove world opinion from its priorities once again as the uprising of 1984–86 gained momentum and international criticism of apartheid stepped up accordingly. The prospects for Namibian independence grew steadily more remote. Deaths in detention, which had become rare after the murder of Steve Biko, became regular occurrences once more. Aggressive destabilization of neighboring states, assassination of South Africans in exile, and full-scale military raids against suspected ANC offices and facilities in neighboring countries all became expected behavior for the "regional powerhouse." Intense military and economic pressure were brought to bear on Lesotho, Swaziland, Mozambique, Zimbabwe, and Botswana to eliminate the ANC missions in those countries, causing widespread suffering in Mozambique and, in early 1986, toppling the government of Lesotho.

The ANC, meanwhile, stepped up its sabotage campaign and became a much more visible presence inside South Africa, with its flag now unfurled on a regular basis at rallies and resistance funerals. In August 1985, at a mass funeral near Duncan Village, in the Eastern Cape, a crowd estimated at seventy thousand repeatedly chanted, "Tambo, give us guns!" The exiled leadership announced a new strategy, "people's war," and growing numbers of grenades began turning up alongside the bricks and homemade petrol bombs in the arsenals of untrained black youths. Anti-apartheid leaders like 1984 Nobel Peace Prize laureate Bishop Desmond Tutu spoke more and more softly about the virtues of nonviolent resistance. Some townships began to be described in resistance circles as "liberated zones," and there was much talk of "making the country ungovernable." The first land mines of what looked increasingly like the long-awaited South African "civil war" exploded in late 1985.

The Botha government, for its part, gave no indication that it was considering sitting down at the negotiating table with the real leaders of the black majority. Polls showed that the still-imprisoned Nelson Mandela was by far the most popular political leader in South Africa, yet the government continued to deal only with dubious figures like Chief Gatsha Buthelezi and the Reverend Allan Hendrickse.

I have stayed in touch with some of the people I knew in Cape Town, and have heard secondhand about others.

Most of my Standard Six students stayed in school for at least another year after I taught them. Many of them passed their Standard Eight exams, some after two or three years of trying, and then left school. Oscar went back to school and managed to finish Standard Eight. Charmaine found teachers more her style and also passed Standard Eight. I don't know what became of Terence. Hester, Shireen, and Marius Le Roux made unsuccessful attempts at Standard Nine. The handful of my students who went straight through high school without failing included Malcolm, Josef, Mieta, Amy, and Wayan. Malcolm went on to the University of Cape Town. Josef became a nationally recognized chess player. Wayan, who is now, according to one informant, deep-voiced and muscular and "terribly handsome," entered the University of the Western Cape last year. Aubrey September, at last report, was still at Grassy Park High— trying Standard Nine for the third time. I don't know if he and Wayan are still friends. Of my geography students, I know even less. Nico and Shaun both failed Standard Nine and went to work, Nico bricklaying like his father. Wayne never passed Standard Eight.

The pass rate for the 1980 matrics at Grassy Park High was even lower than for the previous year's class, and only a few achieved "exemption." Of those, three, none of whom I had counseled extensively, went to UCT. A large percentage of the matrics who passed went to "Bush." A few went to the local teacher-training college. Some of those who failed reenrolled at Grassy Park High for another try. Most went to work, as clerks and secretaries and salesmen. Glynnis, who wanted to be a veterinarian, failed. Hector, who wanted to be an industrial engineer, failed. Adam, who wanted to be an airline pilot, went to teacher-training college, as did Jillian, who had decided not to become an architect. Ishmail, who wanted to be a doctor, passed but did not achieve exemption, and decided to study accountancy at UWC. Warren went to UWC and majored in theology. Elliot failed, and went to a technical college to study computers. Michael, who wanted to be a marine engineer, passed, but his mathematics results did not qualify him for the apprenticeship programs offered by the local shipping companies. The last time I spoke to him, Michael was considering joining the South African Navy.

Meryl went to UCT, earned a B.A. (Ed.), and returned to teach at Grassy Park High. She married a fellow teacher. The last time I heard from her, Meryl complained that some of our former colleagues, people who had been friendly to her when she was an underpaid, unqualified teacher, resented her now that she received a higher salary than they did and was better educated than they were, and snubbed her.

Nelson left Grassy Park High after one more year and resumed his studies at UCT. The last I heard, he had nearly completed a science degree and was living with a divorced woman and her two children.

Jacob did not return to teaching in 1981. When I left South Africa, he was in jail, convicted of possession of banned literature.

Mario Da Silva left Grassy Park High after one more difficult year for his long-awaited post at a "white" school.

Alex took his savings from teaching and flew off to Europe, first traveling around Italy by motorcycle, then staying in London with our mountain-climbing friend, Louis. Fiona made arrangements to travel by ship to the remote South Atlantic island of St. Helena, where she planned to do nothing, she said, but live quietly in a house far away from everything. At the last moment, Fiona abandoned this plan, however, and joined Alex in England. After several months there, they returned to Cape Town, where Fiona went to work as an architect and Alex began studying for his master's in history at UCT.

George Van den Heever left Grassy Park High to run for the new "colored" House of Representatives. He was elected by a turnout of less than 5 percent of the qualified voters in his constituency. As the MP for Grassy Park, his salary is many times what it was as a school principal. Van den Heever holds the "Home Affairs and National Education" portfolio for the Reverend Allan Hendrickse's "colored" Labour Party.

There was a heated succession battle for the post of principal at Grassy Park High. The main antagonists were Napoleon and Africa. Africa won and, by all accounts, proceeded to change drastically the atmosphere at the school. Enrollment was cut back, driving the teacher-pupil ratio down to barely half that of schools in the nearby townships. Africa's goal, people said, was to boost Grassy Park into the ranks of the top "colored" schools in Cape Town. The heavy emphasis on academic achievement reportedly weakened the SRC and student politics in general. Grassy Park High began to gain a reputation as a non-activist school.

Then came the devastating boycott of 1985. Less a student-initiated protest than a gesture of solidarity with the countrywide uprising already in progress, the 1985 boycott produced confrontations with the authorities at Cape Flats schools, including Grassy Park High, far heavier than anything we saw in 1980. Armed soldiers and police, exempt from all civil and criminal liability under the state of emergency, rampaged through schools again and again, beating, whipping, shooting, and teargassing students. If troops or police, when they entered a classroom, decided "normal" education was not in progress—if, say, there was no writing on the blackboard—both teacher and students were often arrested. At Grassy Park High, large numbers of children simply dropped out. There were attempts to force students to write their final examinations at gunpoint. In the end, the entire school year was lost. The boycott was suspended in early 1986, but black high schools throughout the country were still in chaos at the time of writing.

The government had actually made attempts to improve black education after the 1980 boycott. Spending on black education was increased. The number of blacks graduating from high school rose. The permit system restricting black admission to white universities was scrapped. But per capita spending on black education remained a small fraction of per capita spending on white education, the percentage of black matrics who earned "exemption" fell, and blacks still represented less than 10 percent of the students at white universities. The government remained committed to apartheid in education—to segregated schools, "mother tongue instruction," and the "Christian National" syllabus. Meanwhile, "the goal of equal education," to which the government was ostensibly pledged, remained, in the words of one Afrikaner researcher, "a dream for the distant future."

This endlessly deferred dream was, of course, precisely what drove hundreds of thousands of black students out of their inferior schools and into the streets, where the resonant chant in 1985 became "Liberation now, education later." That chant encapsulated much of what distinguished this new generation of students from the boycotters of 1980. Gone was the emphasis on political education, on community organization, on developing an "analysis." Under the state of emergency, more and more black youths seemed to focus exclusively on "action," forming themselves into small, virtually independent "fighting units"—whether in response to the ANC's call to form such units or not was an open question—and battling the authorities in the streets. Petrol-bombing buses and delivery vans, burning down the houses of policemen and township administrators—even burning alive suspected "collaborators"—these were the projects that replaced awareness sessions, study groups, and political theater. The "comrades," although feared in the townships for their ferocity, remained hopelessly outmatched by the security forces and continued to suffer far more casualties than they inflicted. But a desperate idea had clearly gained sway over great numbers of young blacks: the idea that victory was within reach—if they could just keep up the pressure, if they could just keep refusing to return to "normal" life. "Liberation now, education later." In Cape Town, the handful of black matrics who tried to write their final examinations in 1985 did so at central facilities under armed guard. Their results were never even published.

As for those two shining stars of the Class of 1980, Clive and Mattie: Clive passed his matric, but did not gain exemption. In 1981, he went to work—in factories and shops, on construction and road crews, changing jobs almost every month, it seemed. Clive continued to visit me regularly for as long as I stayed in Rondebosch. His plan to save money and leave South Africa to travel and write kept going in and out of focus. Every job Clive worked seemed to outrage him: he said he was always being put in charge of African laborers by white foremen who abused him, then advised him to abuse his underlings. Clive was drifting and angry and often asked my advice about what he should do with his life. More than once, I was on the verge of suggesting that he simply leave the country and join the ANC. I guessed he was thinking the same thing, but I was ashamed to say it, knowing so little myself about what that would involve, beyond great hardship and danger and an irrevocable commitment—perhaps the decision to kill. In the end, Clive did not leave South Africa. He enrolled at UWC, and the last I heard he was about to start teaching at a Cape Flats high school.

I also saw a lot of Mattie during my last months in Cape Town. She was going to UWC, and liked to stop by on her way home from classes. We would sit on the porch outside my room, drinking *rooibos* tea and talking. Mattie was discouraged by the number of *jollers* at UWC, she said, but she was extremely active in student politics herself, and, just to bug me, often applauded in my hearing her own decision not to go to UCT. I met Mattie's family and saw where she got some of her fire. Once or twice we played Ping-Pong at a community center near her house, though Mattie refused to play squash at the multiracial sports complex in town because "some creep might take our photograph, and they'll use it overseas as 'evidence' that sport is being integrated here."

When I was nearly ready to leave Cape Town, I phoned Mattie's house. Her mother answered and, when I asked for Mattie, burst into tears. Had I not heard? Mattie had been detained by the Security Police. They did not know where she was being held. They did not know anything.

Mattie was still in jail—in solitary confinement—when I left

South Africa. By the time she was released, she had missed her exams and failed her first year at UWC. Months later, I received a letter. In it, Mattie sounded fine. She sent her deepest sympathies to me and to everyone living in Reagan's America, and asked that I relay her critical opinion of the film *Reds* to its maker. ("The next time you pick up the phone there, Bill, I hope it's Warren Beatty on the line so that you can just tell him from me that he made an ABSOLUTE mess of John Reed's great book. . . .") The only part of the film she had liked, she said, was the singing of the "Internationale."

In that letter, Mattie described her time in detention as "almost meaningless" compared to what other detainees had suffered, although she did refer to "days of terror and loneliness in the company of the Security Branch and a Bible." She was going to UWC again, she said, but throwing "eighty percent" of her energy into a township youth group. "The struggle has intensified to such a degree that students, those with the least responsibilities and the least to lose, have been forced by circumstances to play a supportive role and no longer the seemingly leading role as in '76 and '80." Mattie enclosed with her letter the youth group's newsletter, noting with pride that "even workers who dropped out of Standard Six are writing articles for it —or part of an article." Across the bottom of the newsletter were drawn the silhouettes of people working in a field over the slogan, "Let Us Speak Together of Freedom."

To my suggestion, made in cards and letters written while I was traveling north through Africa, that she should see those countries herself sometime, Mattie replied that that would "not be possible— now or in the near future. There are just too many complications brought about by going outside S.A. and then coming back. One always stands the risk of being picked up by the Security Branch and accused of going for military training." But she didn't mind being unable to leave the country, Mattie wrote. "One thing which I realized when I hitched to Johannesburg and Durban with you was that there is still so much to learn about South Africa."

San Francisco
March 1986

INDEX